Practice of

INPATIENT BEHAVIOR THERAPY

A Clinical Guide

Practice of INPATIENT BEHAVIOR THERAPY

A Clinical Guide

Edited by

Michel Hersen, Ph.D
Professor of Psychiatry and Psychology
Western Psychiatric Institute and Clinic
University of Pittsburgh School of Medicine
Pittsburgh, Pennsylvania

G&S

GRUNE & STRATTON, INC.
(Harcourt Brace Jovanovich, Publishers)
Orlando San Diego New York
London Toronto Montreal Sydney Tokyo

Grune & Stratton, Inc.
Orlando, FL 32887

Distributed in the United Kingdom by
Grune & Stratton, Ltd.
24/28 Oval Road, London NW 1

Library of Congress Catalog Number 85–071036
International Standard Book Number 0-8089-1715-3
Printed in the United States of America
85 86 87 88 10 9 8 7 6 5 4 3 2 1

To Victoria

Contents

PART 3. TREATMENT OF CHILDREN AND ADOLESCENTS

Preface

Behavior therapists have had a long and fruitful relationship with inpatient units in state hospitals, Veterans Administration hospitals, university hospitals, city hospitals, and community mental health centers. This association has resulted in excellent treatment programs for adults and children with a wide range of diagnostic entities. In addition to the earlier work on token economy with the more regressed and chronic inpatients, in the last 15 years or so, behavior therapists on psychiatric inpatient units have enjoyed an increasing role in treating depression, severe obsessive-compulsive disorder, agoraphobia, conversion reactions, anorexia nervosa and bulimia, alcoholism, drug abuse, hysterical spasmodic torticollis, sexual deviation, uncontrollable hallucinations, tension headaches, and psychogenic seizures. In light of the nature of the inpatient populations so treated, behavior therapists have worked in close collaboration with their medical colleagues, thus combining the best of behavioral and biological approaches extant.

Surprisingly, to date, there have been very few texts on inpatient behavior therapy that cover the spectrum of issues and diagnostic populations treated. Moreover, none deals with the pragmatic day-to-day issues faced by the behavior therapist working on the psychiatric ward. Indeed, when inpatient behavior therapy is considered, the focus is directed to the research literature. Thus, the present volume is devoted to a somewhat more pragmatic approach to how behavior therapists function on inpatient psychiatry services.

The book is divided into three parts, with Part I detailing general issues, including an overview, an analysis of staff training and consultation, and a description of the medical aspects of care. Part II deals with the treatment of adults, and Part III with the treatment of children and adolescents. Each of the nine chapters in Parts II and III include a precise clinical description of the disorder, how to evaluate it psychiatrically and behaviorally, a description of behavioral treatments and how they interface with pharmacology, one or two comprehensive case illustrations, and consideration of problem areas.

Many people have contributed their time and effort to the development and production of this volume. I first thank my colleagues who agreed about the need for this book and willingly contributed chapters detailing their unique expertise. Next, I extend appreciation to my secretaries and research technician (Mary Newell, Kim Sterner, and Jan Twomey) for their invaluable help. Finally, I thank my friends at Grune & Stratton for their willingness to undertake this project.

Michel Hersen, Ph.D.
Pittsburgh, Pennsylvania

Contributors

Geary S. Alford, Ph.D. Department of Psychiatry and Human Behavior, University of Mississippi Medical Center, Jackson, Mississippi

Christine L. Cole, Ph.D. Department of Studies in Behavioral Disabilities, University of Wisconsin, Madison, Wisconsin

James P. Curran, Ph.D. Veterans Administration Medical Center and Brown University Medical School, Providence, Rhode Island

Michael G. Dow, Ph.D. Brown University Medical School, Providence, Rhode Island

John A. Fairbank, Ph.D. Jackson Veterans Administration Medical Center, and the University of Mississippi Medical Center, Jackson, Mississippi

Stephen V. Faraone, Ph.D. Veterans Administration Medical Center and Brown University Medical School, Providence, Rhode Island

Wendy S. Feldman, M.S.W. Department of Social Work, Orthopaedic Hospital, Los Angeles, California

Ralph R. Ford, Jr., M.S. Department of Psychology, University of Georgia, Athens, Georgia

Rohan Ganguli, M.D. Western Psychiatric Institute and Clinic, University of Pittsburgh School of Medicine, Pittsburgh, Pennsylvania

William I. Gardner, Ph.D. Department of Studies in Behavioral Disabilities, University of Wisconsin, Madison, Wisconsin

Francis C. Harris, Ph.D. Western Psychiatric Institute and Clinic, University of Pittsburgh School of Medicine, Pittsburgh, Pennsylvania

Georgina Harris, Ph.D., C.Psych. University Hospital, London, Ontario, Canada

Sandra L. Harris, Ph.D. Department of Psychology, Rutgers University, Piscataway, New Jersey

Michel Hersen, Ph.D. Western Psychiatric Institute and Clinic, University of Pittsburgh School of Medicine, Pittsburgh, Pennsylvania

Carol S. Hickman, M.A. Department of Psychology, University of California, Los Angeles, California

L.K. George Hsu, M.D. Western Psychiatric Institute and Clinic, University of Pittsburgh School of Medicine, Pittsburgh, Pennsylvania

Rolf G. Jacob, M.D. Western Psychiatric Institute and Clinic, University of Pittsburgh School of Medicine, Pittsburgh, Pennsylvania

James W. Langenbucher, Ph.D. Problem Drinkers Program, Butler Hospital, Providence, Rhode Island

Timothy J. O'Farrell, Ph.D. Veterans Administration Medical Center, Brockton, Massachusetts, and Harvard Medical School, Cambridge, Massachusetts

Brian F. Shaw, Ph.D., C.Psych. Clarke Institute of Psychiatry, University of Toronto, Ontario, Canada

Karen L. Thompson, M.A. Department of Psychology, University of Southern California, Los Angeles, California

Carolyn A. Thorwarth, Psy.D. Division of Youth and Family Services, State of New Jersey, Trenton, New Jersey

Samuel M. Turner, Ph.D. Western Psychiatric Institute and Clinic, University of Pittsburgh School of Medicine, Pittsburgh, Pennsylvania

James W. Varni, Ph.D. Behavioral Pediatrics Program, Orthopaedic Hospital, and University of Southern California, Los Angeles, California

Charles J. Wallace, Ph.D. Fuller Graduate School of Psychology, Pasadena, California

PART 1
General Issues

1
Overview

Michel Hersen

When examining behavior therapy from its historical context, it becomes quite clear that the inpatient setting provided a major thrust for this therapeutic movement (see Kazdin, 1978). Clinicians employed in psychiatric institutions who were dissatisfied with the vagaries of the milieu approach in the late 1950s and early 1960s began the systematic application of behavioral principles both to individual patients and entire wards. Hospital administrators and directors of psychiatric programs, who were somewhat doubtful of the value of this challenge to the psychiatric establishment, often only permitted such behavioral innovations in state hospital "back wards" (Ayllon & Azrin, 1968; Ayllon & Michael, 1959; Paul & Lentz, 1977), long-term care facilities for veterans (Atthowe & Krasner, 1968), psychiatric units for delinquent soldiers (Boren & Colman, 1970), programs for hard core drug addicts (Eriksson, Götestam, Melin, & Ost, 1975; O'Brien, Raynes, & Patch, 1971), wards for chronic alcoholics (Narrol, 1967), and cottage programs for retarded individuals (Girardeau & Spradlin, 1964). In general, the initial populations exposed to inpatient behavioral treatment were chronic, previously resistive to other approaches, institutionalized, often disinterested in extra-hospital living, and frequently symptomatic in spite of massive doses of neuroleptics and other drugs. Prior to behavioral intervention their "back ward" status relegated them to custodial care at best.

Despite the chronicity of the patients initially subjected to applications of ward wide token economies (Carlson, Hersen, & Eisler, 1972; Kazdin, 1977), many impressive successes were documented in the literature. Not only were

PRACTICE OF INPATIENT BEHAVIOR THERAPY
ISBN 0-8089-1715-3

there marked changes in eating, grooming, and dressing behavior, as well as overall level of activity (e.g., McReynolds & Coleman, 1972), but there even were improvements in social contact, cooperation, communication, and movements off the back wards and essentially into the community (Paul & Lentz, 1977; Rybolt, 1975; Shean & Zeidberg, 1971).

In general, rather simple contingency management arrangements typified these earlier examples of ward wide applications of the token economy. Patients received points or tokens contingently for performing specified activities (see Table 1-1). These points or tokens then could be exchanged for a variety of privileges, referred to in operant terminology as "back-up reinforcers" (see Table 1-2).[1]

After being able to document therapeutic movement with the worst patients from a prognostic viewpoint, behavior therapists turned their attention to contingency management in open wards with acutely symptomatic psychiatric inpatients (Agras, 1976; Arann & Horner, 1972; Crowley, 1975; Hersen, Eisler, Smith, & Agras, 1972; Moss & Rick, 1981). In addition, more individualized approaches to specific problems were carried out, including the reduction of excessive prescription of pills for minor physical discomfort (Parrino, George, & Daniels, 1971), reduction of delusional speech (Liberman, Teigen, Patterson, & Baker, 1973), and enhancement of social interaction with other patients and ward staff (Frederiksen & Williams, 1977).

Despite the improvements in the overall functioning of chronic patients on token economy wards, it was apparent that all of them did not respond positively (Kazdin, 1972, 1973). Indeed, some did not respond at all, totally ignoring the contingency system and seemingly preferring to remain listlessly on the ward due to their economic inability to purchase "back-up reinforcers" (i.e., privileges). Commenting on such nonresponsiveness, Kazdin (1972) argues that

> First, in many instances where patients do not respond to ward-wide contingencies, individualized contingencies should be attempted. Individualized contingencies adjust reward magnitudes and response requirements individually to enhance response acquisition. Second, reinforcer sampling can be used. . . . Here exposure to the reinforcer is given to enhance its utilization, and to augment its incentive value. . . . Third, group contingencies may be used which employ group pressure for performance. This permits the performance of one person to determine some or all of the reinforcers which are distributed to the group. The advantage of such a contingency is that it aligns the social contingencies with the token reinforcement contingencies administered by the staff. Fourth, the patient himself can help design the contingencies under which he will perform (pp. 417–418).

In addition to Kazdin's suggestions for modification within the token economic system, other approaches to nonresponse and resistance have been fol-

[1] The reader should note that this token economy program was conducted in Sweden and may not be totally representative of the back-up reinforcers available in hospitals in the United States (i.e., ale).

Table 1-1
Common and Bookable Activities

	Points
A. COMMON ACTIVITIES	
1. Up and dressed in the morning	1
2. Morning conference	2
3. Bed making	1
4. Clean own room	2
5. Exercise walks (with personnel)	3
6. Physical education	5
7. Giving a urine sample	1
8. Planned excursion	4–11
9. Garden work	6–12
10. Work in the woods	20
11. Courses	5
12. Treatment conference	3
13. Cooking course	5
14. Social errands	10
B. BOOKABLE ACTIVITIES	
1. Purchase	2
2. Coffee making	2
3. Kitchen work	3
4. Serving meals	2
5. Cleaning the day room	3
6. Cleaning the dining room	4
7. Cleaning the music room	2
8. Cleaning the bathroom	3
9. Cleaning the toilets	5
10. Cleaning the washroom	3
11. Occupational therapy	5/hr
12. Inviting visitors	2
13. Host/hostess for visitors	3
14. Preparation for ward meeting	3
15. Work outside the hospital	6–16
16. School attendance	6–16
17. Baking	10
18. Collecting money for baking	5
19. Purchasing ingredients for baking	5
20. Collecting flowers in the garden	2
21. Taking care of the flowers on the ward	2

From Ericksson JH, Götestam KG, Melin L, & Ost LG. (1975). A token economy for drug addiction (Table 1). *Behaviour Research and Therapy 13*, 113–125, with permission.

Table 1-2
Back-up Reinforcers

	Cost in Points
1. Leaving the ward *after* 4 p.m.	0
2. Leaving the ward *before* 4 p.m.	5
3. Leave of absence, *weekdays*	15/day
4. Leave of absence, weekends	5/day
5. Cigarettes: small packet	3
large packet	5
6. Ale, lemonades	2/bottle
7. Sweets	1–5
8. Fruit	1
9. Newspapers, weekly papers, comics	1–4
10. Ticket to the cinema or football	8

From Eriksson JH, Götestam KG, Melin L, & Ost LG. (1975). A token economy for drug addiction (Table 2). *Behaviour Research and Therapy 13*, 113–125, with permission.

lowed. Included are the combination of token economic and milieu approaches (Greenberg, Scott, Pisa, & Friesen, 1975), a therapeutic contract program as an alternative to the token economy (Levendusky, Berglas, Dooley, & Landau, 1983), and a highly sophisticated and complex program involving a levels system, pharmacology, milieu principles, social and task-functional skills training, and family treatment (Curran, Sutton, Faraone, & Guenette, 1985). Curran et al. (in press) have five principles that underlie the clinical operation of their behavioral unit:

The first and most important of these is a biopsychosocial model of illness. The biopsychosocial model recognizes that most psychiatric disorders are complex and often are long standing, thus requiring attention to biological, psychological and social factors. . . . The second principle dominating our inpatient care is the philosophy of the patient as a co-participant in his treatment. . . . A third principle is an emphasis on interactional patterns. . . . A fourth principle is that while quality patient care is seen as the primary task which takes precedence over other areas, it is not always appropriate to meet all of our patients' expressed needs. . . . The fifth principle is the value that teaching and research both enhance patient care and promote staff growth. Research and teaching are not regarded as competing with clinical care but complementing it.

Token economies and other operant programs for chronic patients were the first real behavioral inroads into the psychiatric inpatient setting. Subsequent to these intitial successes, behavioral clinicians found themselves receiving better reception from ward psychiatrists and nursing personnel, who were eager for innovative approaches for patients resistive to other forms of psychiatric intervention. Thus, in the last 15 years or so, behavior therapists on psychiatric wards have had an increasing role in treating such varied problems as depression, severe obsessive-compulsive disorder, agoraphobia, conversion reactions, anorexia nervosa and bulimia, alcoholism, drug abuse, hysterical spasmodic torticollis, sexual deviation, hallucinations uncontrolled by neuroleptics, tension headache, and psychogenic seizures. Many of the inpatient behavioral treatments referred to have been evaluated with single-case experimental designs (Barlow & Hersen, 1973, 1984; Hersen & Barlow, 1976), thus providing empirical confirmation of the treatment strategies carried out.

GENERAL ISSUES

My colleagues and I have implemented some behavioral interventions in two inpatient settings (VA Medical Center, Jackson, Mississippi; Western Psychiatric Institute and Clinic, Pittsburgh, Pennsylvania) over the last two decades. Certain issues have emerged in our experience that we believe are universally faced by inpatient behavioral practitioners. These include staff training and cooperation; confounding treatments; time limitations; ethical issues; pharmacologic treatment; targets for change; and single-case experimental analyses.

Staff Training and Cooperation

This issue is treated more fully in Chapter 2. It should be noted, however, that for the implementation of specific behavioral techniques, a highly trained staff that is fully cooperative is mandatory (see also Hersen & Bellack, 1978). This especially is the case given the highly technical operations of instructions, feedback, prompting, reinforcement, extinction, flooding, response prevention, and overcorrection, just to name a few operations typically carried out on a daily basis in the psychiatric unit. Not only is it important that techniques be carried out consistently in standardized fashion, but their timing is equally critical.

Writing on the training of psychiatric inpatient staff, Maxmen, Tucker, and LeBow (1974) astutely note that

> First, training courses ought to emphasize concrete practical skills consistent with what staff actually do on the unit; it differs from an exclusively theoretical discourse on patient care that seeks to primarily impart abstact knowledge. Second, the goals of the teaching experience should be clear to every participant. . . . Third, attention must be paid to the methods employed in teaching. . . . Fourth, and perhaps most neglected, it is necessary to consider possible ways of maintaining and reinforcing desirable staff behavior in relation to patients; this requires a constant attention to the continued application of the skills derived from training (p. 226).

Confounding Treatments

Strictly from the standpoint of experimental analysis, the clearest effects of behavioral treatment can be determined if there are no other treatments being administered concurrently on the ward. Given the typical ward structure, however, even in behavioral programs, this is most unlikely. Patients are medicated, they attend group psychotherapy, they partake in the expressive therapies (e.g., art, music, dance), social workers see their families, and other unplanned interventions occur as a matter of daily routine. The next best solution, of course, is if these additional treatments are kept constant. Then, when alternating baseline and treatment phases are contrasted, a meaningful conclusion may be reached (see Bellack & Hersen, 1978). To ensure such stability and continuity of care, the behavior therapist on the ward either must exert considerable control or be able to elicit the cooperation of all treating staff, including the psychiatrist. If, for example, a patient's change in medication were to coincide with introduction of the behavioral intervention, the resulting difference in behavior could not unequivocally he attributed to either the drug or the behavioral approach. Thus, confounds in the overall treatment scheme have considerable implications from both clinical and research perspectives.

In our own work we have found that head nurses and charge nurses are most instrumental in helping behavior therapists to implement programs and to ensure that possible treatment confounds will be minimized. A treatment plan sheet for each patient undergoing behavioral intervention has proven to be quite helpful. Under the best of circumstances, however, acute changes in the patient's condition will at times necessitate unusual extra intervention that for clinical reasons cannot be avoided (e.g., modification of medication dosage, addition of medication).

Time Limitations

Time constraint is an important issue to consider when planning a behavioral inpatient program. Basically, time constraint will be a function of the patient's life circumstances (e.g., job pressures, family interests in his or her returning home or remaining hospitalized); willingness of third party payers to accept the financial obligations imposed by continuing hospitalization; and deliberations of the hospital's utilization review committee as to prolonged inpatient stays. These three factors tend to be more prevalent for psychiatric inpatients in general hospitals, private hospitals, university hospitals, and mental health centers. Time constraints, however, have less bearing on those inpatients in the longer term state hospital and Veterans Administration facilities. Time limitations not only are relevant with respect to completing requisite baseline and treatment phases, but they can be important as motivating elements to enhance the patient's cooperation; i.e., they often provide the needed impetus for bringing about therapeutic movement.

In the evaluation of behavioral treatments in single-case experimental analyses, the therapist, of course, is well advised to consider the inevitable delays in obtaining medical and psychiatric diagnostic tests before behavioral assessment and treatment are carried out. Also, when drugs are part of the experimental analysis, sufficient time periods for "wash-out" phases must be planned in addition to anticipating the possible delayed action of some drugs (e.g., the tricyclics) in bringing about behavioral change. The neophyte at carrying out single-case analyses in the inpatient setting at times will find the patient discharged prior to full completion of all phases of treatment.

Ethical Issues

In the last two decades, ethical–medical judicial decisions in the courts have had a marked influence on the practice of behavior therapy in the inpatient setting (cf. Bazelon, 1974; Goldiamond, 1975; Hersen, 1976; Stuart, 1978). In many ways, albeit beneficial to the inpatient over time, several of the judicial decisions have made it more difficult for behavior therapists to achieve control over their patients' hospital environments in order to implement behavioral programs. As noted in an earlier publication (Hersen, 1976), "artificial" states of deprivation on the ward were created in order to bring about greater therapeutic control:

> As most institutional settings do not have an abundance of additional reinforcers that might be used as incentives for patients (i.e., the program director is unable to shape patient behavior in a positive direction with existing reinforcers), the naturally occurring contingencies in the environment are restructured such that an "artificial" state of deprivation is engineered. That is, privileges formerly granted noncontingently, or even capriciously, such as ward passes, day, night, and weekend passes, and better sleeping arrangements, are now automatically removed and subsequently distributed strictly on a contingency basis in accordance with a predetermined schedule. Now the patient must earn his/her way by displaying good behavior as so identified in the protocol for a given token economy. Depending on the particular institution or the particular state in which the institution is located, in some token economies patients are even required to earn their meals by displaying a specified set of appropriate behaviors (p. 208).

The latter point, of course, no longer applies. All patients, irrespective of their diagnoses or behavior, are to be allotted adequate food, clothing, sleeping arrangements, and access to basic privileges. It now behooves token economists to provide *extra* privileges to motivate their patients to perform. Also, if patients do actual physical work in the hospital, they are not paid in points or tokens but must be offered regular hourly wages. Furthermore, gone are the days when electrical aversive procedures are to be routinely applied (see Turner, Hersen, & Bellack, 1977). Indeed, this now is a rarity. To be able to carry out such aversive procedures today requires approval by institutional review boards and human-use committees, and then only if a persuasive case can be presented that this is the remaining treatment alternative, as all others have failed.

Given the impetus of the patients' rights movement and the attendant loss of control perceived by some behavior therapists, the focus of behavioral treatment for hospitalized psychiatric patients had changed. Rather than finding other strategies to enhance behavioral control per se, behavior therapists in the inpatient setting have turned their attention to a more psycho-educational approach. That is, there now seems to be considerable interest in identifying the behavioral deficits of psychiatric patients with the goal of developing remedial techniques. These techniques often are directed to teaching patients prosocial skills required in maintaining satisfactory interactions with peers and family at home, in the community, and at work (see Bellack & Hersen, 1979; Curran et al., 1985). Whereas token economy was the major overall behavioral treatment for inpatients in the 1960s, it now has been supplanted by the social skill strategy in the 1970s and 1980s (Brady, 1984).

Pharmacologic Treatment

Pharmacologic treatment is an integral feature of all inpatient settings, irrespective of the psychotherapeutic orientation of the ward milieu. Earlier, for a variety of reasons, behavior therapists employed in psychiatric inpatient units were quite threatened by the pharmacologic approach. Often this was due to their perceived loss of control, especially as most behavior therapists tend to be psychologists, not psychiatrists. This was *and still is* a needless fear, however. Indeed, there is no drug available at this time that is able to replace a behavioral technique in the teaching of new skills.

Behavioral and pharmacologic approaches can be applied either in concert or in succession, yielding very good results for both adults and children. There are some instances where behavioral treatment cannot be applied successfully until the patient's psychotic symptoms remit (e.g., Agras, 1976; Hersen, Turner, Edelstein, & Pinkston, 1975). In other instances the patient is interested in obtaining very rapid symptomatic relief, and a pharmacologic approach will be implemented. This may be followed by the concurrent application of pharmacologic and behavioral treatment, with the pharmacologic component eventually faded out (Turner, Hersen, & Alford, 1974). In still other instances the behavioral approach will be followed to bring about the patient's full pharmacological compliance (see Liberman & Davis, 1975).

In historical context, it is clear that the pharmacologic and behavioral approaches to inpatient psychiatry have the greatest empirical bases. It is not surprising then that we are seeing an increased number of inpatient programs where the two strategies are used concurrently in clinical applications. Moreover, the National Institute of Mental Health, in recent years, has funded many clinical-research projects that aim to evaluate the separate and combined effects of pharmacologic and behavioral treatment. There can be no doubt that this approach represents the wave of the future.

Targets for Change

The hallmark of the behavioral approach has always been the targeting and modification of overt behavior; i.e., motor behavior (Hersen & Bellack, 1981). Behavior therapists are certainly interested in self-reports and physiological indices as well, thus forming the tripartite division of measurement (see Hersen, 1973). Self-report and physiological measurement, however, do not represent the unique contribution from the behavioral movement. Quite the contrary, the major contributions to measurement are the precise operational definitions of motor targets that are measured continuously on a time-sampled basis in the natural environment (see Bellack & Hersen, 1978).

The psychiatric inpatient unit provides the ideal setting for observing a large variety of pathological behaviors, none of which could be observed as closely, carefully, or as long anywhere else. For example, it would not be possible to observe the actual drinking habits of alcoholics elsewhere, except perhaps in bars (Miller, Hersen, Eisler, & Elkin, 1974). Nor would it be possible elsewhere to monitor rate of psychomotor seizures on a 24-hour basis (Wells, Turner, Bellack, & Hersen, 1978). And how else can you repeatedly monitor the standing and walking behavior of a conversion reaction (Kallman, Hersen, & O'Toole, 1975) or the handwashing and checking behavior of an obsessive-compulsive (Turner, Hersen, Bellack, Andrasik, & Capparell, 1980)? Indeed, the inpatient unit provides the closest opportunity to observe the natural frequency of occurrence of behaviors targeted for modification repeatedly and continuously.

The inpatient unit also has personnel that can be trained to observe and record many targeted behaviors at one time. This is vastly different from the outpatient setting (see Hersen, 1983), where self-reports of patients predominate, even in behavior therapy. We have had the opportunity to assign nurses and nursing assistants on very well-staffed inpatient units in hospitals on a 24-hour basis to observe and record specified behaviors (Turner et al., 1980). Thus, a true picture of the patient's disorder emerges, showing the possible diurnal variations. On the other hand, time-sampling procedures often prove to be sufficient for less well-staffed behavioral inpatient units. Given the aforementioned, the importance of staff training and cooperation should be underscored.

Single-Case Experimental Analyses

The inpatient setting has been documented as a fruitful ground for conducting single-case experimental analyses (see Barlow & Hersen, 1973, in press; Bellack & Hersen, 1978; Hersen, 1982; Hersen & Barlow, 1976). When time limitations are not a factor and staff cooperation is at a high level, the inpatient unit permits sufficient control to carefully evaluate a large variety of behavioral techniques, independently and also with respect to their interaction with pharmacologic treatments (Liberman & Davis, 1975). Indeed, the relevant motoric, physiological, and self-report measures can be assessed repeatedly in baseline and treatment phases. And, to reiterate, the inpatient unit is *the ideal* place to observe and record the natural rate of occurrence of motor behaviors reflecting psychopathology.

The single-case approach to research dovetails beautifully with the clinical functions of the inpatient unit. Baseline assessment, except where the patient's clinical condition dictates otherwise, should precede therapeutic intervention. Secondly, the empirical evaluation of a treatment's efficacy is fortunately becoming more common in the inpatient psychiatric setting. Moreover, the precise description and monitoring of targets for modification are concordant with the goals of problem-oriented record keeping. And finally, the single-case approach to evaluating the efficacy and quality of clinical care is most consistent with governmental and third-party payer concerns that our treatments be proven efficacious.

Many varieties of single-case designs have been carried out in the inpatient psychiatric setting.[2] For the most part, however, variants of two basic strategies have been used: (1) A–B–A–B, and (2) multiple baseline designs. In the A–B–A–B design, baseline (A) phases are alternated with treatment (B) phases of approximately equal length. Target measures are observed and recorded repeatedly throughout baseline and treatment in standardized fashion. The controlling effects of treatment are documented when improvements in the targeted behavior appear in the B phase. Worsening of the target behavior should once again be seen when B is reintroduced (A–B–A–B). Results are portrayed graphically and evaluated through visual inspection, although statistical analysis is possible when sufficient data points are present (Kazdin, 1976).

In the multiple baseline design, two or more targeted behaviors in the same patient are selected for modification. Baseline assessment of these targets is conducted simultaneously. As described by Bellack and Hersen (1978), "Treatment is administered to each baseline *sequentially in time-lagged fashion,* and control is demonstrated if each baseline changes when and only when it becomes the focus of treatment" (p. 33). Results here too are portrayed graphically and evaluated through visual inspection.

ILLUSTRATIONS OF BEHAVIORAL INTERVENTIONS

Token Economy for Young Patients

One of the earliest studies we conducted in the inpatient setting involved a token economy unit on a rapid-turnover open ward for young veteran psychiatric patients (Hersen, Eisler, Smith, & Agras, 1972). The maximum number of patients at any time on this unit was six. They ranged in age between 18 and 35 (mean = 25.96). For about half of the patients throughout the 24-week study, admission to the unit was their first psychiatric hospitalization.

Physically, the token economy unit (located on an individual corridor) contained six private rooms, a lavatory, and a kitchenette. A shower room, a small day room, and the token economy banking office were on the main ward. The staff included a psychologist, psychology assistant, psychiatrist, and nurses and nursing assistants who also were responsible for patients on the main ward.

---

[2]For a more complete description of design possibilities, see Hersen (1982) and Hersen & Barlow (1976).

Procedurally, patients received tokens (blue index cards with their names, job descriptions, and supervisor's signatures included) contingently for completion of target behaviors in the following categories: (1) work, (2) occupational therapy, (3) responsibility, and (4) personal hygiene. Work assignments were off the ward and administered by *nonpsychiatric* hospital personnel. This was a unique feature of the program that deemphasized institutional living. Another unique feature of the program involved patients planning *all* of their daily activities each morning at "banking hours," where points earned and expended on privileges were recorded. Privileges were issued on orange index cards that contained the supervisor's signature. Privileges most sought after were day, evening, and weekend passes, and other off-ward activities.

When admitted to the unit patients were given a program description outlining responsibilities, requirements, method of earning points, privileges, and the system of fines for behavioral infractions. Patient–staff meetings were held once a week to discuss issues related to the operation of the token economy.

As the data will reflect, the unit was open-ended, with patients admitted and discharged throughout the 24-week period. Results of this program are presented in Figure 1-1. During the first six weeks of the study (baseline = 12 time blocks) privileges were given noncontingently, leading to few points being earned. One new patient (see triangle 1) was admitted during the fourth week, and his point earnings parallel those of the rest of the group. In time blocks 13 to 16 (contingent reinforcement) privileges were issued contingentley (i.e., privileges now cost patients specified numbers of points). This led to an increase in the number of points earned. In blocks 17 to 19 (inflation) the number of points required for privileges was doubled, but patients *did not earn* substantially more points. Indeed, they went "on strike," essentially worked very little, and stayed in the hospital for those two weekends instead of going on pass. In blocks 21 to 22, and 23 to 24, five- and ten-dollar bonuses in canteen booklets were offered to increase work output.[3] Resulting data suggest that the ten-dollar bonus was effective, but not the five-dollar one. In blocks 25 to 28 inflation was maintained but the bonuses were dropped. Performance, however, was maintained at a high level. In blocks 29 to 32 (contingent reinforcement) inflation was removed and privileges now were at their original cost. This resulted in a decrease in performance. When contingent reinforcement was totally removed in blocks 33 to 36 (baseline) earnings diminished considerably. Then, when contingent reinforcement was restored in blocks 37 to 40, earnings once again increased. The second inflation period occurred in blocks 41 to 44, but this time there were proportional increases in earnings. Finally, in blocks 45 to 48 (inflation plus a ten-dollar bonus), there were some increases in earnings displayed.

In looking at these data, a number of features should be underscored. First, left to their own devices (baseline), it is clear that even young, nonchronic psychiatric patients earn few points and begin to evince the listless behavior

[3] Canteen booklets were redeemable at the hospital canteen for material goods.

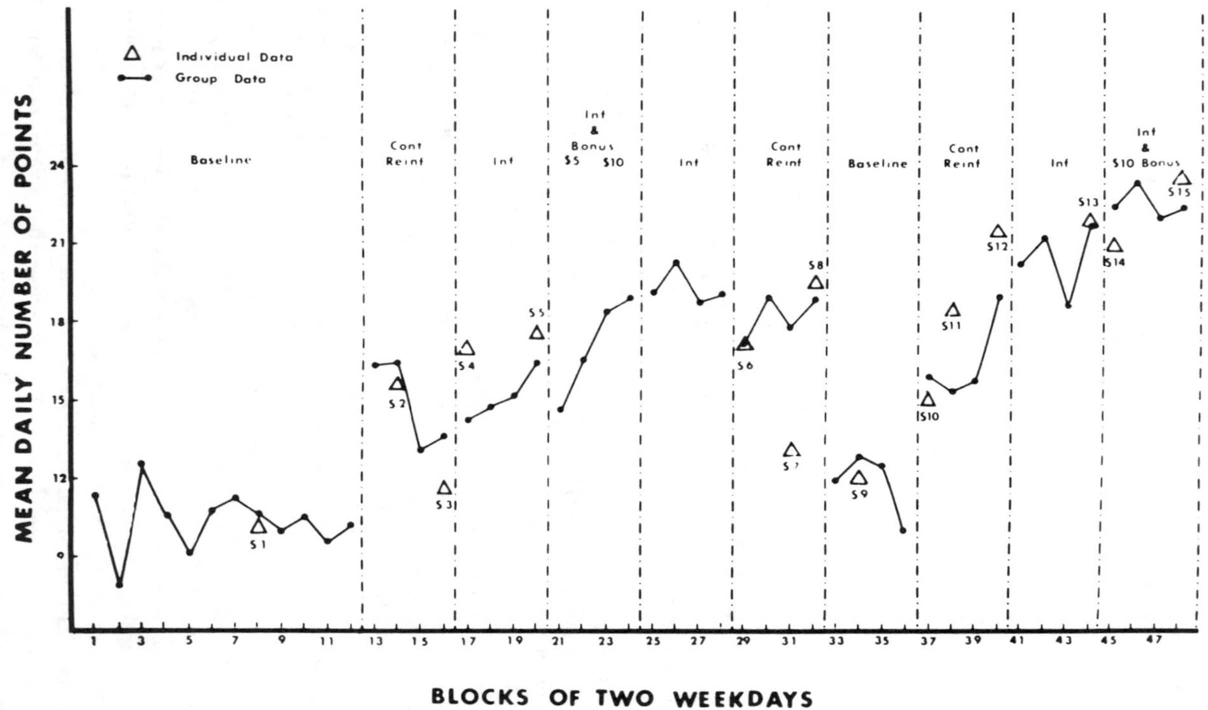

Fig. 1-1. Mean daily number of points plotted in blocks of two weekdays. From Hersen M, Eisler RM, Smith BS, & Agras WS. (1972). A token reinforcement ward for young psychiatric patients. *American Journal of Psychiatry 129*, 228–233, Copyright 1972, the American Psychiatric Association. Reprinted by permission.

characteristic of the older chronic patient. Second, it is important to note that regardless of the point in time a patient entered the program (i.e., baseline, contingent, inflation, bonus), he or she almost immediately adapted to the earning power of the rest of the group. This is documented with the triangle symbol, representing individual data at that juncture. Third, although an operant program, it is clear from these data that young psychiatric patients do not *automatically* respond to the contingency in force; i.e., as evidenced in the first inflation period, our patients were able to *resist* the contingency despite the consequences of earning insufficient numbers of points to obtain privileges. Fourth, these data suggest that token economy programs for younger psychiatric patients on open wards are feasible. Moreover, they may function to prevent or forestall patterns of institutionalization usually associated with any psychiatric hospitalization.

Hysterical Gagging

A 25-year-old, married, black male exhibited sustained gagging symptoms for two years prior to his admission on a VA psychiatric unit. Gagging and the inability to swallow food at breakfast began after medical control of a gastrointestinal ulcer that previously had resulted in vomiting episodes. There appeared to be no pattern with regard to time or place of gagging episodes. All prior medical interventions had failed, and as a result of time lost the patient eventually was relieved of his job as a plasterer. Furthermore, because of subsequent financial problems the patient's relationship with his wife and daughter deteriorated.

Prior to behavioral intervention, laboratory tests failed to reveal a medical etiology for gagging. Throughout baseline and treatment phases the patient was given Maalox for "nervous" stomach and Sopar, 300 mg, H.S., for sleep difficulties.

During baseline the patient was instructed to record time and frequency of gagging episodes on an index card. Figure 1-2 indicates that these ranged from 8 to 12 per day. Treatment involved a very simple contingency; that is, the patient was given two dollars in canteen books (redeemable at the hospital canteen for material goods) each day there was an N-1 decrease from the previous day's count. Also, when a zero rate was maintained the patient still received the two-dollar reinforcement. Because of the zero rate obtained on day 14, the criterion for day 15 was determined on the basis of the rate obtained on day 13 (i.e., $9 - 1 = 8$).

The patient was not given specific instructions as to how gagging must be controlled—thus enhancing the element of self-control—but he actually was observed by nursing personnel gagging during the course of baseline and treatment. Data in Figure 1-2 show marked improvements to a zero level (days 18–24) that were maintained through 12 weeks of follow-up. The exception was week 9 (Thanksgiving) when the patient exhibited some interpersonal difficulties with his family. In addition, during treatment the patient only required Sopar for sleep on one occasion. Follow-up improvements in gagging were corroborated by the patient's wife. Moreover, he was reported to have improved interpersonally as

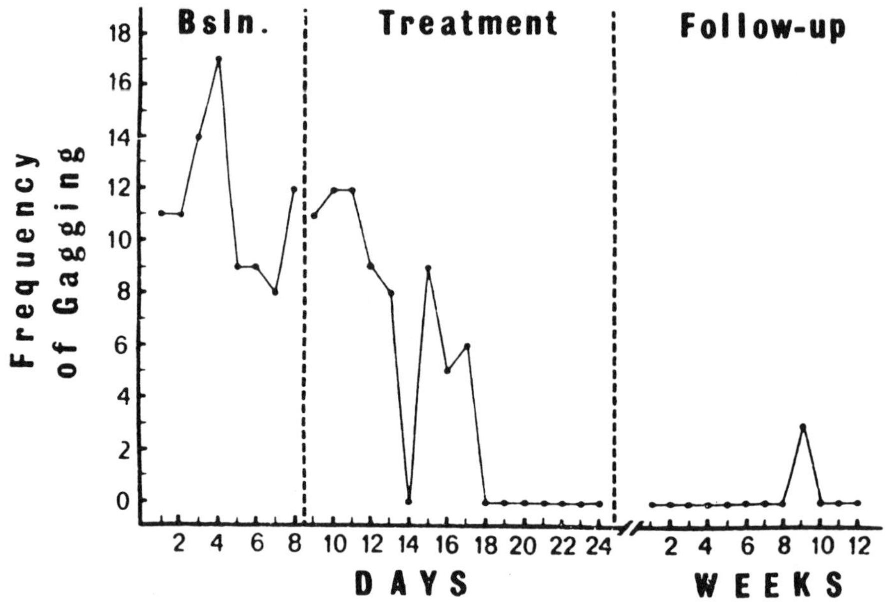

Fig. 1-2. Frequencies of gagging in baseline, treatment and follow-up periods. From Epstein LH, & Hersen M (1974). Behavioral control of hysterical gagging. *Journal of Clinical Psychology 30*, 102–104, with permission.

well. As summarized by Epstein and Hersen (1974), "application of a simple reinforcement technique resulted in the rapid control of a long-standing, debilitating disorder that appeared refractory to medical intervention. While inpatient treatment required external reinforcement to motivate the patient to control his disorder, maintenance of gains during follow-up suggests that the patient was then able to generate self-control over his behavior" (p. 103).

Conversion Reaction

A somewhat more complicated behavioral procedure was followed in a case of conversion reaction (Kallman, Hersen, & O'Toole, 1975). Also, the case exemplifies an initial error in treatment in that the patient's family was not involved in the original behavioral program:

The patient, a 42-year-old white, married male, was admitted in a wheelchair to the psychiatric service of the Veterans Administration Center, Jackson, Mississippi. When admitted he was bent forward at the waist (45-degree angle) and unable to straighten his body or move his legs. For the past 15 years, he had consistently complained of lumbosacral pain. On two occasions (12 and 5 years prior to admission) he underwent orthopedic surgery; however, complaints of pain persisted. In the last five years the patient had numerous episodes of being totally unable to walk. These episodes referred to by the patient as "drawing over," typically lasted 10 to 14 days and occurred every 4 to 6 weeks.

The patient was frequently hospitalized and treated with heat applications and muscle relaxants. Five years prior to this admission the patient had retired on Social Security benefits and assumed all household duties as his wife was compelled to support the family.

Orthopedic and neurologic evaluations failed to reveal contributory causes. An assessment of the patient's family life revealed that there were numerous stresses coinciding with onset of "drawing over" episodes. Included were the patient's recent discharge from the National Guard after 20 years of service, difficulties with his son and youngest daughter, and "guilt" feelings about the role reversal he and his wife had assumed. Moreover, it was clear that the patient received considerable social reinforcement from family members when he presented with symptoms of "illness" (e.g., receiving breakfast in bed, being relieved of household chores, etc.). In light of the above data, the patient was given a psychiatric diagnosis of Hysterical neurosis, conversion type (Astasia-abasia) (p. 411).

Throughout all phases of treatment, a young, attractive female research assistant visited the patient in his room thrice daily for 10 minutes at a time. She talked to him about issues unrelated to his psychiatric admission. At the end of each visit she asked him to stand and walk as far as possible. Time spent standing, steps taken, and distance walked were all recorded. In the first phase of the study the research assistant socially reinforced all of the patient's attempts to stand (e.g., "You're standing very well today"). But as depicted in Figure 1-3, this did not result in improved walking. In the next phase she reinforced both standing and walking, leading to his walking about 20 yards. Then she only reinforced standing, and walking appeared to plateau. When reinforcement for standing and walking was reinstated the patient was able to walk even further. In the next two phases the same reinforcement condition was in force but the patient was given a walker, and then it was removed when he showed progress. Considerable improvements in walking were observed and the patient was discharged.

The four-week follow-up indicated that the patient was walking normally. Shortly after this follow-up assessment, however, he was readmitted to the psychiatry service with the same symptoms. Apparently, in the interim the patient's family had reinforced all of his "sick role behaviors," resulting in renewed symptomatic expression. Thus, in the second attempt at behavioral treatment the family was included in the process.

Procedures carried out initially were repeated in our second treatment. The research assistant first reinforced standing and then standing and walking. This resulted in significant improvements (see Fig. 1-3) and eventual discharge. During the last phase of treatment (reinforce standing and walking), two family-therapy sessions were held. Videotaped sections of the first indicated that the family ignored the patient's positive initiatives but reinforced "sick talk." Therefore, in the second session attention was directed to reversing this trend. Specifically, the family was instructed to ignore symptomatic complaints and issue praise for positive behaviors.

Follow-up assessments at 2, 6, 10, and 12 weeks indicated that the patient was walking normally. Family members were responding appropriately as per

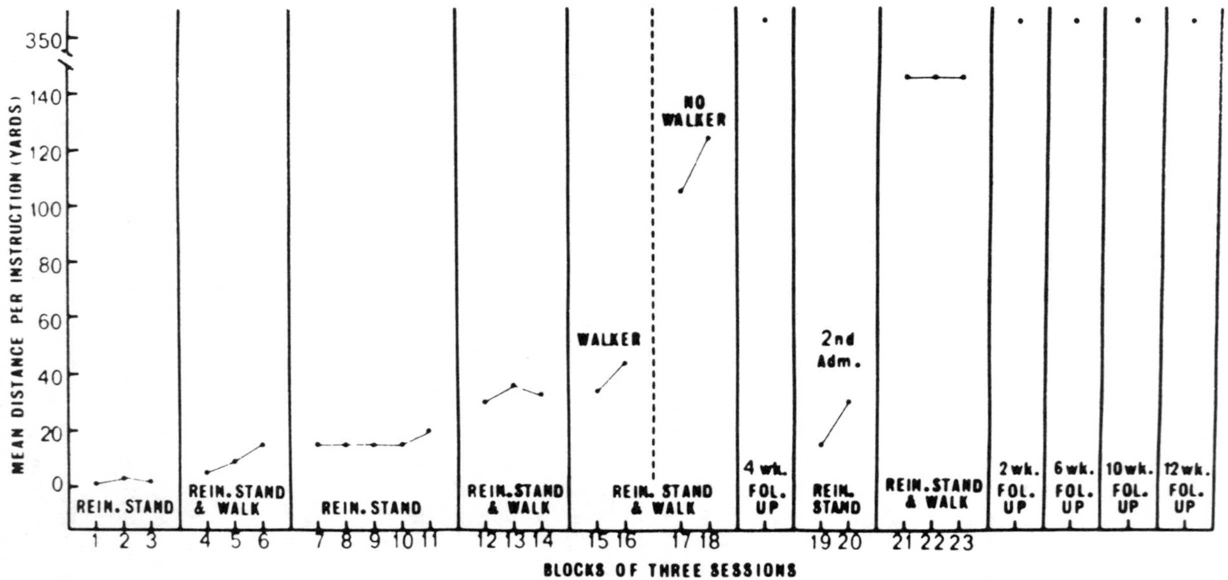

Fig. 1-3. Mean distance walked during all phases of treatment and follow-up. From Kallman WM, Hersen M, & O'Toole DH. (1975). The use of social reinforcement in a case of conversion reaction. *Behavior Therapy 6*, 411–413, with permission.

instructions in the second family-treatment session. Although not in the published report, this patient was followed-up an additional two years and was asymtomatic. He did complain, however, that the family members failed to pay attention to him when he complained of minor physical symptoms.

Our single case analysis suggests "that transfer to and maintenance of gains in the natural environment should not be expected in the absence of additional environmental structuring" (Kallman et al., 1975, p. 413). This indicates that inpatient behavior therapists obviously need to consider the possibility that not only will gains not transfer automatically to the natural environment when the patient is discharged, but that family members inadvertantly may be counterproductive in their reactions. Thus, family members should be an integral part of treatment right from its inception on the ward.

Spasmodic Torticollis

A 45-year-old married male was admitted to a VA Center psychiatric unit (Turner, Hersen, & Alford, 1974). He had suffered from spasmodic torticollis for one-and-a-half years prior to his admission. All previous treatments were unsuccessful, including chiropractic massage, biofeedback, and haloperidol and diazepam. The patient's "particular form of spasmodic torticollis was characterized by a slightly downward positioning of the head, with jerky movements directed towards the right shoulder. A routine physical examination revealed hypertrophy of the left sternocleidomastoid muscle, but neurological studies failed to reveal contributory causes" (Turner et al., 1974, p. 259).

Throughout all phases of treatment, the patient was videotaped three times daily while engaged in neutral conversations with a psychology technician. This was carried out to obtain a relatively naturalistic sample of tic behavior in order to determine the controlling effects of treatment.

Figure 1-4 indicates that tic rate per minute was extremely high and increasing during baseline (mean rate = 21 per minute). Beginning in session 10, massed practice treatment was instituted. This basically is a paradoxical treatment approach in which the patient is expected to duplicate tic movements *volitionally* as accurately and rapidly as possible. This was done 400 times per session, with four sessions held a day. The rationale for the strategy is that such massing will cause fatigue, leading to eventual extinction of the tic as the response to fatigue. In any event, data in the massed practice phase reflect a downward trend, but not below baseline levels. At this point the ward psychiatrist added meprobamate 400 mg, q.i.d., as he felt that insufficient progress had been documented. Thus, in the third phase, where meprobamate was added to massed practice, we see a continuation of the downward trend (i.e., improvement). We then persuaded the psychiatrist to discontinue meprobamate while massed practice was maintained (phase 4). Data in Figure 1-4 show continued improvement to about seven tics a minute. At this juncture treatment was discontinued and baseline procedures were reinstituted. Resulting data show a worsening of the disorder, suggesting that massed practice had an initial effect in reducing rate of tics. This was

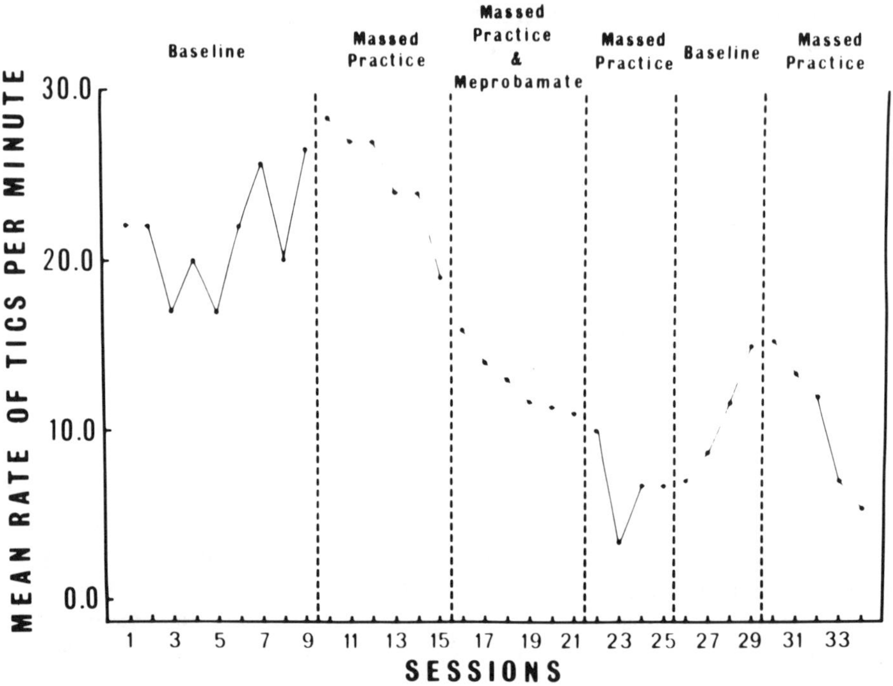

Fig. 1-4. Mean rate of tics (involuntary torticollis movements) per minute for 10-min probe sessions during baseline and treatment phases. From Turner SM, Hersen M, & Alford H. (1974). Effects of massed practice and meprobamate on spasmodic torticollis: An experimental analysis. *Behavior Research and Therapy 12*, 259–260, with permission. Copyright 1974, Pergamon Press, Ltd.

confirmed in the last phase when massed practice was reinstated and the patient once again evinced significant improvement.

Unfortunately, our patient was discharged against medical advice before full completion of treatment and subsequent intended follow-up. The available data in the last three phases of treatment, however, do document the controlling effects of massed practice treatment. Although not confirmed experimentally, introduction of meprobamate in the third phase *may* have contributed to the efficacy of massed practice by diminishing the patient's anxiety.

Psychomotor Seizures

A single-case study involved a 22-year-old, unmarried woman in the "border line" range of intelligence who suffered from psychomotor seizures of 19 years duration (Wells et al., 1978). Prior to her admission to a university-based psychiatric inpatient unit she had been medicated with the following: Tegretol 1000 mg per day, Clonapin 2 mg t.i.d., and Prolixin 2.5 mg t.i.d. Despite such pharmacologic treatment the patient still was having seizures at a rate of 2 to 8

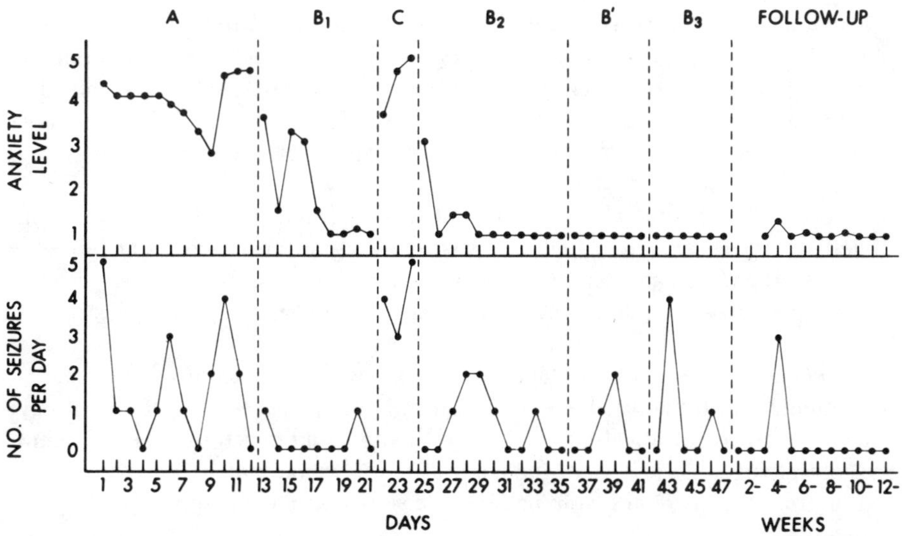

Fig. 1-5. Frequency of seizure activity and ratings of anxiety level across experimental phases: A = Baseline; B1 = cue-controlled relaxation; C = Attention-placebo; B2 = cue-controlled relaxation; B′ = cue-controlled relaxation with a novel therapist; B3 = cue-controled relaxation. From Wells KC, Turner SM, Bellack AS, & Hersen M. (1978). Effects of cue-controlled relaxation on psychomotor seizures: An experimental analysis. *Behaviour Research and Therapy 16*, 51–53, with permission. Copyright 1978, Pergamon Press, Ltd.

per day. These seizures consisted of dilated pupils, a fixed stare, muscle rigidity, and falling to the floor. Often they were preceded by what the patient described as a "tight queasy feeling" in her stomach, leading to fear that a seizure would occur. In light of her anticipatory fear we decided to evaluate the effects of cue-controlled relaxation as a possible treatment.

Throughout all phases of our single-case analysis the patient received Tegretol 200 mg. t.i.d. In addition to recording rate of seizures per day she was asked to evaluate her level of anxiety on a 1 to 5 point basis. In the first phase (A) baseline measures were taken. Examination of Figure 1-5 indicates that anxiety level was high (3–4.5) and seizure activity was variable (0–5). In the following phase (B1) cue-controlled relaxation procedures were instituted. This involved teaching the patient deep muscle relaxation, having her imagine the aura, relax, and verbalize the word "relax" 25 times while exhaling. Figure 1-5 suggests that cue-controlled relaxation brought about decreases in anxiety level and seizure rate. Therefore, in the next phase (C) cue-controlled relaxation was discontinued, but the therapist saw the patient on a daily basis to discuss non-seizure-related problems. During this phase there was a recurrence of high anxiety and frequent seizure episodes. Analysis of the experimental data suggests that cue-controlled relaxation was effective in reducing anxiety and diminishing seizures. This clearly was documented in B3, when cue-controlled relaxation was reinstated: both anxiety level and seizures were decreased. In the week following phase (B′) the original female therapist (KCW) was replaced by a male therapist, who continued cue-controlled relaxation procedures. Anxiety level remained at 1 but there still was some moderate seizure activity. In B3 the former therapist (KCW) resumed training. Anxiety level still remained at 1 but there was increased seizure activity on day 44.

After B3 the patient was discharged with instructions to practice cue-controlled relaxation at home, and she was followed-up for 12 weeks at biweekly intervals. Data indicate low levels of anxiety and seizure-free weeks, with the exception of week 4 (Christmas time) when she experienced family stress at home.

In general, the experimental case study shows that cue-controlled relaxation was effective in bringing about reduction in both anxiety level and rate of psychomotor seizures. Data also indicate that therapists administering the procedure are interchangeable and that cue-controlled relaxation can be used upon discharge from the hospital by the patient as a self-control technique.

Organic Brain Syndrome and Mild Mental Retardation

One of the most difficult cases that we have ever tackled proved to be both a diagnostic and treatment problem (Turner, Hersen, & Bellack, 1978). This was a 19-year-old adopted son of an upper middle class family who had a 15-year history of treatment on both an out- and inpatient basis in some of the most renowned facilities in the United States, but with few beneficial results. He had received a good number of previous diagnoses, including depression, schizophrenia, mental retardation, and obsessive-compulsive personality. Also, at various times he had been placed on major tranquilizers and antidepressants, but with atypical reactions. IQ testing was similarly variable, yielding scores ranging from 20 to 80. To compound the aforementioned, the young man's parents tended to be belligerent when they were not in accord with the therapists' views on the case.

This patient initially was admitted to our Partial Hospitalization Service (Western Psychiatric Institute and Clinic) but frequently required full hospitalization as an inpatient due to extreme aggressiveness: "The patient would yell and scream, pound his fists, and verbally threaten others. This behavior further deteriorated so that he began to show aimless running behavior, chair throwing, stereotyped behaviors, purposeless arm movements, and periods of apparent amnesia. A diagnosis of psychomotor epilepsy was considered, but could not be confirmed" (Turner et al., 1978, p. 254). Over close to six months the patient was tried on a variety of medications and behavioral programs, but generally to no avail. Finally, he appeared to respond to a very low dose of haloperidol of 1 mg daily. Given historical data and our behavioral observations, he was diagnosed as having an organic brain syndrome and mild mental retardation.

Prior to this extensive period of acting out on the ward the patient had been given a course of social-skills training to improve his rate of verbalizations, affect, and social interaction. This was accomplished by training him to respond appropriately to scenarios requiring assertive responding (i.e., the Behavioral Assertiveness Test-Revised: Eisler, Hersen, Miller, & Blanchard, 1975). Initial data collected and evaluated in a multiple-baseline design across behaviors revealed good improvements in eye contact, response latency, speech loudness, appropriate intonation, number of words spoken, number of smiles, physical gestures, and overall assertiveness.

Surprisingly, even after the patient's six-month period of behavioral disruption (after which he finally was stabilized on haloperidol 1 mg daily) some of the gains initially made on specified target behaviors were still in evidence. At this point booster training for his social-skill deficits was administered. Figure 1-6 presents the results of such booster training for both training scenes and generalization scenes (for which no training was given). These results, presented in multiple baseline fashion, clearly document that improvement in deficits was restored through our booster training sessions. As noted by Turner, Hersen, and Bellack (1978), "Booster sessions are infrequently used by behavior therapist to augment treatment gains during follow-up. However, in training individuals in complex interpersonal skills, booster sessions could be extremely facilitative. In this particular instance, the patient rapidly regained his initial training level in several relatively short sessions" (pp. 257–258).

Obsessive-Compulsive Disorder

A 25-year-old married woman had a seven-year history of handwashing and other cleaning rituals—e.g., toothbrushing for inordinately long periods of time (Turner, Hersen, Bellack, Andrasik, & Capparell, 1980). As a result of these rituals, she experienced considerable stress when family members were not compliant with her demands. The patient had been hospitalized several times and had received a variety of treatments, including ECT, but the rituals seemed to persist.

Due to their high rate of occurrence and long durations, handwashing and toothbrushing were the main targets for inpatient treatment. As can be seen in Figure 1-7, both behaviors were at high duration during baseline assessment. Flooding, the first behavioral treatment administered, appeared to have a negligible effect. Therefore, in the third phase response prevention was carried out. This consisted of nursing staff (who were observing her on a 24-hour basis) physically restraining her from handwashing and toothbrushing beyond normal limits. The fourth phase (baseline), however, fails to reflect improvements as a consequence of this behavioral strategy. Therefore, an extensive course of imipramine was begun in the fifth phase (days 28–51). Treatment progressed from 75, 125, 175, 200, 225, to 250 mg daily. The effects of this tricyclic drug began to appear when the dosage was increased to 200 mg. When the dosage decreased to 100 mg in the next phase ritualistic behavior once again increased. But when it was increased again in the following phase duration rituals once more decreased (especially at a level 250 mg daily).

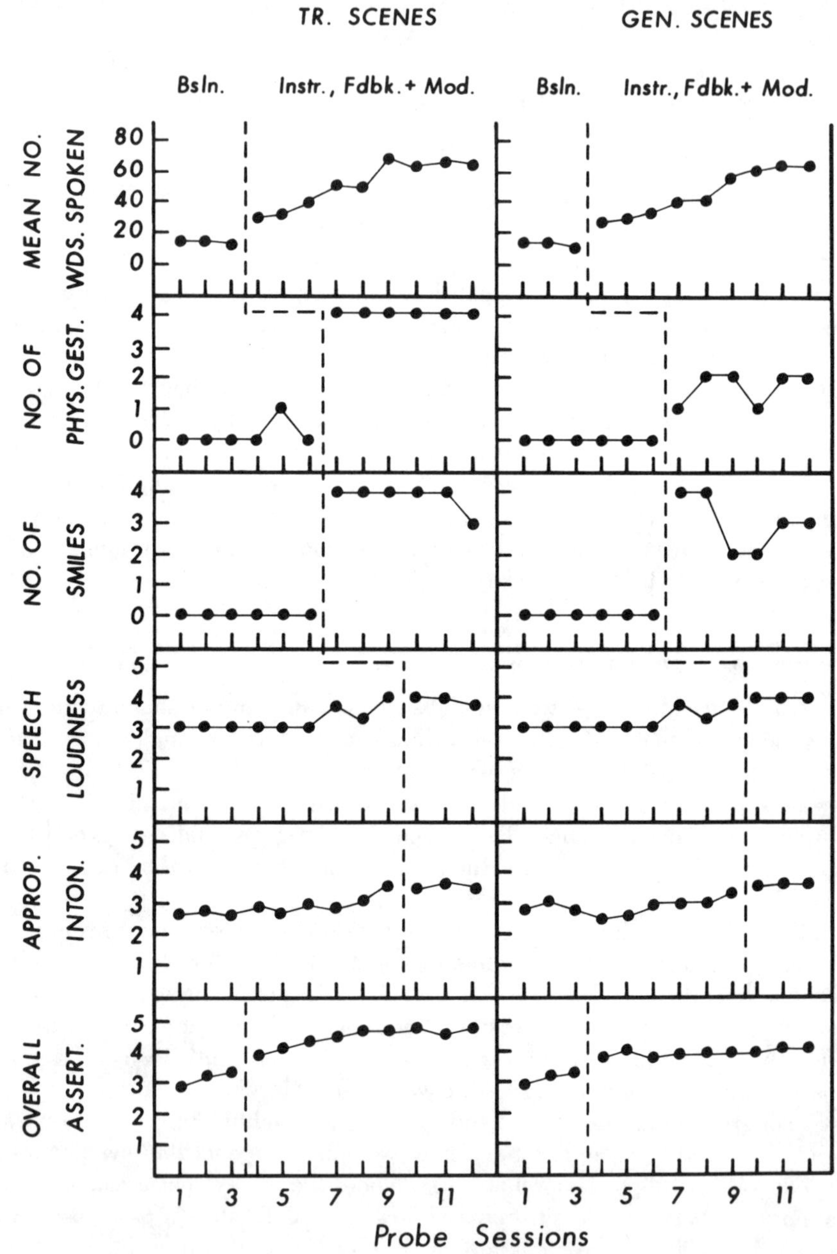

Fig. 1-6. Booster sessions. From Turner SM, Hersen M, & Bellack AS (1978). Social skills training to teach prosocial behaviors in an organically impaired and retarded patient. *Journal of Behavior Therapy and Experimental Psychiatry* 9, 253–258, with permission.

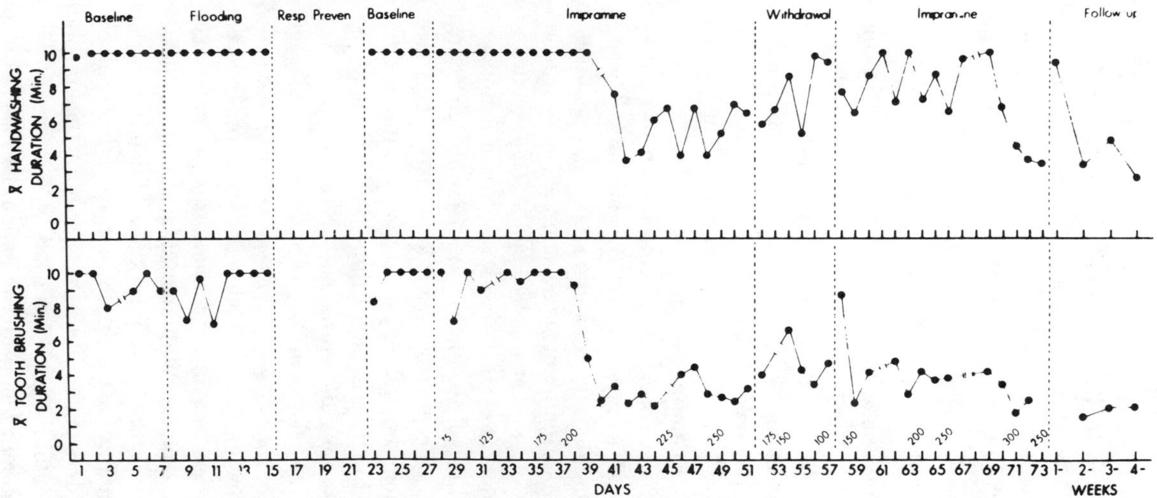

Fig. 1-7. Mean duration of handwashing and toothbrushing per day. From Turner SM; Hersen M, Bellack AS, Andrasik F, & Capparell HV. (1980). Behavioral and pharmacological treatment of obsessive-compulsive disorders. *Journal of Nervous and Mental Disease 168*, 651–657, with permission.

The patient was discharged on a maintenance dose of imipramine, briefly followed-up for four weeks, and then referred to her local mental health center for continued outpatient treatment. In spite of her improvement in duration of rituals when on imipramine, we were not successful in dealing with the interpersonal problems with family members.

This single-case analysis clearly documents the ineffectiveness of the two behavioral strategies tried (i.e., flooding and response prevention). On the other hand, it clearly shows the controlling effects of imipramine (200–250 mg level) for these same two target behaviors. This was confirmed in the imipramine phases of the experimental analysis.

Anorexia Nervosa

A 16-year-old female anorectic (5′7″) weighed 95 pounds when admitted to our inpatient unit at Western Psychiatric Institute and Clinic (Cinciripini, Kornblith, Turner, & Hersen, 1983). Four months prior to her admission she experienced severely decreased appetite and fears of becoming obese, self-induced vomiting, and lost a considerable amount of weight. She then refused solid food altogether and only drank fruit juice and milk. Amenorrhea occurred one month after she began her caloric restriction.

A variety of behavioral treatments known to be effective with anorectics were carried out in succession and concurrently. These appear in Table 1-3, which also documents weight, caloric intake, emesis urges, and emisis episodes during baseline and treatment stages and the two-year follow-up.

During baseline weight was 97 pounds, caloric intake was 850, and emesis urges and episodes were at a high level. When contingency management procedures (hospital privileges made contingent on caloric intake and weight gain) were instituted in the next phase, caloric intake increased to 2650, weight increased to 112 pounds, and emesis urges and episodes decreased significantly. With a return to baseline in phase three there was decreased caloric intake and increased emesis urges and episodes.

The next three phases involved: *contingency management for ideal weight, contingency management and response prevention* ("the patient was accompanied by a staff member in all postmeal activities in order to prevent emesis"), and *contingency management and self-monitoring* (weight = 114–117; caloric intake = 1300–1700; no emesis). With institution of response prevention, emesis urges and episodes dropped to zero. With the addition of self-monitoring, the patient was able to maintain her weight and intake of 1700 calories per day. She then was discharged and placed on a home-contracting program that consisted of specified caloric intake and weight goals.

At the two month follow-up the patient had lost 10 pounds (weight = 107), was only consuming 800 calories a day, and was self-inducing vomiting. She therefore was rehospitalized, and self-monitoring procedures were reinstated. Subsequent to discharge, 9-month, 1-year, and 2-year follow-up contacts revealed maintenance of gains.

Table 1-3
Summary of results of Case Involving 16-year-old Anorectic

Phase[a]	Daily Weight (lbs)	Caloric Intake	Emesis Urges[b]	Emesis Episodes[b]
BL	97	850	12/21 (57%)	10/21 (48%)
CM only	112	2650	2/27 (7%)	1/27 (4%)
BL II	113.5	2100	6/21 (29%)	6/21 (29%)
CM for ideal weight	115	2150	10/30 (33%)	10/30 (33%)
CM and response prevention	115	2100	0/9 (0%)	0/9 (0%)
CM + SM	119	1700	0/30 (0%)	0/30 (0%)
Follow-up Home Contracting				
1 month	117	1500	0 (0%)	0 (0%)
2 months	107	800		12/24 (50%)
9 months	117			0
1 year	117			
2 years	114			0

[a]BL = baseline; CM = contingency management; SM = self-monitoring.
[b]Total frequency/total number of meals (per cent).
From Cinciripini PM, Kornblith SJ, Turner SM, & Hersen M. (1983). A behavioral program for the management of anorexia and bulimia (Table 2). *Journal of Nervous and Mental Disease 171*, 186–189, with permission. © 1983 by The Williams & Wilkins Co., Baltimore.

In addition to the above, "Serum levels of follicle-stimulating hormone and luteinizing hormone (a.m. samples) rose, respectively, from an average of 1.6 and 2.8 mIU/ml at baseline to within a normal range of 12.5 and 10.0 mIU/ml at discharge. Menses had resumed at 2 years postdischarge" (Cinciripini et al., 1983, p. 188).

SUMMARY

Behavior therapists have had many successes while working in the inpatient setting, first in developing ward-wide programs such as the token economy, and more recently in conducting single-case experimental analyses and treatments for a large variety of psychiatric disorders. Some of these cases have involved implementation of behavioral treatments while medication was left at a constant dosage; others have been concerned with the interactive effects of pharmacotherapy and behavior therapy. In some instances pharmacologic approaches have been applied after initial failure of behavior therapy, but the effects of pharmacologic intervention were evaluated using behavioral targets and single-case experimental strategies.

Staff training and cooperation, confounding treatments, time limitations, ethical issues, pharmacological treatment, targets for change, and single-case experimental analyses are important considerations. Token economy programs are effective for young patients. And behavioral treatments have been developed to treat hysterical gagging, conversion reaction, spasmodic torticollis, psychomotor seizures, organic brain syndrome and mild mental retardation, obsessive-compulsive disorder, and anorexia nervosa.

REFERENCES

Agras WS. (1976). Behavior modification in the general-hospital psychiatric unit. In Leitenberg H. (Ed), *Handbook of behavior modification and therapy* (pp. 547–565). Englewood Cliffs, New Jersey: Prentice-Hall.

Arann L, & Horner VM. (1972). Contingency management in an open psychiatric ward. *Journal of Behavior Therapy and Experimental Psychiatry 3*, 31–37.

Atthowe JM, Jr, & Krasner L. (1968). Preliminary report on the application of contingent reinforcement procedures (token economy) on a "chronic" psychiatric ward. *Journal of Abnormal Psychology 73*, 37–43.

Ayllon T, & Azrin N. (1968). *The token economy*. New York: Appleton-Century-Crofts.

Ayllon T, & Michael J. (1959). The psychiatric nurse as a behavioral engineer. *Journal of the Experimental Analysis of Behavior 2*, 323–334.

Barlow DH, & Hersen M. (1973). Single-case experimental designs: Uses in applied clinical research. *Archives of General Psychiatry 29*, 319–325.

Barlow, DH, & Hersen M. (1984). *Single-case experimental designs: Strategies for studying behavior change (2nd ed)*. New York: Pergamon Press.

Bazelon DL. (1974). The perils of wizardry. *American Journal of Psychiatry 131*, 1317–1322.

Bellack AS, & Hersen M. (1978). Assessment and single-case research. In Hersen, M & Bellack AS (Eds), *Behavior therapy in the psychiatric setting* (pp. 3–39). Baltimore: Williams & Wilkins.

Bellack AS, & Hersen M (Eds), (1979). *Research and practice in social skills training*. New York: Plenum Press.

Boren JJ, & Colman AS. (1970). Some experiments on reinforcement principles within a psychiatric ward for delinquent soldiers. *Journal of Applied Behavior Analysis 5*, 33–43.

Brady JP. (1984). Social skills training for psychiatric patients, I: Concepts, methods, and clinical results. *American Journal of Psychiatry 141*, 333–340.

Carlson CG, Hersen M, & Eisler RM. (1972). Token economy programs in the treatment of hospitalized adult psychiatric patients: Current status and recent trends. *Journal of Nervous and Mental Disease 155*, 192–204.

Cinciripini PM, Kornblith SJ, Turner SM, & Hersen M. (1983). A behavioral program for the management of anorexia and bulimia. *Journal of Nervous and Mental Disease 171*, 186–189.

Crowley TJ. (1975). Token programs in an acute psychiatric hospital. *American Journal of Psychiatry 132*, 523–528.

Curran JP, Sutton RG, Faraone SV, & Guenette S. (1985) In-patient approaches. In Hersen M, Bellack AS (Eds), *Handbook of clinical behavior therapy with adults*. New York: Plenum Press.

Eisler RM, Hersen M, Miller PM, & Blanchard EB. (1975). Situational determinants of assertive behaviors. *Journal of Consulting and Clinical Psychology 43*, 330–340.

Epstein LH, & Hersen M. (1974). Behavioral control of hysterical gagging. *Journal of Clinical Psychology 30*, 102–104.

Eriksson JH, Götestam KG, Melin L, & Ost LG. (1975). A token economy treatment of drug addiction. *Behavior Research and Therapy 13*, 113–125.

Frederiksen LW, & Williams JG. (1977). Individualized point systems with a chronic schizophrenic: Component analysis and management in the natural environment. *Journal of Behavior Therapy and Experimental Psychiatry 8*, 205–209.

Girardeau FR, & Spradlin JE. (1964). Token rewards in a cottage program. *Mental Retardation 2*, 345–351.

Goldiamond I. (1975). Singling out behavior modification for legal regulations: Some affects on patient care, psychotherapy, and research in general. *Arizona Law Review 17*, 105–126.

Greenberg DJ, Scott SB, Pisa A, & Friesen DD. (1975). Beyond the token economy: A comparison of two contingency programs. *Journal of Consulting and Clinical Psychology 43*, 498–503.

Hersen M. (1973). Self-assessement of fear. *Behavior Therapy 4*, 241–257.

Hersen M. (1976). Token economies in institutional settings: Historical, political, deprivation, ethical, and generalization issues. *Journal of Nervous and Mental Disease 162* 206–211.

Hersen M. (1982). Single-case experimental designs. In Bellack AS, Hersen M, & Kazdin AE (Eds), *International handbook of behavior modification and therapy* (pp. 167–203). New York: Plenum Press.

Hersen M (Ed). (1983). *Outpatient behavior therapy*. New York: Grune & Stratton.

Hersen M, & Barlow DH. (1976). *Single-case experimental designs: Strategies for studying behavior change*. New York: Pergamon Press.

Hersen M, & Bellack AS. (1978). Staff training and consultation. In Hersen M, & Bellack AS (Eds), *Behavior therapy in the psychiatric setting*. Baltimore: Williams & Wilkins.

Hersen M, & Bellack AS (Eds). (1981). *Behavioral assessment: A practical handbook (2nd ed)*. New York: Pergamon Press.

Hersen M, Turner SM, Edelstein BA, & Pinkston SB. (1975). Effects of pheothiazines and social skills training in a withdrawn schizophrenic. *Journal of Clinical Psychology 31*, 588–594.

Hersen M, Eisler RM, Smith BS, & Agras WS. (1972). A token reinforcement ward for young psychiatric patients. *American Journal of Psychiatry 129*, 228–233.

Kallman WM, Hersen M, & O'Toole DH. (1975). The use of social reinforcement in a case of conversion reaction. *Behavior Therapy 6*, 441–413.

Kazdin AE. (1972). Nonresponsiveness of patients to token economies. *Behaviour Research and Therapy 10*, 417–418.

Kazdin AE. (1973). The failure of some patients to respond to token programs. *Journal of Behavior Therapy and Experimental Psychiatry 4*, 7–14.

Kazdin AE. (1076). Statistical analyses for single-case experimental designs. In Hersen M, & Barlow DH (Eds), *Single-case experimentals designs: Strategies for studying behavior change* (pp. 265–316). New York: Pergamon Press.

Kazdin AE. (1977). Assessing the clinical or applied importance of behavior change through social validation. *Behavior Modification 1*, 427–452.

Kazdin AE. (1978). *History of behavior modification: Experimental foundations of contemporary research.* Baltimore: University Park Press.

Levendusky, PG, Berglas S, Dooley CP, & Landau RJ. (1983). Therapeutic contract program: Preliminary report on behavioral alternative to the token economy. *Behaviour Research and Therapy 21*, 137–142.

Liberman RP, & Davis J. (1975). Drugs and behavior analysis. In Hersen M, Eisler RM, & Miller PM (Eds), *Progress in behavior modification: Vol. 1* (pp. 307–330). New York: Academic Press.

Liberman RP, Teigen J, Patterson R, & Baker V. (1973). Reducing delusional speech in chronic paranoid schizophrenia. *Journal of Applied Behavior Analysis 6*, 57–64.

Maxmen JS, Tucker GJ, & LeBow MD. (1974). *Rational hospital psychiatry: The reactive environment.* New York: Brunner/Mazel.

McReynolds WT, & Coleman J. (1972). Token economy: Patient and staff changes. *Behaviour Research and Therapy 10*, 29–34.

Miller PM, Hersen M, Eisler RM, & Elkin TE. (1974). A retrospective analysis of alcohol consumption on laboratory tasks as related to therapeutic outcome. *Behaviour Research and Therapy 12*, 73–76.

Moss GR, & Rick GR. (1981). Application of a token economy for adolescents in a private psychiatric hospital. *Behavior Therapy 12*, 585–590.

Narrol HG. (1967). Experimental application of reinforcement principles to the analysis and treatment of hospitalized alcoholics. *Quarterly Journal of Studies on Alcohol 28*, 105–115.

O'Brien JT, Raynes AE, & Patch VD. (1971). An operant reinforcement system to improve ward behavior in in-patient drug addicts. *Journal of Behavior Therapy and Experimental Psychiatry 2*, 239–242.

Parrino JJ, George L, & Daniels AD. (1971). Token control of pill-taking behavior in a psychiatric ward. *Journal of Behavior Therapy and Experimental Psychiatry 2*, 181–185.

Paul GL, & Lentz RJ. (1977). *Psychosocial treatment of chronic mental patients.* Cambridge: Harvard University Press.

Rybolt, GA. (1975). Token reinforcement therapy with chronic psychiatric patients: A three year evolution. *Journal of Behavior Therapy and Experimental Psychiatry 6*, 188–191.

Shean GD, & Zeidberg Z. (1971). Token reinforcement therapy: A comparison of matched groups. *Journal of Behavior Therapy and Experimental Psychiatry 2*, 95–105.

Stuart RB. (1978). Protection of the right to informed consent to participate in research. *Behavior Therapy 9*, 73–82.

Turner SM, Hersen M, & Alford H. (1974). Effects of massed practice and meprobamate on spasmodic torticollis: An experimental analysis. *Behaviour Research and Therapy 12*, 259–260.

Turner SM, Hersen M, & Bellack AS. (1977). Effects of social disruption, stimulus interference, and adversive conditioning on auditory hallucinations. *Behavior Modification 1*, 249–258.

Turner SM, Hersen M, & Bellack AS. (1978). Social skills training to teach prosocial behaviors in an organically impaired and retarded patient. *Journal of Behavior Therapy and Experimental Psychiatry 9*, 253–258.

Turner SM, Hersen M, Bellack AS, Andrasik F, & Capparell HV. (1980). Behavioral and pharmacological treatment of obsessive-compulsive disorders. *Journal of Nervous and Mental Disease 168*, 651–657.

Wells KC, Turner SM, Bellack AS, & Hersen M. (1978). Effects of cue-controlled relaxation on psychomotor seizures: An experimental analysis. *Behaviour Research and Therapy 16*, 51–53.

2
Staff Training and Consultation

Charles J. Wallace

With the continuing emphasis on deinstitutionalization of the long-term residents of inpatient psychiatric facilities, the role of inpatient staff members has shifted from custodian to educator. In addition to ensuring a safe and habitable living environment, staff members must now design and implement services to increase patients' capabilities to adjust successfully to the demands of community living. Since many staff members have not been trained to provide these services, there has been a proliferation of specialized programs to assist them to assume their new duties as educators. Unfortunately, the few studies that have evaluated the effects of these programs have yielded contradictory results. As Bernstein (1980, 1984) summarizes in her excellent critical reviews, some programs have had positive effects (e.g., Schinke & Wong, 1977, 1978), many have had no effects (e.g., Delamater, Conners, & Wells, 1984), and a minority have even had detrimental effects (e.g., Plaska, Burgess, & Tillman, 1979).

These large differences in effectiveness are not likely to be due solely to differences in the programs' curricula and formats. Considering that training is but one of the many components that constitute the treatment system of an inpatient ward, it is far more likely that the major determinant of the effectiveness of a training program is its interactions with these other components. Thus, identification of these interactions is perhaps the critical step in designing a successful training program.

This chapter discusses training from the perspective of "sociotechnical

PRACTICE OF INPATIENT BEHAVIOR THERAPY
ISBN 0-8089-1715-3

systems" theory. The theory provides a set of conceptual tools that will assist in identifying the components of an inpatient treatment system and their interactions.

SOCIOTECHNICAL SYSTEMS THEORY

Sociotechnical systems theory (Davis & Taylor, 1979) can be used to describe the operations of organizations as diverse as an automobile manufacturing plant, a classroom, or an inpatient treatment ward. An organization is considered to be a bounded entity whose goal is to transform inputs into specified outputs. Two systems are used to accomplish this transformation: a technical system and a social system. The technical system consists of the tools and techniques that achieve the desired transformation, and the social system consists of the individuals who implement these tools and techniques. The specific form of each of the systems is the result of a deliberate design process that seeks to maximize the systems' joint operations. Because the two are designed, they reflect the social, political, and economic values of both the designers and the organization's major "stakeholders" such as its employees and its stockholders. Thus, an organization is not only an entity that transforms inputs into outputs, but also an economic entity that consumes public and private resources, and a social entity that uses the efforts of individuals to achieve its goals.

Furthermore, since an organization does not exist in a vacuum, it is affected by events in its environment such as variability in customers' demands, fluctuations in suppliers' capacities, and changes in economic and social policies. The technical and social systems must be designed so that an organization can adapt to the changing environment in which it operates. Figure 2-1 illustrates how an organization can be depicted as a sociotechnical system.

Technical System

The design of the tools and techniques of the technical system is based on an underlying technology and is affected not only by the quality of that technology but also by the expected variability of the inputs to an organization. Davis (1977) defines a technology as a body of knowledge that fulfills five criteria: (1) knowledge of the cause–effect relationships of particular actions, (2) methods of measuring the effects of these actions, (3) standards for judging the acceptability of the actual effects, (4) replicability of the cause–effect relationships, and (5) communication of the knowledge such that others can become proficient in its application. The quality of the technology depends primarily on the clarity of the knowledge of the cause–effect relationships. Clearly, known relationships will result in designing tools and techniques that are precisely specified with easily measured effects and readily available feedback mechanisms to correct any faulty uses. Less clearly known relationships will result in designing less precisely

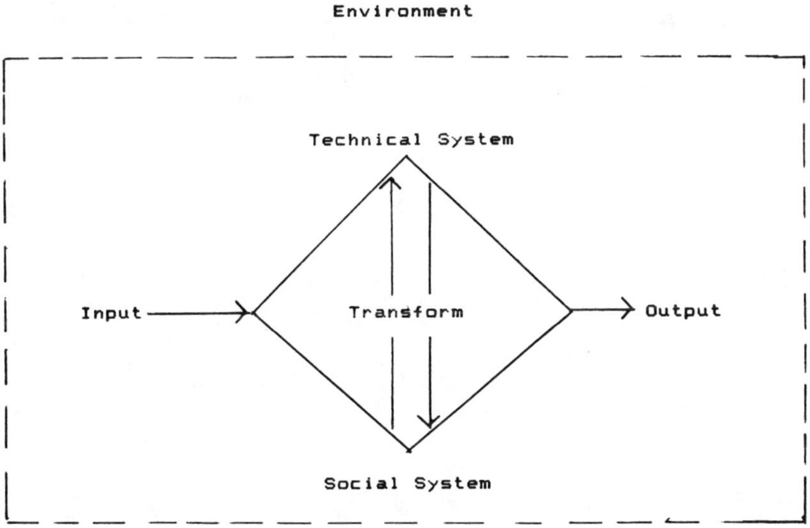

Fig. 2-1. The basic components of an organization.

specified tools and techniques that, when combined with variable inputs, yield a technical system characterized by many trial and error activities. Perrow (1967) has developed a fourfold classification of organizational structures based on dichotomizing the quality of the techology into well and poorly developed, and the variability of the inputs into high and low (see Table 2-1). No structure is a perfect example of any one of these four types since the quality of the technology and the variability of the inputs are continuous rather than discrete. The classification scheme has important implications for the design of the social system, however.

The tools and techniques of the technical system are designed as a sequence of "unit operations," with the output of one operation serving as the input to the next sequential operation. As Davis and Englestadt (1966) note, unit operations describe "the processing steps to be completed; i.e., the work to be done by men and machines" (p. 171). The design of these operations is based on a consideration of the variabilities in the inputs received by each, their integration, the distribution of work to be performed by men and machines, the skills required of the workers, and the extent to which each operation is perceived as a distinct element in the sequence. There are five general classes of unit operations: (1) those that repair or maintain the other unit operations, (2) those that change the location of the raw materials, (3) those that transform the characteristics of the materials, (4) those that inspect the quality and quantity of the outputs of the other operations, and (5) those that store the materials for later transformation. Because of their generic nature, these classes of unit operations apply equally to the production of goods or services.

Table 2-1
Four Types of Organizational Structure

Technology	Variability of Inputs: Low	Variability of Inputs: High
Well Developed	Routine	Engineering
Poorly Developed	Craft	Nonroutine

Social System

An organization seeks a predictable state in which to conduct its unit operations to ensure that it will accomplish its objectives. To achieve this predictable state, an organization may decide to reduce the scope of its transformations to a narrow range of inputs and environmental conditions, or it may develop a range of responses that allows it to cope with changing environmental conditions and inputs. The technical system tends to be fixed at any one point in time, however, and difficult to modify in the event of unanticipated changes in the environment or extreme variability in the inputs. It is the major responsibility of the social system to provide the requisite range of responses that allows an organization to adapt to changing conditions.

The social system consists of a set of individuals who occupy roles. Each role is a set of expectations that define the behaviors that the role occupant is permitted to perform. These include the prescribed tasks of an organization's unit operations, the discretionary tasks that allow the role occupant to exercise a range of judgment in applying the prescribed tasks to variable inputs, and the social behaviors that are considered "acceptable" (e.g., the individuals and groups with whom the role occupant can interact). It is, of course, the discretionary tasks that are the critical elements in determining an organization's adaptability. Because the prescribed tasks are generally the only ones that are explicitly stated (i.e., job descriptions), the actual behaviors of a particular role occupant depend upon that occupant's perception of these expectations and his or her preferences for certain behaviors. The behaviors of different occupants of the same role may be quite different, and the formal representation of an organization's structure by means of charts and job descriptions may be quite inaccurate.

These are four functions and four corresponding "subsystems" that must be considered in the design of the social system. The first is the goal attainment subsystem, which ties the technical and social systems together and consists of the prescribed tasks that define each unit operation, the workers and the abilities they need to perform each task, and the communications that support these performances. The second is the adaptation subsystem, which consists of the discrectionary tasks necessary to adapt each unit operation to changing conditions plus the means of recognizing these changes and of designing and distributing the discretionary tasks. These means can range from decisions by individual workers, to temporary task forces, to permanent planning and budgeting departments.

The third is the integration subsystem, which provides for coordination among the unit operations and consists of the formal and informal communications that are used to identify and resolve organizational conflicts. Also included are organization-wide mechanisms, particularly its means of distributing rewards that reinforce competitive or cooperative behavior among its workers.

The fourth is the long-term maintenance subsystem that provides the means by which an organization recruits, retains, and ultimately replaces its members with a minimum of disruption to the achievement of its goals. Included in this subsystem are an organization's mechanisms for indoctrinating its members and shaping their behaviors such as its "culture," its training programs, its opportunities for learning and for career advancement, its support for inter- and intrapersonal crises, and its tools for evaluating and rewarding performances. Of course, these mechanisms may serve the functions of more than one subsystem. The tools of evaluation and reward may reinforce cooperative behavior for a high level of integration by means of monetary and career rewards that satisfy and retain its members.

Application to an Inpatient Psychiatric Ward

An inpatient psychiatric ward can be conceptualized as an organization that transforms patients from a state of illness to a state of health. Many regulations govern the conduct of this type of organization, but the unit operations that "store" and "transport" patients (i.e., maintain a safe and habitable living environment), that medically transform them (i.e., administer psychotropic drugs and other medically based interventions), and that monitor the quantity and quality of these other unit operations (i.e., documenting in patients' charts) are much the same from organization to organization. Indeed, these unit operations are the core of the formal education of many of the organization's members, such as its nursing staff.

The unit operations designed to increase patients' abilities to adjust to the demands of community living are, however, often different from organization to organization. There are a number of technologies that may be used alone or in combination to design these unit operations, including psychodynamic psychotherapy, milieu therapy, and behavior therapy. The choice of a technology and the design of the unit operations ultimately depend upon the values of the staff about the appropriate methods of modifying and maintaining patient behaviors. The advantages to choosing a behavioral technology are that the cause–effect relationships are more clearly known, have been more frequently replicated, and are communicated and monitored more easily than those of the other psychotherapeutic technologies. Two inpatient organizations subscribing to a behavioral technology may be quite different in their actual operations, however, depending upon the range of psychopathology they choose to treat and the range of environmental conditions in which they expect to operate. These differences in choices and expectations will sustantially affect the design of their sociotechnical systems, including the methods they use to train and maintain their staff members' behaviors.

Tharp and Wetzel (1969) have characterized the social system of an inpatient behavioral organization in terms of three roles: behavioral manager, behavioral engineer, and behavioral consultant. A behavioral manager applies the specific unit operations that have been designed by a behavioral engineer, who has been advised by a behavioral consultant about these operations and the overall structure of the sociotechnical system. Depending upon the design of the social system, staff members may fulfill one or more of these roles, and not all of them will be equally important at any one time (Bernstein, 1980).

An inpatient organization that chooses to treat a wide range of psychopathology and expects to remain in operation for an indefinite period of time will, in terms of Perrow's (1967) classification scheme, develop either a nonroutine or an engineering structure. To adapt to the variable inputs using behavior change unit operations that may or may not be relatively well developed, an organization must design a social system that has a wide range of responses. The capabilites of the role occupants would have to be high, there would be many discretionary tasks, communications to resolve conflicts and to integrate the unit operations would be frequent, monitoring and feedback would be extensive and immediate so that the unit operations could be readily changed, and training would be provided in a wide range of behavior change unit operations. Indeed, it has been suggested that all staff members should be trained as behavioral engineers (Bernstein, 1980). The principal advantage to this type of sociotechnical system is that it better ensures the long-term survival of an organization by building in the response capability to adapt to changing inputs and environmental conditions. Additionally, the continual use of new unit operations may create a "corporate culture" of change and excitement that reduces "burn out" and enhances the long-term career objectives of the staff. The major disadvantage is the high cost of the constant communications and the use of highly qualified personnel.

An inpatient organization that chooses to treat a narrow range of psychopathology and, perhaps, is tied to a limited existence through funds provided by a research grant will develop either a routine or a craft structure. There will be fairly constant inputs for which the behavior change unit operations may or may not be relatively well developed. As an organization matures, the effects of the unit operations will become more clearly known, and it will shift from a craft to a routine structure. The range of responses required of the social system will be narrow and will become even narrower. Once the unit operations have been designed, only infrequent engineering and consultation would be necessary, the number of discretionary tasks would be low, the capabilities of the staff members could be low, feedback would be standardized, monitoring and communication would be infrequent and highly routine, and training would be provided for only a limited range of behavior change unit operations. The principal advantage to this type of sociotechnical system is the low cost of its implementation because of its high degree of standardization. The disadvantage is the inflexibility of the organization, which augurs poorly for its long-term survival. Additionally, the routine nature of the tasks lowers the quality of work for the staff and does not contribute to their long-term career objectives.

IMPLICATIONS FOR TRAINING PROGRAMS

The implications of sociotechnical systems theory for the design and implementation of a staff training program are twofold. First, a training program must be designed to fit the sociotechnical system in which it is embedded. If the desired outcome of training is, for example, staff members' ongoing implementations of sessions to improve patients' social skills, then these sessions must be a scheduled, monitored, and rewarded unit operation. If they are not, then training is a costly waste of time.

Second, training is itself a sociotechnical system that uses several unit operations to achieve the objective of transforming trainees' knowledge and behaviors. Its effectiveness will be determined by variations in the trainees, by the unit operations chosen by the trainers, and by the trainers' social system.

These two sets of implications must be viewed in terms of three major components of any sociotechnical system: the environment, the technical system, and the social system.

Environment

Fit of Training to the Sociotechnical System

The environment of an inpatient organization will limit the range of psychopathology that can be treated, the goals and unit operations that can be chosen by an inpatient organization, and the skills and knowledge of the individuals who are available to fulfill the roles of the social system. These limitations will directly affect the design of the organization's sociotechnical system, and indirectly the design of its training procedures.

Bernstein (1980), for example, suggests that training should be focused on the patient problems that "behavior managers, behavior engineers, and behavior consultants must be able to solve . . . there is little point in teaching people to apply behavioral analysis to problems they will not be called upon to solve, and there is much to be gained from using frequently occurring problems as examples during training" (p. 7). Implicit in this suggestion is the assumption that an organization's sociotechnical system has been designed to transform a specified range of patient behaviors to which the training should be tailored. Although this range may be explicitly stated, the maturing of an inpatient organization may have resulted in changes in the types of patient problems treated by the organization that should be assessed prior to training. Also implicit in Bernstein's suggestion is the assumption that the didactic instruction and practicum experiences that form the training of behavioral consultants and engineers should match the wider range of patient problems they are expected to solve (Linehan, 1980).

Changes in the social mores and values of groups and individuals in the organization's environment will result in changes in the ethical and legal requirements that determine the acceptability of an organization's goals and unit operations. The current emphasis on "social validation" reflects the need to fit explicitly an inpatient organization's sociotechnical system to the values and requirements of its major stakeholders, including the institution of which it is a part, its consumers and their significant others, its own members, and the larger mental health system with which it interacts. Maley and Harshbarger (1976) note, for example, that the mental health system in general must be accountable, and this accountability "must lead to an evaluation that can be consenually validated apart from the jingoism of professional dialogue" (p. 381). Training will, of course, have to be tailored to the acceptable goals and behavior change unit operations chosen by the organization. It may also be necessary to explicitly train behavioral engineers and consultants in the techniques of social validation (Bernstein & Ziarnik, 1984).

Changes in the personnel policies of the institution of which an inpatient organization is a part and in the demographic characteristics of the population will affect the quantity and quality of the labor pool available to fill the roles of the social system. For example, the declining birth rate has led to the voluntary entrance of many women into the labor force who have chosen careers in the human services field (Broskowski & Smith, 1976), and there has been a proliferation of community college programs that award students Associate of Arts degrees as Mental Health Workers. Their curricula tend to be quite heterogeneous (Young, Ture, & Packard, 1974), and there are few standards that regulate the quality of these programs. Considering that the design of an inpatient organization's sociotechincal system is based upon assumptions about the skills and knowledge of the role occupants, a mismatch between these assumptions and the actual skills and knowledge of individuals available to occupy the roles may pose serious problems. If the actual skills and knowledge are lower than assumed, the discretionary tasks may not be implemented correctly and the behavior change unit operations may be ineffective. If the actual skills and knowledge are higher, the unit operations may be implemented correctly but at the cost of the occupants' dissatisfaction with the quality of their work. To solve the problems posed by these mismatches, either the sociotechnical system can be redesigned or training can be provided to remediate deficiences in occupants' skills and knowledge.

There also has been a proliferation of self-help programs that increase the pool of potential caregivers, particularly individuals who can provide post-discharge services (Caplan, 1973). Designing unit operations to integrate these services into the inpatient organization's sociotechnical system may be quite difficult, and providing training to impart the necessary skills and knowledge may be even more difficult given the self-help philosophy of explicitly avoiding the use of professional personnel.

Even changes in the general educational system may affect the design of training programs. As enrollment declines, colleges and universities seek new markets for their services (Broskowski & Smith, 1976). A partnership may be formed between the mental health system and the colleges and universities in which the latter contract to supply some or all of the training needs of the former.

Training as a Sociotechnical System

Considering that training is itself a sociotechnical system, its environment is the larger sociotechnical system in which it is embedded. Any variable that affects the larger sociotechnical system, including the environmental variables discussed above, will affect the design of the training program. This design process is discussed in more detail in the next section.

Technical System

Fit of Training to the Sociotechnical System

In general, training is a "repair" and "maintenance" unit operation that provides role occupants with the skills and knowledge necessary to correctly perform their prescribed tasks. Its effectiveness can be evaluated in terms of trainees' acquisition of the requisite skills and knowledge and their correct performance of the prescribed tasks. Although the acquisition of skills and knowledge are clearly the "core" of a training program and should form the basis of its evaluation, correct performance of the prescribed tasks is a function of the entire sociotechnical system including its training program. Role occupants must not only acquire the skills and knowledge necessary to perform their prescribed tasks, but they must receive accurate and timely feedback, the social system must support them, and the unit operations must be clearly specified. Inaccurate performance may not be rectified by implementation of a training program because that performance may be the result of problems in components of the sociotechnical system other than deficiencies in the role occupants' skills and knowledge.

Specifically discussing training programs for inpatient organizations, Bernstein (1980) suggests that they be evaluated in terms of five areas: (1) trainees' subjective impressions of the program, (2) increases in trainees' knowledge, (3) changes in trainees' behaviors, (4) changes in patients' behaviors, and (5) generalization of the trainees' skills and knowledge across time, settings, and patients. Outcomes in the first two areas are clearly within the province of a training program, as are changes in the trainees' behaviors when these are measured within the context of the training sessions (e.g., pre–post changes in behaviors measured by ratings of videotapes of trainees' performances in analogues of the unit operations). Trainees' actual implementation and generalization of the skills and changes in patients' behaviors are, however, far less a function of the training program than they are of the design of the sociotechnical system and the quality of the behavior change technology that underlies it. It may be too much to expect that training alone will lead to sustained changes in either trainees' or patients' behaviors.

Indeed, if training is not a panacea for the ills of an inpatient organization's sociotechnical system, it may be appropriate in any situation in which training is conducted to question its necessity. Bernstein (1979) found that 80 percent of the difficulties encountered by behavioral engineers and consultants concerned inaccurate performance of the behavior change unit operations by the behavioral managers. Rather than providing unnecessary training, improved performance may be accomplished by more clearly specifying the unit operations, by instituting feedback (e.g., Panyan, Boozer, & Morris, 1970), or by enlisting the approval of the appropriate levels of management (Gladstone & Spencer, 1977; Wallace, Davis, Liberman, & Baker, 1973).

An experiment conducted by Delamater et al. (1984) exemplifies the difficulty of instituting a training program whose goal does not fit with the inpatient organization's sociotechnical system. The goal of their program was to increase staff members' correct use of six skills to shape the behaviors of their 6- to 12-year-old patients during twice daily, 30-minute "free play" periods. The skills, which were directly observed during each period and rated as responses to the children's appropriate and inappropriate behaviors, included rewarding, attending, punishing, redirecting, ignoring, and vocalizing. Training consisted of 14 weeks of instruction using Brown and Presbie's (1974) multi-media programmed curriculum, 2 weeks of direct feedback to selected trainees about the frequency with which they used the trained skills, and 2 weeks of role-playing of the skills. The results indicated that, at best, role-playing had a moderate and short-term effect, with instruction and feedback having no effect. Although these results are in accord with those reported previously, particularly for the ineffectiveness of instruction (e.g., Gardner, 1972; McKeown, Adams, & Forehand, 1975), a major difficulty with this study is that training was conducted to increase skills for which there was no corresponding unit operation. During the free-play period, the children were allowed to do as they pleased, and no unit operations were specifically structured to transform their behaviors. Thus, staff members were being trained to use skills during a period for which there were no prescribed tasks.

Of course, there are training programs that are deliberately designed not to fit a particular sociotechnical system. The training of behavioral engineers and consultants, for example, is designed to give them skills that can be generalized to a wide range of sociotechnical systems. Their training is focused on the underlying behavior change technology and the techniques necessary to adapt that technology to specific inpatient organizations. Linehan (1980) provides an extensive discussion and model of training behavioral engineers and consultants, and Bergan, Kratochwill, and their colleagues have demonstrated that the effects of this type of training can be clearly specified and objectively evaluated (Bergan & Tambari, 1976; Bergan, Kratochwill, & Luiten, 1980; Kratochwill, Bergan, & Mace, 1981).

Similarly, continuing education conferences and workshops are often designed to provide general information about a new aspect of behavior change technology that must be transformed by attendees to fit the particular sociotechnical system in which each one works. However, this transformation into a unit operation that is "adopted" by a particular system depends upon the current design of that system, the skills of the attendees, and their authority to make such changes. It may be too much to expect that workshops and conferences will result in adoption of the technology, since that may be achieved only by attendees actively involved in the design of their sociotechnical systems.

Training as a Sociotechnical System

Training is itself a sociotechnical system that uses a set of unit operations to transform trainees' skills and knowledge. Its inputs are the trainees and the variations in their abilities; its outputs are the desired skills and knowledge; its unit operations are the various elements of the curriculum; its social system is the role of the trainer. As with any sociotechnical system, a training program must be deliberately designed with consideration of the range of inputs (trainees) that can be accommodated, the outputs (skills and knowledge) that are desired, the unit operations (the curriculum and the methods of presentation) that transform the inputs to the outputs, and the means of adapting to unanticipated variations in the inputs to all stages in the transformation process (trainers adapting the curriculum).

Perhaps the first step in this design process is to list the skills and knowledge to be acquired. This list not only forms the basis for further specification of the curriculum, but it also affords an opportunity to consider explicitly the necessity of training. For example, if the desired outcome of training is staff members' implementation of sessions to improve patients' social skills, then the requisite staff skills and knowledge include identifying patients' problem social situations, translating these into correctly enacted role-plays, praising patients' positive behaviors, suggesting behaviors to be improved, correctly enacting a second role-play, praising patients' improvements, and recording the results of the intervention. This list of skills defines the curriculum of the training program by specifying the "boundaries" of each of the training unit operations. Training, however, should be provided only for those skills supported by the sociotechnical system and not previously acquired by the staff.

Assuming that training is necessary, the next step is to determine the specific outputs of each of the training unit operations. Rather than "re-inventing the wheel," it may be possible to adapt the curriculum used by similar training programs. If not, then this step involves a comprehensive analysis of the specific behaviors required to perform each skill. For example, praising patients about their positive behaviors consists of several behaviors, including accurately selecting a positive patient behavior to be praised, clearly describing the positive behavior, giving a verbal indication of praise, giving a concomitant nonverbal indication of praise, and recording the outcome of the intervention. Each of these behaviors is one of the outputs that define the unit operation that trains staff to praise patients' positive behaviors.

Of course, there is a degree of subjectivity in this analysis such that the same skill analyzed by different individuals may result in different lists of requisite behaviors. This subjectivity may be reduced by striving for consensual agreement among "experts" about the adequacy of the analysis, a process similar to social validation or the content validation of a test.

Once the outputs of the unit operations have been specified, the actions required to achieve these outputs must be determined. In the case of learning to provide praise, this may involve the trainees watching a model, then practicing the behaviors in role-plays with other trainees who act as patients, receiving feedback from the trainers who themselves should be models of praising, and continuing to practice the behaviors until the desired outputs are achieved. The role-plays should be tailored to the range of patients and problems likely to be encountered by the trainees (Bernstein, 1980). Although the actions of the unit operations could be entirely didactic, this has proven to be less effective than modeling, role-playing, and feedback (Gladstone & Spencer, 1977; Kazdin & Moyer, 1976; Komaki, 1977).

The effects of each of the training unit operations may be monitored by rating trainees' performances using checklists of the requisite behaviors. Not only do the results of the ratings provide feedback about the effectiveness of the unit operations, they may also be used to shape and reinforce trainees' behaviors. Furthermore, the checklists may be used to monitor staff members' actual implementation of the skills, thus directly linking training to the larger sociotechnical system. The trainees may even use the checklists as cues for their behaviors during and after training (Bornstein & Hamilton, 1978; Komaki, 1977).

There is, however, a "place" for instruction, particularly at the beginning of training. It may be important to "set the stage" for learning the skills by discussing the rationale for their design and development. This may include discussions about the variabilities of the environment in which the inpatient organization operates, the goals of the organization and the means by which these are continually validated, and the quality of the technology underlying the design of both the overall sociotechnical system and the specific unit operations for which the skills are being trained. This discussion not only provides an opportunity to explicitly communicate the inpatient organization's "culture," but it may also allow airing of conflicts at a time deliberately structured by the trainers to be least destructive to achieving the goals of training. It may even be the case that the conflicts are so extensive and intensive that training must be delayed until they are resolved.

Once the actions of the training unit operations and the methods of their evaluation have been specified, the methods of modifying them must be designed to account for the variations in both trainees' abilities and their progress through the unit operations. Implicit in the design of the training unit operations is a specifiable range of trainees' abilities for which they are appropriate. Measuring these abilities with a pretest, as would routinely be done if effectiveness were to be evaluated on the basis of pre–post changes, may identify trainees who are outside of this range. Remedial sessions may be conducted for those who are below this range, and certain unit operations may be skipped by those who are above this range. Trainees will also progress through the unit operations at different rates, and the program may be explicitly designed to allow individual pacing, with trainees even choosing to engage in different steps such as self-paced texts versus lectures within each unit operation (Clark & Macrae, 1976). It may be best, however, to exclude trainees who are markedly discrepant from the expected range since they may be more efficiently trained by other methods.

Social System

Fit of Training to the Sociotechnical System

A major consideration in the design of a training program is the fit of the skills being trained to the quantity and quality of prescribed tasks, discretionary tasks, and social behaviors perceived by the trainees as appropriate for their roles. The poorer the fit, the less likely that trainees will learn and implement the skills. The fact that only the prescribed tasks are explicitly stated, however, makes this consideration particularly difficult. Yet failure to account for the "approved" discretionary tasks and social behaviors that define the "politics" of the inpatient organization may doom an otherwise well designed training program to failure.

For example, Delamater et al. (1984) report that their training program was instituted as part of an administrative decision to shift the sociotechnical system from one based on a psychodynamic technology to one based on a behavioral technology. The shift created a split among the staff members, and introduction of the training program coalesced the split, which substantially contributed to the program's ineffectiveness. Hersen and Bellack (1978) also note the importance of explicitly considering the organization's politics. They suggest the "introduction of a behavioral system on a given psyciatric ward can only intensify the struggles already found in the system. Consequently, the focus of the struggle will often shift, and the behavioral system will bear the brunt of the existing conflicts" (p. 37).

A key element of the inpatient organization's politics is the "turf" that is considered appropriate for each role given the role occupants' professional identities. Turf disputes seem to be never ending (Klein, 1976; Stuckey, 1973), and may be intensified in sociotechnical systems based on a behavioral technology. Roles such as "behavioral engineer" and unit operations such as sessions to improve patients' social skills bear little relationship to the prescribed tasks traditionally established for each professional discipline. A training program should be designed with sensitivity to these disputes since they can surface during training and severely reduce its effectiveness. Specifically discussing the goals and technology of the sociotechnical system early in training may highlight these disputes, which must then be resolved outside of the training sessions.

Consideration should also be given to the organization's politics in deciding who is to be included in the training sessions, what behaviors will be required of the trainees, and who will conduct the training. The approved social behaviors may include proscribed and prescribed relationships among certain roles and their occupants. The "mix" of trainees included in a session should be designed with sensitivity to the proscribed relationships, particularly if the training program involves intensive interaction among trainees over a number of sessions. Role expectations may also differ about the behaviors that are appropriate when each role occupant functions as a trainee. Trainee behaviors such as role-playing may be unacceptable for occupants of certain roles. The behaviors required of trainees should be explicitly stated at the beginning of training, and the unit operations modified, if possible, to match trainees' expectations. Role expectations may also differ about the individuals who can function as credible trainers. Occupants of certain roles may expect to be trained only by high status individuals, and efforts should be made to enhance the trainers' credibility by emphasizing their expertise and their similarity with the trainees. The training program should be supported by the appropriate levels of management, assuming that this does not exacerbate existing conflicts (Ziarnik & Bernstein, 1984), and by "internal change agents" who have been accorded a high status in the organization's politics.

In addition to receiving this "stamp of approval" from high status individuals, the value of training may be substantially enhanced if it is seen as one of the components that advances the long-term career objectives of the organization's members. This may be particularly important for trainees who have been granted degrees as "Mental Health Associates" or "Mental Health Workers" and for whom career opportunities are often limited (Klein, 1976). Collaborating with local educational institutions to provide credit for participation may be an imortant reinforcer for trainees.

Training as a Sociotechnical System

The social system of the trainers must be designed so that the training unit operations may be implemented, adapted, and integrated to achieve the training program's objectives. Given the crucial importance of adapting training to the sociotechnical system in which it is embedded, the trainers must function as "system analysts" (Nadler, 1970), adapting the unit operations as necessary. Methods to integrate the trainers' activities should be designed so that there is a smooth and credible flow of communication to the trainees. Consideration should also be given to the long-term career development of the trainers. As Malott (1976) suggests, reinforcers for the trainers are often publications in professional journals and presentations at conventions of professional societies. However, requirements for acceptable publications and presentations in terms of their research design may conflict with the organization's goals. These conflicts should be aired and resolved so that the training component of the organization's sociotechnical system can function effectively.

SUMMARY

The design of a training program is a complex process that requires careful thought and sensitive analysis to be successful. The specification of the program's desired goals requires a comprehensive analysis of the inpatient organization's sociotechnical system that leads to explicitly questioning the very necessity of the program. Development of the training unit operations requires a thorough behavioral analysis of the desired outputs and the methods by which these may be achieved. Implementation of the program requires both the itnerpersonal sensitivity to be aware of the many social system variables that may moderate its effectiveness and the flexibility to adapt the program accordingly. Yet this complexity should not deter attempts to design successful training programs; they are essential to the growth and long-term development of the organization and its members.

REFERENCES

Bergan JR, & Tambari ML. (1976). Consultant skill and efficiency and the implementations and outcomes of consultation. *Journal of School Psychology 13*, 3–14.

Bergan JR, Kratochwill TR, & Luiten J. (1980). Competency-based training in behavioral consultation. *Journal of School Psychology 18*, 91–97.

Bernstein GS. (1979). Development and evaluation of an instrument to assess the competence of behavioral managers (Doctoral dissertation, Univeristy of Wisconsin, 1979). *Dissertation Abstracts International 39*, 4567B.

Bernstein GS. (1980). Training behavior change agents: A conceptual review. *Behavior Therapy 13*, 1–23.

Bernstein GS. (1984). Training of behavior change agents. In Hersen M, Eislen RM, & Miller PM (Eds), *Progress in behavior modification, vol. 17* (pp 167–199). New York: Academic Press.

Bernstein GS, & Ziarnik JP. (1984). Training behavior change agents in outcome selection. *The Behavior Therapist* 7, 103–104.

Bornstein PH, & Hamilton SB. (1978). Positive parental praise: Increasing reactivity and accuracy of self-observation. *Journal of Abnormal Child Psychology 6*, 503–509.

Broskowski A, & Smith TP. (1976). Manpower development for the human service system. In Maley RF, & Harshbarger D (Eds), *Community mental health systems* (pp 291–315). New York: John Wiley.

Brown PL, & Presbie RJ. (1974). *Behavior modification skills*, Hicksville, New York: Research Media.

Caplan G. (1973). *Support systems and community mental health: Lectures in concept development*. New York: Behavioral Science.

Clark HB, & Macrae JW. (1976). The use of imposed and self-selected training packages to establish classroom teaching skills. *Journal of Applied Behavior Analysis 9*, 105.

Davis LE. (1977). Job design: Overview and future direction. *Journal of Contemporary Business 6*, 85–102.

Davis LE, & Englestadt PN. (1966) Unit operations in sociotechnical systems: Analysis and design. *International Journal of Production Ressearch 4*, 171–178.

Davis LE, & Taylor JC. (1979). *Design of jobs*. Santa Monica, CA: Goodyear Publishing Co.

Delamater AM, Conners CK, & Wells KC. (1984). A comparison of staff training procedures. *Behavior Modification 8*, 23–39.

Gardner JM, (1972). Teaching behavior modification to nonprofessionals. *Journal of Applied Behavior Analysis 5*, 517–521.

Gladstone BW, & Spencer CJ. (1977). The effects of modeling on the contingent praise of mental retardation counselors. *Journal of Applied Behavior Analysis 10*, 75–84.

Hersen M, & Bellack AS. (1978). Staff training and consultation. In Hersen M, & Bellack AS, (Eds), *Behavior therapy in the psychiatric setting*. Baltimore: Williams & Wilkins.

Kazdin AE, & Moyer W. (1976). Training teachers to use behavior modification. In Yen S, & McIntire R. (Eds), *Teaching behavior modification*. Kalamazoo, MI: Behaviordelia.

Klein DC. (1976). Community change agents. In Maley RF, & Harshbarger D (Eds), *Community mental health systems* (pp 345–375). New York: John Wiley.

Komaki J. (1977). Using behavioral self-control strategies in the training of beginning counseling skills. *Behavior Therapy 8*, 99–101.

Kratchowill TR, Bergan JR, & Mace FC. (1981). Practitioner competencies for implementation of behavioral psychology in the schools: Issues in supervision. *School Psychology Review 10*, 434–444.

Linehan MM. (1980). Supervision of behavior therapy. In Hess AK (Ed), *Psychotherapy supervision: Theory, research, and practice* (pp 148–180). New York: John Wiley.

Maley RF, & Harshbarger D. (1976). The integration of behavior analysis and systems analysis. In Maley RF, & Harshbarger D (Eds), *Community mental health systems* (pp 379–384). New York: John Wiley.

Malott PW. (1976). A behavioral-system approach to the design of human services. In Maley RF, & Harshbarger D. (Eds), *Community mental heatlh systems* (pp 319–342). New York: John Wiley.

McKeown D, Adams HE, & Forehand R. (1975). Generalization to the classroom of principles of behavior modification. *Behavior Research and Therapy 13*, 85–92.

Nadler L. (1970) Developing human resources. Houston: Gulf Press.

Panyan M, Boozer H, & Morris M. (1970). Feedback to attendants as a reinforcer for applying operant techniques. *Journal of Applied Behavior Analysis 3*, 1–4.

Perrow C. (1967). A framework for comparative analysis of organizations. *American Sociological Review 12*, 243–272.

Plaska, T, Burgess J, & Tillman M. (1979). The Boulder training model. Presented at the annual convention of the Association for Behavior Analysis, Dearborn, Michigan.

Plaster GA, & Mohler RS. (1979). The development, implementation, and assessment of a new staff training model. *Mental Retardation 5*, 251–255.

Schinkle SP, & Wong SE. (1977). Evaluation of staff training in group homes for the mentally retarded. *American Journal of Mental Deficiency 82*, 130–136.

Schinke SP, & Wong SE. (1978). Teaching child care workers: A behavioral approach. *Child Care Quarterly* 7, 45–61.

Stuckey GL. (1973). Challenges in mental health for new professionals. *American Journal of Orthopsychiatry 43*, 164–167.

Tharp RG, & Wetzel RJ. (1969). *Behavior modification in the natural setting*. New York: Academic Press.

Wallace CJ, Davis JR, Liberman RP, & Baker V. (1973). Modeling and staff behavior. *Journal of Consulting and Clinical Psychology 41*, 422–426.

Young CE, True JE, & Packard ME. (1974). A national survey of associate degree mental health programs. *Community Mental Health Journal 10*, 313–320.

Ziarnik JP, & Bernstein GS. (1984). Effecting change in community-based facilities: Putting staff training in perspective. *The Behavior Therapist* 7, 39–41.

3
Medical Aspects

Rohan Ganguli

Physicians have, historically, led the treatment of psychiatric inpatients. In many state hospitals, Veterans Administration hospitals, and other chronic care facilities, psychologists (often behavior therapists) have actually directed treatment for some years now. Even in these places, however, there is usually a "physician of record" who allegedly heads the treatment team. The implication that psychologists must be supervised by physicians in institutional settings has led to the recommendation that independent practice is the ideal clinical setting for them (Blau, 1983). This is quite unfortunate since behavior therapy has greatly influenced current treatment practices in many inpatient hospital settings. There is also every indication that the range of disorders and problems amendable to a behavioral treatment is expanding, and hence the influence of behavior therapists will continue to increase. The precise role of the physician (psychiatrist) in the collaborative management of inpatients will inevitably come under review. The part that a physician ought to play in the management of psychiatric inpatients should be considered in terms of assessment, treatment, and research.

ASSESSMENT

The first skill that a medical practitioner contributes in the assessment phase is the detection of physical disorders that may be causing mental symptoms. A host of common conditions such as diabetes (Sachar, Anis, Halbreich,

PRACTICE OF INPATIENT BEHAVIOR THERAPY
ISBN 0-8089-1715-3

Nathan, & Halpern, 1980), cancer (Peterson, Popkin, & Hall, 1981), cardiovascular disease (Frohlich, Tarazi, & Dustan, 1969), and epilepsy (Williams, 1956), as well as some rarer ones, could present with only psychological symptoms. The consequences of failing to diagnose these conditions and to treat them properly could be serious and includes death (Leeman, 1975). An extensive discussion of the diseases and their psychological symptoms is presented elsewhere (Ganguli, 1983a). It may still be suggested that these conditions could simply be screened by using a battery of laboratory tests without the involvement of a physician. Unfortunately, this is unlikely to be possible in the forseeable future. The diagnosis of physical disorders, especially when they present in an atypical fashion, is quite difficult. No battery of laboratory tests could possibly screen for all the causes of psychological symptoms. Furthermore, diagnosis is rarely a matter of one abnormal test but a synthesis of information from the history, examination, and laboratory. I have argued elsewhere (Ganguli, 1983) that many psychiatrists may actually not be sufficiently medically skilled to do this task. Inpatient physicians, on the whole, are exceptions to this generalization, and tend to deal with physical examinations and laboratory tests enough to maintain their diagnostic skills. However, in any setting it is advisable to have a system established where consultation with an internist, neurologist, and other medical specialists is possible. This approach is illustrated by several case studies.

Case 1

A 23-year-old man was admitted to the hospital for the third time complaining of insulting and threatening hallucinations. He had previously been diagnosed as schizophrenic, had lost his psychotic symptoms when given antipsychotics, and had been in follow-up for five years. On examination, the psychiatrist noted that he had stiffness and marked tremor on one side of his body but not the other—a finding that is uncommon in drug-induced parkinsonism. The psychiatrist also noted that he had a peculiar lability of affect similar to that seen in persons with brain stem disease. Earlier neuropsychological testing and EEG had been "normal." Nevertheless, the psychiatrist had a sufficiently strong clinical suspicion of an organic problem to order another EEG. This one was slower than the earlier one but still only equivocally abnormal. Nevertheless, it added to the accumulating evidence for a brain lesion. A CAT scan showed a massive hydrocephalus caused by a cyst blocking the third ventricle. This condition frequently results in sudden death, and so the patient underwent emergency neurosurgery the next day. On follow-up over one-and-a-half years, his abnormal movements and stiffness had disappeared and his psychotic symptoms were minimal.

It should be noted that this patient's psychotic symptoms had responded to his medications and a successful behavioral program had been instituted to deal with his "temper outbursts." The psychiatrist, however, had detected several subtle clues, none by themselves sufficient to make a diagnosis, that suggested neurological involvement, and his actions saved this patient's life. Had he been satisfied with the previous "screening" tests, i.e., EEG and neuropsychologic testing, he would not have been able to do this.

Case 2

A 44-year-old black woman who was already being treated for depression was seen by the psychiatrist. She was on antidepressants and said that her depression was much better but that she still felt very sluggish. The psychiatrist noted that she had a coarse voice and rough dry skin. When asked about it, she said she found cold difficult to tolerate. He checked her reflexes and noted a slow relaxation of the muscles. The psychiatrist diagnosed hypothyroidism despite the fact that laboratory tests of thyroid functioning were equivocal. He ordered a check of her thyroid stimulating hormone (TSH) blood level. The patient was found to have a level nine or ten times normal, confirming the clinical diagnosis.

Medical surveillance is, therefore, essential for patients who present continuing or recurrent symptoms. In both cases presented, the diagnosis might not have been made initially, even by a vigilant physician because the conditions hadn't progressed very far. Patients may also, at a single examination, leave out information that would alert a physician to the diagnosis.

Inpatient settings are, by definition, in hospitals and, therefore, this is the ideal setting for the treatment of individuals with a combination of physical and psychological problems. It is also a legal and reasonable requirement that patients admitted to a hospital receive a medical evaluation to detect incidental health problems. Indeed, my own clinical experience is replete with instances in which asymptomatic heart disease, diabetes, and hypertension have been detected because of a good medical evaluation.

Case 3

Behavioral methods of assessment can, conversely, be of great benefit even when the "physical" etiology of disturbed behavior is quite certain. A 16-year-old boy with long-standing and partially intractable epilepsy was admitted to our inpatient unit because of allegedly unprovoked aggressive outbursts at home. He was well known to the psychiatrist, the unit staff, and the consulting neurologist. The consensus was that his behavior would "improve" once the seizures were controlled. Manipulation of his anticonvulsants did little for either his seizures or his behavior, however. A behavioral therapist on the faculty was consulted. He identified the problem behaviors and instituted round-the-clock observation. He also talked to the patient and his mother and constructed a list of reinforcers. To our surprise, many of the reinforcers were unknown to the staff. The behavioral observation showed clearly that the patient's outbursts were most frequent on the days he had the most seizures. Despite this, the assessment technique had a marked effect on the attitude of the staff. Earlier they had been reluctant to try any behavioral measure with this "organic" problem. After the assessment, they agreed to try a differential reinforcement program for the outbursts. The patient's behavior did improve enough for him to be able to return home. On a subsequent admission, the behavioral assessment technique was also used to monitor the manifestations of his seizure disorder while testing an experimental anticonvulsant.

TREATMENT

In the area of treatment, the need for collaboration between psychologists and psychiatrists is, if anything, even greater than in the case of assessment. Etiologic research addresses the questions of how much genetics, neurochemistry, and environmental variables contribute to the pathogenesis of disorders. We are very far from any definitive answers, however. Besides which, the etiologic considerations do not always bear directly on the most effective or efficient treatment. For example, stage fright and its deleterious effects on performance (about as environmentally determined as you can get) can be effectively eliminated with a blocker of the adrenergic system (Kelly, 1980). This is accomplished by blocking some of the disabling autonomic responses to the anxiety-provoking situation. On the other hand, incontinence due to brain damage in the elderly (about as organic as you can get) has been successfully modified by a behavioral technique (Jarvis, 1981). Furthermore, some clinical distinctions, which predict therapeutic success, have no known etiologic significance. For example, patients with anxiety who experience panic attacks seem to benefit from tricyclic drugs, while those without panics do not (Klein & Gittleman-Klein, 1976). Depressed patients with "endogenous" symptoms respond well to eletroconvulsive therapy (Kiloh & Garside, 1963), but these symptoms do not predict the response to other antidepressant treatments such as tricyclic drugs or monoamine oxidase inhibitors.

Psychiatrists do not only contribute knowledge about pharmacologic or somatic treatments. This knowledge can be acquired by any intelligent person who reviews and exhaustively keeps up with the literature. The experience of having used somatic treatment with a large number of patients is an invaluable attribute of the practicing physician. Pharmacotherapy is considerably more of an art than a science. The latest advances in sleep (Kupfer, 1976) or endocrine studies (Caroll, 1982) help to guide treatment only to a limited extent. Similarly, blood or serum levels of drugs have specific valuable assessment functions but cannot be the sole guide for treatment decisions. A review of rational prescribing practices is presented elsewhere (Ganguli, 1983b).

The area in which collaboration between behavior therapists and psychiatrists has proved most fruitful is in the combination of psychotropic drugs with behavioral treatment. A comprehensive discussion is contained in a chapter by

Ganguli and Detre (1981). Obsessional disorders inflict an unusual amount of suffering and have fascinated psychiatrists and psychologists for a long time. They are also extremely resistant to treatment (Detre & Jarecki, 1971). Separate clinical trials of behavior therapy (Rachman, Hodgson, & Marks, 1971; Rachman, Marks, & Hodgson, 1973) and of tricyclic antidepressant drugs (Capstick, 1971; Slater & Roth, 1969) indicate that both reduce some symptoms in obsessionals. It was postulated that behavior therapy could reduce compulsive rituals but had less effect on obsessional thinking. Tricyclics reduced rumination (or made it less bothersome) but affected rituals only secondarily (Philpott, 1976). A natural extension of this thinking led to a clinical trial combining clomipramine with behavior therapy (Rachman, Cobb, Grey, McDonald, Mawson, Satory, & Stern, 1979). The results indicate that behavior therapy did reduce rituals and produce improvement in most behavioral measures. Clomipramine improved mood and reduced anxiety.

RESEARCH

In much of the behavioral research, behavioral techniques have focused on aspects of behavior that are assumed to have little biomedical contribution. Such an example is social-skill training with chronic schizophrenics (Bellack & Hersen, 1978). The patients are usually on medication but the behavioral intervention is generally carried out without medical collaboration because the problem behaviors are not felt to be amenable to "medical" treatment. This arises from dichotomous thinking, which dictates that drugs are of use to treat active symptoms and maintain remission while psychological methods are effective against psychosocial deficits. The theory is simple and attractively practical. However, evidence is steadily accumulating that patients with severe social deficits may have structural and metabolic changes in their brains (Andreasen & Olsen, 1982). More than one pathological disease entity could lead to the same behavioral end state (Crow, 1980). It would, therefore, be wise to continue to look for methods of treatment from all possible angles. Further evidence of a complex dynamic interplay between biology and the psychological environment is in the functioning of the immune system in response to stress. Conditioning has been shown to produce marked immunosuppression (Ader & Cohen, 1975). Inescapable shock produces a profound immunosuppression while escapable shock does not (Laudenslager, Ryan, Drugan, Hyson, & Maier, 1983). Bereavement produces marked immunosuppression, while the chronic stress preceding this does not (Schleifer, Keller, Camerino, Thornton, & Stein, 1983). The effect of psychological stress on the neuroendocrine system is another case in point (Ackenheil, 1980).

Some areas of mental health research, such as chronobiology, deal with complex interrelationships between internal events, such as hormone secretion and temperature changes, and external variables, such as light and dark cycles, environmental time cues, and finally, psychological issues such as mood, motivation, and cognition. It seems silly for any discipline to lay claim to primacy in such a field, and unquestionably all disciplines can contribute.

SUMMARY

Physicians ought to remain an essential part of the assessment and treatment of psychiatric inpatients. Their involvement in the detection of physical disorders should not be limited to the initial assessment but ought ot continue if the patient's symptoms persist. In many instances, nonsomatic treatments are by themselves the most effective ones. Many of the more serious psychiatric illnesses, however, can be best treated by a combination of somatic and psychological approaches. Our current state of knowledge about the etiology and pathogenesis of mental illnesses only emphasizes our ignorance, and collaboration between the various disciplines is mandatory.

REFERENCES

Ackenheil M. (1980). Hormonal response to stress in mental illness. In Van Praag HM (Ed), *Handbook of biological psychiatry (Part III)* (pp 195–216). New York: Marcel Dekker.

Ader R, & Cohen N. (1975). Behaviorally conditioned immunosupression. *Psychosomatic Medicine 37*, 333–340.

Andreasen NC, & Olsen S. (1982). Negative vs positive schizophrenia. *Archives of General Psychiatry 39*, 789–794.

Bellack AS, & Hersen M. (1978). Chronic psychiatric patients: Skills training. In Hersen M, & Bellack AS (Eds), *Behavior therapy in psychiatric setting* (pp 169–195). Baltimore: Williams & Wilkins.

Blau TH (1983). Roles and professional practice. In Hersen M., Kazdin AE, & Bellack, AS (Eds), *The clinical psychology handbook* (pp 57–62). New York: Pergammon Press.

Capstick N. (1971). Clomipramine in obsessional states. *Psychosomatics 12*, 332–335.

Caroll BJ. (1982). The dexamethazone suppression test for melancholia. *British Journal of Psychiatry 140*, 292–304.

Crow TJ. (1950). Molecular pathology of schizophrenia: more than one disease in process. *British Medical Journal 280*, 1–9.

Detre TP, & Jarecki HG. (1971) *Modern psychiatric treatment*. Philadelphia: Lippincott & Co.

Frochlich ED, Tarazi RC, & Dustan HP. (1969). Hyperdynamic-adrenergic circulatory state. *Archives of Internal Medicine 123*, 1–7.

Ganguli R. (1983a). Medical assessment. In Hersen M, Kazdin AE, & Bellack AS. (Eds), *The clinical psychology handbook* (pp 455–465). New York: Pergammon Press.

Ganguli R. (1983b). The rational use of psychotropic drugs. *Urban Health 12*, 42–48.

Ganguli R, & Detre TP. (1981). Psychopharmacology and behavior therapy. In Michelson L, Hersen M, & Turner SM (Eds), *Future perspectives in behavior therapy* (pp 83–102). New York: Plenum Press.

Jarvis GJ. (1981). Controlled trial of bladder drill and drug therapy in the management of detrusor instability. *British Journal of Urology 53*, 565–566.

Kelly D. (1980). *Anxiety and emotions: Psysiological basis and treatment*. Springfield, IL: Charles C. Thomas.

Kiloh LG, & Garside RF. (1963). The independence of neurotic and endogenous depression. *British Journal of Psychiatry 109*, 451–463.

Klein DF, & Gittleman-Klein R. (1976). *Progress in psychiatric drug treatment*. New York: Brunner Mazel.

Kupfer DJ. (1976). REM latency: A physiologic marker for primary depressive disease. *Biological Psychiatry 11*, 159–174.

Laudenslager ML, Ryan SM, Drugan RC, Hyson RL, & Maier SF. (1983). Coping and immunosuppression: Inescapable but not escapable shock suppresses lymphocyte proliferation. *Science 221*, 568–570.

Leeman CP. (1975). Diagnostic errors in emergency room medicine: Physical illness in patients labelled psychiatric. *International Journal of Psychiatry Medicine 6*, 533–540.

Peterson LG, Popkin MK, & Hall TCW. (1981). Psychiatric aspects of cancer. *Psychosomatics 22*, 774–793.

Philpott R. (1976). The assessment of drugs in obsessional states. *British Journal of Clinical Pharmacology 3*, 91–95.

Rachman S, Cobb J, Grey S, McDonald B, Mawson D, Statory G, & Stern R. (1979). Behavioural treatment of obsessive-compulsive disorders, with and without clomipramine. *Behaviour Research and Therapy 17*, 467–478.

Rachman S, Hodgson R, & Marks IM. (1971). The treatment of chronic obsessive compulsive neurosis. *Behaviour Research and Therapy 9*, 237–247.

Rachman S, Marks IM, & Hodgson R. (1973). The treatment of obsessive compulsive neurotics by modelling and flooding in vivo. *Behaviour Research and Therapy 11*, 463–471.

Sachar EJ, Anis G, Halbreich U, Nathan S, & Halpern F. (1980). Recent studies in the neuroendocrinology of depressive disorders. *Psychiatric Clinics of North America 3*, 313–326.

Schleifer SJ, Keller SE, Camerino M, Thornton JC, & Stein M. (1983). Suppression of lymphocyte stimulation following bereavement. *Journal of the American Medical Association 250*, 374–377.

Slater E, & Roth M. (1969). *Clinical psychiatry (3rd ed)*. London: Bailliere, Tindall & Casell.

Williams D. (1956). The structure of emotions reflected in epileptic experiences. *Brain 79*, 29–67.

PART 2
Treatment of Adults

4
Obsessive–Compulsive Disorder

Rolf G. Jacob, Ralph R. Ford, and Samuel M. Turner

Behavioral treatments and, more recently, psychopharmacological treatments have significantly improved the prognosis for obsessive–compulsive disorder. Consequently, more than ever before, obsessive–compulsive patients now have reason to feel optimistic about the benefit that they can expect from treatment. Obsessive–compulsive disorder, however, still constitutes one of the most severe and chronic forms of the anxiety disorders. Even after having accomplished significant behavioral changes, most obsessive–compulsive patients will have to continue to make efforts to retain their treatment gains.

Considerable skill, resources, and time are required from the therapist treating patients with obsessive–compulsive disorder. General therapeutic and social skills are needed to be able to persist in the planned implementation of the treatment program despite repeated questions and requests for change by the patient. Familiarity with the psychiatric ward as an administrative unit is required to enlist the assistance of the staff. Channels of communication need to be actively maintained with all categories of the ward personnel, including nurses aides, nurses, social workers, and other professionals. Key members of the staff need to be trained in the principal components of behavioral intervention, i.e., response prevention and flooding. In addition, staff members assigned to observe the patients need to be trained in behavioral observation and recording techniques. Since many of these staff members work during the nonbusiness hours of the day, most beginning therapists do not realize the time commitment necessary for this type of liaison work.

PRACTICE OF INPATIENT BEHAVIOR THERAPY
ISBN 0-8089-1715-3

The present chapter describes the inpatient behavioral treatment of patients with obsessive–compulsive disorder, delineating the main features of the disorder, reviewing the behavioral literature from a practical standpoint, and concluding with a description of the treatment of two cases. For more detailed and scholarly reviews, we refer the reader to books written or edited by Beech (1974), Beech and Vaughan (1978), Emmelkamp (1982), Rachman and Hodgson (1980), and Yaryura-Tobias and Nezigolu (1983).

CLINICAL DESCRIPTION

As the name implies, obsessive–compulsive disorder is characterized by a high rate of obsessions and compulsions. Usually, both obsessions and compulsions occur together, although some patients suffer from obsessions only.

Obsessions refer to an excess of certain thoughts, ideas, images, impulses, or urges, which are experienced as intrusive, unwanted, difficult to control, and causing distress. They frequently involve themes of contamination with germs or dirt and forbidden violent or sexual acts. Examples of obsessions include recurrent concerns of acquiring or inflicting disease by exposure to or transmission of germs, thoughts of stabbing somebody with a knife, or thoughts of having injured someone while driving.

Obsessions may sometimes involve preprogrammed sequences of thoughts. Such sequences of obsessions are called *cognitive rituals*. Often these sequences of obsessions involve neutralizing thoughts aimed at undoing the effect of an original "harmful" obsession. Cognitive rituals can be interwoven with compulsive behaviors. For example, one patient needed a glass of water at his bedroom table at all times. However, he had to make sure that the water was not poisoned. Therefore, he would look behind the glass, beside the glass, lift the glass, think the thought "let's see what's there," then mentally name all the objects located close to the glass, and conclude with the thought "I guess it's O.K."

Obsessions should be differentiated from *overvalued ideas*. Patients with overvalued ideas will defend their beliefs as being entirely rational, whereas patients with obsessions regard their obsessional beliefs as unreasonable or irrational. For example, one patient was engaging in extensive house-cleaning rituals because she believed that the house was contaminated with asbestos. Even though the degree of contamination was insufficient to cause health concerns, the patient firmly maintained her view that the risk was significant and that she therefore was justified in her excessive cleaning behaviors. Treatment was never initiated because the patient did not agree with our rationale for response prevention. Overvalued ideas thus constitute a poor prognostic sign (Foa, 1979).

Obsessions should also be differentiated from *delusions*. This differentiation can be difficult in some cases. For example, fears of contamination can be either delusional or obsessive. The degree of insight and conviction is a differentiating factor; delusions also tend to be more bizarre and less founded in reality.

Compulsions refer to an excess of certain purposeful behaviors, which the patient engages in under a sense of pressure, despite recognizing that the frequency of their performance is irrational. Furthermore, these behaviors result in significant distress and social impairment of the patient. Most compulsive behaviors tend to belong to one of two classes: checking or cleaning. Compulsive *checkers* may repeatedly check items such as if doors are locked, gas stoves are turned off, or that the parking brake of their car is engaged. For example, one patient fearful of injuring somebody while driving would repeatedly return to sites of presumed accidents. Each patient will have different checking behaviors, and checking behaviors can assume ritualistic qualities. Compulsive *cleaners* are characterized by increased frequency of washing or cleaning behaviors. For example, they may wash their hands more than 50 times per day and spend hours on cleaning their living quarters. One patient seen in our clinic would clean the entire living room floor and furniture with bleach every day, causing considerable damage not only to the furniture, but also to his hands, which had assumed a raw exematous appearance.

Not all compulsive behaviors fall neatly into either the washing or checking categories. Compulsive hoarding involves the patient being unable to discard items that should be thrown away. For example, one patient seen in our clinic saved all her old magazines and newspapers in the trunk of her car. In another patient, the hoarding compulsions included her paychecks. When evaluated at our clinic she had not cashed her paychecks for several months.

In the preceding discussion, obsessions and compulsions were treated as separate entities. They really are closely related, however. Compulsive behaviors are usually related to obsessive ideation. For example, compulsive washing is usually an expression of an obsessional concern about contamination.

The clinical description of the main features of obsessive–compulsive disorder is enunciated in the current edition of the *Diagnostic Manual of the American Psychiatric Association* (*DSM-III*: APA, 1981). *DSM-III* lists the following criteria as necessary conditions for diagnosing obsessive–compulsive disorder:

A. Either obsessions or compulsions:
   Obsessions: recurrent, persistent ideas, thoughts, images, impulses that are ego dystonic, i.e., they are not experienced as voluntarily produced, but rather as thoughts that invade consciousness and are experienced as senseless or repugnant. Attempts are made to ignore or suppress them.
   Compulsions: repetitive and seemingly purposeful behaviors that are performed according to certain rules or in a stereotyped fashion. The behavior is not an end in itself, but is designed to produce or prevent some future event or situation. However, either the activity is not connected in a realistic way with what it is designed to produce or prevent, or may be clearly excessive. The act is performed with a sense of subjective compulsion coupled with a desire to resist the compulsion (at least initially). The individual generally recognized the senselessness of the behavior (this may not be true for young children) and does not derive pleasure from carrying out the activity, although it provides a release of tension.

B. The obsessions or compulsions are a significant source of distress to the individual or interfere with social or role functioning.

C. Not due to another mental disorder, such as Tourette's Disorder, Schizophrenia, Major Depression, or Organic Mental Disorder.

The first *DSM-III* criterion (Criterion A) constitutes a succinct description of obessions and compulsions. Mild forms of obsessions and compulsions can also be found present in normals, however. To qualify for a diagnosis of obsessive–compulsive disorder, the obsessions or compulsions need to be a significant source of distress or cause a significant deterioration of the patient's social functioning (Criterion B). For example, one patient evaluated for an unrelated problem admitted to spending 45 minutes each day washing his face. This behavior was not a source of distress for him, however, nor did it interfere with his social functioning. Therefore, this patient was not diagnosed as having obsessive–compulsive disorder. The deterioration of social functioning in obsessive–compulsive patients can be marked. Many will give up their jobs, drop out from school, or show gross impairments in their roles as family members.

Criterion C refers to the differential diagnosis of obsessive–compulsive disorder. Before discussing the differential diagnosis, however, we need to describe other characteristics of patients with obsessive–compulsive disorder that are not diagnostic but that are often present and further complicate the treatment of these patients.

Associated Features

Besides obsessions and compulsions, patients with obsessive–compulsive disorder show certain other characteristics which further contribute to their social incapacitation. These characteristics, which emerged as separate factors in a factor-analytic study reported by Rachman and Hodgson (1980), include conscientiousness, doubting, and obsessional slowness.

Conscientiousness and doubting involve an excessive fear of making mistakes, coupled with indecisiveness regarding the correct course of action. These features may be manifest during the patient interview: Because of fears of leaving out details that may be important, the discourse tends to be overelaborate and full of unnecessary details. As further expression of their doubtfulness, obsessive–compulsive patients frequently will ask about minute details of the treatment program. Rather than enabling the patient to reach a decision, however, the new information will prompt a geometric progression of further questioning, leaving the patient even more confused and indecisive.

The tendency toward conscientiousness can cause the patient significant distress. For example, one patient developed pervasive concerns that he might have provided the government with incorrect information on his income tax return. Another patient hesitated to enter treatment for the following reason: When questioned about the time of onset of his condition, he began to suspect that some of his obsessive–compulsive problems might have predated his current medical insurance policy; because the policy included a clause ruling out the coverage for conditions preexisting the initiation of the policy, he became concerned that letting the insurance company pay for the treatment would be a dishonest act.

In patients suffering from *obsessional slowness*, normal routine behaviors, such as brushing teeth, combing hair, and dressing or undressing, take an excessive amount of time. The components of these behaviors are often ritualized. For example, a patient evaluated at our clinic would spend at least 15 minutes trying to part her hair. This was because she felt the need to have the part be absolutely straight. Furthermore, she would attempt to remove any irregularities or curves by merely looking at them, hoping that a certain look magically would straighten it out. Obsessive slowness usually occurs in conjunction with other symptoms of obsessive–compulsive disorder. However, Rachman (1974) and Rachman and Hodgson (1980) also described a comparatively rare condition, called *primary obsessive slowness*, in which the slowness is present without concomitant compulsions.

Differential Diagnosis

Obsessive–compulsive disorder usually is not difficult to diagnose. This is especially true if the obsessive–compulsive symptoms constitute the principal reason for the patient to seek treatment. However, as implied by criterion "C" of the *DSM-III*, obsessions or compulsions are sometimes seen in other psychiatric conditions. These conditions include depression, Tourette's syndrome, dysmorphophobia, schizophrenia, and brain injury. Obsessive or compulsive symptoms may also be present in agoraphobia, hypochondriasis, anorexia nervosa, and bulimia. Finally, a person may show behaviors that seem to be compulsive to bystanders but do not fulfill criteria for obsessive–compulsive disorder. These behaviors include egosyntonic behavioral excesses, such as "compulsive" gambling or drinking, which do not constitute a source of subjective distress, at least while the person engages in them. The perfectionistic housekeeping behaviors of the "houseproud" housewives of Cooper (1970) constitute another example. In some individuals, however, tendencies toward perfectionism can become the source of distress for the person's social environment. Provided that certain other symptoms are also present, these persons are given a diagnosis of compulsive personality disorder. Compulsive personality disorder will be described later in this section.

Depression

Depression and obsessive–compulsive disorder are intimately linked. Depression can occur as a reaction to the social incapacitation produced by the obsessive–compulsive disorder. On the other hand, obsessive–compulsive symptoms can occur as a secondary symptom of depression. In either case, exacerbation of one tends to cause worsening of the other, thus establishing a vicious cycle. In current diagnostic practice, depression is diagnosed if the obsessive–compulsive symptoms are considered "due to" depression. In practice, this assessment is made if the onset of depression occurred before the onset of obsessive–compulsive symptoms. Conversely, if the depression is considered as secondary to the obsessive–compulsive disorder, both diagnoses are made. The compulsive symptoms of patients with primary depression may improve after successful treatment of the depression. We recently evaluated a patient with primary depression and severe obsessive–compulsive symptoms, which included handwashing rituals and fear of contamination to the point of refusing a physician to perform a physical examination. In this patient, the obsessive–compulsive symptoms improved dramatically after treatment for depression. Conversely, Foa (1979) reports that patients with severe depression do not show habituation during exposure treatment and thus are poor candidates for behavioral treatment.

Some patients with bipolar disorder may show obsessions or compulsions during the depressive phase. One such patient was treated with the new antidepressant agent fluoxetine (Turner, Jacob, Beidel, & Griffin, 1984). The improvement of his obsessions and compulsions was dramatic; however, shortly after his recovery he switched into a manic episode during which he became so fascinated with the idea of death that he took an overdose of his medication.

Schizophrenia

The delusions of schizophrenics can sometimes resemble obsessions. For example, somatic delusions, which involve convictions of infestation (e.g., with lice or worms [Munro, 1980]), superficially resemble the fears of contamination frequently reported by obsessive–compulsive patients. Furthermore, some schizophrenics engage in ritualistic behaviors, which can resemble compulsions. Usually, the differential diagnosis is not difficult, since schizophrenics lack the internal attribution of their delusions or of their ritualistic behaviors. That is, whereas obsessive–compulsive patients basically feel responsible for their obsessions or compulsions, schizophrenic patients do not feel responsible for their delusions or for their rituals.

Dysmorphophobia

Dysmorphophobia is a condition in which patients have overvalued ideas about their appearance (Turner, Jacob, & Morrison, 1984). For example, one patient, concerned with facial acne, would spend hours in front of the mirror checking his face for pimples, even though objectively the problem was minor. Little to nothing is known about behavioral treatment for these cases. However, since overvalued ideas are at the core of the disorder, the prognosis probably is poor.

Tourette's Syndrome

Tourette's syndrome is a movement disorder characterized by involuntary repetitive movements and vocal tics. The vocal tics consist of grunting, clicking, and barking sounds along with words. Some patients display coprolalia, or an urge to utter obscenities. Patients with Tourette's syndrome frequently have obsessions and also can display behavioral rituals, such as touching strangers, which resemble compulsions. In our experience, attempts at behavioral treatment with these patients has not been encouraging.

Brain Injury

Obsessive–compulsive symptoms can occur during the recovery from head injury (McKeon, McGuffin, & Robinson, 1984). The symptoms persist for years, even though neurological findings in most of the cases normalize. Jenike and Brotman (1984), using the chart review data of 12 patients with severe obsessive–compulsive disorder who had received EEG evaluations during their routine evaluations, found that EEG abnormalities were present in four of the patients. The changes appeared consistent with the diagnosis of temporal lobe epilepsy. It is unclear, however, whether the EEG changes were causally related to the obsessive–compulsive symptoms.

It is comparatively rare for any of the anxiety disorders to have an onset after age 35 to 40. Therefore, it is generally recommended that organic conditions, including neurological dysfunction, be ruled out especially in cases with late onset of anxiety disorder (Jacob & Rapport, 1984).

Compulsive Personality Disorder

DSM-III describes a person with compulsive personality disorder as (1) being serious, conventional, stingy, with restricted ability to express warm emotions; (2) being perfectionistic, overly concerned with details at the expense of the big picture; (3) insisting that others submit to their way of doing things without showing concerns for the feelings of others; (4) showing excessive involvement with work at the expense of pleasure and interpersonal relationships; (5) being indecisive, tardy, and procrastinating. For a diagnosis of compulsive personality disorder, at least four of these five qualities need to be present. Patients with obsessive–compulsive disorder may or may not have concomitant compulsive personality disorder. However, many obsessive patients had *compulsive personality traits* before onset of their obsessive–compulsive disorder. Persons are said to have compulsive personality traits when they show some but not all of the characteristics of compulsive personality disorder.

Prevalence, Incidence, and Natural History

Obsessive–compulsive disorder is a rare condition; its prevalence is estimated to be only 0.05 percent in the general population, 0.3 to 2.9 percent in psychiatric outpatients, and 3.5 to 4.6 percent in neurotic inpatients (Black, 1974). Men and women are approximately at equal risk of developing obsessive–compulsive disorder. The onset usually occurs in early adult life, but in some cases childhood onsets is seen (Rapoport, Elkins, Langer, Sceery, Buchsbaum, Gillin, Murphy, Zahn, Lake, Ludlow, & Mendelson, 1981). Based on the available literature, Black (1974) estimated that 30 percent had an onset before age 15, 55 percent before age 25, 84 percent before age 35, and 95 percent before age 45.

Even before the onset of obsessive–compulsive disorder, many patients show compulsive personality traits. As mentioned earlier, such traits include excessive cleanliness, orderliness, uncertainty, rigidity, punctuality, and over-dependability. These traits were present in 64 to 84 percent of the cases (Black, 1974; McKeon, Roa, & Mann, 1984).

A question frequently asked by patients is whether their condition is genetically determined. Turner, Beidel, and Nathan (in press) reviewed the pertinent literature and concluded that a consensus of studies on the prevalence of obsessive–compulsive disorder in twins lends some support for a genetically determined biological predisposition for obsessive–compulsive disorder as well as for other anxiety disorders. It also appears that obsessive–compulsive disorder has a higher prevalence in first degree relatives of obsessive–compulsive patients than in the normal population. For example, Carey and Gottesman (1981) reported that obsessive–compulsive illness was present in 6.2 percent of parents, 6.2 percent of children, and 3.2 percent of siblings of index cases. Compulsive personality traits were even more common: at least 8.3 percent of parents, 9.3 percent of children, and 6.4 percent of siblings. Compared to the overall prevalence of obsessive–compulsive disorder, it appears that relatives, including children, of patients with obsessive–compulsive disorder are at increased risk. However, the prevalence of 6.2 percent in children also implies that 94 percent of the children were unaffected. Perhaps this figure could be even higher if the effect of modeling obsessive–compulsive behaviors to the children were eliminated by successful treatment of the parent.

The natural history of obsessive–compulsive disorder is not known. However, the effect of traditional psychiatric treatment is reflected in a number of follow-up studies. The results have been quite inconsistent. One of the better designed follow-up studies found that 55 percent were worse or unchanged, 33 percent were slightly improved, and 23 percent were much improved (Kringlen, 1965). The follow-up time was 13 to 20 years. Presence of obsessive personality traits and greater severity of the disorder predicted poor prognosis. The patterns of development of illness was as follows: 8 percent showed a steady worsening of their condition, 30 percent were unchanged, 27 percent showed steady improvement after some years of no improvement, 20 percent showed a varying course without complete remission, 7 percent showed a phasic course with symptom-free intervals, 6 percent showed constant improvement, and one patient (2 percent) showed a fluctuating course but was gradually worsening. The improvement figures of Kringlen (1965) appeared to be lower than those reported in most other studies. For example, Lo (1967), in a Chinese sample, reported an improvement rate of 84 percent. Even if we accept the more pessimistic data reported by Kringlen, however, the 27 percent improvement rate should be kept in mind when evaluating the long-term effects of treatments for obsessive–compulsive disorder.

Assessment

Obssessive–compulsive disorder involves disturbances in a number of dimensions, including the motoric, affective, cognitive, and physiological domains. For an assessment strategy to be comprehensive, all these domains would need to be assessed. In most clinical outcome studies the primary assessment tools have been clinical interviews, self-report symptom inventories, and global rating scales. Some of the more widely used instruments are discussed here.

Global Ratings of Specified Symptoms

Global ratings appear to have widespread use in clinical treatment studies. They can be used to assess a wide variety of response dimensions. Typical variables rated include frequency or duration of rituals or obsessions, degree of avoidance, intensity of overall distress, and anxiety. These ratings tend to be powerful instruments of measuring change (Agras & Jacob, 1981). It has been suggested that these devices be used in conjunction with other measures, particularly obsessive–compulsives inventories and objective behavioral measures (Mavissakalian & Barlow, 1981; Turner & Michelson, 1984).

Self-Report Inventories

A number of self-report inventories have been used as assessment and treatment outcome measures with obsessive–compulsives. Personality inventories include the *MMPI* and the *Eysenck Personality Inventory*. Obssesive–Compulsive Checklists include the *Leyton Obsessional Inventory*, the *Maudsley Obsessional Compulsive Inventory* and the *Sandler-Hazari Obsessional Inventory*. Mood state and behavioral inventories include the *Beck Depression Inventory*, the *Wolpe-Lange Fear Survey*, and the *Social Avoidance and Distress Scale*. In general, these instruments help to provide more information in areas of nature of symptoms, differential diagnosis, and treatment planning.

Leyton Obsessional Inventory (LOI). This is a 69-item questionnaire developed by Cooper (1970) which distinguishes both obsessional symptoms and traits. The format includes a procedure in which cards are sorted into "yes" or "no" categories. The scale is unique in that it provides scores not only of obsessional trait and symptoms, but also of resistance to the obsessions and the degree of interference caused by the obsessions.

The criterion groups used for normative purposes consisted of 60 normal women, 25 "houseproud" housewives, 41 normal males, 25 husbands of houseproud wives, and 17 obsessional patients at the Maudsley Hospital. Preliminary results indicated that all four scores of the LOI could discriminate between obsessionals and normals. The test–retest reliability was established at r = .87 for the symptom score and r = .91 for the trait score (Kendell & DiScipio, 1970). The discriminant and concurrent validity appears to be acceptable. Marks, Hodgson, and Rachman (1975) found acceptable correlations between LOI scores and clinical ratings (r = .61–.69), behavioral avoidance test (r = .43–.52), fear thermometer (r = .47–.53) and somatic differential (r = .57–.73). Snowden (1980), recognizing the need for a less cumbersome and time-consuming instrument, developed a paper and pencil questionnaire based on the card-sort test and found the ultimate form to correlate r = .73 with the card-sort test. The test–retest reliability of the paper and pencil questionnaire was r = .77.

Maudsley Obsessional Compulsive Inventory (MOCI). The Maudsley Obsessional Compulsive Inventory, developed by Hodgson and Rachman (1977), is a 30-item questionnaire that derives the total score from four subscores: checking, washing, slowness/repetition, and doubting. Preliminary evidence indicated the the MOCI can discriminate between obsessionals and other neurotics; the test–retest reliability was r = .89. The correlation with the LOI was r = .60 (Rachman & Hodgson, 1980). It appears that this measure will become more popular among researchers due to its ease of administration and scoring.

Other obsessive compulsive inventories that have been reported in the literature include the Lynfield Obsessional–Compulsive Questionnaire (Allen & Tune, 1975), the Obsessive/Compulsive Checklist (Philpott, 1975), the Sandler and Hazari Obsessional Inventory (Sandler & Hazri, 1960), and the Hysteroid/ Obsessoid Questionaire (Foulds, 1965). These instruments have received much less attention than the LOI or the MOCI, and empirical evidence supporting their use is scant.

Behavioral Assessment

The use of behavioral measures in the assessment of obsessive–compulsive disorder has been noticeably lacking, despite the fact that one of its most prominent symptoms involves observable motor behaviors. Rachman and his associates (Rachman, Hodgson, & Marks, 1971; Hodgson, Rachman, & Marks, 1973; Roper, Rachman, & Marks, 1975) have utilized and adapted version of the Behavior Advoidance Test (Lang & Lazovik, 1963). Although the authors report significant changes between pre- and post-treatment measures, no data concerning the validity and relaibility of this measure were reported. In a later study, Rachman, Cobb, Grey, McDonald, Mawson, Sartory, and Stern (1979), comparing behavioral treatment and clomipramine, rated the performance on a behavioral avoidance test along both a performance and discomfort dimension. However, again validity and reliability were not reported.

Mills, Agras, Barlow, and Mills (1973) ingeniuously developed an automatic direct recording procedure of handwashing behavior. Handwashing would only take place in a specifically designed "washing pen." The patient's entrance into the washing pen triggered an electric recording device that recorded both the frequency and duration of visits to the washing pen. In addition, in one of the cases, a video camera was placed in the patient's room for constant monitoring of other ritualistic behaviors.

Two studies conducted by Turner and his colleagues (Turner, Hersen, Bellack, & Wells, 1979; Turner, Hersen, Bellack, Andrasik, & Capparell, 1980) involved behavioral observations by inpatient staff. Washing, checking, and other ritualistic behaviors were assessed during 30-minute or one-hour time intervals for three distinct observation periods each day. The interrater reliability was reported to be .99 both for duration and frequency of compulsive behaviors.

Physiological Assessment

Psychophysiological assessments have not received the same intensive research attention in obsessive–compulsive disorder as they have in other anxiety disorders. The few studies reported in the literature have examined a number of variables, including heart rate, skin conductance, and blood pressure (Turner & Michelson, 1984).

Hodgson and Rachman (1977) examined the effects of exposure to contimination, performance of rituals, and interruption of rituals on pulse rate variability in 12 compulsive washers. They found that subjective ratings of distress significantly increased when touching a contaminated object and decreased with the performance of the ritual. Pulse rate also showed a trend to increase under contamination and decrease with ritual performance; however these changes were not statistically significant. An interesting note was that neither pulse rate nor ratings of distress displayed significant changes during the interruption of the rutuals. In another study, Roper, Rachman, and Hodgson (1973) monitored pulse rate and distress levels in compulsive checkers and found similar trends of increased levels of distress while under provocation; again the pulse rate results were inconclusive.

Other researchers have studied skin conductance as well as heart rate (Rabavilas & Boulougouris, 1974; Boulougouris & Stefanis, 1977; Hornveld, Kraaimatt, & Van Dam-Baggin, 1979). These studies demonstrated significant changes in subjective distress and both physiological variables under conditions of exposure. These trends were present both comparing phobic to neutral stimuli as well as comparing obsessive–compulsive with normal subjects.

In an attempt to use physiological measures of arousal as an aid in treatment, Adrasik, Turner, and Ollendick (1980) treated a 25-year-old female with a seven-year history of compulsive handwashing. Self-report and pulse rates were recorded during eight exposure sessions. Exposure was terminated when significant decreases in pulse rate had occurred. Sessions ranged from 55 to 170 minutes in length. Interestingly, in half of the session, no correspondence was found between self-report of anxiety and pulse rate. Correlations were higher in shorter sessions. The authors concluded that had self-report measures of distress been utilized in deciding when to terminate the treatment, sessions would have resulted in minimal exposure times. Although no outcome or follow-up data were presented, the results suggested that adding physiological measures during exposure sessions could lead to more refined decisions as to session length.

BEHAVIORAL TREATMENT

The two core components of the behavioral treatment of obsessive–compulsive disorder are prolonged exposure to feared stimuli (flooding) and prevention of the compulsive behaviors (response prevention). These interventions were first applied to patients with obsessive–compulsive disorder by Meyer (1966). One of the two patients in this study had a three-year history of washing and cleaning rituals associated with fear of contamination by dirt. The other had a 36-year history of checking rituals associated with religious and sexual preoccupation. Treatment consisted of (1) making the patients engage in anxiety/fear-provoking behavior (i.e., touching door knobs; imagining having sex with the Holy Ghost); and (2) monitoring patients on a 24-hour basis to prevent them from carrying out their ritualistic behaviors. To accomplish response prevention, mild physical restraint, persuasion and distraction were employed. Remarkable reduction in the frequency of rituals and compulsive urges were evident after a few weeks (2.5, 4 weeks) of treatment. An interesting note is that symptoms did not totally disappear and follow-up outpatient sessions were given. Nevertheless, at 14 and 22 months of follow-up, treatment gains were maintained. More importantly, however, the patients were more functional, occupationally and socially, as compared to their pretreatment incapacitation. Meyer's contention is that treatment should be intensive and strict control over the patient's behavior is necessary for effective outcome.

Meyer's work (Meyer, 1966; Meyer & Levy, 1973) was succeeded by more than 15 years of research into various aspects of the bahavioral treatment of obsessive–compulsive disorder. Two parallel lines of investigation, particularly in the U.S. and Europe, examined the differential effects of response prevention and exposure to feared stimuli. A well-controlled study systematically varied response prevention, instructions, placebo expectancy, and exposure (Mills et al., 1973). Five compulsive washers were studied utilizing clinical ratings, subjective report of anxiety/discomfort, and time spent in the "washing pen," which recorded both frequency and duration of handwashing behavior. In each case there was an impressive reduction in handwashing behaviors following response prevention. Exposure was found to particularly influential in eliminating the subjective feeling of distress.

Other researchers (Catt & McConaghy, 1975; Turner et al., 1979; Turner et al., 1980) have also produced impressive results with use of supervised response prevention. For example, in the Catts and McConaghy study, six patients were treated and followed for 9 to 24 months. Though the average hospital stay was 3.5 months, most improvement occurred within a few weeks. It is difficult to determine whether response prevention was the major factor in treatment, however, since aspects of graduated exposure and modeling were utilized as well as milieu therapy for interpersonal, marital, and social skills problems.

While the efficacy of response prevention was being established in the previous studies, other researchers pursued different lines of investigation to study the effect of various modes of exposure treatment with obsessive–compulsive disorder. Rachman and his colleagues at Maudsley Hospital in London, in a series of studies (Rachman, Hodgson, & Marks, 1971; Hodgson, Rachman & Marks, 1972; Rachman, Marks, & Hodgson, 1973), investigated various ways of implementing exposure to feared situations in 20 severe obsessive–compulsive patients. In the initial study (Rachman, Hodgson, & Marks, 1971), 10 chronic obsessive–compulsive patients were given 15 control sessions of relaxation with 10 minutes of imaginal exposure to fear-provoking stimuli. In one experimental group (modeling), the therapists demonstrated the expected behaviors of the patient (i.e., touching contaminated items) and then requested the patient to perform those same behaviors; the patients were gradually exposed to fear-provoking stimuli based on a hierarchical arrangement. In the other experimental group (flooding), the therapist did not demonstrate behaviors and the patients were immediately exposed to the most fear-provoking situation. Thus, the two groups differed in two respects: therapist modeling and gradual exposure versus exposure to the most feared item at once (flooding). Patients were also instructed in response prevention. It was found that both the modeling and flooding groups showed significantly more improvement in the experimental phase than the relaxation control phase.

In a second study, Hodgson, Rachman, and Marks (1972) introduced a modeling with flooding group. They found that at six-month follow-up, this group showed significantly more improvement on a number of dependent measures than the previously treated gradual-exposure/modeling group and the flooding/no-modeling group. At the two-year follow-up (Marks, Hodgson, & Rachman, 1975), the treatment effects remained but the combined group (flooding and modeling) failed to maintain its previous superiority. Results at that time also indicated an overall 75 percent success rate with improvement after three weeks being predictive of good outcome at six and twelve months. These studies certainly established treatments based on exposure to feared stimuli as effective procedures in treating compulsive rituals. Similar findings were obtained in other studies (Boersma, Den Hengst, Dekker, & Emme Lkamp, 1976; Emme Lkamp & Kraanen, 1977; Marks, Stern, & Mawson, Cobb, & McDonald, 1980; Roper, Rachman, & Marks, 1975).

The Maudsley group made several additional conclusions regarding treatment of obsessive–compulsive disorder: (1) depression is a common affective state before, during, and after treatment, which suggests an indication for combining pharmacotherapy with behavior therapy; (2) domiciliary treatment with involvement of other family members enhances motivation and aides in maintaining treatment gains; (3) continuous *supervised* response prevention is not necessary for successful treatment (Marks, Hodgson, & Rachman, 1975).

More recently, Foa and her associates at Temple University Medical Center completed a number of studies investigating the relationship of exposure (imaginal and in vivo) and supervised response prevention (Foa & Goldstein, 1978; Foa, Steketee & Milby, 1980; Steketee, Foa, & Grayson, 1982; Foa, Grayson, Steketee, Doppelt, Turner, & Latimer, 1983). In the Foa, Steketee, and Milby (1980) study, eight obsessive–compulsive washers were treated in a crossover design with exposure and response prevention. Results indicated that whereas the exposure-only group had significantly greater reduction in anxiety levels than the response-prevention group, the response-prevention group showed the greatest reduction in rituals. When treatments were combined, the differences between the groups disappeared. Since an order effect could not be ruled out, a second experiment was conducted examining the three treatments separately (Steketee, Foa & Grayson, 1982). The results in this study confirmed the earlier findings, with the combined group showing the most pervasive treatment effects.

Another question addressed by Foa and her coworkers concerned the effect of imaginal exposure compared to exposure in vivo. Exposure to some of the patient's "ultimate" calamitous fears, such as those involving death or mutilation, are impossible, for obvious reason, to arrange in vivo. Yet anxieties connected to such fantasies may provide powerful stimuli for compulsive behaviors. Foa, Steketee, Turner, and Fischer (1980) conducted a study in which one group of compulsive checkers received gradual exposure in vivo plus response prevention, and the other group received the same treatments plus exposure in imagination. They found that whereas at post-treatment there was no difference in the effect of these two approaches, at follow-up there was a significantly superior maintenance of treatment gains in the group that had also received imaginal desensitization. A second study essentially replicated these results (Steketee et al., 1982). Thus, these findings imply that carefully analyzing the patient's "ultimate" fears and providing an appropriate exposure to these fears is important for long-term treatment outcome.

A final question addressed by Foa et al. related to predictors of treatment outcome. In a major follow-up study, Foa, Grayson, Steketee, Doppelt, Turner, and Latimer (1983) examined the treatment outcomes of 46 patients who had participated in various earlier studies. Regression analyses of demographics, pretreatment neurotic symptoms (depression and anxiety), and responses to exposure (habituation within and between sessions) were conducted. Results indicated that age of onset correlated with outcome; the earlier the onset of symptoms, the better the maintenance of treatment gains. Furthermore, habituation of reported anxiety both within and between sessions was positively associated with outcome. Finally, high levels of depression and anxiety were negatively correlated with successful outcome. Indeed, other researchers have reported a high incidence of depression in clinical samples (Vaughan, 1976; Rachman & Hodgson, 1980) and have proposed concomitant treatment for depression and obsessive–compulsive symptoms (Mavissakalian, Turner, & Michelson, 1984).

Treatment of Obsessions

Obsessions constitute a special problem in the behavioral assessment and treatment of obsessive–compulsive disorder. Since obsessions are verifiable only by the patients themselves, the effect of any treatment is difficult to assess. In those cases where obsessions are accompanied by compulsions, behavioral treatment aimed at reducing compulsive behavior often also will affect the incidence of obsessions, but this does not invariably happen. Furthermore, some patients are suffering from obsessions without accompanying compulsions. The success rate of behavioral treatment in these cases is limited. The procedures that have been reported in the literature to treat obsessions primarily include thought-stopping techniques and techniques based on forced exposure to the offending thought.

Thought-Stopping

Thought-stopping involves the deliberate interruption of a distressing thought by the use of a cue word such as "stop," or a loud noise. In addition, in some variants of the technique, neutral or pleasant alternative images are introduced after stopping the obsessive thought. The actual techniques vary from study to study (Tryon, 1979). In one technique the patient first practices to interrupt neutral thoughts. Once interrupting the neutral thoughts is mastered, the patient applies thought-stopping to the obsessions themselves. During the initial session, the patient is asked to imagine a neutral scene, raising his index finger on obtaining the image. The therapist then rings a bell and emphatically shouts the word "stop." When the patient has succeeded in stopping the thought, he lowers his finger and then begins to imagine a preselected pleasant scene, again signaling with the finger when the switch has been accomplished. In the next one to two sessions, the bell is faded out, and gradually the loudness of the word "stop" is reduced to a whisper. The patient himself then begins to verbalize the word "stop," fading it from loud to a whisper, and finally thinking it covertly. At this stage, homework assignments are given to practice thought-stopping to neutral thoughts for 5 to 10 minutes per day. Once the technique is mastered, the neutral thoughts are replaced by the least distrubing obsessive thoughts. Upon success, the more disturbing obsessive thoughts are gradually introduced.

A version of this technique was employed in a single-case study by Lombardo and Turner (1979). The patient, who was a 25-year-old male day-hospital patient, spent a significant amount of time fantasizing over heterosexual relationships, the unattainability of which caused him feelings of depression. During thought-stopping, the obsessive ruminations decreased from a median level of 40 minutes per day down to virtually zero after four days of practice. During a reversal phase, obsessive ruminations increased to exceed the original baseline level. During a second thought-stopping phase, however, the obsessive ruminations were again brought under control after five days of treatment.

In some cases, ruminations or cognitive rituals occur only in specific situations and cannot be elicited in the sessions. In these cases, thought-stopping can be rehearsed in the session in imagination by re-creating as many eliciting cues as possible and then imaginally applying the thought-stopping procedure. A case described by Turner, Holtzman, and Jacob (1983) engaged in various ritualistic looking behaviors, including looking at a certain crack on the wall upon descending the stairs, at certain corners of her bathtub while taking a shower, at certain spots on the bathroom wall upon leaving the shower, and at a certain spot in her bedroom wall while undressing. Self-administered response prevention had been unsuccessfull in all of these behaviors except looking at the crack of the wall upon descending the stairs. With imagined thought-stopping, the remaining looking behaviors decreased substantially.

While these and other case studies indicate that thought-stopping can have value for treating obsessions, the overall results are rather mixed. For example, Stern, Lipsedge, and Marks (1973) reported that thought-stopping according to taped instructions resulted in marked improvement in only four of eleven patients, and a slight improvement in an additional three patients. Furthermore, the thought-stopping procedure did not differ in effectiveness from the control procedure involving thought-stopping applied to an imagined blank television screen. Stern (1978) found that only two of eleven patients showed slight improvement with thought-stopping. Thus, while thought-stopping may be worth a trial in some cases, success is not guaranteed.

Habituation Training

Obsessions can be regarded as noxious stimuli to which the patient fails to habituate (Rachman, 1976). Dysphoric mood, neutralizing obsessions, and reassurance may contribute to the lack of habituation.

The procedures of satiation training and imaginal flooding involve "exposure" to the distressing obsessions. Theoretically, prolonged exposure should result in habituation, especially if the patient is in a relatively calm state of mind and the exposure is sufficiently prolonged or repeated. *Satiation training* as a strategy involves imaginal exposure to the "bad" thoughts while preventing the occurrence of neutralizing or "good" obsessions. Preferrably, patients should be in a calm state of mind to facilitate habituation. They should also not be reassured by the therapist. Satiation training resulted in significant improvement in two of seven patients in the study by Stern (1978) referred to in the section of thought-stopping. Interestingly, both these patients had the emotion of "horror" attached to their obsessions; the technique did not work in patients in whom obsessions were associated with "pleasure" or "guilt." Beech and Vaughan (1978), in their detailed analysis of two cases, failed to find evidence for habituation occuring with satiation training.

Flooding or prolonged exposure involves more active therapist guidance and longer sessions than satiation training (Emmelkamp, 1982). Reviewing two of his own studies, Emmelkamp (1982) concluded that exposure to relevant obsessions had a larger effect than exposure to irrelevant cues. Overall, prolonged exposure and thought-stopping were about equal in effectiveness, although the effect of thought-stopping was reported to be more variable. Similar results, i.e., no difference between flooding and thought-stopping, were obtained in a study by Hackmann and McLean (1975).

Other Techniques

Assertiveness training (Emmelkamp, 1982), cognitive restructuring (Robertson, Wendiggersen & Kaplan, 1983), paradoxical intention (Gerz, 1966), and faradic disruption (Kenny, Mowbray, & Lalani, 1978; Kenny, Solyom, & Solyom, 1973) are other techniques that have been employed for the treatment of obsessions. With the exception of the first two, these techniques appear to be variants of thought-stopping or habituation training. The fact that so many different techniques are being attempted attest to the difficulty of treating obsessions.

Treatment of Obsessive Slowness

For patients with obsessive slowness, special measures may be necessary. The goal of treatment is to have the patient perform the target behavior within a "normal" period of time. The treatment begins by setting a maximum time limit for the behavior in question, which may then be gradually reduced further. In some cases, the therapist may have to instruct the patient how to perform the behavior in a "normal" fashion. Furthermore, prompting and pacing may be necessary to bring the behavior down to acceptable durations. For example, Rachman (1974) described a patient with primary obsessive slowness who needed 45 minutes to brush his teeth because he would brush one small group at a time. He was first instructed in how to brush his teeth within a shorter period of time. After instructions, he was able to bring the duration of tooth brushing down to 15 minutes. The therapist then modeled the correct behavior and provided feedback of how much time had elapsed every 30 seconds. After this additional intervention, duration of tooth brushing decreased to below 10 minutes, although the target 5-minute limit was never reached.

The cases reported by Bennun (1980), Bilsbury and Morley (1978), Clark, Sugrim, and Bolton (1982), and Rachman (1974) show that instructions, modeling, and pacing are at least moderately effective in some cases. They also point out, however, the remarkable lack of generalization of the treatment effect from one target behavior to another. Although this lack of generalization is a welcome feature for those wishing to assess the effect of their intervention in a multiple-baseline design, it also points toward the difficulties in treating obsessional slowness. Furthermore, efforts at "counter control" appear to be common, such as those of the patient treated by Bilsbury and Morley (1978). This patient admitted to performing those rituals, that he had been forced to skip during the intervention, at a time later during the day when the therapist was absent.

COMBINATIONS OF BEHAVIOR THERAPY WITH PHARMACOTHERAPY

Besides behavior therapy, pharmacotherapy with antidepressant drugs provides a significant addition to the treatment arsenal for obsessive–compulsive disorder. The drug that has received the greatest systematic attention is clomipramine, an antidepressant agent thought to have primarily serotonin reuptake blocking action (Yaryura-Tobias & Neziroglu, 1983). After initial informal trials in the early 1970s, controlled trials for clomipramine were performed independently in England and Sweden. Thoren, Asberg, Croholm, Jornestedt, and Traskman (1980) conducted a study comparing clomipramine with nortriptyline and placebo in a three-group double-blind design with 24 patients. After an initial five-week phase during which patients were given their assigned drugs without concomitant behavior therapy, patients entered an open-treatment phase in which behavior therapy and an increased dosage of clomipramine were combined. The investigators found that after five weeks of medication only, clomipramine but not nortriptyline was significantly superior to placebo on an interview-based measure of obsessive–compulsive symptoms. The treatment effect took the entire five-week period to develop. After the combined behavioral and clomipramine treatment of the open-treatment phase, 12 of the 22 patients improved. These included three patients who had not shown any improvement on nortriptyline only. To test whether the effect of the program was due to relief of depression, the responders were compared to nonresponders on pretreatment depression measures. No difference was found between responders and nonresponders on pretreatment depression or other clinical variables, including severity of illness, sex, or age.

From a behavioral standpoint, it was unfortunate that the design of the Thoren et al. study did not permit a comparison of the clomipramine/behavior therapy combination with drug only, since the dose of the drug was increased during the combined open-treatment phase. A more systematic evaluation of the effect of drugs, behavior therapy and their combination was reported by Marks, Stern, Mawson, Cobb, and McDonald (1980) and Rachman, Cobb, Grey, McDonald, Mawson, Sartory, and Stern (1979). Forty-seven subjects were first put on clomipramine or placebo during an initial four-week outpatient phase. Four of these patients were subsequently admitted to a six-week inpatient program. During the first three weeks of the inpatient program, patients received either 15 sessions of exposure (plus unsupervised response prevention) or relaxation therapy, by random assignment. Thus, the first three weeks of the inpatient program permitted comparison of the effect of four treatment conditions: placebo plus relaxation (PR), placebo plus exposure (PE), clomipramine plus relaxation (CR), and clomipramine plus exposure (CE). During a second three-week inpatient period, the PR and CR groups crossed over to exposure treatment. After discharge, patients received their assigned drug for six months; the drug was then tapered off over four weeks. The patients remained in follow-up over an additional period of up to 18 months.

Of particular interest for the present discussion are the results of the first three weeks of inpatient treatment, because they permitted the assessment of the relative effectiveness of clomipramine and behavioral treatment. A rather clear pattern emerged: clomipramine but not behavior therapy resulted in an improvement of measures reflecting mood, such as ratings of anxiety and scores on the Wakefield and Hamilton Depression Scales. Conversely, behavior therapy tended to improve behaviorally focused measures such as the rated performance on a behavioral avoidance test. The combination of exposure treatment and clomipramine had additive effects. In contrast to the findings of Thoren et al. (1980), however, the clomipramine effect was limited to patients who had evidenced a significant degree of depression before treatment. In the ten subjects with the least amount of depression, clomipramine and placebo did not differ in effectiveness. Interestingly, there seemed to be a "therapeutic window" relating the effectiveness of clomipramine to plasma levels. Patients with levels less than 100 or exceeding 250 ng/ml showed less therapeutic effect. Thus, raising the dose above a certain critical level was associated with less effect.

The side effects of clomipramine, as reported by Stern, Marks, Mawson, and Luscombe (1980), included dry mouth, sweating, unsteady hands, temporary drowsiness, constipation, and difficulty focousing eyes. These side effects were more prevalent in the clomipramine group compared to the placebo group. It should be noted, however, that the placebo treated patients also exhibited side effects.

The choice of clomipramine in these studies is a reflection of an interest in the "serotonergic hypothesis" of obsessive–compulsive disorder, which postulates that obsessive–compulsive disorder is due to a specific disturbance in the activity of the neurotransmitter serotonin in the brain (Yaryura-Tobias, 1977). Further development of pharmacotherapy will involve the testing of antidepressant drugs that have a more specific effect on serotonin than clomipramine. For example we recently completed an outpatient-based study in which the drug fluoxetine, a selective serotonin reuptake blocker, showed considerable promise (Turner, Jacob, Biedel, & Himmelhoch, in press).

Clomipramine and fluoxetine are not yet commercially available in the United States. Other antidepressants have, however, also shown promise. For example, in a series of single-case designs involving four cases, Turner, Hersen, Bellack, Andrasik, and Capparell (1980) evaluated the effect of imipramine with or without concomitant behavioral treatment. Of the four patients, one responded to neither response prevention nor medication. In the first of the remaining three cases, imipramine alone appeared to somewhat reduce checking, possession placing (placing possessions in a particular order), urges to wash and urges to check, but not handwashing. Response prevention resulted in further improvement in all of these behaviors. Interestingly, this occurred at the expense of a deterioration of the patient's mood, as evidenced by an increase of the scores on the Beck Depression Inventory during response prevention. In the second case, flooding and response prevention were ineffective in reducing the duration spent in handwashing and tooth brushing rituals. Imipramine resulted in a decrease of these behaviors once it was prescribed at a dose exceeding 200 mg. per day. Upon withdrawal of the medication, performance again deteriorated but again improved upon reinstitution of a high dose of imipramine.

TREATMENT PROGRAM

The inpatient treatment of a patient with obsessive–compulsive disorder requires not only knowledge of behavior therapy, but also management skills to coordinate the activities of the interdisciplinary team comprised by the various staff members involed in the treatment. The key individual of the program is the primary clinician who develops the treatment plan, coordinates the implementation of assessment and treatment procedures, and provides follow-up for the patient after discharge. The program followed at our institution can be conveniently subdivided into preadmission, admission, and follow-up phases.

During the *pre-admission phase*, the initial contact with the patient is made. The assessment is conducted, including a psychiatric evaluation, a collateral interview with family members or significant others, and administration of paper and pencil tests and inventories. This initial evaluation provides the necessary information to develop preliminary target behaviors for observation and treatment.

A thorough assessment is also essential for making decisions concerning inpatient versus outpatient treatment and the desirability of psychopharmacologic treatment. We have been able to treat a number of patients entirely on an outpatient basis. Outpatient treatment is feasible if the patient is able to co-operate with self-implemented response prevention and the exposure treatment. Inpatient treatment is indicated when the patient requires close supervision for the purpose of response prevention, if current stressors in the home or work environment preclude successful implementation of outpatient treatment, or if the patient's problems are so pervasive or complicted that inpatient observation would significantly add to the overall assessment of the patient. Finally, inpatient treatment may be necessary for patients who live so far away from the treatment facility that they cannot commute back and forth for intensive daily outpatient sessions. Other clinicians have used similar rationales for decisions concerning inpatient treatment (Foa, Steketee, & Milby, 1980; Marks, 1981). To help reduce misunderstanding, it is important to discuss the general rationale and strategies of treatment with the patient and elicit consent prior to hospitalization, without, however, necessarily going into an excessive amount of detail.

The *admission phase* consists of two periods: baseline and intervention. During baseline, which lasts one week, no restrictions are placed on the patient's behavior. A primary nurse or nurse clinician is assigned as the treatment team leader and is responsible for the daily routine care of the patient. The primary clinician designates the target behaviors to be monitored and provides the treatment team with the necessary recording devices, such as data sheets, counters, etc. When the patient is admitted to the treatment unit, additional interviews and routine medical examinations are performed. Staff are instructed to observe and record target behaviors; they are also encouraged to make informal observations that might provide clues for additional target behaviors that the patient had not volunteered. The primary clinician, after consulting with the team and reviewing observational data, prepares with the patient an exposure hierarchy to be used during exposure sessions. Items used in Case 1 are listed in Table 4-1.

During the intervention period, the behavioral treatment is implemented. The main components of the program are respose prevention and flooding. The patients are instructed to refrain from engaging in the target behaviors (i.e., handwashing), except for specified and agreed upon episodes. For example, handwashings are limited to 30-second duration before and after meals; showers are limited to one daily for 10 minutes. In implementing response prevention, we rely mostly on patient's self control, although some prompting is usually necessary. We implement the response prevention on a 24-hour basis.

Many patients display a general fear of "contamination" with dirt or germs. They typically cope with this fear by cleaning and washing. Often they covertly create uncontaminated "safe zones" in the hospital. For example, one patient was found to store her clothes in a plastic bag, thus avoiding contamination. She had cheerfully gone along with various exposure treatments, without, however, showing much anxiety. It was only when the hidden clothes were found and "contaminated" that she began to show an increase in anxiety. Contamination involved the patient touching her clothes after her hands had been in contact with "unclean" items. It is important to make sure that all of the patient's "safe" environment is contaminated. For example, such items as the patient's clothing, books, etc., are brought in contact with "contaminated" objects; the patient is instructed not to decontaminate (wash) these items throughout hospitalization. Also, after washing, the patient is instructed to recontaminate himself or herself by touching contaminated articles.

In vivo flooding sessions are conducted by the primary clinician and assisted by other treatment team staff. The patient is exposed to items listed on the exposure hierarchy during the sessions. Sessions are typically conducted for 90 minutes or whatever time period necessary for the patient to report that anxiety levels are reduced to tolerable levels. Research has indicated that longer exposure periods produce greater treatment gains (Andrasik, Turner, & Ollendick, 1980; Foa & Chambless, 1978; Rabavilas, Boulougouris, & Stefanis, 1976).

We also conduct imaginal flooding sessions, particulary when the patient's fears involve disasters not arrangeable in vivo, or if patients appear to engage in cognitive avoidance strategies, such as distraction, during in vivo sessions that prevent them from feeling anxious.

The *follow-up phase* begins with the discharge of the patient. Early in this phase, we schedule therapist's contacts fairly frequently, such as several times per week. These contacts include home visits during which further exposure sessions are held and any safe zone in the patient's living quarters is contaminated. Family members are advised not to cooperate with possible reemerging compulsive behaviors. Several such home visits may be necessry. Once the treatment gains appear to have transferred to the home environment and show signs of maintenance, therapist contacts can be gradually withdrawn. Clinical judgement will dictate the frequency of continued appointments.

Case 1

The patient was a 31-year-old female with a 20-year history of checking and handwashing behaviors that were related to her obsessive fears of becoming contaminated by dog feces, worms, grass, newspaper, books, and cleaning chemicals. Her problems began at age 12, which the patient associated with her parent's marital difficulties and her problems interacting with her siblings. She was often subjected to severe criticism concerning her clothes, grooming habits, and overall appearance by her parents and her sisters. The patient gradually developed fears concerning contamination by dirt and began to perform elaborate cleaning rituals. The contamination fears subsequently began to predominate her thoughts; as a result the patient began to avoid friends and public places as a means of controlling contamination. There were some periods of amelioration; however, the problems began to exacerbate when she began experiencing marital difficulties. Handwashing behaviors and cleaning rituals began to dominate her daily activities and she became virtually housebound. Previous interventions had included hypnosis and trials of antidepressants and anti-anxiety agents.

Table 4-1
Case 1 Exposure Hierarchy

Item	Anxiety Rating
1. Hold books in lap without checking	3
2. Read newspaper and turn pages without checking	4
3. Walk past room trash container several times touching slightly with foot	5
4. Hold pair of scissors, place in therapist hand, and then receive open scissors back from therapist	5
5. Hold scissors to forehead and check	6
6. Face therapist while he makes sudden move with scissors	7
7. Hold brown bag containing jar with soil and earthworms	8
8. Walk down street touching sign posts, fire hydrants, and trees	8
9. Walk on grass without checking	9
10. Sit down on grass; check once, no more	10
11. Hold jar of worms; poke at worms with stick	10
12. Lift worms from jar; hold in hand; pass to therapist and receive back again	10
13. Approach pile of dog feces; hold foot over pile	10
14. Hold foot over pile of feces; bend over and touch top of shoes; rub hands over body	10
15. Walk back and forth across dry feces without checking	10

Treatment

The patient was admitted to the adult inpatient unit and given a routine psychiatric interview, medical examination, and completion of a battery of personality and anxiety inventories. After a five-day observation period she was put on reponse prevention and on a 90-minute daily exposure program for ten days, during which she was exposed to contaminated items based on a self-rated hierarchy (Table 4-1). For example, the patient was escorted outside and asked to approach piles of dog feces. She was next asked to stand next to the feces, to tap with the bottom of her shoe, and hold her foot over the pile. Then without moving away, she was required to bend over, touch the top of her shoes, and rub her hands all over her body and place them on her face. (Note that the patient was not required to directly touch the fecal material, as this would constitute a nonhygienic behavior to be avoided even by normals.) The therapist provided support for approach behaviors and refrained from providing reassurance to self-defeating inquiries (i.e., "what if . . .?"). Another procedure involved touching each item in her room including books, papers, etc., with contaminated clothes. The patient was not permitted to clean her room or wash her hands until directed by staff to do so. In addition to the in vivo exposure program outlined above, the patient also received one session of imaginal flooding with images involving having intestinal parasites and worms, a fantasy that was close to her "ultimate" fear.

The results of treatment are depicted in Figure 4-1. As can be seen, there was a rapid decrease in the frequency of handwashing and toileting behaviors,

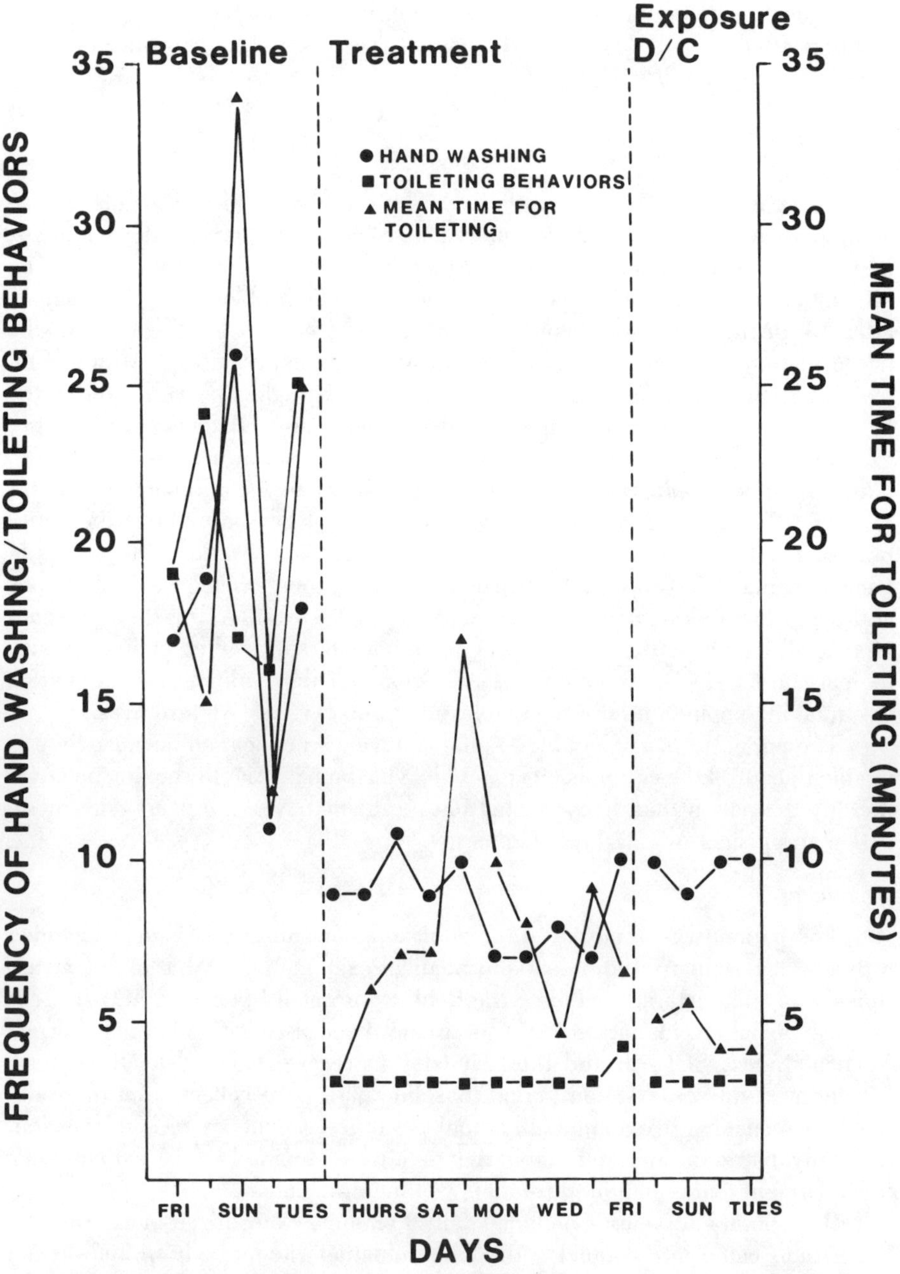

Fig. 4-1. Frequency of handwashing and toileting behaviors (i.e., wiping, flushing) per day and mean duration in minutes for toileting per day.

as well as a reduction of the amount of time that the patient spent engaging in toileting rituals. Upon discharge, the patient was given a self-exposure program to practice daily for prevention of relapse.

Case 2

The patient was a 28-year-old male with a 15-year history of obsessive–compulsive symptoms including contamination fears involving dirt, dead animals, and dog excrement; excessive handwashing, frequent showers and car washing; difficulties touching money and kitchen utensils. His problems began at age 13 after the death of a close friend who was a victim of suicide. The patient who had a history of strict morals and religiosity began experiencing extreme guilt feelings for having failed to include the friend in his nightly prayers. During the first year, symptoms were characterized by compulsive religious behavior. For example, the patient performed nightly an elaborate set of prayers for himself, family members, and friends. If the patient forgot to include someone in his prayers before getting into bed, he would get out of bed and restart the entire prayer. The patient also went to church for "confession" several times per week. Handwashing behavior initially began when the patient would wash his hands and arms for a skin rash, as instructed by a physician. As his fears of guilt increased, he developed fears of dirt contamination that resulted in an excessive increase in handwashing behaviors. As a result of these difficulties the patient was unable to maintain full-time employment due to excessive tardiness.

The patient was also unable to pursue advanced education because he was unable to control the compulsions before leaving home. Prior to seeking behavior therapy the patient had been treated for approximately seven years with medication and insight-oriented psychotherapy.

Treatment

The patient was admitted to the adult inpatient unit. Assessment included a thorough psychiatric interview and medical examination. A battery of inventories was administered including the Beck Depression Inventory, MMPI, Fear Survey, Social Avoidance and Distress Scale, Fear of Negative Events, Cornell Medical Index, SCL-90, and the Maudsley Obsessive–Compulsion Inventory. During a six-day observation period, baseline data were collected on three dependent measures: frequency of compulsive urges, frequency of handwashing, and daily distress scale. Self-monitoring data were recorded by the patient while the treatment team monitored frequency of handwashing.

Behavioral intervention included daily 90-minute exposure sessions whereby the patient came into contact with "contamination" items both on and off the unit. These sessions were conducted over a 14-day period. The patient was monitored on a 24-hour basis by the assigned staff and was prevented from washing hands or taking showers except for specified times during which explicit time limits were enforced for handwashing and showers. In Figure 4-2 the results of the treatment relative to baseline data are displayed. As can be seen, during

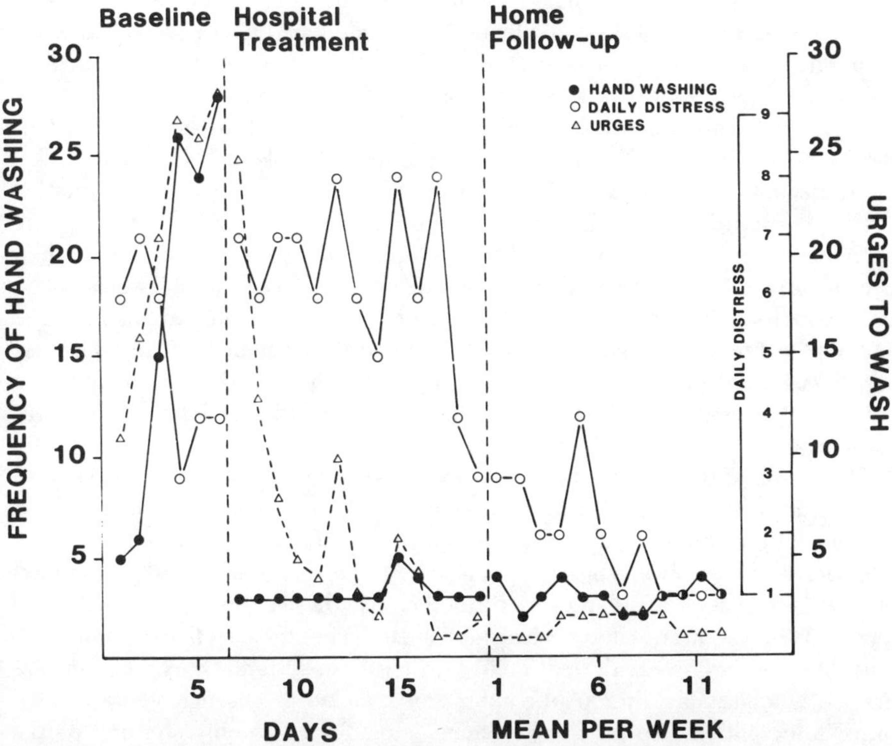

Fig. 4-2. Frequency recording of daily handwashing, urges, and daily distress ratings during baseline and hospital treatment phases. Mean frequency for handwashing, urges, and distress per week for three-month home follow-up.

treatment a rapid decline in urges and frequency of handwashing was evident. Self-report of distress, however, remained at relatively high levels.

After discharge the patient was followed as an outpatient for three months. He was seen on a biweekly basis and received exposure sessions for feared stimuli. Follow-up data for mean frequency of handwashing, handwashing urges, and self-report of distress were compiled on a weekly basis. As is evident in Figure 4-2, the treatment gains were maintained and, additionally, the distress ratings were lower in this outpatient phase compared to the inpatient levels.

PROBLEM AREAS

In our experience, most patients completing the entire inpatient program experience at least some improvement, although they will need to continue to work to maintain their treatment gains. The treatment is not without problems, however. One such problem is that not all patients will accept the program. For example, some patients develop strong anxieties immediately after admission and leave before the treatment is implemented. During his first hospital day, one such patient, with an obsessional fear of warts, identified a nurse who had warts on her hand. When this nurse entered his room, the patient requested immediate discharge. Thus, treatment was never implemented.

Patients with concomitant personality disorders, such as histrionic or borderline personality disorder, pose a different kind of problem. They often develop interpersonal problems with the staff that impede the successful implementation of the program. For example, during a time when two compulsive patients were hospitalized simultaneously, one of them closely monitored the amount of attention the other received from the treatment team. She would angrily protest when the balance appeared not to be in her favor. Another female patient began to look forward to the exposure sessions conducted by her male therapist, because they constituted precious moments during which she was the sole recipient of concentrated male attention. Since she exhibited little anxiety during these sessions they obviously had little functional value.

Patients with extreme forms of obsessive indecisiveness and those with concentration difficulties due to depression also require special attention. These patients often complain that they are uncertain if they performed a certain behavior and therefore repeat the behavior just to make sure. Adding antidepressant medication might improve the outcome in these cases. At a more general level, further research is needed to establish guidelines for selection of candidates most likely to improve with treatment. Furthermore, systematic explorations are needed of multimodal therapeutic approaches, including pharmacotherapy, cognitive interventions, social skills training, etc., for cases only showing partial improvement with the basic program.

Throughout the treatment, but perhaps particularly during the outpatient follow-up phase, family issues will often surface as the main impediment for maintenance of gains or further progress. Thus, family and marital problems, including sexual ones, may need specific intervention (e.g., Stern & Marks, 1973).

Another question that needs to be studied is how to assign patients to inpatient or outpatient treatment. With hospitalization costs amounting to hundreds of dollars per day, it would seem important to further develop outpatient based programs. For example, a home-based program might be more cost-effective than a hospital stay even if the home-based program would necessitate a therapist to spend 24 hours in the patient's home to supervise response prevention.

SUMMARY

Obsessive–compulsive disorder is a rare but debilitating condition characterized by a high frequency of obtrusive thoughts (obsessions) and imperative washing, cleaning, checking, hoarding, or other behavioral rituals (compulsions). Associate features include obsessive slowness, indecisiveness, and conscientiousness. In the differential diagnosis of obsessive–compulsive disorder, depression, delusional states, dysmorphophobia and brain injury should be considered.

The mainstay of the treatment of obsessive–compulsive disorder is exposure to feared thoughts and situations, and response prevention of the compulsive behaviors. Furthermore, treatment with antidepressant medication may significantly enhance treatment effectiveness, especially in patients with impaired ability to concentrate due to depression. The treatment of patients with obsessions without compulsions and the adaptation of behavioral treatment to patients with concomitant personality disorders needs further development. The involvement of the spouse in treatment and other family issues need further study. In the follow-up of treated obsessive–compulsive patients, home visits and outpatient contacts are needed to reinforce response prevention and to provide booster sessions in case of re-emerging fears. However, maintenance strategies are relatively unexplored and in need of further research.

The treatment of patients with obsessive–compulsive disorder is difficult. It is difficult because the patients often pose management problems, and because of the high degree of staff coordination necessary. However, with correctly implemented programs, the improvement can be quite significant and gratifying both for patients and staff.

REFERENCES

Agras WS, & Jacob RG. (1981). Phobia: Nature and measurement. In Mavissakalian M, & Barlow DH. (Eds), *Phobia, psychological and pharmacological treatment* (pp 35–62). New York: Guilford Press.

Allen JJ, & Tune GS. (1975). The Lynfield Obsessional Compulsive Questionnaires. *Scottish Medical Journal 20*, 21–24.

Andrasik F, Turner SM, & Ollendick TH. (1980). Self-report and physiologic responding during in vivo flooding. *Behavior Research and Therapy 18*, 593–595.

Beech HR (Ed). (1974). *Obsessional states.* London: Methuen Ltd.

Beech HR, & Vaughan M. (1978). *Behavioural treatment of obsessional states.* New York: John Wiley.

Bennun I. (1980). Obsessional slowness: A replication and extension. *Behaviour Research and Therapy 18*, 595–598.

Bilsbury C, & Morley S. (1978). Obsessional slowness: A meticulous replication. *Behaviour Research and Therapy 17*, 405–408.

Black A. (1974). The natural history of obsessional neurosis. In Beech HR (Ed), *Obsessional states.* London: Methuen.

Boersma K, Den Hengst S, Dekker J, & Emmelkamp PM. (1976). Exposure and response prevention in the natural environment: A comparison with obsessive–compulsive patients. *Behaviour Research and Therapy 14*, 19–24.

Boulougouris JC, & Stefanis C. (1977). Psychophysiological responses in obsessive–compulsive patients. *Behaviour Research and Therapy 15*, 221–230.

Carey G, & Gottesman II. (1981). Twin and family studies of anxiety, phobic, and obsessive disorders. In Klein DS, & Radkin JB (Eds), *Anxiety: New research and changing concepts.* New York: Raven Press.

Catts S, & McConaghy N. (1975). Ritual prevention in the treatment of obsessive compulsive neurosis. *Australian and New Zealand Journal of Psychiatry 9*, 37–41.

Clark DA, Surgrim I, & Bolton D. (1982) Case histories and shorter communications. *Behaviour Research and Therapy 20*, 289–292.

Cooper J. (1970). The Leyton Obsessional Inventory. *Psychological Medicine 1*, 48–64.

Emmelkamp, PMG. (1982) *Phobic and obsessive–compulsive disorders: Theory, research, and practice*. New York: Plenum Press.

Emmelkamp, PMG, & Kraanen J. (1977). Therapist controlled exposure in vivo versus self-controlled exposure in vivo: A comparison with obsessive–compulsive patients. *Behaviour Research and Therapy 15*, 491–495.

Foa EB. (1979). Failure in treating obsessive–compulsives. *Behaviour Research and Therapy 17*, 169–179.

Foa EB, & Chambless DL. (1978). Habituation of subjective anxiety during flooding in imagery. *Behaviour Research and Therapy 16*, 391–399.

Foa, EB, & Goldstein A. (1978). Continuous exposure and complete response prevention in treatment of obsessive–compulsive neurosis. *Behavior Therapy 9*, 821–829.

Foa EB, Grayson JD, Steketee GS, Doppelt HG, Turner RM, & Latimer PR. (1983). Success and failure in the behavioral treatment of obsessive–compulsives. *Journal of Consulting and Clinical Psychology 51*, 287–297.

Foa EB, Steketee G, & Milby JB. (1980). Differential effects of exposure and response prevention in obsessive–compulsive washers. *Journal of Consulting and Clinical Psychology 48*, 71–79.

Foa EB, Steketee G, Turner RM, & Fischer SC. (1980). Effects of imaginal exposure to feared disasters in obsessive–compulsive checkers. *Behaviour Research and Therapy 18*, 449–455.

Foulds GA. (1965). Personality and personal illness. London: Tavistock Publications.

Gerz HO. (1966). Experience with the logotherapeutic technique of paradoxical intention in the treatment of phobic and obsessive–compulsive patients. *American Journal of Psychiatry 123*, 548–553.

Hackmann A, & McLean C. (1975). A comparison of flooding and thought-stopping in the treatment of obsessional neurosis. *Behaviour Research and Therapy 13*, 263–269.

Hodgson R, & Rachman S. (1977). Obsessional–compulsive complaints. *Behaviour Research and Therapy* 15, 389–395.

Hodgson R, Rachman S, & Marks IM. (1972). The treatment of chronic obsessive–compulsive neurosis: Follow-up and further findings. *Behaviour Research and Therapy 10*, 181–189.

Hodgson R, Rachman S, & Marks IM. (1973). The treatment of obsessive–compulsive neurotics by modeling and flooding in vivo. *Behaviour Research and Therapy 11*, 463–471.

Hornveld RHJ, Kraaimatt FW, & Van Dam-Baggen RMJ. (1979). Anxiety, discomfort and handwashing in obsessive–compulsive and psychiatric control patients. *Behaviour Research and Therapy 17*, 223–228.

Jacob RG, & Rapport M. (1984). Panic Disorder. In Turner SM (Ed), *Behavioral treatment of anxiety disorders*. New York: Plenum.

Jenike MA, & Brotman AW. (1984). The EEG in obsessive–compulsive disorder. *Journal of Clinical Psychiatry 45*, 122–124.

Kendell RE, & Discipio WJ. (1970). Obsessional symptoms and obsessional personality traits in patients with depressive illness. *Psychological Medicine 1*, 65–72.

Kenny FT, Mowbray RM, & Lalani S. (1978). Fradic disruption of obsessive ideation in the treatment of obsessive neurosis: A controlled study. *Behavior Therapy 9*, 209–221.

Kenny FT, Solyom L, & Solyom C. (1973). Faradic disruption of obsessive ideation in the treatment of obsessive neurosis. *Behavior Therapy 4*, 448–457.

Kringlen E. (1965). Obsessional neurotics. *British Journal of Psychiatry 111*, 709–722.

Lang PJ & Lazovik AD. (1963). Experimental desensitization of a phobia. *Journal of Abnormal and Social Psychology 66*, 519–525.

Lo WH. (1967). A follow-up study of obsessional neurotics in Hong Kong Chinese. *British Journal of Psychiatry 113*, 823–832.

Lombardo TW, & Turner SM. (1979). Thought-stopping in the control of obsessive ruminations. *Behavior Modification 3*, 267–272.

Marks IM. (1981) Review of behavioral psychotherapy in obsessive–compulsive disorders. *American Journal of Psychiatry* 138, 584–592.

Marks IM, Stern RS, Mawson D, Cobb J, & McDonald R. (1980). Clomipramine and exposure for obsessive–compulsive rituals: I. *British Journal of Psychiatry 136*, 1–25.

Marks IM, Hodgson R, & Rachman S. (1975). Treatment of chronic obsessive–compulsive neurosis by in vivo exposure. *British Journal of Psychiatry 127*, 349–364.

Mavissakalian MR, & Barlow DH. (Eds), (1981). *Assessment of obsessive–compulsive disorders*. New York: Guilford Press.

Mavissakalian M, Turner S, & Michelson L. (In press). Future directions in the assessment and treatment of obsessive–compulsive disorder. In Mavissakalian M, Turner S, & Michelson L. (Eds), *Obsessive compulsive disorder: psychological and pharmacological treatment. New York: Plenum Press.*

McKeon J, McGuffin P, & Robinson P. (1984). Obsessive–compulsive neurosis following head injury: A report of four cases. *British Journal of Psychiatry 144*, 190–192.

McKeon J, Roa B, & Mann A. (1984). Life events and personality traits in obsessive–compulsive neurosis. *British Journal of Psychiatry 144*, 185–189.

Meyer V. (1966). Modification of obsessive–compulsive behavior. *Behaviour Research and Therapy 4*, 273–280.

Meyer V, & Levy R. (1973). Modification of behavior in obsessive–compulsive disorders. In Adams HE, & Unikel P. (Eds), *Issues and trends in behavior therapy*. Springfield, IL: Charles C. Thomas.

Mills HL, Agras WS, Barlow DH, & Mills JR. (1973). Compulsive rituals treated by response prevention. An experimental analysis. *Archives of General Psychiatry 28*, 524–529.

Munro A. (1980). Monosymptomatic hypochondrical psychosis (MHP): New aspects of an old syndrome. *Journal of Psychiatric Treatment and Evaluation 2*, 79–86.

Philpott R. (1975). Recent advances in the behavioural measurement of obsessional illness: Difficulties common to these and other measures. *Scottish Medical Journal 20*, 33–40.

Rabavilas A, & Boulougouris J. (1974). Physiological accompanying of ruminations, flooding, and thought stopping in obsessive patients. *Behavior Research and Therapy 2*, 239–243.

Rabavilas AD, Boulougouris JC, & Stefanis C. (1976). Duration of flooding sessions in the treatment of obsessive–compulsive patients. *Behaviour Research and Therapy 14*, 349–355.

Rachman S. (1974) Primary obsessional slowness. *Behaviour Research and Therapy 12*, 9–18.

Rachman S. (1976). The modification of obsessions: A new formulation. *Behaviour Research and Therapy 14*, 437–443.

Rachman R., Cobb J, Grey S, McDonald B, Mawson D, Sartory G, & Stern R. (1979). The behavioral treatment of obsessional–compulsive disorders, with and without clomipramine. *Behaviour Research and Therapy 17*, 467–478.

Rachman S, & Hodgson R. (1980). *Obsessions and compulsions*. Englewood Cliffs, N.J.: Prentice Hall.

Rachman S, Hodgson R, & Marks IM. (1971). The treatment of chronic obsessive–compulsive neurosis. *Behaviour Research and Therapy 9*, 237–247.

Rachman S, Marks IM, & Hodgson R. (1973). The treatment of obsessive–compulsive neurotics by modeling and flooding in vivo. *Behaviour Research and Therapy 11*, 463–471.

Rapoport J, Elkins R, Langer DH, Sceery W, Buchsbaum MS, Gillin JC, Murphy DL, Zahn TP, Lake R, Ludlow C, & Mendelson W. (1981). Childhood obsessive–compulsive disorder. *American Journal of Psychiatry 138*, 1545–1554.

Robertson J, Wendiggensen P, & Kaplan I. (1983). Towards a comprehensive treatment for obsessional thoughts. *Behaviour Research and Therapy 21*, 347–356.

Roper G, Rachman S, & Hodgson R. (1973). An experiment on obsessional checking. *Behaviour Research and Therapy 11*, 271–277.

Roper G, Rachman S, & Marks IM. (1975). Passive and participant modeling in exposure treatment of obsessive–compulsive neurotics. *Behaviour Research and Therapy 13*, 271–279.

Sandler J, & Hazari A. (1960). The obsessional: Or the psychological classification of obsessional character and symptoms. *British Journal of Medical Psychology 33*, 113–122.

Snowden J. (1980). A comparison of written and post box forms of the Leyton Obsessional Inventory. *Psychological Medicine 10*, 165–170.

Steketee G, Foa EB, & Grayson JB. (1982). Recent advances in the behavioral treatment of obsessive compulsives. *Archives of General Psychiatry 39*, 1365–1371.

Stern RS. (1978). Obsessive thoughts: The problem of therapy. *British Journal of Psychiatry 132*, 200–205.

Stern RS, Lipsedge MS, & Marks IM. (1973). Obsessive ruminations: A controlled trial of thought-stopping technique. *Behaviour Research and Therapy 11*, 659–662.

Stern RS, & Marks IM. (1973). Contract therapy in the obsessive–compulsive neurosis with marital discord. *British Journal of Psychiatry 123*, 681–684.

Stern R, Marks I, Mawson D, & Luscombe D. (1980). Clomipramine and exposure for compulsive rituals: II. Plasma levels, side effects and outcome. *British Journal of Psychiatry 136*, 161–166.

Thoren P, Asberg M, Cronholm B, Jornestedt L, & Traskman L. (1980). Clomipramine treatment of obsessive–compulsive disorder. *Archives of General Psychiatry 37*, 1281–1285.

Tyron G. (1979). A review and critique of thought stopping research. *Journal of Behaviour Research and Therapy 10*, 189–192.

Turner SM, Beidel DC, & Nathan S. (In press). Biological factors in obsessive–compulsive disorders. *Psychology Bulletin*.

Turner SM, Hersen M, Bellack AS, Andrasik F, & Capparell HV. (1980). Behavioral and pharmacological treatment of obsessive–compulsive disorders. *Journal of Nervous and Mental Disease 168*, 651–657.

Turner SM, Hersen M, Bellack AS, & Wells KC. (1979). Behavioral treatment of obsessive–compulsive neuroses. *Behaviour Research and Therapy 17*, 95–106.

Turner SM, Holzman A, & Jacob RG. (1983). Treatment of compulsive looking by imaginal thought-stopping. *Behavior Modification 7*, 576–582.

Turner SM, Jacob RG, Beidel DC, & Griffin S. (In press). A second case of mania with fluoxetine. *American Journal of Psychiatry.*

Turner SM, Jacob RG, Beidel DC, & Himmelhoch. (In press). Treatment of obsessive–compulsive disorder with fluoxetine HCL. *Clinical Psychopharmacology.*

Turner SM, Jacob RG, & Morrison R. (1984). Somatoform disorders. In Sutker P, & Adams HE (Eds), *Handbook of psychopathology.* New York: Plenum Press.

Turner SM, & Michelson M. (1984). Obsessive–compulsive disorders. In Turner SM (Ed), *Behavioral theories and treatment of anxiety.* New York: Plenum Press.

Vaughan M. (1976). The relationships between obsessional personality, obsessions and depression and symptoms of depression. *British Journal of Psychiatry 129*, 36–39.

Yaryura-Tobias JA. (1977). Obsessive–compulsive disorders: A serotonergic hypothesis. *Journal of Orthomolecular Psychiatry, 6*, 317–326.

Yaryura-Tobias A, & Nezigolu FA. (1983). Obsessive–compulsive disorders: Pathogenesis–diagnosis–treatment. New York: Marcel Dekker.

5
Affective Disorders

Brian F. Shaw and Georgina Harris

This chapter outlines the use of cognitive-behavior therapy (CBT: Beck, Rush, Shaw & Emery, 1979) in the inpatient treatment of individuals suffering from depression. The largest group of patients admitted to psychiatric units of general hospitals suffer from an affective disorder. In the United States it has been estimated that 18 percent of the population will have a lifetime diagnosis of definite major depression (Weissman & Myers, 1978). The past 15 years has heralded the greatest advances in the understanding of these conditions both from biological and psychological viewpoints. One of the most promising approaches in the treatment of ambulatory, depressed patients is cognitive-behavior therapy (Blackburn, Bishop, Glen, Whalley & Christie, 1981; Rush, Beck, Kovacs & Hollon, 1977; Murphy, Simons, Wetzel and Lustman, 1984). To date there have been no systematic outcome trials with inpatients.

This chapter is a clinical guide designed to delineate the use of cognitive-behavior therapy within a multi-disciplinary treatment approach. Descriptions of the disorders, methods of evaluation, and the integration of cognitive-behavioral treatment with other interventions are provided. Two cases illustrate the importance of careful assessment and the consistency and concentration of treatments. Finally, problem areas in the inpatient treatment of depressed patients are addressed.

PRACTICE OF INPATIENT BEHAVIOR THERAPY
ISBN 0-8089-1715-3

CLINICAL DESCRIPTION

The *Diagnostic and Statistical Manual (DSM-III:* American Psychiatric Association, 1980) lists four main diagnoses within the affective disorders group (major depression, bipolar disorder, cyclothymic disorder, and dysthymic disorder). Patients with major depression and bipolar disorder account for most of the hospitalizations. In addition to the Axis I diagnosis, diagnoses on Axis II (personality disorders) and Axis III (associated medical disorders) are common in patients who require hospitalization. This chapter focuses primarily on those patients suffering from major depression.

By adopting the *DSM-III* classification we accept the notion of a syndrome, a collection of signs and symptoms that define individuals and relate to issues of treatment strategy and prognosis. We recognize that the research on the prediction of the course of the disorder for many depressed individuals is inprecise. Nevertheless, it is our position that the classification scheme adds to our understanding of the individual by allowing a comparison to other patients via normative research. We realize that behaviorally-oriented practioners may object to the use of a diagnostic system (Schact & Nathan, 1977) rather than following a system of behavioral analyses. Psychologists often prefer a psychosocial–interpersonal model to behavioral or diagnostic classifications. (Smith & Kraft, 1983). In our view depression is not simply a symptom that needs to be modified, however, but rather is a syndrome representing a number of interrelated symptoms. Thus, when treating the depressed patient we expect that a change in one symptom area (e.g. reducing apathy) will have a positive effect on other symptoms (e.g. dysphoria).

Major depression involves dysphoric mood or loss of interest or pleasure in all or almost all usual activities and pastimes and at least four other symptoms (e.g. fatigue, sense of worthlessness, suicidal ideation, insomnia). These symptomatic changes must have persisted every day for at least two weeks. The symptoms cannot include mood incongruent delusions nor hallucinations. The changes must not be a function of schizophrenia, paranoid disorder, organic mental disorder, or uncomplicated bereavement. Some patients admitted with major depression will have the specific features of melancholia (distinct quality of mood, early morning awakening, marked psychomotor agitation or retardation, significant anorexia, and excessive guilt). This chapter does not review the criteria for the other affective disorders, but highlights only major depression.

ASSESSMENT ISSUES

Frank (1976) states that "behavior therapy and behavioral assessment are part of one and the same process" (p xi). The use of a cognitive-behavior orientation similarly requires the therapist to assess outcomes in specific areas. From our perspective, the clinician should first determine the patient's diagnosis. If the patient suffers from an affective disorder, he or she should proceed to assess the severity and chronicity of the disorder and the associated cognitive and/or behavioral change.

The first step involves making a diagnosis with particular attention to other psychological and medical disorders that may influence the severity and chronicity of the affective disorder. As will be emphasized throughout this chapter, the multi-disciplinary model of the inpatient unit offers significant advantages for assessment. Patients are observed in a variety of contexts and the staff can address the same assessment issues from their different perspectives. To make a diagnosis the clinician requires information about the patient from a variety of sources. The Schedule of Affective Disorders and Schizophrenia (SADS: Endicott & Spitzer, 1978) is particularly useful as a basis for the diagnosis combined with other data. The severity *and* chronicity of the disorder should be determined. A measure of the severity of depression is best obtained from the clinician's judgment and the patient's self-report. The Hamilton Rating Scale for Depression (HRSD: Hamilton, 1960) is a 17-item scale designed for use by the clinician to rate the severity of depression (there is in fact a 24-item scale but only the first 17 items are used as the severity index). The Beck Depression Inventory (BDI: Beck, Ward, Mendelson, Mock & Erbaugh, 1961) or the Carroll Rating Scale (Carroll, Feinberg, Smouse, Rawson, & Greden, 1981) are two commonly used self-report scales to determine severity. The chronicity of the episode is typically evaluated by the length of the episode (in months) and the number of previous episodes. Some patients report that they have been depressed for much of their adult lives. When the clinician hears such a report it is useful to consider the diagnosis of dysthymic disorder (see Akiskal, 1981). More information on these measures and others may be found in Shaw, Vallis, and McCabe (in press) or Lewinsohn and Lee (1981).

Cognitive-behavior therapy (CBT) requires a systematic documentation of the symptom pattern of the affective disorder. Frequently, individuals are hospitalized because of suicidal ideation or behavior, severe hopelessness, and/or melancholia. Prominent sleep disturbance and appetite loss are other commonly observed symptoms in inpatients. After documenting the pattern of symptoms, one decides what areas to address first. Hopelessness and apathy are two typical early targets. Notably in outpatient studies of pharmacotherapy or cognitive therapy, a specific pattern of symptom change as the depression remits has not been observed (Simons, Garfield & Murphy, 1984; Zeiss, Lewinsohn & Munoz, 1979). It appears that with successful treatment the cluster of symptoms lessen following an idiosyncratic pattern. For this reason the cognitive-behavior therapist initially selects target symptoms with the answers to these questions in mind: (1) how severe is the depression; (2) what symptom(s) is most distressing to the patient and (3) what target is most amenable to intervention in the short term?

Self-report measures of severity are frequently useful to document symptom change but there are limitations that need to be recognized (see Prusoff, Klerman, & Paykel, 1972). For example, in our experience it is rare that a patient will obtain a score of greater than 50 on the BDI (range 0–63). Patients who obtain very high scores should be assessed for response bias problems (e.g., exaggeration). Typically BDI scores in the 20s or 30s are reported. For example, the mean scores on the BDI and the HRSD (17 item) in a group of 59 patients meeting RDC criteria for major depression across three settings was 28.1 and 24.4, respectively (Hamilton & Abramson, 1983; Eaves & Rush, 1984; Dobson & Shaw, in press). In a past report (Shaw, 1981), the value of observational scales for staff has been reviewed. It is particularly useful to identify specific symptoms, such as apathy or sleep disturbance, and to devise a behavioral assessment through the use of a systematic checklist to record the staff's observations several times per day. Indeed, Williams, Barlow, and Agras (1972) found that behavioral measures were better predictors of post-hospital course than either the HRSD or the BDI. The behavioral assessment used in their work included talking, smiling, motor activity, and time out of room.

A number of outpatient studies have suggested that there are subtypes of depression. Some of the most common subtypings involve the psychotic–nonpsychotic and endogeneous–nonendogeneous groupings (cf. Klein, 1974). Considerable attention has also been given to the relationship between anxiety and depressive disorders (see Fowles & Gersh, 1979). More recently the division between primary and secondary depression has been described (Feighner, Robins, Guze, Woodruff, Winokur, & Munoz, 1972). This distinction depends on the chronology of affective and nonaffective disorders. A major depression preceded by any other nonaffective illness is considered secondary; otherwise, the depression is considered primary. Each of these dimensions can be reviewed for its usefulness as variables to describe the patient's disorder. At the present time, however, with the exception of the psychotic–nonpsychotic dimension, there is little evidence that subtyping depressed patients has a significant role in treatment planning. Patients who are psychotic are not candidates for cognitive interventions but instead require a structured environment and concrete behavioral interventions. In our experience, patients with severe depression (particularly those with melancholia) also benefit initially from behavioral interventions.

TREATMENT ISSUES

The general trend in mental health is to provide outpatient treatment, and we endorse this effort. Nevertheless, it has been our experience that an admission to a hospital can be beneficial to provide a greater consistency in concentration of treatment that may bring earlier relief to the patient. Furthermore, there are many practical issues that warrant hospitalization, including stress reduction, careful assessment of suicidal risk, and the adjustment of medication. As noted previously, we use a problem-oriented approach in the treatment of the depressed patient. Certain symptoms are identified and listed in the patient's medical record as problems for all staff to assess and to provide consistent records of their interventions. Later in this chapter, we concentrate on two typical problems: *helplessness* with associated apathy, withdrawal, and anhedonia, and *hoplessness* with related irritability and suicidal ideation.

Perhaps the most essential issue in the inpatient treatment of patients with affective disorders is clear communication among the patient, the family, and the disciplines involved in the patient's care. We have observed many traditional psychiatric inpatient units where the prevailing treatment approach involves psychopharmacology and the role of the nonmedical disciplines is primarily one of assessment of, for example, daily activities, marital functioning, and support systems. We support these activities but strongly recommend a more active psychological treatment modality combined with medical approaches. The disciplines involved in most inpatient units include psychiatry, nursing, occupational therapy, social work, and psychology. These disciplines have developed expertise based on a variety of theoretical orientations. The result can be a broad and comprehensive understanding of the patient's difficulties leading to a multifaceted treatment plan.

Our position is that a cognitive-behavioral orientation in the treatment of affective disorders can be an effective modality but the approach requries a *consistent* application by the staff. Most importantly, it is critical that all staff understand the basic principles of the treatment orientation so that they will know when their recommendations may run counter to other advice given to the patient. For this reason, the most difficult issue in utilizing a cognitive-behavioral approach is not the one-to-one interaction with patients but the coordination of the staff. Power and control issues interact with the beliefs of the clinicians about what factors are important in the development and maintenance of the patient's disorder. Routine educational sessions to teach the basic assumptions of cognitive-behavior therapy are important.

The staff's attitude to depressed patients requires attention if a consistent approach to treatment is to be achieved. Working with patients who suffer from affective disorders can be a frustrating and difficult task. Depressed patients are frequently caught in a cycle of a sense of worthlessness, helplessness, and hopelessness that is exacerbated by changes in their vegetative functioning and a loss of motivation. What Beck (1967) has described as the depressed individual's "paralysis of will" may lead staff to conclude that the depressed patient wants to be depressed and is being reinforced (or receives secondary gain) from his or her disorder. The assumption of a cognitive-behavioral oriented program is that no one wants to be depressed. Motivational explanations for the disorder are not ignored but do not receive the central emphasis. Within the cognitive-behavioral framework, the apathy and motivation observed in depression is intimately connected with the individuals' belief that they are incapable of solving their problems and/or that effort will further deplete already reduced energy resources. Such expectations and beliefs are essential areas for staff attention and provide the early material for the goal of changing dysfunctional thinking.

Helplessness in patients, particularly those who have made a suicide attempt, may at times result in antagonism toward open criticism. On the other hand, some staff members are prone to give depressed patients unrealistically positive feedback in the belief that the power of positive thinking or unsolicited compliments will have a therapeutic effect. Both of these reactions usually backfire (see Coyne, 1976a). In our experience, the ideal staff attitude and strategy is a collaborative, scientific one. Staff members assess the patient's symptoms, teach the person ways to problem solve and cope with pessimistic thinking, offer advice and suggestions to alleviate symptoms, and observe whether their interventions have a positive effect. Units that are comfortable with the trial-and-error methods of psychopharmacology will readily see parallels between their treatment strategy and the empirical ("let's test it out") strategy used in cognitive-behavior therapy units. The difference is that staff members provide a concentrated effort to intervene to change the patients' thinking versus a more passive observational role.

The goal of inpatient care is to treat the patient's major symptoms and to make gains to the point where he or she can move to an outpatient status. The overall rationale given to patients is one of learning how to cope with their disorder and to work toward solving life problems rather than one of curing their disorders. Affective disorders tend to be recurrent, and it is important not to give the patient an overly optimistic outlook. Again, a realistic perspective is advisable, with patient's being told that their condition may recur; the purpose of treatment is to teach them the skills to cope with their depression. Patients are trained to recognize the first signs and symptoms of depression so that they will have an early warning system that will lead to their reapplication of the techniques they have learned, or to further treatment if necessary. By adopting an attitude that the therapy's major purpose is not to cure the disorder but to learn how to manage it, patients often take a more active problem-solving approach to their depression (e.g., "I have a disorder that flares up occasionally. There are certain steps I must follow when it does"). This attitude also eases the difficulty that many patients have in acknowledging that some symptoms of depression may return in the future.

Before detailing specific treatment interventions, consideration should be given to the structure of the inpatient unit. Behavioral assessment requires a regular schedule of observations, as well as the previously described, careful descriptions of the behaviors of interest. The emphasis is on the patient and staff working together rather than on the patient receiving treatment from the staff as is typically associated with the biologic approach. All staff are encouraged to list their observations and assessments in the form of a problem-oriented record (Weed, 1968). In this way it is clear what interventions or what changes have been observed. This method also allows easy comparisons between objective observations and subjective reports. A number of basic rules apply to the unit. The first is that "beds are for sleeping"; all patients are expected to be out of bed and out of their rooms. In extreme cases room doors are locked to prevent the withdrawal and avoidance characteristic of patients with affective disorders. In order to encourage collaboration, it is critical that the rationale for therapy intervention be outlined for patients. Most depressed patients will acknowledge that when they withdraw from others or try to rest by laying in bed they actually feel worse. This reaction is understandable, because when they isolate themselves they are bombarded with their own negative thinking and sense of helplessness. It often is necessary to use a graded task approach to have patients engage in other activities on the unit; but we have found a clear limit-setting rule around napping and avoidance to be the best with depressed patients. All patients are encouraged to walk and exercise as part of their daily routine. In addition to the encouraging findings that increased activity (walking or running) has an antidepressant effect (Griest, Klein, Eischens & Faris, 1978), there is an opportunity for patients to distract themselves and even to experience an increased sense of self-efficacy.

All patients are encouraged to involve themselves in the activities of the unit. Occupational therapy is particularly useful in this respect in that it provides a forum for patients to check out their thinking. Prior to any task it is important that staff evaluate the patient's expectations and predictions. We have consistently found that depressed patients will report that they "can't" engage in certain activities or that they will "fail." If staff takes the time to examine the patient's predictions and reasons for these predictions (e.g., "I'm no good; I can't concentrate"), they can often lower such pessimism with specific strategies (e.g., set lower initial goals, break the task into components, watch for images of the consequences of failure). It is important to document these negative predictions before the patient has carried out the task. Actual achievements are monitored, and the staff work consistently to provide feedback of achievements versus expectations. This kind of feedback to the patient is essential, as it directly addresses the issue of self-esteem and avoidance. Patient's failures are also noted followed by a discussion of the expected consequences (e.g., criticism from others).

Many of the cognitive and behavioral methods have been described in the literature (cf. Beck, Rush, Shaw, & Emery, 1979; Bellack, Hersen & Himmelhoch, 1980; Lewinsohn, Biglan, & Zeiss, 1976). The severity of the patient's depression dictates the types of interventions initially attempted. As previously mentioned, behavioral assignments are common early in the therapy and with more severely depressed patients. Initially, patients are encouraged to engage in tasks that will lead to mastery (versus pleasure) experiences. A mastery experience refers to a sense of accomplishment when performing a specific task (Beck, Rush, Shaw, & Emery, 1979). In prescribing mastery exercises the clinician must emphasize that the judgments are made relative to the patient's current level of functioning and the degree of negative expectations. In other words, when depressed the person may find it difficult to cook a meal. He or she may be convinced that the task cannot be completed because it is viewed as an overwhelming whole. The steps required to accomplish the task are reviewed and the patient is helped to understand that viewing the task as a series of smaller steps make it more manageable. With this type of intervention the patient is encouraged to imagine himself or herself accomplishing each step while watching for obstacles. Then the patient is encouraged to work through the various stages and to see each one that is completed as a mastery experience. This method is only one way of reducing the patient's sense of helplessness, by viewing tasks in more realistic terms and by lowering standards to account for one's current level of functioning.

Patients are often asked to keep a journal or diary of their thoughts and images. It is often useful to have the patient write down what he or she sees as his or her major problems followed by a list of different alternatives or solutions. Writing establishes a record, but even more importantly serves to make the patient's thinking specific and concrete. By writing, patients may avoid the type of circular, no-solution thinking associated with patients who ruminate about their difficulties. They can also identify those aspects of their lives they cannot control in the present. It should be noted that some obsessional patients are adversely affected by nonspecific assignments and in these cases specific examples should be generated during the session as examples for later use.

Inpatient treatment involves not only the cognitive-behavioral approach but also biological and social treatments. We have found few major problems interfacing cognitive-behavioral therapy with psychopharmacologic treatments for depression (see Shaw & Dobson, in press). At present a wide range of antidepressants is available, including both tricyclics and monoamine oxidase inhibitors. Electroconvulsive therapy is indicated in some depressed patients, and again, there is no reason to combine this modality with a cognitive-behavioral treatment. The one caveat is the post-ECT period, when behavioral rather than cognitive interventions should be employed.

The clinicians' conceptualizations about the cause of depression and the necessary treatment components significantly affect the patients' involvement with their treatment. One important issue is to avoid raising the patient's expectations for change with a single modality. A more therapeutic stance is to indicate that the unit has a number of psychological and pharmacologic treatments at its disposal. Patients should be informed that the cause of depression is not known but that there are many treatment options. Managing the patient's expectations is essential to good treatment and a major emphasis in cognitive-behavior therapy. Unless there is a research protocol or clinical contraindications there is little reason to avoid combined treatments. Rush and Shaw (1983) caution against using cognitive-behavioral therapy alone when the patient presents with a major depression with melancholia. The one area that we have found difficult in the past involves concomitant marital counseling when the patient is moderately to severely depressed. While some theories of depression clearly point to the importance of social relationships in the maintenance of depression (see Coyne, 1976b) our preference is to provide the family members with specific advice in interacting with the depressed patient. Education about the effects of depression is extremely important for the family. Marital therapy is often best left until the patient is improved and able to consider decisions and function from a less negative perspective.

Some inpatients will have an affective disorder secondary to other illness, adding another complicating factor in the individual's treatment. Medical illness may alter the conceptualization of the factors maintaining the patient's symptoms. It may also alter the types of problems encountered by the clinician.

CASE STUDIES

The two case studies in this section are typical of those seen in a general hospital. The first one describes a patient who was so severely depressed on admission that he was even unable to look after his personal hygiene. His depression was readily recognized both by his general practitioner and by his family but was less readily acknowledged as depression by the patient. The second case is one where the depression went unrecognized, hidden by both a severe illness and by an angry and aggressive manner. It is important to recognize the presence of depression in people with severe physical illness. Unfortunately one often hears that a person "has good reason to be depressed." Thus, the depression is seen as inevitable and no intervention is made. As a result patients suffer pain and distress that the proper treatment could at least reduce and perhaps remediate.

Case History 1

Mr. A. was admitted to inpatient psychiatry having been troubled with depression for several months. He owned his own business but had been increasingly unable to cope with his work and had been absenting himself from his office more and more often. His work had always been a source of pride and pleasure to him, but he felt himself losing the ability to enjoy both his work and his social and family life. He began to experience pain in his abdomen after working for a few hours at his business and when this pain developed he would leave for home. The amount of time that he could spend at work became shorter until, finally, he was experiencing the pain and feelings of intense anxiety before leaving the house. For two-and-a-half months before coming to hospital he did not go to work at all and felt so hopeless that he would weep. On the weekend before his admission to the hospital he had become almost unable to move, and his family insisted that he must get help.

Seven months before his admission to the hospital, Mr. A.'s father had died. Although they had been business partners for 30 years the father had left his half of the business to other family members and nothing to his son. This effectively put the business in danger of failing as Mr. A did not have enough money to buy the heirs out of the other half of his business. He had had no prior knowledge of the provisions of his father's will, but denied having been upset by it. He said that he was saddened by his father's death but not as intensely as he had been by his mother's death. His bereavement was complicated by feelings that his relationship with his father had not been as good as he might have wished.

The diagnosis made on admission to the hospital was a major depressive episode. He met the diagnostic criteria set forward in the *DSM-III:* He had lost interest in all of his usual activities and past times, which had lasted for two months. There had been no shifts in his mood, which had stayed uniformly low and helpless. He had a poor appetite and had sustained a weight loss of 25 pounds over the two-month period. He was having difficulty sleeping and showed signs of psychomotor retardation, being almost unable to get out of his chair. There had been a decided decrease in sexual drive and he judged himself to be without energy. Though he did not have any active plans for suicide, he nevertheless thought that it would be for the best should he just die. Personality testing was completed, and the results of the MMPI showed a severe depression with anxiety and perfectionist tendencies. A Beck Depression Inventory resulted in a score of 30, indicating a severe depression.

Initially the attending psychiatrist believed that Mr. A.'s depression would resolve when the underlying anger and disappointment, thought to be the root cause of his difficulty, were recognized and ventilated. To that end an insight-oriented approach was used and Imipramine, 125 mg q.h.s. was prescribed. In spite of valiant efforts, the hoped for change did not occur. Mr. A. was a practical man and he remained bewildered in the face of attempts to help him with regard to an understanding of his underlying emotions. His view of his condition was that of a person who does not spend time analyzing his feelings but rather thinks that there must be some biological means (i.e., a pill) to correct the malfunction. He continued to lose weight and was still having difficulty sleeping. Nozinan 50 mg q.h.s. p.r.n. was added to his medications.

During an interview with a cognitive-behavior therapist, Mr. A. was asked what he thought the events of the previous month meant. A torrent of self-abuse ensued. Mr. A. said it was perfectly obvious that he was "less than a man, a complete failure." He said that he had reached the point where if he even thought about going to work he got a pain in his stomach that was only relieved by deciding to stay home. He would then weep because he was "so useless and cowardly." He believed that he would never be able to cope at work again and that this was probably the first of many hospital admissions. The fact that he had been a successful business and family man for 30 years was set at naught.

Mr. A. had been in the hospital for four weeks at the time of this interview and during that time had been extremely difficult to engage in conversation. He would answer in monosyllables, or not at all, his face full of despair. When the focus was changed from his possible anger toward his father, to his thoughts about himself, his behavior changed. The content of his response in the interview suggested that a cognitive approach might be helpful. Several target symptoms were identified; the first was Mr. A.'s habit of severe self-denigration. The second, determined from psychological testing and confirmed in conversation with Mr. A., was his perfectionism. Part of his inability to act was thought to be related to his belief that unless he could do something perfectly he should not do it at all. The third was Mr. A.'s severe level of anxiety, and the fourth was the extreme dependence on his wife and children, which had developed during the time prior to his hospital admission. For example, he sat in a chair all day with the family coaxing him to eat the meals that they brought to him. If he was left alone he cried and reported that he was fearful.

The nurses, social workers, occupational therapists, psychologists, and psychiatrists on the inpatient team were all familiar with the cognitive-behavioral approach to treatment. In Mr. A.'s case, once the four major target symptoms were identified, the team worked out a treatment plan that was designed to modify each of them.

To counter Mr. A.'s sense of inner tension, his primary nurse began to teach him relaxation techniques on a one-to-one basis, as he was unable to join the relaxation group. Gradually, he was able to increase the amount of time he could sit and began to feel some relief from his agitation. Mr. A. found that by relaxing his abdomen he could induce a state of general relaxation. Once this pattern was identified, Mr. A. was able to induce relaxation more quickly by concentrating on that area. He was eventually able to join the relaxation group, and it was counted as a triumph when he fell asleep during one session.

The occupational therapist on the team provided an extremely useful part of Mr. A.'s therapy. While assessing his concentration and work skills, she suggested a project that was closely allied to his business. The knot in Mr. A.'s stomach returned and the staff was presented with a first hand opportunity to observe and to intervene in this behavior. He was encouraged to use relaxation techniques, and in spite of his initial distress he was able to do so. The rewards were twofold: (1) the resolving of the tension and (2) an objective lesson that greatly helped Mr. A.'s understanding of his difficulty in going to work. In short time it was seen that by using relaxation techniques in order to stay at the task his tension gradually decreased until finally it did not occur at the beginning of a session in occupational therapy. Mr. A. composed a motto for himself, typically framed in negative fashion. It was "Avoid something that worries you and you'll keep on getting knots." Though his motto frightened him a little, he found it easier to remember and use at first than one that was stated more positively. He began to use his strategy of staying with a task, recognizing that in time he would feel relieved.

Mr. A. tended to predict failure in any task that he undertook. For this reason, before beginning a task, Mr. A. was asked to describe his expectations of the result. At first these expectations were invariably negative: that he was not going to be able to perform the task at all. He was then encouraged to go ahead with the task, which he usually completed to a very high standard. Immediately upon completion, he would begin to find fault with every aspect of his performance. As the occupational therapist had documented, the patient's prediction that he would not expect to be able to do the task at all, it was possible to show him that he had performed beyond his expectations. The patient learned that his pattern of thinking involved changing his expectations throughout a task. As he began to attain his goal he raised the requirement of the task until it was impossible to attain. Once he realized this pattern, it was possible to discuss alternatives with him that gave him a chance of succeeding.

For example, one alternative was that he might be satisfied with simply attempting a task because his usual prediction was that he could not do so. Another might be that the task was completed whether or not it was perfectly done. When he met those goals he was able to feel pleased that he had done so. Most importantly, tasks were broken down into steps. It was Mr. A.'s habit to see a job as one overwhelming whole and to berate himself if it was not totally completed. By breaking jobs into steps he was able to see that even if he did not completely finish he had carried out a certain number of steps toward his goal. During this time the other staff were helpful in gently turning him away from his self-denigration and perfectionism, toward an appreciation of the great efforts he was making.

At the same time that staff members were working with Mr. A. on mastery tasks, one of us (G.H.) met with him daily for one-hour sessions to explore the continuing flood of negative thoughts. For example, Mr. A. said that his father had often told him that he was incompetent, and this opinion became part of his own view of himself. Rather than attempting to reassure Mr. A. that he was competent, he was asked to provide evidence for the view of himself as incompetent. He found this assignment very difficult to do. In fact, he disclosed that he had spent some years secretly correcting his father's mistakes, helping him to believe that he was the mainstay of the business. Mr. A. often told his father that he was needed to run the business, and had begun to accept it as at least partly true himself. After his father's death he had thought it disloyal to suggest anything else. When the same approach was applied to Mr. A.'s belief that he was useless and a coward, he became resistant, saying that he did not have to provide evidence; it was simply true. It was helpful to use a technique at that point that gave him a little distance from the topic. His circumstances were described as belonging to another person and he was asked to consider the possibility that the person was or was not useless and a coward. This method capitalizes on the observation of any discrepancy between judgments on the self and others in depression (for an experimental study, see Garber & Hollon, 1980). His kindness toward others immediately asserted itself, and he was unable to say that a person who had worked hard all his life and had been a loving husband and father deserved to be condemned because he was depressed.

Mr. A. progressed very well over the three-week period that he was seen daily for intensive cognitive-behavior therapy. His BDI scores went from the original 30 to 9, in the normal range. Behaviorally, he was observed to be talking freely to other patients, to smile frequently, and his posture improved. Interestingly, the staff commented that Mr. A. was taller than they had thought he was on admission. He began eating and gaining weight. Although his sleep disturbance remained a problem, it did improve to a point where he only had one poor night in every four. It was decided that Mr. A. was ready for discharge. Indeed, it was essential that he return to his family and business in order to practice the techniques he had learned in the hospital. He returned to work and only experienced mild anxiety at the beginning of the first day. Although he was happy about his ability to cope, his perfectionistic standards led to a judgment that he did not complete everything as competently and efficiently as he "should." He continued to be apprehensive about some aspects of his work, particularly having to speak to customers about outstanding debts. During his outpatient appointments he was worked hard at role-playing different alternatives and, while he still dislikes the task of debt collection, he does not procrastinate over it. Importantly, he negotiated an agreement with the heirs that allowed him to continue with his business.

The level of his dependency on his family that developed during his depression was, as is frequently the case, uncomfortable for all concerned. His supportive and sensible wife, however, made the transition easier than it is for some people. She readily recognized that the support that had been needed was now, in fact, excessive, and she gradually withdrew it, returning to her usual activities. Mr. A. at first felt a little lost about this withdrawal but, when he realized that he continued to cope even when she was not there, he was grateful to her and felt stronger and happier. Two years after the end of therapy he has had no recurrence of symptoms and his business is thriving.

Case History 2

It is frequently the case in a general hospital that one finds cases of major depression secondary to a physical illness. Mr. B. is an example of this type of patient. He is a 39-year-old man who was diagnosed as having chronic renal failure. He was having renal dialysis three times a week and was a candidate for a kidney transplant. Unfortunately, his course on dialysis was extremely rocky because he was not adhering to the fluid restrictions of his diet. Such noncompliance meant that he was gaining up to 7 kg between dialysis treatments. As a consequence, during dialysis he had severe chest pain and muscle cramps, became hypotensive, and twice went into failure.

Mr. B. was first referred for assistance with the control of his fluid intake. At the first interview Mr. B. presented himself in a "hail-fellow-well-met" light, denying any difficulty, and saying that he did not need a "shrink" because he was happy and well. The problem that he was having in dialysis was of no consequence. Mr. B. was a sales representative, though he had been unable to work for some months. He belonged to a service club, organized many charitable functions, and considered it both a duty and a pleasure to visit club members who were ill, doing any errands or jobs that they were unable to do. The possibility that he would ever be on the receiving end of such kindnesses had never occurred to him, and seemed entirely inappropriate in his view. Indeed, his eyes filled with tears when he told of receiving some flowers from his friends, but he said that he had tried not to let people know of his difficulties. These facts and further psychological assessment strongly suggested that he was a person who needed to be in control of his life and disliked seeing himself as unable to take that control. The excessive fluid (nonalcoholic) intake seemed to be an almost defiant gesture, asserting his right to do as he wished.

The scores on the MMPI suggested a depression of severe intensity, and the interview showed that this depression was not entirely covered by his bravado and laughing manner. His BDI score was 28, indicating severe depression. Mr. B. also met the diagnostic criteria for a major depressive episode according to *DSM-III*. Though he dismissed such things as unimportant, Mr. B. had been experiencing a loss of interest in his usual activities, had excessive feelings of guilt about his illness, and felt that he might as well be dead if he had to live by way of coming in for dialysis. There was considerable psychomotor agitation and he appeared to have difficulty concentrating.

At first Mr. B. was seen as an outpatient each time he came to hospital for dialysis. The approach was to stress the possibility of him taking greater control of his physical health. The method was behavioral and included the keeping of records and use of reinforcers when certain targets were met. He noted down everything he drank and the circumstances under which he did so. The reinforcers, which he decided upon himself, included such things as getting himself a new book that he had wanted when he kept to his fluid restriction for two days. The best reinforcer, however, turned out to be the short time that he had to spend on the dialysis machine as his fluid retention subsided. Over a two-week period he had reduced his weight increase (fluid retention) from 7 kg to 4 kg between dialysis sessions, but this was still excessive. While his progress was being reviewed during an outpatient session he suddenly burst out that he should have been able to reduce his fluid intake by himself, furthermore, if he were not such a failure he would have done in order to accomplish this goal. When the therapist spoke of his gains and the negative consequences of self-criticism in this situation, he replied that he should have been much harder on himself. The therapist recognized that the patient berated himself for having no willpower and courage, and after saying these things to himself he would usually have a glass of water. He believed that this was absolute proof that he was useless. The possibility that such negative self-statements might lead to feelings of discouragement and a reduced, rather than an enhanced, ability to take positive actions was discussed. Mr. B. was surprised to find that he agreed, because he said that he also felt unable to control his intake after the nurses and his wife scolded him. At this point it was clear that the intervention had to become more broadly based.

First it was suggested that Mr. B. become an inpatient so that a more comprehensive and concentrated approach could be taken, It was clear that Mr. B. was severely depressed. While there had been some lessening of depression as measured by the Beck Inventory (scores changed from 28 to 20), he was still endorsing items that showed he felt hopeless about the future and negative and guilty about himself. He agreed to come into hospital, though amid much rather hollow laughter. He said that he hoped no one would find out that he was in the "crazies" rather than in the renal unit.

The target symptoms were identified as follows: first, hopelessness about the future, which was related to the second symptom of excess fluid intake. Another factor that required some modification was the behavior of both nurses and family members, who were seen to be provoking the very behavior that they wished to eliminate. The more they scolded him the more he drank.

The behavioral approach to reducing fluid intake was continued while Mr. B. was an inpatient. Mr. B. was given as much control of the situation as possible. He was not placed under close observation and kept records himself. Contingencies were dependent upon weight alone, and in this way he began to feel that he was again responsible for himself.

It was decided that a cognitive approach would be used to address Mr. B.'s depression. The daily sessions with his psychologist and his meetings with other staff focussed on his automatic thoughts (Beck, Rush, Shaw, & Emery, 1979). Mr. B. kept a journal, which provided many instances of his dysfunctional thinking. For example, Mr. B. said if he could not do all the things that he had accomplished in the past before his illness he was useless. By using role-playing technique (Mr. B. was asked to present the case that a person in his exact circumstances was useless), he quicky realized that he would never condemn another person for being in his situation and yet he was applying these cruel standards to himself.

It was believed that Mr. B.'s fluid intake was also affected by the reactions of others around him. It appeared that he was receiving a great deal of attention, albeit negative, for drinking too much. An interview with his wife revealed that he would call attention to himself "like a little boy" when they were at social gatherings or at his service club by drinking glasses of water with ice, which he would clink. When his friends would mention his drinking he would roar with laughter and say that he was strong and would be fine. Mrs. B. said that she had tried to frighten her husband into complying with the fluid restrictions by telling him that if he did not care what would happen to her and their daughter he should die. Mr. B. was always distressed by these statements, thinking that his case was hopeless. Such reactions were usually followed by drinking secretively. Thus, he was getting *attention* from others and was also having his negative and hopeless thoughts reinforced.

A meeting with the nurses in the renal unit showed that they were so worried about his excessive fluid retention that they would criticize him when he came for dialysis. His effort and success in reducing the excess gain from 7 kg to 4 kg had not been remarked upon beyond a comment that, despite improvement, it was still not good enough. Mr. B.'s actions presented a difficult situation for the dialysis staff. The evidence that a person is actively harming himself leads to tension and anxiety in the staff, with resultant attempts to change behavior by criticism. Reversing the behavior so that they did not comment about excess fluid retention, but praised any move in the healthy direction, was an important therapeutic step. Mr. B. was praised and given much attention as weight gain subsided. On the two occasions when his weight inceased slightly, the staff adopted a very matter of fact air and made no comment on the gain.

After the first week there was a gradual but steady improvement in the area of fluid weight gain. Mr. B.'s depression began to lift, as he began to believe that he could control himself and help in his treatment. Happily, a suitable kidney became available when Mr. B. had reached the point where surgery was feasible, a period of approximately one month. He had a difficult time postsurgically in that the new kidney was slow in infusing. Also, he had to continue on dialysis for one week. With assistance, however, he used the cognitive techniques that he had learned to deal with his negative thoughts. His mood remained stable and he was able to cope with pain well.

Now, approximately six months since surgery, he remains rebellious, occasionally eating forbidden foods, but he is back at work and appears to be coping well. He now says that he used to think that if he was going to have to live in such a restricted way as he did before the surgery that he might as well die; so that in that sense his behavior can be seen to have been suicidal. Being in the hospital helped reduce the negative feedback he was getting at a crucial time and also allowed for a more concentrated effort to decrease his depression and feelings of hopelessness.

SPECIAL ISSUES

A change of treatment orientation toward a cognitive-behavioral modalilty naturally will develop slowly. Training of staff is critical to provide the consistency of intervention.

The Suicidal Patient

The suicidal patient presents an important challenge to clinicians. The frequent assessment of suicidal ideation is essential. In addition to the demographic indicators of risks (e.g., lives alone, unemployed, drug and alcohol abuse, past history of attempts, and family or friend history of suicide completion), a scale such as the Suicide Ideation Scale (Beck, Kovacs & Weissman, 1979) may be used to determine the content areas of the assessment of risk. It is important to differentiate from the patients' intentions to kill themselves and the lethality of their method (e.g., hanging and jumping from high places are high lethality). Often we have observed that patients who use low lethality methods are viewed as only making a gesture when in fact their intent is high, creating a dangerous judgment of low risk. Research in this area continues to grow and revise our notions about risk for suicide. In addition to the usual precautions of close observation and the removal of objects that may be used in an attempt, cognitive therapy provides some specific strategies. For the most part patients who are suicidal have a high degree of hopelessness. The two most common reasons for suicidal behavior involve a desire or wish to escape the intense negative effect and a desire to influence others. Many suicidal patients act on the basis of both reasons. It is important to pursue patients' alternative coping strategies, recognizing that while their answer may be "none," it is often the case that they have prematurely rejected reasonable plans. If staff direct their attention to the patient's level of hopelessness and the fantasized consequences of his or her attempt (e.g., people will know how I'm suffering), then efforts can focus on realistic attempts to solve problems. Suicidal patients frequently express extreme thinking (e.g., I can't live without John). Identifying the dysfunctional nature of the person's thinking and providing more moderate alternatives (e.g., I enjoyed life before John; I have several friends) can have an effect on the patient's hopelessness. Goldberg (1984) compared a *single interview* cognitive intervention with an approach focused on the patient's affective and interpersonal experience and a wait-list control group. The cognitive interview resulted in a lower self-report of depression, hopelessness, and anger, and was more effective than the other conditions. Specific treatment approaches with the suicidal patient are outlined in detail by Beck, Kovacs, and Weissman (1979).

The Problem of Anxiety

A second problem involves the anxiety experienced by many depressed patients once their depression improves. This anxiety if often observed at the time of discharge from hospital. Recognizing that the period of three months post-hospitalization is a time of increased risk for suicidal behavior, it is important to address the cognitive underpinnings of the patient's anxiety. The philosophy of a cognitive-behavioral inpatient unit is based on a coping model. Patients learn to change their behavior and challenge their ability during their periods of depression. As usual, it is advisable to take a graded approach to the patient's anxiety, encouraging him or her to use weekend or day passes prior to leaving the hospital to complete homework assignments. In this way, the patient is gradually reintroduced to his or her environment and can test out whether the skills and attitude change has a beneficial effect. A treatment strategy whereby staff inquires of the patient's expectations, recording these expectations and role-playing various alternate solutions, is often useful.

Staff Variability

Another problematic issue involves staff variability, both providing the treatment and being available. Turnover can be viewed as a discouraging development, particularly given that a consistent behavioral orientation takes some effort to achieve. Inpatient units, particularly in teaching settings, characteristically involve an influx of students, interns, and residents, as well as the usual turnover of staff. Ground rules for the new staff should emphasize the consistency of the approach, and teaching materials often serve a valuable function. Major problems involve drift from the therapeutic model. Cognitive-behavioral therapists have emphasized accountability and the exposure of one's work through the detailing of procedures in manuals and the use of audiovisual aids to monitor their work. The major concern is that the patient will through ignorance be given inconsistent advice about their disorder and coping strategies. There is interesting research (Luborsky, McLellan, Woody, O'Brien, & Auerbach, 1984) with drug addicts that indicates consistency (or purity) of conceptualization and treatment is related positively to outcome. Although the predicted outcome of many therapeutic modalities is uncertain at this point, we wish to underscore the importance of consistent communications among the staff and patients. An emphasis on record-keeping and a clear specification of the interventions are two methods of working toward better communication.

Summary

Cognitive-behavioral treatments have been proposed for a number of disorders ranging from anorexia nervosa to pain. The work on the treatment of unipolar, major depressions has probably been the most concentrated. We would like to encourage practitioners working on inpatient units to see these methods as part of their treatment armamentarium.

ACKNOWLEDGMENT

The assistance of the 10th Floor Staff of University Hospital, London, Ontario is appreciated. Thanks also to Sheila McCormick, Jane Burnie, and Marlene Stewart for secretarial assistance. This work was aided by a grant from the National Institute of Mental Health (MH38231-01) to Brian F. Shaw.

REFERENCES

Akiskal H. (1981). Subaffective disorders: Dysthmic, cyclothymic and bipolar II disorders in the "borderline" realm. *Psychiatric Clinics of North America 4*, 25–46.

Beck AT. (1967). *Depression: Clinical, experimental and therapeutic aspects.* New York: Harper and Row.

Beck AT, Kovacs M, & Weissman A. (1979). Assessment of suicidal intent: The scale of suicide ideation. *Journal of Consulting and Clinical Psychology 47*, 343–352.

Beck AT, Rush AJ, Shaw BF, & Emery G. (1979). *Cognitive therapy of depression.* New York: Guilford Press.

Beck AT, Ward CH, Mendelson M, Mock J, & Erbaugh J. (1961). An inventory for measuring depression. *Archives of General Psychiatry 4*, 561–571.

Bellack AS, Hersen M, & Himmelhock JM. (1980). Social skills training for depression: A treatment manual. *JSAS Catalogue of Selected Documents 10*, 92 (Ms No. 2156).

Blackburn IM, Bishop S, Glen AIM, Whalley LJ, & Christie JE. (1981). The efficacy of cognitive therapy in depression: A treatment trial using cognitive therapy and pharmacotherapy each alone and in combination. *British Journal of Psychiatry 139*, 181–189.

Carroll BJ, Feinberg M, Smouse PE, Rawson SG, & Greden JF. (1981). The Carroll rating scale for depression. I: Development, reliability and validation. *British Journal of Psychiatry 138*, 194–200.

Coyne JC. (1976a). Depression and the response of others. *Journal of Abnormal Psychology 85*, 186–193.

Coyne JC. (1976b). Toward an interactional description of depression. *Psychiatry 39*, 14–27.

Dobson KS, & Shaw BF. (in press). Cognitive assessment of major depressive disorder. *Cognitive Therapy and Research.*

Eaves G, & Rush AJ. (1984). Cognitive patterns in symptomatic and remitted unipolar depression. *Journal of Abnormal Psychology 93*, 31–40.

Endicott J, & Spitzer R. (1978). A diagnostic interview: The schedule for affective disorders and schizophrenia. *Archives of General Psychiatry 35*, 837–844.

Feighner JP, Robins E, Guze SB, Woodruff RA, Winokur G, & Munoz R. (1972). Diagnostic criteria for use in psychiatric research. *Archives of General Psychiatry 26*, 57–63.

Fowles DC, & Gersh F. (1979). Neurotic depression: The endogeneous-neurotic distinction. In Depue RA (Ed), *The psychology of depressive disorders: Implications for the effects of stress*. New York: Academic Press.

Frank CM. (1976). Foreword. In Mash EJ, & Terdal LG, *Behavioral therapy assessment*. New York: Springer Verlag.

Garber J, & Hollon SD. (1980). Universal versus personal helplessness in depression: Belief in uncontrollability or incompetence. *Journal of Abnormal Psychology 89*, 55–56.

Goldberg JO. (1984). The immediate effects of cognitive versus affective interviews: A study of suicide attempters. Unpublished doctoral dissertation. University of Waterloo, Canada.

Griest JH, Klein MH, Eischens RR, & Faris JW. (1978). Antidepressant running: Running as a treatment for non-psychotic depression. *Behavioral Medicine*, June 19–24.

Hamilton M. (1960). A rating scale for depression. *Journal of Neurology, Neurosurgery and Psychiatry 23*, 56–62.

Hamilton EW, & Abramson LY. (1983). Cognitive patterns and major depressive disorder: A longitudinal study in a hospital setting. *Journal of Abnormal Psychology 92*, 173–184.

Klein DF. (1974). Endogenomorphic depression. *Archives of General Psychiatry 31*, 447–454.

Kovacs M, & Beck AT. (1978). Maladaptive cognitive structures in depression. *American Journal of Psychiatry 135*, 525–523.

Lewinsohn PM, Biglan A, & Zeiss AM. (1976). Behavioral treatment of depression. In Davidson PD (Ed), *The behavioral management of anxiety, depression and pain*. New York: Brunner/Mazel.

Lewinsohn PM, & Lee WML. (1981). Assessment of affective disorders. In Barlow DH (Ed), *Behavioral assessment of adult disorders*. New York: Guilford Press.

Luborsky L, McLellan AT, Woody GE, O'Brien CP, & Auerback A. (1984). Therapists' success and its determinants. Unpublished manuscript, University of Pennsylvania.

Murphy GE, Simons AD, Wetzel RD, & Lusterman PJ. (1984). Cognitive therapy and pharmacotherapy, singly and together in the treatment of depression. *Archives of General Psychiatry 41*, 33–41.

Prusoff BA, Klerman GL, & Paykel ES. (1972). Pitfalls in the self-report assessment of depression. *Canadian Psychiatry Association Journal 17*, 101–107.

Rush AJ, Beck AT, Kovacs M, & Hollon SD. (1977). Comparative efficacy of cognitive therapy and pharmacotherapy in the treatment of depessed outpatients. *Cognitive Therapy and Research 1*, 1–17.

Rush AJ, & Shaw BF. (1983). Treatment failures in the cognitive therapy of depression. In Foa EB, & Emmelkamp P (Ed), *Failures in behavior therapy*, New York: John Wiley.

Schact T, & Nathan PE. (1977). But is it good for psychologists? Appraisal and status of *DSM-III*. *American Psychologist 32*, 1017–1025.

Shaw BF. (1981) Matching depressed subjects to treatment in an inpatient setting. In

Rehm L (Ed), *Behavior therapy for depression: Present status and future directions*, New York: Academic Press.

Shaw BF, & Dobson KS. (in press). Cognitive therapy in the treatment of depression. In Friedman E, Mahn J, & Gersham S (Eds), *Depression and antidepresants*. New York: Raven Press.

Shaw BF, Vallis TM, & McCabe SB. (in press). The assessment of the severity and symptom patterns in depression. In Beckam E, & Leber B (Eds), *Depression: Treatment, assessment and research*. New York, Dorsey Press.

Simons AD, Garfield SL, & Murphy GE. (1984). The process of change in cognitive therapy and pharmacotherapy of depression: Changes in mood and cognition. *Archives of General Psychiatry 41*, 45–51.

Smith D, & Kraft WA. (1983). *DSM-III*—Do psychologists really want an alternative? *American Psychologist 38*, 777–785.

Weed LL. (1968) Medical records that guide and teach. *New England Journal of Medicine 278*, 593–600.

Weissman MM, & Myers JK. (1978). Rates and risks of depressive symptoms in a United States urban community. *Acta Psychiatry Scandinavia 57*, 219–231.

Williams J, Barlow D, & Agras W. (1972). Behavioral assessmenet of severe depression. *Archives of General Psychiatry 72*, 303–337.

Zeiss AM, Lewinsohn PM, & Munoz RF. (1979). Nonspecific improvement effects in depression using interpersonal skills training, pleasant activity schedules or cognitive training. *Journal of Consulting and Clinical Psychology 47*, 427–439.

6
Schizophrenia and Other Psychotic Disorders

James P. Curran, Stephen V. Faraone, and Michael G. Dow

The criteria for schizophrenia as listed in DSM-III are as follows: (1) a symptom reflecting a major marker for schizophrenia, including delusions, hallucinations, or a formal thought disorder; (2) deterioration from premorbid level of functioning in such areas as work, social relations, and self-care; (3) continuous signs of the illness for at least six months at some time during the person's life, with some signs of the illness at present; (4) the full depressive or manic syndrome, if present, developed after any psychotic symptoms or was brief in duration relative to the psychotic symptoms; (5) onset of prodromal or active phase of the illness before age 45; (6) not due to any organic mental disorder or mental retardation.

Types of schizophrenic disorders include: (1) disorganized type (characterized by frequent incoherence, absence of systematized delusions, and blunted, inappropriate or silly affect); (2) catatonic type (characterized by either catatonic stupor, mutism, negativism, rigidity, excitment or posturing; (3) paranoid type (characterized by delusions and/or hallucinations of persecutory, grandiose, or jealous nature); (4) undifferentiated type (characterized by prominent delusions, hallucinations, incoherence, or grossly disorganized behavior and does not meet the criterion for the other three types listed or meets the criterion for more than one of these types); (5) residual types (characterized by a previous episode of schizophrenia without any present prominent psychotic symptoms but with continuing evidence of the illness such as blunted affect and social withdrawal).

The other psychotic disorders include the paranoid disorders, schizophreniform disorder, schizoaffective disorder, and atypical psychosis. Paranoid dis-

PRACTICE OF INPATIENT BEHAVIOR THERAPY
ISBN 0-8089-1715-3

orders are characterized by persistent persecutory delusions or delusional jealousy of at least one-week duration, emotion and behavior appropriate to the context of the delusional system, and no prominent hallucinations, bizarre delusions, or thought disorders. The criteria for schizophreniform disorder are the same as for schizophrenia except for duration. To meet the criteria for schizophreniform disorder the illness (including prodromal, active, and residual phases) must last more than two weeks but less than six months. Brief reactive psychosis is characterized by psychotic symptoms immediately following a recognizable psychosocial stressor that would evoke significant symptoms of distress in almost anyone. These psychotic symptoms last more than a few hours but less than two weeks, with an eventual return to premorbid level of functioning. Schizoaffective disorder is retained in *DSM-III* without diagnostic criteria and is used for those instances in which a clinician is unable to make a differential diagnosis with any degree of certainty between affective disorder and either schizophreniform disorder or schizophrenia. Finally, atypical psychosis is a residual category used for cases in which there are psychotic symptoms but they fail to meet the criteria for any specific mental disorder.

Schizophrenia constitutes the vast majority of psychotic disorders. Several features of the *DSM-III* definition of schizophrenia are worth noting. The criteria employed in *DSM-III* are "narrower" and have been better operationalized than the criteria used in the previous DSMs. This "narrower" definition of schizophrenia reflects a trend toward increased reliance on empirical development and verification of disorders. The criteria reflect both the positive symptoms of schizophrenia (i.e., delusions, hallucinations, and formal thought disorders) as well as the negative symptoms of schizophrenia (i.e., deterioration from previous level of functioning in areas such as work, social relations, and self-care). This is an important distinction because such symptoms may be the result of different processes and these symptoms may respond differentially to treatment. For example, neuroleptic medications have proven useful in controlling many of the positive symptoms of schizophrenia but appear to be less useful in treating and may, in fact, contribute to the negative symptoms of schizophrenia (Van Putten & May, 1978).

The age criterion (i.e., onset before 45 years of age) reflects the Kraepelinian notion of praecox or early onset of the disorder. However, the criteria do not reflect Kraepelin's other notion of dementia, a progressive intellectual deterioration as a result of the disorder. It is now felt that the course of the disorder is quite varied (Lauria & Meltzer, 1977). While it appears that some schizophrenics follow a progressive deteriorating course, others may have only one or two episodes and achieve a good recovery. In fact, one model of schizophrenia developed by Zubin and Steinhauer (1981) states that schizophrenia is episodic. While schizophrenics have a vulnerability to future episodes, these episodes are time-limited. Episodes arise in the wake of triggering life events and abate when the stress and aftermath dissipatate.

The types and magnitudes of symptoms do not appear to be good predictors with respect to the course of the illness (Hawk, Carpenter, & Strauss, 1975;

Strauss & Carpenter, 1974). What seems to be a better predictor is the patient's premorbid history. Schizophrenics with a good premorbid history (i.e., adequate social and sexual functioning) appear to exhibit a less deteriorating course than patients' with a poor premorbid history.

Another major issue regarding schizophrenia is whether it should be considered a unitary or multi-model disease entity (Zubin & Steinhauer, 1981). A number of etiotypes or causes have been postulated regarding a predisposition to schizophrenia involving genetic, biochemical, neurophysiologic, developmental, learning, and ecological factors. Perhaps no single etiotype in itself may be either necessary or sufficient to produce the illness. Various etiotypes and their interactions may interact with environmental stressors to produce similar appearing phenotypes. Consequently, although the symptoms may appear similar, their origins might differ. Evaluation and assessment are obviously necessary in order to make a correct diagnosis, in examining the course of the illness, and evaluating the effectiveness of various treatment procedures.

ASSESSMENT

A comprehensive psychiatric and behavioral assessment of schizophrenia is a prerequisite to effective treatment. This section examines three major areas of evaluation: psychopathology, the family environment, and social competence.

Assessment of Psychopathology

The assessment of psychopathology has three major goals: (1) establishing a correct diagnosis, (2) evaluating prognosis, and (3) monitoring the course of the disorder. The first two goals are best achieved through a comprehensive structured psychiatric interview such as the National Institute of Mental Health's Diagnostic Interview Schedule (DIS). An excellent review of available interviews is given by Hedlund and Vieweg (1981). A structured interview is preferable to an unstructured interview because it ensures that the clinician will ask the patient about areas of psychopathology unrelated to the signs and symptoms needed to diagnose schizophrenia. This additional information may have prognostic significance.

For example, prevalance of problem drinking among schizophrenics may be as high as 63 percent (Gottheil & Waxman, 1982). Concomitant alcoholism bodes poorly for prognosis and has significant implications for treatment planning. The presence of affective symptoms prior to or during a schizophrenic episode predicts good outcome (Taylor & Abrams, 1975; Vaillant, 1964). Better outcome is also found for paranoid as compared with nonparanoid schizophrenics (Tsuang & Winokur, 1974), and the former benefit more from phenothiazines than the latter (Goldstein, 1970).

For the purpose of monitoring the longitudinal course of psychopathology, an evaluation instrument should permit a relatively brief assessment of severity along multiple dimensions of symptomatology. A thorough review of rating scales that meet these requirements is available (Endicott & Spitzer, 1980). One scale used extensively is the Brief Psychiatric Rating Scale (BPRS). A comprehensive review of the BPRS is given by Hedlund and Viewig (1980). The version we use consists of 21 seven-point scales of psychopathology rated on the information collected during a semi-structured 20- to 40-minute interview. Ours is based on an abbreviated form of the Present State Examination (Wing, Cooper, & Sartorious, 1977). Periodic BPRS ratings can be used to document patient responsiveness to theraputic interventions and to explore the functional relationships between psychopathological behavior and the environment.

In addition to the standard BPRS, our assessment program includes the Target Symptom Ratings suggested by Falloon, Boyd, McGill, Williamson, Razani, Moss, Gilderman, and Simpson (in press). For each patient, we specify three schizophrenic symptoms that are characteristic of his or her disorder. During the BPRS interview, questions are asked to enable the interviewer to rate these "target symptoms." Since these three scales are individualized, the ratings can be based solely on the unique phenomenology of each patient's symptoms. Although the incremental validity of using target symptoms in addition to the BPRS has yet to be established, their sensitivity to treatment induced changes has been demonstrated (Falloon, Boyd, McGill, et al., in press).

Both the DIS and the BPRS should be administered at the beginning of the patient's hospitalization because they will serve as the foundation for important aspects of treatment planning. The DIS will take three or more hours to administer to inpatient schizophrenics. Thus, for most patients, several sessions are required to complete the DIS. In many settings, the length of the interviews will be too costly for use by professional staff. However, the structure of the interview make it feasible to use nonprofessional staff after they have been appropriately trained. In fact, high levels of diagnostic agreement between nonprofessional interviewers and psychiatrists have been reported (Robins, Helzer, Crougham, & Ratcliff, 1981). The BPRS can also be administered by a nonprofessional after appropriate training. A useful schedule of BPRS assessments is the following: at the beginning of hospitalization, the end of hospitalization, and every three months thereafter on an outpatient basis.

When assessing the psychopathology of schizophrenia, careful attention should be given to differentiating the psychotic thought disorder from nonpsychotic cognitive distortions, irrational beliefs or assumptions, and maladaptive automatic thoughts. The latter cognitions are usually less absurd and will be evident both before and after the onset of an acute episode. After an episode, depessive cognitions increase in likelihood as a concomitant of the postpsychotic depession experienced by many schizophrenics.

The assessment of maladaptive cognitions should be an ongoing component of all contacts with the patient. A longitudinal perspective of such cognitions during hospitalization will facilitate their discrimination from psychotic symptoms. Those that wax and wane with obviously psychotic symptoms should not be targeted for cognitive therapy. Those that continue or become more prominent when the acute phase has subsided should be considered for cognitive treatment.

Behavioral Family Assessment

There is a substantial body of evidence indicating that patients who live in a stressful family environment characterized by high "expressed emotion" (EE) have increased risk for relapse (e.g., Vaughn & Leff, 1976; Vaughn et al., 1982). EE measures the degree of criticism and/or emotional overinvolvement expressed about the patient during the Camberwell Family Interview (CFI: Brown & Rutter, 1966). The CFI is a semi-structured interview that encourages relatives to discuss the impact that the patient's disorder has had on them and the emotional atmosphere of their home. The CFI is a regular component of our family assessment program. Unfortunately, implementation of the correct procedure for rating EE requires intensive training, lengthy interviewing, and careful, time-consuming coding. For many practitioners, this limits its usefulness as a clinical tool. However, it is practical for clinicians to perform a less rigorous EE assessment by becoming familiar with: (1) the structure and style of the CFI so as to be able to interview relatives in a manner that allows for experssion of criticism and emotional overinvolvement without directly eliciting such expression, and (2) the definitions of criticism and overinvolvement used in the EE studies. These dimensions can be used to structure the evaluation of the patient's relatives.

An alternative to the CFI providing additional information about communication and problem-solving skills is the Direct Family Intervention (DFI) procedure used by the UCLA family project (Doane, West, Goldstein, Rodnick, & Jones, 1981; Valone, Norton, Goldstein, & Doane, 1984). Briefly, the DFI is composed of four steps. First, each family member is individually asked to identify two family problems. The patient identifies problems created by other family members and they identify problems created by the patient. The respondent is asked to role-play a statement that describes the issue to the offending party. These statements are audiotaped. The second step requires family members to respond to audiotaped problem statements about their behavior. Their responses are audiotaped contiguous to the original problem statement. Then, the audiotapes corresponding to the two most emotionally laden problem areas are played for the entire family as a stimulus for two separate ten-minute family discussions, which are videotaped. Finally, these two discussions are coded for affective style (AS) and problem-solving style (PSS). The AS codes are described by Doane et al. (1981). They include supportive, critical, guilt inducing, and intrusive statements. PSS includes codes such as statement of problem, solution proposals, plan for implementation, paraphrase of feelings, and seeking clarification. Although we have found it to be useful in a clinical/research setting, the DFI can be difficult to implement if needed resources are not available. However, informal behavioral observations of the family can be substituted for the more rigorous videotaping and coding procedures.

Assessment of Social Competence

The goal of a social competence assessment is to determine: (1) where inadequacies exist in the patient's repertoire of social behaviors, and (2) whether these deficiencies are due to the lack of an appropriate response or the interference of inappropriate responses. Ideally, social competence would be assessed by direct observation of patients in a variety of naturalistic environments. Since this is rarely feasible on an inpatient unit, two alternatives are recommended: (1) direct observation of patient behavior on the inpatient unit, and (2) the use of role-play measures.

Observations of social behavior should be integrated into a behavioral observation system and can be used for the development and implementation of token economies. Observational systems can be implemented with a wide range of sophistication, from informed impressions to highly structured observations recorded on a mobile data storage system. A structured, yet practical approach, involves the following steps: (1) define the behaviors of interest; (2) decide which situations should be observed; (3) decide how long behavior should be observed in each situation; and (4) decide how the observational interval should be broken up into time intervals.

For the purpose of assessing social competence, direct observation provides important information. However, observation on the inpatient unit faces the problem of a lack of situational variabililty. Such variability can be obtained by the use of role-play measures. Our role-play measure of social competence is the Simulated Social Interaction Test (SSIT) (Curan, 1982). The patient is videotaped while responding to a series of eight standardized situations, which cover the range reported to be most difficult for psychiatric patients (Goldsmith & McFall, 1975). Thus, the SSIT can be used by a clinician to determine which situations are most difficult for a given patient. Social competence programs can be designed in accordance with this assessment by using knowledge of patient-situation interactions to choose role-plays during therapy sessions and to assign between-session practice tasks. The disadvantage of the SSIT is that most clinicians will not have the resources needed to administer it. In addition to videotape equipment and trained raters, the SSIT requires a narrator, who describes the scenes, and two confederates who take turns role-playing with the patient. For the practicing clinician, a less rigorous but practical approach may be taken. First, the clinician should become familiar with the range of situations covered by the SSIT. The clinician can then use these situations to engage in role-plays with the patient. Informal observations of these role-plays provide the clinician with a guide for assessing the situation-specific skill needs of patients.

For purposes of discharge planning and transition into the community, the clinician should assess social competence in terms of measures of social support and social adjustment. The methodological issues involved in assessing the social supports of schizophrenic patients have received a good deal of attention (e.g., Lin, Dean, & Ensel, 1981; McFarlane, Neale, Norman, Roy, & Streiner, 1981; Sokolovsky & Cohen, 1981). Nevertheless, there is no consensus as to how social support should be measured. Our assessment program uses a semi-structured interview to collect the following information about patients: (1) the size of their social network, (2) the degree of interconnectedness of their network members, (3) the average duration that others have been in their network, (4) the average amount of contact they have with the network, (5) the degree to which they enjoy the company of network members, (6) the degree of frankness with which they can discuss problems with network members, and (7) the degree to which their network members are helpful.

The comprehensive assessment of social support is a useful clinical tool. At the molar level it enables one to classify patients into one of three groups: those who need to develop a support network, those who need to repair an existing network, and those who need to maintain an existing network. This means of classification has specific treatment implications inasmuch as the development, repair, and maintenance of networks require different behavioral skills. At a molecular level the social support assessment provides information about the details of a support network's functioning. This provides further information about skills deficits. For example, patients who receive little enjoyment from their network may need to learn leisure skills, whereas patients who cannot discuss their problems frankly may need to learn the skills underlying self-disclosure. Another benefit of a comprehensive social support assessment is that it identifies individuals who may help the patient's treatment by entering into family therapy, helping with case management decisions, and providing needed resources (e.g., housing, money, transportation).

The assessment of social adjustment among psychiatric patients can be done via self-report inventory or with a personal interview. A comprehensive review of 27 useful social adjustment instruments is provided by Weissman (1975; Weissman, Sholomakas, & John, 1981). Our project uses the Social Adjustment Scale-II (SAS-II), an adaptation of the original Social Adjustment Scale designed specifically for use with a schizophrenic population (Schooler, Hogarty, & Weissman, 1979). The SAS-II is administered by a trained rater in a semi-structured one-hour interview. The informant can be either the patient or a significant other. The 52 questions asked by the SAS-II cover the following areas of social adjustment: work role, relationships, sexual adjustment, romantic involvement, family roles, social leisure activities, and personal well-being. Thus, the SAS-II provides a comprehensive assessment of the adjustment of schizophrenics in the community.

BEHAVIORAL TREATMENTS

Operant Procedures and Token Economies

Operant procedures, including schedules of reinforcement, shaping, fading, and so on have been applied successfully to both positive and negative target symptoms of schizophrenics. For example, operant procedures have been used to reduce delusional speech in schizophrenic patients (Rickard & Dinoff, 1962; Winzce, Litenberg, & Agras, 1972) and increase the amount of rational speech (Isaacs, Thomas, & Goldimond, 1960; Liberman, Wallace, Teigen, & Davis, 1974). While such applications have provided useful and necessary demonstrations that operant procedures have potential utility as treatments for schizophrenia, they have been often instituted in such a circumscribed fashion that they generally do not have much significant clinical impact for the patient. A more systematized, detailed, and comprehensive approach utilizing operant procedures in the treatment of schizophrenics is a token economy.

Token economies were developed in response to the need for more control of the ward environment and to provide a more pervasive therapeutic milieu. Token economies can be perceived as a means of ward management, but more importantly as a means to teach and maintain appropriate behavior in patients (e.g., personal hygiene, social conversation) and to suppress inappropriate behavior (e.g., hallucinations, delusions). The comprehensiveness of a token system is a reflection of both the goals of the program and the nature of the clinical unit. For example, in dealing with a chronic debilitated population where the goal of the program is discharge to the community, a very pervasive and thorough token economy system is needed. In our own acute care unit, which has a more functional population, a less comprehensive token system is adequate. In a comprehensive token unit all privileges, such as ground passes, private rooms, consummables such as candy, cigarettes, and so on, must be purchased with tokens that are contingent upon appropriate behaviors. Such programs require application of systematic and structured learning procedures in order to teach patients targeted behaviors. Token programs focusing on more functional patients may not require such elaborate procedures for teaching various instrumental skills, because these skills exist in the patients' repertoires. Thus, the contingency system alone serves to maintain the desired performance. Likewise, in working with less debilitated patients, it may not be necessary to depend upon primary reinforcement as "backups" to the token system.

Establishing a Token Economy

No matter how detailed and comprehensive a token program is established, a common set of problems and issues needs to be addressed. It is obviously important to decide which criterion behaviors and components ought to be reinforced. In working with a debilitated chronic population where a major rehabilitation effort is required for deinstitutionalization, a host of behaviors must be targeted. It may be useful to group these behaviors in numbers of categories and organize them in a hierarchical fashion. Major groupings may involve self-care, occupational, educational, and social activities. Under each of these headings an exhaustive list of all behaviors must be stipulated and operationalized. It is critical to have these criterion behaviors operationalized in such a fashion so as to prevent inconsistencies and unrealiability in the individuals responsible for dispensing the tokens. The targeted criterion behaviors and their operationalized definitions must be constantly monitored in order to determine whether they remain consistent with the goals of the program and with environmental realities.

In working with a less debilitated or more acute population it probably is not necessary to target very low level remedial skills as part of the program. By and large these patients know how to bathe and shave, make change, use a telephone, and so on. We currently use a contingency system on our own acute inpatient unit. Here the contingencies are established specifically in order for the patients to conform to the rules of the unit and take an active part in their treatment program. Patients progress through our unit through a series of levels. At each step more is required from the patient while more privileges are available. The earlier steps are more restrictive, while the higher step levels are more consistent with community functioning.

Particularly with schizophrenics, activities must be arranged in which criterion behaviors are to be expected; teaching devices must be employed in order to elicit and develop criterion behaviors. These activities and teaching devices may be quite systematic, such as self-help classes for personal hygiene, classes for work-related skills, and training programs to teach social skills. Various teaching devices may be implemented, such as shaping, fading, modeling, use of prompts, and so on.

Within a contingency system, skills are developed in a more systematic and direct fashion than is usually the case in a natural environment. Unless generalization is programmed, it is quite likely that when the patient is returned to the natural environment a deterioration of skills will be exhibited. A useful procedure for promoting transfer back into the natural environment is the concept of step levels within the token system. As a patient progresses through the step levels, less time is spent in the artificial token system and more time is spent in the natural environment. Often, in the case of chronic patients, some programs such as a day hospital or half-way house are needed in order to "bridge the gap" between the hospital and the natural environment. Care should be taken so that the goals and structure of these "bridging" programs are consistent with the goals and structure of the hospital program. Other strategies for reacclimating patients to the natural environment are community trips, overnight passes, prerelease work programs, and so on.

In order for a token system to operate, it obviously is necessary to secure "backup" reinforcers that patients will find reinforcing. What is reinforcing for any particular patient can be quite idiosyncratic. A good deal of time must be devoted to determine what is particularly reinforcing for any particular resident. Both a depressed and inflated economy must be avoided. If the economy is too inflated there is no reason for a patient to work; if it is too depressed patients may give up trying to earn tokens. As in any economy, various types of tampering with the economy, such as black marketing, counterfeiting, and stealing should be monitored.

A token economy is basically a reward system. Consequently, in most cases, inappropriate behavior such as delusional talk is handled by an absence of reinforcement. Inappropriate behavior is often incompatiable with earning tokens, and consequently the staff is trained to ignore these behaviors. Intolerable behaviors such as presenting a clear danger to self or others are usually handled in a number of ways, including response cost, time-out, restitution procedures, and a demotion to a lower level.

Some form of data collection is necessary in order to maintain a token economy system. One needs to know how tokens are dispensed and to which patients, how many tokens each patient spent, and on what reinforcers. The staff needs to know what the criterion is for any particular patient for any particular activity during the day. Without such data collection a token economy cannot operate.

In order to have an effecive economy it is essential that staff members be thoroughly trained so that their behavior is consistent with the goals of the program. Some skills the staff need to master include (1) the ability to judge reliably whether patients attain their criterion behavior, (2) accurate completion of data recording sheets, and (3) various teaching procedures such as chaining and shaping, and so on. Individual staff members must be assigned to monitor the contingency program and be held responsible for its implementation. When a staff member distributes a token or records a specific behavior as having been attained, he or she should praise the patient and the behavior that is being reinforced. As in any treatment program, communication among staff members is extremely important. Procedures for improving communication (e.g., staff meetings, log books, etc.) and promoting morale (e.g. staff social functions) are important.

It is our contention that the major advantage of a token economy is that it provides a structure and a motivational system wherein patients can acquire or relearn skills and coping strategies through various therapeutic interventions. If a token economy is established with no attempt to teach coping strategies, then one has merely established a system for ward management as opposed to a therapeutic program.

Cognitive-Behavioral Interventions

Cognitive-behavior therapy is based on the experimental-clinical model, which emphasizes the importance of thorough assessment and the development of specific interventions designed to remediate the particular problems that the client presents (Craighead, Kazdin, & Mahoney, 1981). No strong assumptions need to be made regarding the degree of independence or construct purity of the various clinical syndromes, such as anxiety, affective disorders, schizophrenia, substance abuse, or personality disorders. Indeed, while these clinical categories have considerable heuristic and theoretical value, individual clients will often present with overlapping symptoms.

Psychiatric patients often present with other problems in addition to their psychotic symptoms. When these other problems occur, psychotic patients may benefit from the range of cognitive-behavioral interventions designed for specific target problems, such as anxiety management, depression, substance abuse, insomnia, and so on. These interventions will facilitate the individual's adjustment back into the community, decrease stress from the associated problems, and improve daily functioning. Implementation of these programs may, of course, be made much more difficult by the presence of psychotic symptoms. Such treatments might best be viewed as ways to improve the individual's living situation, decrease stress, and thereby help to decrease the individual's vulnerability to schizophrenic relapse.

One problem that deserves special emphasis, given its prevalence among psychotic patients, is depression. In our own clinical work, we frequently use cognitive-behavioral treatments in treating depression in psychotic patients (see Rehm, 1981). Procedures we use include self-monitoring of positive events, planned activity increases, and cognitive restructuring of negative self-evaluations and dysfunctional automatic thoughts. Implementation of these treatments must take into consideration the cognitive deficits and distractibility often present among psychotic patients. Thus, we tend to emphasize the more operant procedures such as schedule activity increases.

Cognitive-behavioral interventions may also be helpful in managing some psychotic-like symptoms. For example, in our inpatient settings, we sometimes receive referrals involving patients who report hearing voices but fail to meet the full diagnostic criteria for schizophrenia. Moreover, they are refractory to neuroleptic medications as well. These individuals most often are diagnosed a atypical psychoses. One patient, for example, heard a voice involved in repetitive counting from 1 to 12. Another patient reported voices telling him to kill himself. In each of these cases, a thorough clinical interview suggested that the patient was experiencing repetitive obsessive thoughts, and was probably not experiencing auditory hallucinations, per se. After determining that these patients were probably experiencing repetitive obsessive thoughts, cognitive-behavioral treatments such as thought-stopping, increases in activity incompatible with dysfunctional thoughts, temporal control (limiting obsessive thoughts to certain time periods), and geographical control (limiting obsessive thoughts to certain locations) proved helpful.

Medication noncompliance is an additional area that is recently gaining attention by cognitive-behavioral psychologists (Epstein & Masek, 1978; Haynes, Taylor, & Sackett, 1979). Given the propensity of some schizophrenic patients to relapse when off medications, cognitive-behavioral strategies are needed to increase medication compliance. Some strategies that may be relevant include better patient education, gradually increasing patient control of medications while in the hospital in order to shape behavior patterns, stimulus control interventions where medication administration is tailored to existing behavior patterns, periodic reminder phone calls, and so on.

Social and Task-Functional Skills Training

Concurrent with the emphasis on deinstitutionalization and pharmacologic treatment of schizophrenia has been the development of a "revolving door" pattern of discharge and readmission to psychiatric facilities. Research has shown that some 30 to 40 percent of schizophrenic patients are readmitted to psychiatric facilities within one year of discharge, with readmission levels increasing to the 50 to 60 percent range after 2 years (Mosher, 1971; Talbott, 1974).

While medication noncompliance is one factor promoting relapse, it alone cannot account for the revolving door pattern. Hogarty, Goldberg, and Schooler (1974) found 48 percent relapse within 2 years among patients who took their medications reliably. As Brown (1982) so succinctly notes, "Drugs do not teach daily living and coping skills necessary for survival and maintenance in the community" (p. 91).

The importance of interpersonal and daily living skills has been emphasized within recent years by behavioral and psychosocial models of psychopathology and treatment. Seminal research by Zigler and Phillips (1961) found that psychiatric inpatients who were relatively low in social competence averaged longer stays in inpatient facilities than patients who were more socially competent. In addition, socially competent individuals had lower relapse and readmission rates.

Social difficulties appear to be fairly prevalent among psychiatric patients. Using strict criteria, Curran, Miller, Swick, Monti, and Stout (1980) found that 7.4 percent of a large group of psychiatric inpatients were judged by a professional staff to be socially inadequate. Bryant, Trower, Yardley, Urbieta, and Letemendia (1976) found that 16.3 percent of a large outpatient sample were judged to be socially inadequate. Moreover, the prevalence of inadequate social behavior appears to be fairly uniform among the major psychological disorders (Bryant et al., 1976; Currran et al., 1980; Youngren & Lewinsohn, 1980). Empirical research and conceptual models have stressed the relevance of social difficulties for such disparate problems as alcoholism (Marlatt & Donovan, 1981), depression (Libet & Lewinsohn, 1973), chronic mental patients (Hersen, 1979), marital distress (Gottman, 1980), and isolated or withdrawn children (Conger & Keane, 1981).

Social skills training is one of the major psychosocial treatment approaches developed in recent years, and it has been applied to a number of social situations and a variety of populations (see Twentyman & Zimering, 1979, for a review). Although broadly defined, social skills training emphasizes the acquisition and improvement of specific social skills, usually emphasizing conversational skills. When applied to psychiatric populations, the goals of this approach include facilitating the development of additional social support, increasing meaningful structured activity, limiting social withdrawal, improving self-concept, avoiding negative social interactions, and improving coping strategies that will help patients respond better to environmental stress.

We regularly employ social skills training with psychotic patients at our inpatient facility. Patients begin the skills program only after they are stabilized, usually with the assistance of neuroleptic medication. Each skills group is led by two experienced therapists. Typically, one of the therapists is a predoctoral psychology intern and the other is a master's-level clinician.

Our groups usually consist of three or four psychotic patients. Groups meet for one hour in the morning and one hour in the afternoon, Monday through Thursday. On Friday, there is a brief review of the week's material, and then a community trip, which usually lasts for two hours and typically includes lunch in a restaurant. This trip provides opportunities for patients to practice their skills in the community. The complete program lasts six weeks.

The Monday through Thursday sessions generally consist of the following components: (1) review of the previous day's material and discussion of the homework assignment; (2) didactic presentation of the current lesson, including rationale; (3) modeling of the skills described in the lesson, usually by therapist, or occasionally by prepared videotape or patient modeling; (4) discussion and some questioning of patients on the major points; (5) role-playing and behavioral rehearsal; (6) observing the videotaped interaction and eliciting feedback from participants and observers; (7) therapist praise for positive aspects of performance and suggestions for improvement; (8) mastery of the skill through repeated practice; and (9) homework assignments to practice skills with other individuals outside of the group to promote generalization and skill mastery.

The major topics covered in our social skills program include the following: presentation of a model of social communication that includes perceiving, processing, and performing; starting a conversation; self-disclosure; speaking skills; nonverbal skills; listening skills, observational skills; receiving criticism; processing information and self-statements; assertiveness training; and remedies for problematic situations such as apologies, explanations, and saving face. We attempt to make each of the topics as relevant as possible for all of the patients by structuring role-plays and examples to fit the circumstances of each. For example when role-playing assertiveness situations with patients who abuse alcohol, we might help them practice refusing a drink. We also emphasize a generative approach (Trower, 1982) to the social skills we teach. That is, we stress observational skills and attempt to provide instruction on appropriate placement, timing, and sequencing of behavior, in addition to the mastery of response delivery. We also attempt to make the groups as lively and enjoyable as possible, as a way of modeling appropriate social interaction.

In addition to the relatively standard social conversational skills format, therapists are allowed considerable flexibility to implement relevant task-functional skills, either in the group format or in one-to-one sessions. By task-functional skills, we refer to daily living skills, such as grooming, job hunting and interviewing, or looking for an apartment. Consultation with other hospital departments, such as Occupational Therapy or Recreation can often be arranged. The unit is structured so that one of the social skill trainers is the primary therapist for each patient in the program. This helps to coordinate patient care. Therapists meet individually with patients several times per week, monitor progress in the social skills program and employ additional interventions to help with other clinical problems such as depression, family problems, etc.

Behavioral Family Therapy

Behavioral family therapy is an attempt to align the professional treatment team with the family and to use the resources of the family to effect the course of schizophrenia in a positive fashion. In traditional family therapy the family was perceived as dysfunctional and as having caused or contributed to the schizophrenic illness. Traditional family therapy was viewed as a means to correct a pathological unit. In behavioral family therapy the family is not regarded as having caused or contributed to the illness, nor is the goal to correct but rather to support the family. The aim of behavioral family therapy is to reduce the probability of relapse and to help the patient achieve as high social and occupational functioning as possible. McFarlane (1983) states that while the goal of the traditional family therapy was to make the family "normal," behavioral family therapy at times fosters somewhat abnormal family processes, such as keeping emotion at a low level, artificially simplifying communication, and establishing age-inappropriate parental control over the patient.

Interest in behavioral family therapy arose from research examining the families of schizophrenics. Although family interactional patterns are not implicated in the etiology of schizophrenia (Goldstein & Rodnick, 1975), there is some evidence that family interactional patterns such as expressed emotion (Brown, Briley, & Wing, 1972), communication deviance (Singer, Wynne, & Toohey, 1978), and faulty problem-solving (Falloon, Doane & Pederson, in press) might affect the course and the relapse rate of schizophrenia. Another major impetus for behavioral family therapy was the deinstitutionalization movement. With deinstitutionalization, patients were returned to their communities of origin and often to their families. Approximately 50 percent of today's discharged schizophrenic patients return to their families (McFarlane, 1983). Although these families have been devastated by the illness, they usually have received little if any communication or education regarding their relatives' problems. Families are often entrusted with the care of their schizophrenic member on a 24 hour, 7 day a week basis. They need to be involved in the total treatment of the patient and not isolated or, even worse, blamed for the illness.

The goal of behavioral family therapy is to work with these families, to help educate them about schizophrenia, and to teach and to be taught by them strategies that help prevent relapse in schizophrenics. Published reports (Anderson, Hogarty, & Reiss, 1980; Falloon, Boyd, McGill, Razani, Moss, & Gilderman, 1982; Goldstein, Rodnick, Evans, May, & Steinberg, 1978; Leff, Kuipers, Berkowitz, Eberlein-Fries, & Sturgeon, 1982) indicate that application of behavioral family therapy results in a good deal of success in the treatment of schizophrenics. The programs in these published reports differ along numerous dimensions, including the number of sessions, when the sessions are initiated (outpatient or inpatient), office versus home-base delivery, and with differential emphasis on education versus skills training. However, all of these programs involve linking the professional team with the family and incorporating the family as part of the treatment team.

Our own behavioral family treatment was developed from these other programs and contains elements common to each of them. The intensive phase of our program lasts for twelve, one-and-a-half-hour, sessions, and is initiated when the patient is hospitalized on our psychiatric unit. During this phase families meet weekly or twice weekly for 12 sessions. If the family opts to meet twice a week, the intensive phase is generally completed during the patient's inpatient hospitalization. This 12-session intensive phase consists of three modules (education, communication skills, and problem-solving training). During our aftercare

Table 6-1
Goal of Family Program

1. Resolution of family guilt
2. Realization of handicap
3. Identification of stressors
4. Neuroleptic medication adherence
5. Management of disruptive behavior
6. Keeping the family healthy

phase the family first meets twice-monthly for two months and then once a month thereafter. Problem-solving is emphasized during the aftercare phase, although education and communication skills training are also continued. Crisis intervention can occur at anytime if needed. In addition, many of our families also participate in a family support group that meets twice-monthly. In our support group we exclude the patients from the family meetings, although other investigators (McFarlane, 1983) include the patient in multiple-family groups.

Education

In the education module material is presented in such a fashion as to set the stage for the accomplishment of the six goals presented in Table 6-1. We feel that the attainment of these goals is pertinent to reducing the relapse rate in our schizophrenic patients and to help them obtain reasonably good community functioning.

Particularly useful information in helping resolve the guilt of family members is information regarding the genetic basis of schizophrenia and neurochemical problems associated with the disorder. We discuss both twin and adoption studies supporting the genetic basis of schizophrenia (e.g., Gottesman & Shields, 1972; Rosenthal, Wender, Kety; Schulsinger, Welner, & Ostergaard; 1968), as well as various biochemical theories, including the dopamine hypotheses (Snyder, 1976). Families are told forthrightly that it is unlikely that they have caused schizophrenia, and that the illness has a genetic basis. Families are also told that the schizophrenic patient indeed has a handicap and that the symptoms displayed are not of a volitional nature.

Families are further informed that, although they did not cause the illness, their interactional patterns may play a role in the course of the illness. They are told that, while high levels of criticism and or overinvolvement are natural responses to the illness, they are counterindicated and may bring on a relapse. Stress, which may be of a positive or negative nature, can prove toxic to patients. Indeed, patients are asked to be good "detectives" and let other members of the family know when they are feeling stressed.

The importance of neuroleptic medication is emphasized. Families are told that neuroleptic medication appears to correct the chemical imbalance and reduces the stress level experienced by the patient. The purpose of the drug, its effectiveness, dose requirements, and side effects are all discussed within the family context.

Families are told that the patients need for low stress is not to be confused with permissiveness. In fact, families are told that clear limits do help maintain a low-stress atmosphere. Finally, the families are urged to keep themselves healthy. They are told that although rallying around a sick member and directing most family resources toward helping the patient is an effective way of treating an acute illness, it is not a very effective way to treat a long-term illness. They are told that both the patient and the family must learn to live with the illness. Both patient and family members are urged to develop their own social support systems.

Communcation Skills Training

The training procedures employed in our communication-skills training module are identical to the training procedures used in the previously discussed social skills training. Consequently, our presentation will be most brief. Given the profound effect schizophrenia has on the family, it is no wonder that communication among family members is often difficult. During the education phase we emphasize the need to lower the stress level in the family, to have direct and simple communication, and to give members feedback in a nonaversive manner. In addition, communication training is a prerequiste for effective problem-solving.

An assessment of each family's communication problems should be made and a treatment intervention developed on the basis of this assessment. It has been our experience and the experience of others (Falloon, Boyd, & McGill, 1984) that the skills frequently lacking in families are the following: listening skills, giving and receiving positive feedback, giving and receiving criticism, feeling talk, making requests, assertive behavior, and reciprocity of conversation. Generally, our communication training module covers five, one-and-a-half-hour sessions during the intensive phase of treatment, although often we refer back to its principles and do further training during the aftercare stage.

Problem-Solving Training

Problem-solving training begins during the last five sessions of the intensive phase and continues throughout the aftercare phase. Families are told that the difference between distressed and nondistressed families is not the number of problems faced by each type of family, but their ability to solve these problems. Families are told that it is not the goal of the program to help them solve all their problems, because this goal is impossible; but rather the goal is to teach them a problem-solving model. Our problem-solving model employs six steps (Table 6-2).

During the problem-solving sessions the therapist is quite task-oriented. If the family drifts from the task, the therapist emphatically refocuses their atten-

Table 6-2
Six Steps Problem-Solving

1. Problem definition
2. Developing options
3. Evaluating options
4. Choosing options
5. Implementation
6. Review

tion. Problem-solving is presented as a collaborative effort that takes a good deal of discipline and patience. Families are urged to attempt problem-solving on their own between sessions. Specific times are set aside for problem-solving when a minimum of interfering factors such as television and telephones are present.

It is important to keep the problem definition step separate from the other steps. Problems are often presented in global and negative terms. It is the therapist's function to help the family operationalize problems and present them in a more positive fashion. Families often get defensive and members engage in cross-complaining , denial, and so on. The therapist reminds the family that one of them has the duty of defining the problem or being a complainer while the others are obliged to be good listeners. Good listening is not an admission of guilt. If families choose to fight, the therapist will label it as fighting and state something to the effect that it does not appear that the family is ready to problem-solve at this time.

In developing options the therapist encourages "brainstorming" and at this time discourages evaluations of any of the ideas presented. All the proposed options are written down to be later examined during stage 3 (evaluating options). In evaluating options all the short- and long-term positive and negative consequences are examined, as well as the probability of each outcome. Once an option or options are choosen, they are written down and a contract developed. Specific responsibilities for specific duties are outlined and a recording procedure developed. The problem solutions are reviewed at each session and minor modifications made as needed. If the solution does not seem to be effective in solving the problem, the family is asked to revert back to step 1 and to redefine the problem.

Aftercare

Good inpatient treatment demands good aftercare. Gains made during hospitalization often dissipate unless a thorough and systematic aftercare program is implemented. All behavioral programs reviewed in this chapter contain provisions for implementing procedures promoting generalization to the natural environment. In general, in our own treatment program we try to arrange it so that our patient's aftercare therapist is one of the therapists who had been responsible for instituting the inpatient program. Consequently, continuity of care is maintained.

Therapists attempt to make home visits so that they have a good idea of the patient's natural environment and the problems that lie within. As mentioned previously, we have a relative's support group that maintains linkage between the hospital staff and the families. For patients, we have a day-treatment program that they may attend on a daily basis. The day-treatment program provides a social network and engages in activities such as trips to ballgames, fishing expeditions, and so on.

Good aggressive case management is important. Helping patients to find jobs, school programs, and residences is extremely important. We have worked with managers of boarding homes and taught them procedures that we have found effective in dealing with schizophrenic patients. Although we have not established half-way homes ourselves, they certainly have proved effective in other programs (Brown, 1982).

INTERFACE WITH PHARMACOLOGY

The behavioral treatment of schizophrenics interfaces with the pharmacological approach employed. Research indicates that regular medication is most important when the patient needs to be protected from a stressful environment. For example, failure to take medication on a regular basis increases the risk for relapse among patients from high-stress family environments. However, medication regularity has less influence on relapse risks among patients from low-stress family environments (Vaughn & Leff, 1976; Vaughn et al., 1982). Stressful life events are associated with relapse (Rabkin, 1980), and medicated patients require more events to precipitate relapse than nonmedicated patients (Birley & Brown, 1970; Leff, Hirsch, Gaind, Rhode, & Stevens, 1973).

The treatment implications of these findings are straightforward. Behavioral treatment programs are designed to provide patients with effective coping skills to negotiate or remove stress in their environments. If a behavioral program is successful, the stress protection provided by medication will be required to a lesser degree. For example, Falloon et al. (in press) demonstrate that, in comparison with an individual psychotherapy control group, schizophrenics receiving behavioral family therapy were much less likely to relapse even though they required less neuroleptic medication.

Since neuroleptic treatment can result in an exacerbation of negative symptoms (Van Putten & May, 1978) and the development of handicapping motoric side effects, patients who succeed in a behavioral program should be considered for a trial of medication reduction. Given the stresses associated with discharge and return to the community, however, medication reduction should not be attempted until the patient has been restabilized to some extent.

Case Example 1

Daniel C. is a 32-year old single white male who was brought to the hospital by his mother, with whom he lives. She had Daniel admitted because he had been overly suspicious and had been walking aimlessly around the neighborhood talking to himself. Daniel had one prior psychiatric admission, three years earlier, prompted by his destroying several television sets in a large department store. At that time, the patient had been diagnosed as having a schizophreniform disorder.

Records from the first admission indicated that the patient had a history of truancy and fights in school, along with heavy marijuana and alcohol abuse. The patient quit school at age 17 and enrolled in the Air Force. He served two years in Viet Nam as an airplane mechanic and received an honorable discharge. Daniel completed the GED (high-school equivalency) after the service and worked intermittently at various blue-collar jobs (construction, mechanic, house painter) until his first psychiatric admission at the age of 29. The patient was described as a loner throughout his adult life. Relevant stressors within a few months prior to the first admission included the death of his father and being fired from a house-painting job because of petty theft.

At the time of the current admission the patient appeared disheveled; his clothes were dirty and torn, and his hair was uncombed. The patient looked sad, was tearful, and spoke hesitantly in a soft voice. He appeared frightened, and asked that the door to the interview room be kept open. The patient was oriented in all spheres. His speech was purposeful, although tangential at times. He performed within normal limits on tests of recall and mathematics. A review of psychiatric symptoms indicated that the patient experienced sleep-onset insomnia, suicidal ideation, suspiciousness, ideas of reference (thoughts that other people were talking about him and planning to kill him), and auditory hallucinations that told him that he was "worthless and no good." The patient denied any drug or alcohol use within 30 days prior to admission, although periodic marijuana and alcohol abuse have been problematic since age 12. The patient reported being unable to work since his last admission because of "nerves." There were no known precipitants of this hospitalization.

Daniel C. was admitted to the inpatient unit with the primary diagnosis of schizoaffective disorder, and secondary diagnoses of alcohol abuse, in remission, and cannabis abuse, in remission. The patient was initially medicated with an antidepressant (Elavil), but became agitated and more disoriented. When tried on a low dose of Haldol, the patient appeared to stabilize. The patient's mood and sleep also improved. After gathering more complete information from the structured diagnostic interview schedule (DIS), the patient's primary diagnosis was changed to schizophrenia, paranoid type.

The patient was assessed for involvement in the social skills program, and the following goals were mutually developed: (1) to learn to initiate conversation with others, (2) to maintain eye contact while speaking, (3) to become more assertive in business situations, and (4) to be able to refuse drinks when others offered. Initial behavioral observations using the SSIT confirmed that the patient exhibited little eye contact, spoke infrequently, and was unassertive.

The patient was involved in the six-week social skills program, and reported progressively greater comfort in initiating conversation with others. Eye contact also improved, based on the Simulated Social Interaction Test (SSIT) assessment at discharge. The patient still had difficulty with assertiveness situations, as became apparent on one of the community trips when a waitress made a mistake on his order. The patient successfully practiced refusing drinks. The individual therapist worked with the patient on task-functional skills such as helping him open a bank account with a relative as a guardian. Cognitive-behavioral interventions for depression were also phased in, and the patient attended an alcohol group on the inpatient unit and was encouraged to attend AA meetings after discharge.

The family component was delayed because the mother was hospitalized for depression shortly after Daniel's admission. Initial assessments using the Camberwell Family Interview suggested that the mother was overinvolved with the patient and was highly critical. She expected him to work full-time and resisted the idea of his obtaining his own apartment. She was also unaware of Daniel's present and prior diagnoses, and exhibited little understanding of schizophrenia. Our behavioral family program involving communication and problem-solving modules was applied. The mother reported some relief when the genetic basis of schizophrenia was discussed. She also learned, for the first time, about some of the psychotic symptoms Daniel had been experiencing. It also became apparent that neither Daniel nor the mother had addressed issues involved in reorganizing the household and distributing responsibility after the father's death. Initial problem-solving of some financial and personal matters occurred in the family sessions. Family assessments at discharge indicated less parental overinvolvement and better problem-solving strategies.

Daniel was discharged after a total of three months of hospitalization. He continued to meet with his individual therapist on an outpatient basis, in addition to the family meetings and periodic medication maintenance. He began attending AA meetings and acquired a part-time house-painting job within a few months. Ratings on the Brief Psychiatric Rating Scale (BPRS) indicated no resumption of Daniel's positive symptoms of schizophrenia. He is still relatively quiet and socially isolated, although he has more social contact now as compared with prior to admission.

PROBLEMS AREAS

Schizophrenia is a disorder with a complex clinical presentation that varies from overt disruptive psychosis to a state of withdrawn apathy. On an inpatient unit the symptomatology is more pronounced and the changes are more rapid. The resulting problems for assessment and treatment are not negligible and are often exacerbated by the need for the therapist to effectively interact with other staff members and relatives of the patient. This section discusses common problems and some proposed solutions.

Assessment Problems

Since many newly admitted schizophrenics are overtly psychotic, the assessment of psychotic features does not usually pose a problem. However, these features often interfere with assessment of other aspects of psychological and behavioral functioning. Such interference will be markedly reduced if one waits until the patient has been stablized on appropriate medication. Since this may require several weeks, this period is ideal for completing family assessments that do not require the presence of the patient.

A more subtle problem caused by psychotic behavior is that it often tempts the clinician to ignore a comprehensive psychiatric assessment because "the patient is obviously schizophrenic." However, schizophrenia is often complicated by substance abuse, simple phobias, and a variety of other disorders, which may be responsive to appropriate treatments. A comprehensive psychiatric evaluation may uncover a substantial affective component. For example, it is not uncommon for an "obviously schizophrenic" patient to admit to a history of hypomania or manic symptomatology. This information has significant pharmacologic implications and cannot be ignored.

After the psychotic symptoms have stabilized, assessment problems are created by the negative symptoms of schizophrenia. During this stage patients are apathetic and emotionally withdrawn. They are easily overstimulated and are likely to be distracted by irrelevant stimuli. These factors dilute the reliability and validity of verbal reports. Therefore, interviews must be conducted with constant attention to the patient's ability to process and convey information. When the patient appears excessively stimulated or distractible, the interview should be terminated and continued at another time. During a social competence assessment, negative symptoms are not a problem; they constitute the behavioral deficits that are the object of the assessment.

A potential difficulty with the family assessment involves families who have had previous experience with the mental health care system. Since many of these families have received inadequate services in the past, they may approach mental health professionals with anger and mistrust. In this case the clinician must earn the respect of the family before a therapeutic alliance can be formed. Assessment contacts lay the foundation for this alliance, as they occur at the beginning of the patient's hospitalization. For these reasons, it is best to begin such assessments with the Camberwell Family Interview (CFI). There are two aspects of the CFI that are very appealing to family members. First, it is a relatively long interview, lasting at least one hour. For families who are used to brief sessions, this provides hard evidence that the clinician values their input. Second, the interview provides an avenue for ventilation of much affect, giving clinicians a context in which to demonstrate their empathic concern for the patient and family.

Treatment Problems

In most cases the patient who refuses to take medication cannot be effectively treated with social skills training or family therapy. Establishing habitual medication compliance is of paramount importance. Some noncompliant patients fail to take their medication because they "forget" due to the cognitive and behavioral deficients associated with schizophrenia. Many of these patients will agree to take an injectible neuroleptic, which can be continued on an outpatient basis. Patients whose noncompliance is directly incorporated into their psychosis are more difficult. For example, a patient may refuse medication because a voice told him he would die if he did. Others may refuse due to paranoid ideation. For these patients, an ongoing token economy program will be helpful. Medication ingestion can be shaped with operant techniques in many recalcitrant patients.

The token economy can also be a useful tool for overcoming the behavioral deficits associated with negative symptoms. Tokens can be made contingent upon behaviors such as attendance of treatment sessions and completion of practice assignments. Active engagement in treatment can also be facilitated by clearly communicating to patients how the social competence and family interventions will help them attain goals they consider to be important. Some patients want jobs, others want friends, and so forth. In most cases, their specific needs can be related to the behavioral treatments discussed in this chapter.

A potential problem in the implementation of family therapy is the existence of psychopathology among the patient's relatives. Schizophrenia is known to be a familial disorder, with the lifetime risk for immediate relatives being approximately 10 percent (Tsuang & Faraone, 1985). Additional relatives may be at risk for schizophrenia "spectrum" disorders such as schizotypal and paranoid personality (Reich, 1976). There is also some evidence for assortative mating (McGue, Gottesman, & Rao, 1983); spouses of schizophrenics may be more likely to be schizophrenic than one would expect from the general population prevalence.

Psychopathology in the family must be diagnosed and treated. Severe cases will require pharmacologic interventions. The maladaptive behaviors created by the milder cases can be treated in the context of the communication and problem-solving phases of family therapy. Significant psychopathology will almost always be related to the problems that family members bring to therapy. Treating the psychopathology in the process of family therapy will provide the family with a means of coping with the associated behavioral problems.

A final problem area encountered in the inpatient behavioral treatment of schizophrenia involves the attitudes of other professionals involved in the patient's treatment. There is no scarcity of therapeutic myths about schizophrenia (e.g., "schizophrenia is a brain disease treatable only with neuroleptics" or "schizophrenia is caused by bad mothering; behavioral treatments are useless"). Such myths are often communicated to patients unintentionally by staff members, by not rewarding patients for progress made in the program, scheduling patients for other appointments during behavior therapy sessions, and exuding a general lack of enthusiasm for the program. One step toward overcoming this problem is to do the public relations work needed to "sell" the behavioral program to the staff of the inpatient unit. Sponsoring workshops and didactic presentations about the behavioral treatments is an effective way to generate interest and enthusiasm. Staff members can be trained to implement the treatment by serving as cotherapists with experienced behavior therapists. To some extent the program will sell itself through the comments of the patients, family, and staff who have observed significant improvement. In short, problems caused by staff members will be minimal if the staff is educated about and actively engaged in the treatment program.

SUMMARY

The criteria for psychotic disorders, most notably for schizophrenia, are better operationalized in *DSM-III* contrasted to previous manuals, thus reflecting an increased reliance on empirical development and verification of disorders. The criteria for schizophrenia include major markers for positive symptoms, including delusions, hallucinations, or a formal thought disorder, as well as criteria for negative symptoms reflecting deterioration from a premorbid level of functioning. There is also considerable debate as to whether these disorders should be considered unitary or multimodel disease entities (Zubin & Steinhauer, 1981). Valid and comprehensive assessment strategies are necessary in order to make correct diagnosis. They are also essential in studying the course of the illness and in evaluating the effectiveness of various treatment procedures. We employ an assessment battery in our own inpatient work that includes assessment of psychopathlogy, family environment, and the patient's social competence. We use a comprehensive structured psychiatric interview (Diagnostic Interview Schedule) in order to determine diagnosis and to obtain other information relevant for prognosis and treatment. We use two instruments (The Brief Psychiatric Rating Scale and Target Symptom Ratings) in order to monitor the patient's psychopathology during treatment and follow-up. The patient's family and environment is assessed using the Camberwell Family Interview and the Direct Family Intervention Procedure. From the Camberwell, attitudinal measures of degree of criticism and family overinvolvement are obtained. From the Direct Family Intervention Procedure, observations are made regarding the degree of support and criticism in the family, as well as the family's ability to problem-solve. The patient's level of social competence is measured from direct but unsystematic observations of the patients on the unit, through a structured role-play test (Simulated Social Interaction Test) and through several self-report and informant-report measures regarding social adjustment and social support.

Behavioral intervention procedures include operant procedures, cognitive-behavioral techniques, social and task-functional skills training, and behavioral family therapy. Token economies are systematized, detailed, and comprehensive applications of operant procedures. Careful attention must be paid to issues regarding token economy so that they function not merely as a ward management system but as a comprehensive therapeutic milieu. Cognitive-behavioral interventions illustrate how these procedures could prove useful in treating problems associated with psychotic behavior, as well as treating psychotic-like symptoms. Social and task-functional skills training appear to be important interventions in preventing the "revolving door" pattern of discharge and readmission to psychiatric facilities. While medications are extremely important in treating psychotic symptoms, they do not teach the daily living and coping skills necessary for survival maintenance in the community. Behavioral family therapy also appears to be a useful strategy in maintaining psychotic patients in the community. Behavioral family therapy is an attempt to align the professional staff with the family and to use the resources of the family to effect a more positive course for schizophrenia.

Behavioral treatment programs are designed to provide patients with effective coping skills to negotiate undue stress in their environments. If the behavioral programs are successful, then the diathesis-stress model of psychotic behavior would indicate a reduction in psychotropic medication.

REFERENCES

Anderson CM, Hogarty GE, & Reiss DJ. (1980). Family treatment of adult schizophrenic patients: A psychoeducational approach. *Schizophrenia Bulletin 6*, 490–505.

Birley JL, & Brown G. (1970). Crises and life changes preceeding the onset or relapse of acute schizophrenia. *British Journal of Psychiatry 116*, 327–333.

Brown M. (1982). Maintenance and generalization issues in skills training with chronic schizophrenics. In Curran JP, & Monti PM (Eds), *Social skills training: A practical handbook for assessment and treatment.* New York: Guilford Press.

Brown GW, Birley JLT, & Wing JK. (1972). Influence of family life on the course of schizophrenic disorder: A replication. *British Journal of Psychiatry 121*, 241–258.

Brown GW., & Rutter M. (1966). The measurement of family activities and relationships: A methodological study. *Human Relations 19*, 241–263.

Bryant B, Trower P, Yardley K, Urbieta H, & Letemendia FJJ. (1976). A survey of social inadequancy among psychiatric outpatients. *Psychological Medicine 6*, 101–112.

Conger JC, & Keane SP. (1981). Social skills intervention in the treatment of isolated or withdrawn children. *Psychological Bulletin 90*, 478–495.

Craighead, WE, Kazdin AE, & Mahoney MJ (Eds). (1981). *Behavior modification: Principles, issues, and applications (2nd ed)* Boston: Houghton Mifflin.

Curran JP. (1982). A procedure for the assessment of social skills: The Simulated Social Interaction Test. In Curran JP, & Monti PM (Eds), *Social skills training. A practical handbook for assessment and treatment* New York: Guilford Press.

Curran JP, Miller IW III, Zwick WR, Monti PM, & Stout RL. (1980). The socially inadequate patient: Incidence rate, demographic and clinical features, and hospital and posthospital functioning. *Journal of Consulting and Clinical Psychology 48*, 375–382.

Doane JA, West KL, Goldstein MJ, Rodnick EH, & Jones JE. (1981). Parental communication deviance and affective style. *Archives of General Psychiatry 38*, 679–685.

Endicott J, & Spitzer RL. (1980). Psychiatric rating scales. In Kaplan HI, Freedman AM, & Sadock DJ (Eds), *Comprehensive textbook of psychiatry III.* Baltimore: Williams & Wilkins

Epstein LH, & Masek BJ. (1978). Behavioral control of medicine compliance. *Journal of Applied Behavior Analysis 11*, 1–9.

Falloon IRH, Boyd JL & McGill CW. (1984). *Family care of schizophrenia.* New York: Guilford Press.

Falloon IRH, Boyd JL, McGill CW, Razani J, Moss H, & Gilderman AM. (1982). Family management in the prevention of exacerbation of schizophrenia. *The New England Journal of Medicine 306*, 1437–1440.

Falloon IRH, Boyd JL, McGill CW, Williamson M, Razani J, Moss, HB, Gilderman AM, & Simpson GM. (in press). Family versus individual management in the prevention of morbidity of schizophrenia: I. Clinical outcome of a two-year controlled study. *Archives of General Psychiatry.*

Falloon IRH, Doane JA & Pederson J. (in press). Family versus individual management in prevention of morbidity of schizophrenia: III. Family functioning. *Archives of General Psychiatry.*

Goldsmith JB, & McFall RM. (1975). Development and evaluation of an interpersonal skill training program for psychiatric inpatients. *Journal of Abnormal Psychology 84*, 51–58.

Goldstein M. (1970). Premorbid adjustment, paranoid status, and patterns of response to phenothiazine in acute schizophrenia. *Schizophrenia Bulletin 1*, 24–37.

Goldstein MJ, & Rodnick EH. (1975). The family's contribution to the etiology of schizophrenia: Current status: *Schizophrenia Bulletin 14*, 48–63.

Goldstein MJ, Rodnick EH, Evans JR, May PRA, & Steinberg MR. (1978). Drug and family therapy in the aftercare of acute schizophrenics. *Archives of General Psychiatry 35*, 1169–1177.

Gottheil E, & Waxman HM. (1982). Alcoholism and schizophrenia. In Pattison EM, & Kaufman E (Eds), *Encyclopedic handbook of alcoholism.* New York: Gardner Press.

Gottman JM. (1980). *Marital interaction: Experimental investigations.* New York: Academic Press.

Gottesman II, & Shields J. (1972). *Schizophrenia and genetics: A twin study vantage point.* New York: Academic Press.

Hawk AB, Carpenter WT, & Strauss JS. (1975). A Diagnostic criteria and five-year outcome in schizophrenia: A report from the International Pilot Study of Schizophrenia. *Archives of General Psychiatry 32*, 343–347.

Haynes RB, Taylor DW, & Scakett DL (Eds). (1979). *Compliance in health care.* Baltimore: Johns Hopkins University Press.

Hedlund JL, & Vieweg BW. (1980). The Brief Psychiatric Rating Scale (BPRS): A comprehensive review. *Journal of Operational Psychiatry 11*, 48–65.

Hedlund JL & Vieweg BW. (1981). Structured psychiatric interviews: A comparative review. *Journal of Operational Psychiatry 12*, 39–67.

Hersen M. (1979). Modification of skill deficits in psychiatric patients. In Bellack AS, & Hersen M (Eds), *Research and practice in social skills training* (pp 189–236). New York: Plenum.

Hogarty GE, Goldberg SC, & Schooler NR. (1974). Drug and sociotherapy in the aftercare of schizophrenic patients: II. Two-year relapse rates. *Archives of General Psychiatry 31*, 603–608.

Isaacs W, Thomas J, & Goldimond J. (1960). Application of operant conditioning to reinstate verbal behavior in psychotics. *Journal of Speech and Hearing Disorders 25*, 8–12.

Lauria R, & Meltzer HY. (1977). *Standard Psychotic History Schedule.* Chicago: Illinois State Psychiatric Institute/University of Chicago Clinical Research Center.

Leff J, Hirsch S, Gaind R, Rhode P, & Stevens B. (1973). Life events and maintenance therapy in schizophrenic relapse. *British Journal of Psychiatry 123*, 659–660.

Leff J, Kuipers L, Berkowitz R, Eberlein Fries R, & Sturgeon D. (1982). A controlled study of social intervention in the families of schizophrenic patients. *British Journal of Psychiatry 141*, 121–134.

Libet JM, & Lewinsohn PM. (1973). Concept of social skill with special reference to the behavior of depressed persons. *Journal of Consulting and Clinical Psychology 40*, 304–312.

Liberman RP, Wallace CJ, Tiegen J, & Davis J. (1974). Intervention with psychotic behaviors. In Calhoun KS, Adams HE, & Mitchell CM (Eds), *Intervention treatment in psychopathology.* New York: John Wiley.

Lin N, Dean A, & Ensel WM. (1981). Social support scales: A methodological note. *Schizophrenia Bulletin 7*, 73–89.

Marlatt GA, & Donovan DM. (1981). Alcoholism and drug dependence: Cognitive social learning factors in addictive behaviors. In Craighead WE, Kazdin AE, & Mahoney MJ (Eds), *Behavior modification: Principles, issues, and applications* (pp 264–285). Boston: Houghton Mifflin.

McFarlane WR (Ed), (1983). *Family therapy in schizophrenia.* New York: Guilford Press.

McFarlane AH, Neale KA, Norman GR, Roy RG, & Streiner DL. (1981). Methodological issues in developing a scale to measure social support. *Schizophrenia Bulletin 7*, 90–100.

McGue M, Gottesman I, & Rao DC. (1983). The transmission of schizophrenia under a multifactorial threshold model. *American Journal of Human Genetics 35*, 1161–1178.

Mosher LR. (1971). Madness in the community. *Attitude 1*, 2–21.

Rabkin JG. (1980). Stressful life events and schizophrenia: A review of the research literature. *Psychological Bulletin 87*, 408–425.

Rehm LP (Ed). (1981). *Behavior therapy for depression: Present status and future directions.* New York: Academic Press.

Reich W. (1976). The schizophrenia spectrum: A genetic concept. *Journal of Nervous and Mental Disease 162*, 3–12.

Richard HC & Dinkoff MA. (1962). A follow-up note on verbal manipulation in a psychotherapeutic relationship. *Psychological Reports 11*, 506.

Robins LN, Helzer JE, Crougham J, & Ratcliff KS. (1981). National Institute of Mental Health Diagnostic Interview Schedule: Its history, characteristics and validity. *Archives of General Psyciatry 38*, 381–389.

Rosenthal D, Wender PH, Kety SS, Schulsinger F, Welner J, & Ostergaard L. (1968). Schizophrenics' offspring reared in adoptive homes. In Rosenthal D, & Kety SS (Eds), *The transmission of schizophrenia.* New York: Pergamon.

Schooler N, Hogarty G, Weissman MM. (1970). Social Adjustment Scale II (SAS II). In Hargreaves WA, Attkisson CC, & Sorenson JE (Eds), *Resource materials for community mental health program evaluators publication no. (ADM) 79–328.* Washington, D.C.: U.S. Government Printing Office.

Singer MT, Wynne LC, & Toohey ML. (1978). Communication disorders and the families of schizophrenics. In Wynne LC, Cromwell RL, & Matthysse S (Eds), *The nature of schizophrenia.* New York: John Wiley.

Snyder SH. (1976). The dopamine hypothesis of schizophrenia: Focus on the dopamine receptor. *American Journal of Psychiatry 133*, 197–202.

Sokolovsky J, & Cohen CI. (1981). Toward a resolution of methodological dilemmas in network mapping. *Schizophrenia Bulletin 7*, 109–116.

Strauss JS, & Carpenter WT. (1974). Characteristic symptoms and outcome in schizophrenia. *Archives of General Psychiatry 30*, 429–434.

Talbott JA. (1974). Stop the revolving door: A study of recidivism to a state hospital. *Psychiatric Quarterly 48*, 159–167.

Taylor M, & Abrams R. (1975). Manic depressive illness and good prognosis schizophrenia. *American Journal of Psychiatry 132*, 741–742.

Trower P. (1982). Toward a generative model of social skills: A critique and synthesis. In Curran JP, & Monti PM (Eds), *Social skills training: A practical handbook for assessment and treatment* (pp 399–427). New York: Guilford Press.

Tsuang MT, & Faraone SV. (1985). Genetic aspects of schizophrenia: An introduction to current theories of the transmission of schizophrenia. In Abuel D (Ed), *Hereditary aspects of neurological and psychiatric disorders* New York: Ware.

Tsuang MT, & Winokur G. (1974). Criteria for subtyping schizophrenia: Clinical differentiation of hebephrenic and paranoid schizophrenia. *Archives of General Psychiatry 31*, 43–47.

Twentyman CT, & Zimering RT. (1979). Behavioral training of social skills: A critical review. In Hersen M, Eisler RM, & Miller PM (Eds), *Progress in behavior modification: Vol. 7*. (pp. 319–400). New York: Academic Press.

Vaillant GE. (1964). Prospective prediction of schizophrenic remission. *Archives of General Psychiatry 11*, 509–518.

Valone K, Norton JP, Goldstein MJ & Doane JA. (1984). Parental expressed emotion and affective style in an adolescent sample at risk for schizophrenia spectrum disorders. *Journal of Abnormal Psychology 93*, 448–457.

Van Putten T, & Mary PRA. (1978). Akinetic depression in schizophrenia. *Archives of General Psychiatry 35*, 1101–1107.

Vaughn CE, & Leff JP. (1976). The influence of family and social factors in the course of psychiatric illness: A comparison of schizophrenic and depressed neurotic patients. *British Journal of Psychiatry 129*, 125–137.

Vaughn CE, Snyder KS, Freeman W, Jones S, Falloon IRH, & Liberman RP. (1982). Family actors in schizophrenic relapse: A replication. *Schizophrenia Bulletin 8*, 425–426.

Weissman MM. (1975). The assessment of social adjustment: A review of techniques. *Archives of General Psychiatry 32*, 357–365.

Weissman MM, Sholomiskas D, & John K. (1981). The assessment of social adjustment: An update. *Archives of General Psychiatry 38*, 1250–1258.

Wing JK, Cooper JE, & Sartorious N. (1977). *Measurement and classification of psychiatric symptoms*. New York: Cambridge University Press.

Winzce JP, Leitenberg H, & Agras WS. (1972). The effects of token reinforcement and feedback on the delusional verbal behavior of chronic paranoid schizophrenics. *Journal of Applied Behavioral Analysis 5*, 247–262.

Youngren MA, & Lewinsohn PM. (1980). The functional relation between depression and problematic interpersonal behavior. *Journal of Abnormal Psychology 89*, 333–341.

Zigler E, & Phillips L. (1961). Social competence and outcome in psychiatric disorder. *Journal of Abnormal and Social Psychology 63*, 264–271.

Zubin J, & Steinhauer S. (1981). How to break the logjam in schizophrenia: A look beyond genetics. *Journal of Nervous and Mental Disease 169*, 477–492.

7
Alcohol Abuse

Timothy J. O'Farrell and James W. Langenbucher

CLINICAL DESCRIPTION

In the past three decades, progressively greater clinical and investigative resources have been brought to bear on this country's foremost public health problem: alcohol abuse and dependence. The increasing sophistication of descriptive approaches to this problem served at once as a product of this focus as well as a guide.

Perhaps most influential of these approaches, the so-called *unitary disease model*, was advanced by the foremost student of alcoholism of his time, Elvin Jellinek (1952, 1960). This model, refined by Glatt (1967, 1974), Keller (1972), Mann (1968), and others, and still the core of most lay and professional approaches, holds in brief that alcoholics differ from normal individuals in terms of metabolic or psychological factors; that these differences predispose the nascent alcoholic to two overwhelming symptoms of disease, *craving* and *loss of control;* and that the sole method to arrest the disease process lies in a life-long commitment to abstinence. Though extraordinarily vital, this model has proved insupportable by the existing evidence (Caddy, 1978; Langenbucher & Nathan, 1983; Pattison, 1976).

A somewhat more sophisticated approach had been undertaken earlier by Knight (1937), who believed that his patients could be divided into two groups: the "reactive" alcoholics, who we might now say suffered from alcohol abuse as an associated feature of another disorder, and "essential" alcoholics, who man-

PRACTICE OF INPATIENT BEHAVIOR THERAPY
ISBN 0-8089-1715-3

ifested a picture of primary and intractable alcohol addiction. Though it continues to resurface on occasion, this model is now obsolete, but it foreshadowed many of the properties of the modern nosological approaches to alcoholism.

Chief among these is the diagnostic model contained in *DSM-III*. Superficially, this model is, like Knight's, a bifurcated or two-category schema, but very poor standardization of the phenomena of *tolerance* and *withdrawal* makes it essentially a unitary, or single-category, diagnostic model. That is, most diagnosticians can uncover signs of tolerance and withdrawal as they are contained in this model, and thus the bulk of patients will fall into the diagnostic category that includes these symptoms (alcohol dependence).

At first glance, however, *DSM-III* posits two categories of alcohol problems. The first, *alcohol abuse*, is marked by (1) a pathological pattern of use (such as daily drinking, an inability to remain abstinent, etc.) and (2) negative consequences of use (such as alcohol-related legal, marital, or job problems.) The second category, *alcohol dependence*, includes these first two features but also requires signs of alcohol tolerance and withdrawal effects when the patient is abstinent from alcohol. We have noted that *DSM-III* fails in its attention to these last two features. Other properties of *DSM-III*, however, deserve a higher regard. First, *DSM-III* contains entire descriptive sections on alcohol-related organic disorders, such as alcoholic amnestic syndromes (Wernicke-Korsakoff syndromes) and alcoholic hallucinosis. Second, *DSM-III* includes in its other diagnostic sections information pertaining to alcohol abuse and dependence as features associated with other primary disorders, such as personality disorders.

Probably the finest of the modern nosological approaches to alcohol disorders is contained in the "Criteria for the Diagnosis of Alcoholism" developed by the National Council on Alcoholism (1972). These criteria were deemed significant enough to receive unprecedented simultaneous publication in two different professional journals—*American Journal of Psychiatry* and *Annals of Internal Medicine*—and are far superior to *DSM-III* as a diagnostic and descriptive guide. The NCA criteria provide for three levels of diagnostic certainty: (1) a "classical, definite, obligatory" diagnosis of alcoholism, (2) a "probable, frequent, indicative" diagnosis, and (3) a "potential, possible, incidental" diagnosis. The NCA criteria also provide discussions of signs and symptoms of alcoholism that are differentially weighted for significance (e.g., gross motor tremor in alcohol withdrawal is very significant, report of "blackouts" is moderately significant, and a history of marital disruption is still less significant). These symptoms or criteria are organized according to "major" and "minor" levels of significance, and are further divided according to (1) a physiological and clinical "track" (Track I), and (2) a behavioral, psychological and attitudinal track (Track II). Moreover, these criteria provide for (and may even require) the use of alternate sources of information to establish diagnostic accuracy. For example, a number of questionnaire-like *alcoholism screening devices* are now available to search for behavioral and psychological phenomena that are contained on Track II, and a broad array of physiological measures (eg., liver function tests, EEGs, etc.) can register the presence of Track I criteria. In general, we find these NCA criteria to be quite specific, yet capable of capturing the diverse manifestations of alcohol problems in people's lives.

On the other hand, what does *not* emerge from the preceding discussion is a description of alcoholism as a precisely detailed and unitary disorder. This failure is intentional: Unlike some disorders discussed elsewhere in this book, alcoholism is not a problem that can be easily defined. Rather, it appears to be a complex constellation of problems, only some of which constitute definable syndromes. For example, a major authority, E. Mansell Pattison (1976), believes that alcohol problems are distributed over a very broad range of human functioning. Similarly, a number of *cluster analysts* (epidemiologists who study "subtypes" of human populations) have identified multiple subtypes of alcohol abusers, only a few of which would fit the classical picture painted by Elvin Jellinek. We know also that pathological alcohol use can be present in individuals who suffer from other, more primary, disorders, such as major mood and thought disorders, adjustment and grief reactions, and stress-related disorders. Thus, in a very real sense, each patient presents a fresh mystery, and we see the need for clinicians to make use of multiple sources of information so that they may arrive at very fine-grained assessments and treatment plans.

ASSESSMENT

In the behavioral inpatient treatment of alcohol abuse, clinical assessment must be a multi-method, multi-targeted process designed to maximize the likelihood of the patient's long-term success. This is best accomplished by focusing on three features of the patient's problems with alcohol, which together constitute a behavioral analysis of the drinking disorder: (1) the *antecedents*, or the circumstances that "set the stage" for abusive drinking, (2) the *behavior*, or the actual drinking pattern, and (3) the short- and long-term *consequences* of the drinking. The goal of assessment is to thoroughly document these components of the behavioral analysis, each of which has itself a number of dimensions. The clinician's and patient's understanding of them all can contribute significantly to treatment planning and ultimate treatment success. It can also identify areas of risk for the patient, should the abusive style of alcohol use persist.

Antecedents

It is important to understand the circumstances that contribute to problem drinking so that the patient can learn to establish alternate life practices in the future. A number of domains must be assessed, and a variety of clinical assessment strategies can be used profitably.

Cultural antecedents. In some measure, the normality or abnormality of a given drinking pattern is partially a function of the *norms* that prevail in the drinker's culture. These may include norms centered in the patient's ethnic group (Greely & McReady, 1980), norms that dominate the workplace (Plant, 1979), and norms that have been established by the patient's own family (Goodwin, 1979; Heath, 1975). From the clinician's point of view, these antecedents may be approached by direct interviews, both intake and therapeutic interviews as well as interviews of co-informants. A relatively new assessment aid, the Lifetime Drinking History Questionnaire (LDHQ: Skinner, 1981) is a standardized interview format that can also provide important information on cultural contributions to problem drinking.

Social antecedents. Along with cultural influences, more immediate social circumstances contribute to problem drinking, and should be assessed. Chief among these are interpersonal *high-risk situations*, including marital and family disruptions, the presence of alcoholic family members, and a preference on the patient's part for membership in heavy drinking social circles. Aversive social events, such as rejection by intimate friends and even pleasant social occasions such as weddings and holiday parties, can also set the stage for a period of heavy drinking. These antecedents too are best approached by direct interviews, with possible confirmation by co-informants.

Individual antecedents. Factors centered in the individual can contribute to problem drinking. These may include transient mood states, the ways in which the patient tends to cope with stress, and a variety of basic personality functions (e.g., impulsivity, sensation-seeking tendencies, basal levels of anxiety and depression, and others). Because these antecedents are so various, an assortment of assessment strategies may be needed, and the clinician may use any of a number of specialized assessment instruments in addition to the clinical interview. Objective personality tests such as the Minnesota Multiphasic Personality Inventory, the Millon Clinical Multiaxial Inventory, or the Sixteen Personality Factor Questionnaire can be useful. Another objective test, the Personality Assessment Survey (Wanberg, 1983), has been developed recently to study personality functions in alcohol-dependent patients. Still more specialized instruments might be applied to very narrow bands of functioning, such as anxiety, depression, and sensation-seeking.

Drinking Behavior

A detailed study of the patient's actual drinking behavior is useful for several reasons. Such a study can shed still more light on antecedent conditions, can be used to estimate the degree of the patient's alcohol-addiction, and can suggest therapeutic measures that will interrupt or extinguish the drinking pattern. All of these, of course, have critical implications for goal-setting and treatment planning.

Again, information obtained by interview of the patient and co-informants is useful here. One of the most promising interviews is a standardized format developed by Sobell, Maisto, Sobell, Cooper, Cooper, and Sanders (1980) that gathers detailed information on treatment history, social and legal consequences of drinking, and daily drinking behavior using a one year "time-line" method. The Lifetime Drinking History Questionnaire is another excellent interview.

Still other measures to assess drinking behavior are available in questionnaire format. In fact, Miller (1976) was able to review no fewer than 10 of these alcoholism screen devices available at that time. Two of these are most prominent. The first, the 24-item Michigan Alcoholism Screening Test or MAST (Selzer, 1971) is widely used, is reliable and valid (Skinner, 1981), but focuses more on alcohol-related impairment than on actual drinking behavior. The second, the relatively new Alcohol Use Inventory or AUI (Horn, Wanberg, & Foster, 1974) is a 147-item test that, like some personality tests, yields a profile of scores. Sixteen specific subscores (e.g., drink to change mood, psycoperceptual withdrawal, daily quantity when drinking) and six general scores (e.g., anxiety related to drinking, alcohol use deterioration, general alcoholism) are generated by this measure. We suggest that the best estimate of the patient's actual drinking style can be obtained by an interview along with one or more of the alcoholism screening devices.

Consequences

Understanding the reinforcing consequences an individual derives from alcohol is important for helping the patient find alternative sources to provide these same benefits. Clinical interview and Marlatt and Miller's (1983) Drinking Profile can be helpful in identifying the short-term benefits of alcohol. Long-term, cumulative negative consequences of a history of excessive drinking need to be thoroughly documented and understood for goal-setting, treatment planning, providing ancillary treatment services (e.g., vocational counseling, legal aid, etc.), and for helping the patient to gain an understanding of his or her present life circumstances. These negative consequences lie in a number of domains, and clinical interviews and examinations can be used to identify those domains that require more specific study.

Social consequences. Abuse of alcohol most often results in some impairment of social and vocational functioning, and our experience indicates that the extent of impairment in these areas can be comfortably assessed with simple interviews. However, some excellent aids arc also available. For example, the Life Events Questionnaire (Horowitz, Schaefer, Hiroto, Wilner, & Levin, 1977) provides an excellent entré to recent stressful events in the drinker's life, many of which are alcohol-induced. Such other instruments as the Addiction Severity Index (McLellan, Luborsky, Woody & O'Brien, 1980) measure several dimensions of the social costs of abusive drinking, and the Marital Satisfaction Inventory (Synder, 1981) provides a profile of subscores that reflect marital assets and problem areas.

Personality consequences. Drinking problems sometimes arise against a background of such personality dimensions as low impulse control, subclinical mood disorders, and other problems. It is also likely that a career of heavy drinking can itself cause distortion of the drinker's personality (Vaillant, 1982), an idea that has steadily gathered momentum in recent years. Because changes in personality, or "postmorbid" functioning, have important implications for such issues as the patient's treatment motivation and ability to learn new coping strategies, the personality consequences of the patient's drinking history should be assessed. We again recommend for this purpose carefully conducted clinical interviews over several occasions, and also suggest the Personality Assessment Survey, which was developed with alcoholic populations. Additional complications for the patient's history, such as depression, hopelessness, and suicidality should also be monitored.

Neuropsychological consequences. Since the early work of David Wechsler (1941), the idea that excessive consumption of alcohol produces impairment of brain function has steadily gained ground. The precise mechanism that produces these changes remains unclear—the impairment may be due to nutritional deficiencies, hypoxia, metabolic imbalance, altered cerebral blood flow, or the direct neurotoxic effects of alcohol on brain tissue—but the observation that alcoholics experience such changes, sometimes very drastic ones, is consistently reported. There is even growing evidence (Ryan & Butters, 1980; 1983) that these changes are not restricted to aged alcoholics, but rather may appear relatively early in the drinking career.

These neuropsychological consequences of alcohol abuse have important implications for both treatment planning and for the patient's postdischarge adjustment. We suggest that clinical interviews, a careful mental status examination, and a review of risk factors (e.g., duration of alcohol problem, nonbeverage alcohol and nonalcohol drug use, head trauma, etc.) be used to assess the need for further study. Should this indication prove positive, a number of measures can be called upon to clarify the patient's neuropsychological status. These include such measures as the EEG or CAT-scan, but the Halstead-Reitan Battery, Luria-Nebraska or Bender-Gestalt tests may prove quite adequate.

Medical consequences. A number of organ systems are vulnerable to alcohol and to the lifestyle implications of its abuse. Damage to these systems has important consequences for treatment selection (e.g., cardiac contraindications of disulfiram), risks associated with relapse, and even patient mortality, and deserves careful medical screening. Hepatic functioning is one of the most sensitive to alcohol. Abnormality of liver metabolytes and cirrhotic liver structures can be assessed by physical examination, liver function tests, and biopsy. The cardiovascular system, however, is also vulnerable, the most severe condition probably being alcoholic cardiomyopathy, a life-threatening degenerative disease of the heart muscle. Nervous system disorders can also result from alcohol abuse; probably the most common, and a cardinal sign of alcohol dependence, is peripheral neuropathy, a loss of motor and sensory function in the patient's limbs. Signs of these disorders should be carefully monitored, and medical consultation requested.

Integrating Assessment Findings

The model of assessment we have proposed is complex, involving analysis of each patient's drinking problems according to antecedent conditions, behavior, and consequences, and requiring attention to several domains within each one of these. According to our assessment plan, findings will be submitted from many disciplines, including nursing staff, clinicians, ancillary service staff, neuropsychologists and psychometrists, and medical specialists. Integrating these findings for the purpose of treatment and maintenance planning may be a weak link in this complex structure. However, several strategies may be useful to forge a coherent whole from this abundance of information.

Leaving the data in the hands of a broadly trained case manager, who may request the services of specialist-consultants, is one common alternative. Especially difficult diagnostic problems need to be brought to the attention of case conferences for a presentation of the data. This is followed with an interview of the patient and a discussion and synthesis of the case material. Finally, use of multidisciplinary treatment teams, with representatives from a number of specialized disciplines, is an increasingly common choice. We realize that the strategy in any given instance may depend largely on such factors as staffing strength and simple institutional tradition. We wish to emphasize two points, however. First is that a modern approach to the assessment of drinking problems requires the search for very diverse, and perhaps discrepant, pieces of information; that is, the diagnostic tasks must at first be analyzed and dispersed. Second point is that, following these diverse procedures, the information must be synthesized and collected into a body that suggests strategies for further assessment, treatment, and maintenance.

DESCRIPTION OF BEHAVIORAL TREATMENTS

Recent thinking about stages in the process of change for a person with a drinking problem (Goldstein & Marlatt, 1985; Prochaska & DiClemente, 1983) is useful for defining the goals of inpatient behavioral treatment of alcoholism. Briefly stated, the process of change for someone with a drinking (or other addictive behavior) problem has three stages: (1) initial commitment to change—recognizing that a problem exists and deciding to do something about it, (2) the change itself—stopping abusive drinking and stabilizing this change for at least a few months, and (3) the long-term maintenance of change.

Given this analysis, what role should inpatient behavioral treatment of alcoholism play in the change process for a person with a serious alcohol problem? A relatively brief three- to four-week inpatient treatment should concentrate on facilitating and consolidating the patient's initial commitment to change, starting the change in drinking behavior, and planning for continued improvement. Specifically, the treatment program's goals are to: (1) enhance the individual's recognition of the extent of his or her alcohol problem, consolidate decision-making about the goal for the drinking behavior, and strengthen commitment to the change in drinking; (2) begin stabilizing change in the drinking problem by decreasing the desire for alcohol, teaching skills to deal with high-risk situations for return to drinking, and strengthening behaviors incompatible with abusive drinking; (3) plan aftercare for further stabilization of change and to promote long-term maintenance. Of course, patients who are physically addicted to alcohol must be detoxified and fully recovered from any alcohol withdrawal syndrome before starting inpatient treatment of the type we have described.

Facilitating and Consolidating Commitment to Change in Drinking

When people are voluntarily admitted to an inpatient program that specializes in alcoholism treatment, they already recognize that they have a drinking problem and need to change. For the patient on a general psychiatric ward (not specializing in alcoholism), although often some initial awareness has begun, this may be more limited because the process of admission has not explicitly labeled the problem as alcohol-related. In both cases, usually much remains to be done to facilitate awareness of the extent and seriousness of the alcohol problem and to consolidate commitment to change.

Often in traditional nonbehavioral treatment programs, staff efforts to promote this goal consist of highly emotionally charged exhortation and confrontation to get the patient to accept the label of "alcoholic." Once the patient accepts this label, staff pay little attention to the idiosyncratic reasons that motivate an individual patient's problem recognition and commitment to change. We suggest an alternative approach that attempts to intensify patients' awareness of the their problem and to make explicit their reasons for not drinking. In this approach, completing and reviewing the assessment results with patients can be used to good advantage to intensify their awareness of the specific negative effects that alcohol has had on their lives. For example, reviewing the results of liver function and other medical tests, neuropsychological testing, and drinking history interviews can provide multiple examples of the negative effects drinking has had on the patient. Similarly, a score card showing the number of days and percent of the previous year spent drinking in light and heavy quantities or incarcerated for alcohol-related reasons generally impresses patients with the extent of their drinking. The therapist gives this feedback in the assessment of a matter-of-fact, nonjudgmental manner, and elicits and discusses the patient's reaction to the feedback. William Miller (1983) describes in detail a similar approach that he calls "motivational interviewing." In addition to carefully reviewing the assessment with the patient, a number of other methods are useful in facilitating commitment to change.

Alcohol education about the long-term negative consequences of excessive alcohol use may help patients strengthen their commitment to not drinking. This includes detailed information about long-range effects of prolonged alcohol abuse on physical health, social and occupational functioning, family life, and psychological well-being. Videotape, a good medium for presenting alcohol education material in a time-efficient and standardized manner, has been found to be superior to live or written presentations of such material (Stalonas, Keane, & Foy, 1979). The alcohol education material is most useful when it is followed by a discussion with the patient in which the educational material is related directly to the specific experiences of the patient revealed by the assessment procedures. For example, information about alcohol-induced liver pathology can be related to the results of the patient's liver function tests by describing current liver functioning and what the likely effect will be of continued drinking and of abstinence from alcohol.

The *decision matrix* (Marlatt, 1982), can aid patients in clarifying their reasons for not drinking and incease commitment to abstinence. Table 7-1 illustrates a sample decision matrix taken from a patient described in the case illustration presented later in this chapter. In the use of the decision matrix the patient is asked to fill out each of the eight cells of the matrix with all the effects that are important to the patient. The therapist can assist in this process in three ways. First, the therapist can help the patient be as thorough as possible in listing all important, personally relevant consequences. In this regard, asking the patient to consider positive (and negative) consequences in each of the following categories, drawn from Janis's balance sheet procedure (Janis, 1982; Wheeler & Janis, 1980), can be helpful: gains (losses) to self, gains (losses to important others, approval (disapproval) from others, approval (disapproval) from self. Also by considering assessment information obtained earlier, the therapist may be able to suggest important consequences that have been omitted and might be considered. Second, the therapist can try to get patients to make each consequence as specific and emotionally meaningful as possible by asking them to provide more details about general statements (e.g., in place of "get along better at home" might go "fewer arguments with wife, can help children with homework, take son fishing like we used to," etc.) Third, the patient can be asked to assign numerical ratings to each of the positive and negative outcomes listed, and then to disclose to the therapist the reasons for the ranking. The overall goal of this process is to have the patient consider possible outcomes of the decision to drink or not in as complete, specific, and emotionally meaningful form as possible, and to share this decision-making with the therapist.

Stabilizing Change in the Drinking

Aversion Therapy to Decrease Desire for Alcohol

Aversion therapies attempt to create an aversion or distaste for alcoholic beverages, thus providing a substantial aid in stabilizing abstinence from alcohol while the alcoholic rearranges his or her life and develops behavioral patterns that are incompatible with alcohol abuse (Miller & Hester, 1980). Although the

Table 7-1
Decision Matrix for Stopping Drinking

	Immediate Consequences		Delayed Consequences	
	Positive	Negative	Positive	Negative
To continue or resume drinking	• relieve depression • escape negative feelings about marriage • relieve tension and fear of impending chest pain • ease initial conversation with clients • help forget job problems • ward off withdrawal symptoms	• verbal/physical abuse to wife • decrease awareness of "real" chest pain • impair judgement in negotiations with clients	• continued gratification	• more depressed suicidal urges/acts • divorce • increase cardiac problems, risk of death • harm professional reputation • job loss • stay addicted to alcohol
To stop drinking or remain abstinent	• talk better with wife • approval of wife and children • feel better physically • feel less depressed • alert with clients • self-worth	• initial tension with clients • hard to not drink when angry at wife	• chance of keeping wife and family • better cardiac functioning • keep job • rebuild reputation • don't commit suicide	• denial of gratification (becomes less intense over time)

original basis in Pavlovian concepts of conditioning has been questioned, aversion therapy is relatively simple procedurally. Alcoholic beverages are repeatedly paired with a very unpleasant stimulus—either (1) a nausea-producing drug, (2) aversive mental imagery, or (3) electrical stimulation. Since the use of electrical stimulation is relatively ineffective in comparison to alternative methods as an approach to abstinence, and an adequate understanding of why it seems to work for certain individuals is not available currently (Miller & Hester, 1980), we will not consider it further here.

Nausea-producing drugs. As described by Miller and Hester (1980), emetine hydrochloride, the most successfully used drug, is given by intramuscular injection. Prior to the onset of nausea and vomiting, the patient consumes alcoholic drinks which he or she later vomits. Typically about five conditioning sessions are held while the patient is hospitalized, and additional booster sessions are often scheduled at regular intervals after discharge. Due to the potential toxic effects of emetine at the high doses used in some treatment centers, an alternative medically conservative procedure has been developed that produces equivalent nausea by using syrup of ipecac and low doses of emetine (Baker, Cannon, Stephenson, & Droubay, 1978). Of course, appropriate medical evaluation and informed consent procedures must be followed in the use of emetine aversion conditioning. A further note of caution comes from a recent review indicating relative success for these procedures with married, employed alcoholics of middle class or higher socioeconomic status, but unclear effectiveness for other populations (Miller & Hester, 1980). However, more recent studies question the influence of these patient characteristics on the outcomes of aversion therapy (Wiens & Menustik, 1983). Thus, the question of which type of patient is likely to benefit from such treatment remains unclear.

Aversive imagery. Covert sensitization (Cautela, 1966) involves the therapist verbally presenting imagery of alcohol and drinking scenes that are associated with imagined nausea and vomiting and other unpleasant scenes. The rationale for covert sensitization is similar to that of emetine chemical aversion in that both seek to condition feelings of nausea to the taste and smell of alcoholic beverages. Elkins and Murdock (1977) indicate that having the alcoholic imagine actually *tasting* the alcohol is essential to the development of conditioned nausea (i.e., becoming nauseous to images of alcohol alone without having to explicitly imagine feeling ill and vomiting). Alcoholics who develop such conditioned nausea to alcohol during covert sensitization treatment have better long-term outcomes than those who do not. Despite the fact that research data are inadequate to reach firm conclusions about the effectiveness of covert sensitization, implementation of this procedure is easier and applicable to more patients than emetine aversion.

Alternative Skills to Deal with Likely Precipitants of Renewed Alcohol Use

Many alcoholics use alcohol as a coping device for dealing with feelings of tension and anxiety, interpersonal stress, and various other life problems. As Marlatt (1982) has shown, such situations present abstinent alcoholics with a high risk of relapse when they are encountered after discharge from the hospital. This rationale and supportive data from outcome studies (e.g., Chaney, O'Leary, & Marlatt, 1978) suggest that inpatient behavioral programs should try to teach their patients alternative skills for dealing with stressful situations.

Relaxation training and systematic desensitization. As Miller and Mastria (1977) point out, relaxation training can be used to help alcoholics reduce their general level of tension and anxiety, reduce cravings and urges to drink, get to sleep more easily, and reduce arousal when confronted with a stressful situation (e.g., job interview). Although controlled studies have shown relaxation training to have quite a modest impact on treatment outcome (Miller & Hester, 1980), we believe on the basis of our clinical experience that relaxation training can be quite valuable as *part* of a multimodal program for patients who show a specific need for this skill. Supporting this notion, systematic desensitization, in which relaxation is paired with specific environmental stimuli (or imagined scenes of such stimuli) that provoke feelings of tension or anxiety in the patient, has shown more promising results than relaxation alone as a component of multimodal programs (Miller & Hester, 1980).

Social skills training. A number of findings support the use of social skills training with alcoholics: (1) alcoholics report significantly greater discomfort in situations requiring *negative* assertion (i.e., refusing an unreasonable request) than nonalcoholics; (2) interpersonal conflict and social pressure to drink are important precipitants of relapse (Marlatt, 1982); (3) response latency for assertive response to role-played scenes while hospitalized significantly predict treatment outcome one year after discharge (Chaney et al., 1978); and (4) practice of assertiveness skills to deal with general interpersonal stressors, and to refuse drinks, effectively benefits alcoholics' treatment outcomes (Van Hasselt, Hersen, & Milliones, 1978).

In the present authors' experience, a group format has been extremely useful in teaching alcoholics social skills (Fortgang, O'Farrell, Cutter, & Bayog, 1981). First, the therapist presents the rationale for social skills training and offers examples of problematic situations. The components of an effective response to situations involving unreasonable requests or pressure to drink are generally written on the board or a flipchart, and include (1) eye contact; (2) convincing affect (i.e., loudness and tone of voice, facial expression, gestures and posture); (3) refusal of the request; (4) request for change in behavior (e.g., in response to drink pressure, "Please, in the future, don't tempt me by asking me to drink. Also, could you tell the other guys not to ask me"); and (5) change the subject and suggest an alternative activity other than drinking (in the case of drink pressure situations).

Next, to overcome patients' initial reluctance to engage in behavioral rehearsal, structured role-play situations, or "scenes," with preset roles, can be used to help reduce anxiety and get the group started role-playing. The following are two sample scenes taken from those we and others (Eisler, Hersen, Miller, & Blanchard, 1975; Foy, Miller, Eisler, & O'Toole, 1976) have used:

Assertiveness scene. You are having lunch with a friend when suddenly he asks you if you would lend him $30 until he gets paid next week. You have the money, but were planning on spending it on something for yourself. Your friend says *(spoken by role partner):* "Please lend me the money; I'll pay you back next week."

Drink refusal scene. At a social gathering, a drinking friend that you have not seen in some time comes over to you with a bottle of liquor. He has been talking to a couple of other old drinking companions. You do not want to drink. He says *(spoken by role partner):*

"It sure has been a long time since we've had a drink together. How about having a couple of rounds with us?"

Follow-up remark by role partner if subject initially refuses: "What kind of man are you who won't drink with his friends?"

In using these structured scenes, the therapist describes to the group what will happen in the role-play, gets volunteers to play the roles of protagonist (i.e., drink pusher or maker of unreasonable request) and alcoholic, narrates the scene and cues the protagonist to deliver his or her lines, and provides feedback on the alcoholic patient's response. In providing feedback, the therapist refers to the components of assertiveness written on the board or chart, provides positive feedback first, followed by suggestions for improvement, and elicits feedback from other group members about the effectiveness of the patient's response. "Instant replays" are conducted, each followed by feedback, until the patient's performance improves to an acceptable level. To make the initial role-playing even less threatening and to provide more instructions and modeling in the desired response, the therapist can first play the role of the patient and demonstrate poor quality responses, and ask then the group for criticisms. Then the scene can be re-played a few times, showing improvement on a specific component of assertive behavior. Trainers should use personally relevant content for each patient in the role-played scenes and combine role-playing with a discussion of the issues raised in the role-play. In addition, breaking into small subgroups or using individual sessions can provide patients with intensive coaching and practice in dealing with the specific troublesome situations they are likely to encounter after hospital discharge.

Problem-solving skills training. When confronted by a problem, alcoholics often act impulsively with little thought to the consequences of their actions and without considering a range of alternative solutions. This often leads to unsatisfactory solutions to problems, especially when drinking is the immediate solution used to avoid dealing with the problem temporarily. Teaching alcoholics to adopt a problem-solving orientation (cf. Goldfried & Davison, 1976) to stressful situations can be very useful in overcoming such maladaptive responses. In both individual and group sessions with our patients, we teach them to use four standard steps in the problem solving process: (1) list all possible solutions; (2) judge the consequences (positive and negative, short-term and long-term) of each solution; (3) rank order the solution from first choice to last choice in terms of their likely overall outcomes; and (4) take action with the first ranked solution, and if that fails, go to the second solution or restart the problem-solving process. These steps are listed on the blackboard or flipchart in the room where the session takes place. In an example from one of our inpatient behavioral groups, an alcoholic recounted an experience in which his car, which he drove to work, had broken down at a time when he did not have sufficient money to pay to have it repaired. Feeling frustrated and uncertain, he had a few drinks "to think about what to do," kept on drinking, and did not report to work or call his employer. As a consequence, he lost the job and began a serious drinking binge. Table 7-2

Table 7-2
Sample Problem-Solving Format

Possible Solution	Positive Consequences	Negtive Consequences
A. Borrow money for the repair.	Could use car again soon.	Don't know when I could pay it back, would feel indebted.
B. Borrow friend's car.	Would have transportation.	Would be taking on responsibility for his car. He might need it at times.
C. Use public transportation until next paycheck.	Would have transportation, no urgency on car, costs little.	Takes longer to get there, would have to allow more time; crowded, less convenient.
D. Drink	Would temporarily forget; wouldn't care.	Would still have no car, lose job, lose even more money, etc.

displays the problem-solving format constructed when this problem was discussed in the group. After some discussion, the potential solutions were ranked as follows (1) public transportation, (2) borrow car, (3) borrow money, (4) drink. When asked in the group, he indicated he had not considered public transportation when the problem had occurred. "Stop and think before you drink" in response to a problem was how this alcoholic described what he learned from this group therapy session.

Strengthening Behaviors Incompatible with Excessive Alcohol Use

Vocational assistance. When admitted for inpatient treatment, alcoholics often are unemployed, working in jobs that promote drinking, or have work-related problems that have precipitated abusive drinking both on and off the job. Effective methods for helping alcoholics learn skills needed to find and keep a job, an important part of a comprehensive inpatient treatment program, have been developed by behavior therapists. Azrin's behavioral approach to vocational counseling, called a job-finding club (Azrin, Flores, & Kaplan, 1975), has been successfully used with hospitalized alcoholics (Azrin, 1976; Hunt & Azrin, 1973). This approach emphasizes use of standardized procedures and group social reinforcement to help alcoholics to identify and pursue job leads. As described by Hunt and Azrin (1973), alcoholics are helped to prepare a resumé, phone all friends and relatives to ask for job leads, call the major employers in the area, place a "situations wanted" advertisement in the local papers, rehearse job interviews and phone calls, search want ads, place applications, and interview for available jobs. Consistent with the emphasis on social support, this program uses mutual assistance and sharing a job leads among job-seekers, a "buddy" system, family support, is done in a group setting, and is monitored in all feasible respects by the counselor. While the alcoholic engages in the above procedures, a counselor or fellow job club group member is physically present and actively assists the client. For example, the counselor or "buddy" stands by while phone calls are made, role-plays interviews, escorts the alcoholic to the job interviews, and immediately following the interview, discusses the results. In addition, the hospital makes a phone readily available and arranges for typing and copying of resumés. Finally, to the extent possible, the types of jobs sought are designed to compete as strongly as possible with drinking. Such jobs are those that are full-time, permanent, reasonably satisfying, and well-paying, and performed in a highly visible social context. Two distinctive features strongly support the adoption of Azrin's methods by inpatient alcoholism programs: (1) extensive experimental evaluations have established the effectiveness of the approach, and (2) a 200-page detailed procedural manual with extensive appendices of all written materials used in inplementing the job club is available (Azrin & Besalel, 1980).

Many alcoholics also need to learn skills to cope with interpersonal and other work-related problems that can lead to renewed drinking. Using the general social skills training approach described above, Foy and colleagues (Foy, Massey, Duer, Ross, & Wooten, 1979) taught their hospitalized alcoholic patients more effective responses to difficult interpersonal situations on the job. Patients role-played stressful job situations (e.g., repeated pressure to do unwanted overtime work) they had experienced or might encounter, and received modeling, feedback, and coaching from the counselor to help them respond more satisfactorily. Miller and Mastria (1977) point to additional work-related problem areas that may lead to drinking and that can be addressed profitably with alcoholics. These include (1) reviewing work schedule and responsibilities to prevent overload, and planning a realistic workload and schedule; (2) rearranging travel routes to and from work to avoid taverns, lounges, or liquor stores that may be a temptation for drinking; (3) dealing with work-related lunches and meetings where alcohol is available; and (4) coping with the stress, loneliness, and availability of liquor associated with work-related travel and conventions.

Improving marital and family relationships. A number of converging lines of evidence indicate the need to improve alcoholics' marital and family relationships. Many alcoholics have extensive marital and family problems (e.g., Billings, Kessler, Gomberg, & Weiner, 1979), and positive marital and family adjustment is associated with better alcoholism treatment outcomes at follow-up (e.g., Finney, Moos, & Mewborn, 1980). Disturbed marital and family interaction often precipitates renewed drinking by abstinent alcoholics (Hore, 1971a, 1971b; Marlatt, 1982). Finally, marital and family therapy have improved alcoholism treatment outcome in several studies (e.g., Steinglass, 1976). Given the obvious need, what can be done in a brief inpatient stay to achieve the two goals of (1) mobilizing the spouse and family to support the alcoholic in adhering to the difficult and stressful decision to stop drinking, and (2) improving marital/family relationships? A series of meetings with the alcoholic and spouse/family can get the couple or family firmly started on a new alcohol-free life together and prepare them for marital/family therapy on an outpatient basis when indicated.

The general purpose of inpatient alcohol-focused marital/family treatment sessions is to specify behavioral changes needed in the alcoholic or the family members that would help achieve the drinking goal. Although needed changes vary widely, certain issues occur with sufficient frequency that they should probably be addressed with most cases. For instance, possible exposure to alcoholic beverages and alcohol-related situations should be discussed. The couple should decide if the nonalcoholic spouse will drink alcoholic beverages in the alcoholic's presence, whether alcoholic beverages will be kept and served at home, if the couple will attend social gatherings involving alcohol, and how to deal with these situations. Particular persons, gatherings, or circumstances that are likely to be particularly stressful should be identified and a plan developed to deal with them.

Maladaptive couple interactions related to alcohol (e.g., nagging about past drinking but ignoring sober behavior) also need to be addressed, since arguments, tension, and negative feelings can precipitate more abusive drinking. Therapists need to confront such patterns and provide specific procedures for the couple to use in difficult situations. For example, Lazarus (1968) and others (Cheek, Franks, Burtle, & Laucius, 1971) have used relaxation training and systematic desensitization to help spouses control their fear and anger about the alcoholic's drinking. Similarly, Eisler and colleagues (Eisler, Miller, Hersen, & Alford, 1974) taught the alcoholic to request assertively that the spouse refrain from comments about drinking. Written behavioral contracts also can be used to structure the spouse's and the alcoholic's role in the recovery process. The Antabuse Contract (described briefly above and in more detail elsewhere: O'Farrell & Bayog, 1984) and Kivlahan and Shapiro's (personal communication, May 18, 1984) Sobriety Trust Contract (in which the alcoholic reiterates his or her desire not to drink once each day in the presence of the spouse, who agrees not to mention past or "possible" future drinking) are examples of such agreements. In our experience, successful agreements, although they may differ in various ways (see O'Farrell, in press b, for other examples) have a number of common elements that make them useful. The drinking behavior goal is made explicit. Specific behaviors for each spouse to help achieve this goal are also detailed. The contract provides alternative behaviors to negative interactions about drinking. Finally, and quite importantly, the agreement decreases the nonalcoholic spouse's anxiety and need to control the alcoholic and his or her drinking.

Preparations for possible outpatient marital therapy that can be accomplished during inpatient treatment include education about the need for such therapy and a detailed assessment of the marital relationship. A brief educational presentation about the marital stress common to the early period of sobriety and the role of marital therapy in coping with this stress and resolving other relationship issues is described in detail elsewhere (O'Farrell & Cutter, 1984). In terms of relationship assessment, the first author frequently conducts a couple evaluation with the alcoholic and spouse in which each spouse separately completes a series of questionnaires about his or her marriage. Assessment includes: (1) the Marital Adjustment Test (Locke & Wallace, 1959), to determine overall relationship satisfaction and areas of disagreement, (2) the Marital Status Inventory (Weiss & Cerretto, 1980), to assess steps toward separation and divorce, (3) the Areas of Change Questionnaire (Margolin, Talovic, & Weinstein, 1983), to establish relationship changes desired, (4) the Conflict Tactics Scale (Straus, 1979) to assess the extent of verbal and physical abuse, and (5) a Sexual Adjustment Questionnaire (O'Farrell, Kleinke, & Cutter, 1984). A videotaped sample of communication while the couple discusses a current marital problem also is obtained. Each spouse is interviewed separately to review questionnaire responses and to provide an opportunity to clarify anything that is ambiguous. After the assessment information has been gathered and analyzed by the therapist, a feedback session is held in which the therapist shares impressions of the nature and severity of the drinking and marital prolems and invites the couple to respond to these impressions. At the end of the feedback session the couple decides whether or not they will begin short-term marital therapy on an outpatient basis. If the decision is to start marital therapy, behavioral marital therapy procedures described elsewhere (O'Farrell, 1985) may be useful. For those not pursuing marital therapy further, a behavioral contract to structure each spouse's role in the recovery process, as described above, can be negotiated if this has not already been done.

Lifestyle analysis and planned modification. Marlatt (1982) has described the role of lifestyle imbalance in setting the stage for relapse. According to this analysis, a lifestyle with a preponderance of activities perceived as external demands (or "shoulds," e.g., routine work, household chores, etc.) over activities engaged in for pleasure of self-fulfillment (or "wants") often leaves the individual feeling deprived, with a corresponding desire for indulgence and gratification. A somewhat different lifestyle pattern we have observed, which has similar negative effects, is that of the individual for whom long stretches of unstructured, unrewarding free time is the problem. In such cases, "shoulds" are not excessive, but "wants" are not often fulfilled either. Cautela's (1984) notion of what he calls the "general level of reinforcement" in an individual's life, if at too low a level, can lead to problematic self-indulgent behavior.

Although hospital treatment does not permit establishing and monitoring new daily lifestyle patterns because the time is too brief and patients are removed from their usual environment, an inpatient stay does provide an opportunity to help them review their daily lifestyles and plan needed changes. For patients with unstructured free time, the task is to identify meaningful activities (e.g., a volunteer job) and potentially pleasurable leisure time activities that are incompatible with drinking. For patients whose lifestyle is characterized by a preponderance of "shoulds" and a dearth of "wants," Marlatt (1982) suggests helping them restructure their daily lives to make room for physical exercise (e.g., jogging), meditation or relaxation, or other "positive addictions" (Glasser, 1976), as well as idiosyncratic pleasurable nondrinking activities. Ideally, such activities should be planned for times when the individual has been in the habit of drinking to take a "time out" from the stresses of excessive perceived obligatory duties.

Pharmacology

Antabuse. Antabuse (Disulfiram), a drug that produces extreme nausea and sickness when the person taking the drug ingests alcohol, is widely used in alcoholism treatment as a deterrent to drinking for persons with a goal of abstinence. Unfortunately, Antabuse therapy is not always effective because the alcoholic frequently discontinues the drug prematurely (Lundwall & Baekland, 1971). Behavior therapists have used a variety of contingency contracting procedures to help maintain Antabuse ingestion that can be initiated during inpatient treatment and continued after discharge from the hospital. In such procedures, the alcoholic agrees to take Antabuse daily in the presence of another person who agrees to provide certain benefits to the alcoholic. For example, a contract can be negotiated in which an employer allows the alcoholic to work each day if the job supervisor observes Antabuse ingestion. Similarly, a spouse or family member may agree that the alcoholic can live at home, and provide praise and refrain from nagging about drinking. When a significant other is not available for daily Antabuse observation, a "self-contract" can also be used. Such an agreement involves specifying in writing the minimum amount of time the patient plans to take Antabuse and involves daily record keeping. The record serves as feedback to patients that they have maintained their commitments. Finally, a monetary deposit made at the outset and earned back through daily compliance with Antabuse can be added to any of the Antabuse contracting procedures.

Psychotropic Medications. A variety of drugs have been used widely in the treatment of alcoholism including minor tranquilizers (e.g., Valium, Librium), antidepressants (e.g., Elavil), lithium, and antipsychotic medications. The general rationale for the use of such medications is that they alleviate problematic affective states that lead to drinking in alcoholics. Unfortunately, recent reviews of the literature indicate little support for this widespread practice. Rada and Kellner (1979) conclude that, "No drug has been conclusively shown to attenuate drinking in controlled studies, and there is little evidence that the elimination of target (affective) symptoms improves the recidivision rate. Presently there apprears to be a discrepancy between clinical practice and research findings" (p 129). Similarly, Miller and Hester (1980) argue that, "The routine prescription of psychotropic medications for problem drinkers remains a practice without scientific support" (p 29). On the basis of these reviews, we feel that use of any psychotropic medication with an alcoholic is justified only when a very careful diagnostic assessment reveals a drug-treatable disorder in addition to the alcoholism. For example, an alcoholic who suffers from a bipolar affective disorder could be prescribed lithium.

Planning Aftercare and Postdischarge Life

Will changes in drinking begun during inpatient treatment continue once the patient is discharged from the hospital? Carefully formulating specific plans for aftercare and postdischarge life with the alcoholic is one of the most important tasks the inpatient therapist has in providing an affirmative answer to this question. Aftercare, which consists of continued help for the alcohol problem, may include any of the following: attendance at Alcoholics Anonymous, outpatient alcoholism counseling, halfway house placement, marital/family therapy, continued Antabuse, and booster sessions for further aversion therapy. The specific type of aftercare should be determined as early during inpatient treatment as possible so that the patient can have at least one aftercare program visit prior to discharge from the hospital. It is highly desirable that the aftercare plan established be able to be continued for a period of one to five years. Logistical factors such as transportation and cost also must be considered carefully to insure they do not present barriers to continued aftercare. Ideally, the inpatient counselor and the patient should meet with the outpatient counselor to share what the patient learned about his or her alcohol problem during inpatient treatment and the patient's plans for postdischarge life. The inpatient counselor can follow-up by phone four to six weeks after discharge to determine whether the aftercare planned and started while in the hospital has been continued. In addition to specific aftercare planning, the patient needs to have a written detailed plan of life changes he or she plans to make to help achieve the drinking behavior goal. Examples of such changes include removing all alcoholic beverages from living quarters, joining an exercise class or working out at a gym after work rather than drinking, and discontinuing contact with alcoholic acquaintances. The specific changes needed emerge from the assessment and treatment conducted during the inpatient stay. The changes should be started while the patient is still in the hospital when possible, and the counselor can inquire about the implementation of these planned changes during the follow-up contact four to six weeks after discharge.

CASE ILLUSTRATION

Identifying Information

Mr. V was a 45-year-old, unemployed, white male, civil engineer and father of six children, ages 13 to 21, four of whom lived at home with their mother, from whom the patient had been separated for five months at the time of his admission to the medical service of the hospital. Events immediately leading to Mr. V's hospitalization were (1) his oldest son had a court hearing following an arrest for theft; (2) he and his wife had argued about the son's difficulties; (3) he had returned to the family home and destroyed several articles of his wife's clothing, in response to which his wife had initiated a court petition for legal separation;

and (4) Mr. V had experienced thoughts of suicide, including an idea of purchasing a gun for this purpose. Mr. V's complaints at the time of admission (as taken from the admitting summary) were difficulty sleeping, tenseness, depression, chest pains, and excessive alcohol use of from one to two quarts of rum daily for four-and-a-half months prior to admission. Given his chest pains and a history of two serious heart attacks and two other episodes of severe chest pain requiring hospitalization in the previous 12 years, the patient was admitted to the medical service for detoxification from alcohol and close monitoring of his cardiac status. After being successfully detoxified from alcohol and completing repeated testing to insure his cardiac condition was stable, the patient entered our inpatient alcoholism treatment program.

Drinking History and Current Status

Mr. V began drinking at age 15 at parties during high school, but did not feel it was a problem then or later during military service and college. His drinking started to increase around age 30, when his work as an engineer began to involve increased drinking with clients and associates. At age 36, when the patient had his first heart attack, his physician advised him to stop drinking, a warning that went unheeded. During the next six years he suffered more cardiac problems and suffered from a ruptured disk that required a spinal fusion. Drinking continued to increase. Despite the extensive history of heavy drinking, both Mr. V and his wife dated onset of what they considered a drinking problem to the period when at age 42, after suffering the health problems, the patient lost his job as a city engineer due to a new mayor, and his oldest son was arrested. Mr. V's drinking escalated to a quart or more per day of rum, and on occasion he became verbally abusive and threatening to his wife, especially when they argued about the oldest son's problems or Mr. V's excessive drinking.

Approximately 18 months prior to the present hospital admission, the patient again suffered serious chest pain and, when his physician diagnosed possible alcoholic cardiomyopathy, entered a seven-day detoxification program. He did not drink and attended Alcoholics Anonymous sporadically for six weeks after his first alcoholic treatment, but resumed drinking after an argument with his wife. The patient found a new job and resumed heavy drinking. Approximately 14 months prior to the present admission, patient and wife were arguing frequently and, after an incident in which the patient became extremely abusive and threatening, the couple separated just prior to their 25th wedding anniversary and remained apart for two months. Six months after their reconciliation, and approximately five months prior to the present admission, Mr. V quit his job after his boss told him he should get help for his drinking problem, and the couple again separated. The patient continued to drink daily and the quantity increased to two quarts of rum on many days. He became increasingly depressed and was very unhappy and dissatisfied with the separation from his wife and children. When his wife refused to let him visit her and the children over the New Year holiday because he was drinking heavily, he inflicted a superficial gash on his wrist with a razor blade and called his wife asking her to contact the police. For two months after this, he remained separated from his wife and family, worked at a new job, and continued drinking very heavily, until the events (described above) that immediately preceded his admission to the hospital.

Assessment Results

Results of the various assessment procedures conducted were consistent with the history reported above. Medical testing and evaluation revealed elevated liver enzymes without liver pathology and a history of coronary artery disease complicated by alcoholic cardiomyopathy. In terms of drinking behavior, the patient's responses to the Time-Line drinking interview (O'Farrell, Cutter, Bayog, Dentch, & Fortgang, 1984) showed that he had spent 80 percent of the previous year drinking, that when drinking he was a daily drinker consuming rum and Coke in quantities from one to two quarts of rum daily, and that he had experienced blackouts and severe shakes and sweats when trying to stop drinking on his own. On the MAST, he received a score of 47, indicating multiple and serious consequences from alcohol abuse. A diagnostic interview was conducted by a psychiatrist in response to patient's complaints of depression, sleep disturbance, and suicidal ideation, and his request for antidepressant medication. The conclusions were that alcohol dependence was the primary diagnosis and that "depression" and other complaints were caused by the alcohol problem and did not represent an affective disorder for which an antidepressant would be helpful. In addition, an obsessive–compulsive personality disorder was suggested as a possible secondary diagnosis. Finally, an evaluation of the marital relationship was conducted, the results of which are presented below in the description of the marital therapy sessions.

Reviewing the assessment and history materials indicated a number of antecedents that had been associated with alcohol consumption. For each antecedent the short-term consequence of the drinking had brought some temporary improvement but the longer-term consequences had been to create or exacerbate serious life problems. The following analysis was presented to Mr. V, and he concurred with this formulation of factors involved in his drinking:

1. He was a rigid, perfectionist individual who experienced considerable anxiety and both mental and physical (muscular) tension in response to daily life events. Alcohol helped temporarily to relieve such tension. In particular, after he had his first episode of chest pain he became quite fearful when he experienced muscular tension that this might lead to another heart attack. Alcohol relieved the tension and his fears about a heart attack in the short run, but exacerbated his heart problem, leading to alcoholic cardiomyopathy in the long run.
2. Business-related social drinking with clients and associates was customary in his work and seemed to help these relationships initially. As time went on, he developed a reputation as a heavy drinker that he reluctantly admitted

may have contributed to his loss of the town engineer position and his leaving the job after that. Drinking helped relieve his distress over this job instability but cost him his current job when he had to enter the hospital for alcoholism treatment.

3. Marital conflict clearly contributed to the drinking, which brought temporary escape from the feelings of frustration, anger, and loss associated with these conflicts. In fact, he felt his marital and family problems were the most important contributors to his drinking problem. Eventually, drinking led to increasingly more frequent and severe abusive and destructive outbursts at his wife, which led to police intervention, marital separation, and finally a court petition awaiting a hearing for legal separation and most likely eventual divorce.
4. The losses experienced led to feelings of depression, sadness, and guilt, at first relieved by, and later seriously increased by, alcohol. When intoxicated he had made a suicidal gesture, and serious suicidal ideas continued to frighten the patient when he was abstinent.
5. He had drunk in sufficiently large quantities so that he had become physically dependent on alcohol. Some of his drinking was done to decrease discomfort associated with falling blood alcohol levels (i.e., to ward off withdrawal symptoms).

Treatment

Inpatient alcoholism treatment consisted of (1) alcohol education, (2) individual and group behavioral therapy to clarify his decision about drinking and to provide alternative behaviors for use to deal with problematic antecedents noted above, (3) marital counseling, (4) Antabuse, and (5) planning for aftercare. Vocational assistance was offered since he was unemployed, but he declined, saying he did not need this, and apparently he was correct. He had located some promising job leads by the time of discharge and started work a few weeks later.

Alcohol education. The patient attended a comprehensive alcohol education program and chose four aspects of the material that were particularly meaningful to him to discuss with his therapist. The medical consequences of excessive alcohol use interested the patient, as he had been a medical technician in the military. The potentially life-threatening effects of alcohol to his heart and the potential of eventual liver damage if he continued excessive drinking proved very important to him. The effects of alcohol on mood and affective state, specifically the immediate positive and delayed deleterious effects, and the elevated risk of suicide among middle-aged, divorced, male alcoholics, was a second area he found particularly important. A third area was alcoholism and marriage, specifically the effect of marital conflicts on drinking and common stages in a wife's reaction to her husband's alcoholism (Jackson, 1954). In relation to the latter, the patient was impressed by the information that the greater the alcohol-related marital stressors (especially verbal and physical abuse and job/financial instability), the more likely the marriage would end in divorce (O'Farrell, Harrison, & Cutter, 1981). Finally, the educational material on Antabuse led to a request to start this drug immediately.

Individual and group behavior therapy. These discussions of the educational material and the review of the assessment and history information resulted in the decision matrix about drinking presented in Table 7-1. The patient said he felt that unless he stopped drinking he could not solve any of the life problems facing him, and that drinking would only make them much worse. He very much wanted to regain his wife and family and provide a stable life for his children, and secondarily to restore his professional reputation. To him, Antabuse seemed like the one way he might manage to remain abstinent, but he almost was refused a prescription. The prescribing physician was concerned that if the patient drank on Antabuse the reaction would kill him, and that Antabuse might have cardiac side effects that could be dangerous in this patient's case. After a cardiology consultation ruled out the side effects as a concern, and the patient insisted that he understood the seriousness of an Antabuse reaction for him, that continued drinking also was life threatening for him, and that he would sign a statement relieving the physician of responsibility for any negative consequences from Antabuse, he received the prescription a week before discharge.

The behavioral therapy group in which the patient participated, described in more detail elsewhere (Fortgang et al., 1981), consisted of fifteen 90-minute sessions devoted to (1) relaxation training; (2) acquisition of problem-solving skills as an alternative to drinking in problematical situations; (3) training, through behavioral rehearsal, in assertiveness and drink refusal; and (4) instruction in self-control skills, including the use of a contract with a significant other to maintain Antabuse ingestion. Since the patient's individual therapist was also a cotherapist in the group, group material of particular relevance was discussed in individual therapy sessions to determine how it applied to specific situations in the patient's life. Relaxation to cope with anxiety and tension and the use of problem-solving to think through alternative ways to deal with work and other situations that frequently caused the patient considerable worry and distress both proved helpful. Drink refusal training for work-related social situations was the focus of repeated role-playing of specific past and likely future situations in individual sessions after the concept was introduced in the group. Finally, the patient indicated strong interest in negotiating an Antabuse contract with his wife, but the therapist did not encourage this because it appeared for most of the inpatient stay that he would not be medically cleared for Antabuse.

Behavioral marital therapy. Six marital sessions with the patient and his wife were conducted by the first author. At the first couple interview, both husband and wife indicated they were willing to try marital therapy to see whether their relationship could be improved enough to justify keeping their marriage intact. The husband was relieved, but then insisted he wanted to return home to live after discharge while they continued for a "trial period" together. The wife refused, saying she was not ready to have the patient back home—she needed time to get over her bitterness about the husband's recent destructive behavior and to feel more secure that she could trust him not to drink. The wife also indicated that the marital separation had been very difficult for her financially and emotionally, and that having to make a decision about the future of their relationship was overwhelming. At the end of the first session, we agreed to meet conjointly (1) to evaluate briefly what needed to be changed in their relationship in addition to the husband's drinking, (2) to attempt to make weekend visits pleasant times for each other to provide an incentive for further reconciliation, and (3) to start communication training so the couple could discuss constructively difficult issues they would face if they went back to living together. In addition, it was agreed that they would not discuss past negative events or the decision of if or when husband would return home to live.

On the Locke-Wallace Marital Adjustment Test (MAT), the wife received a score of 28, indicating extremely poor adjustment. Specifically, her MAT answers indicated that: she was "very unhappy" in the marriage, experienced very frequent disagreement about most aspects of the relationship (e.g., sex, money, friends), never went out with her husband and rarely confided in him, and would marry a different person if she had her life to live over. The husband's MAT score of 84, while clearly indicating a distressed relationship (as do scores <100) and specifying similar problem areas as those rated by the wife, showed an awareness of less intense disagreement and turmoil than perceived by the wife. Similarly, on the Marital Status Inventory (which measures actions taken toward divorce), the wife scored 13 (indicating she had completed all steps but actually filing for divorce). The husband scored 5, indicating serious consideration of the possibility of divorce, but much less action in this direction than had been taken by the wife.

Treatment sessions were spent in planning weekend visits, for which the couple was assigned homework of engaging in an enjoyable recreational activity together, recording pleasing behavior of their partner that each spouse noticed, and setting aside four hours of "caring time" to do something special for one other. These assignments were reviewed after each weekend visit and used as the vehicle for practicing communication skills of listening and expressing feelings directly. Although both spouses reported positive reactions to the couple sessions, at the start of the session held one week prior to scheduled hospital discharge, the wife still was quite reluctant to have her husband return home, and the husband had arranged for another place to stay. During this session the husband announced that his request for Antabuse had been granted, and he proposed an Antabuse contract in which the wife would observe his Antabuse ingestion each day if he returned to live at home on discharge. He also indicated he expected to start a new job within a few weeks and emphasized the financial benefits of not having to maintain two households. The patient also stressed that he planned to attend weekly outpatient aftercare counseling sessions once discharged from the hospital, and that he wanted to continue therapy sessions for couples. After hearing this plan, the wife agreed the patient could return home to live, but indicated she was not interested in additional couples sessions at that time. She wanted to get their lives stabilized financially and observe continued abstinence on her husband's part before investing further in the marital relationship.

Aftercare proceeded as planned, and the wife met periodically with the patient and outpatient counselor so that compliance with the Antabuse contract could be monitored. Four months after discharge, the couple entered a behavioral marital therapy couples group, the format of which is described in detail elsewhere (O'Farrell & Cutter, 1984). At five years post-hospital discharge, the patient remains continuously abstinent and employed, with stable cardiac functioning. The couple's marriage has stabilized, no separations have occurred, and they have returned for further couples therapy sessions when needed to deal with major life stressors and unresolved relationship issues.

PROBLEM AREAS AND ISSUES

Currently, the most controversial issue in the alcoholism treatment field is whether the goal of all such treatment should be lifelong total abstinence or whether controlled drinking is a viable alternative treatment goal. This extremely polarizing controversy has been heated up by the critique by Pendery and her colleagues (Pendery, Maltzman, & West, 1982) of the Sobell's early study on training controlled drinking in hospitalized alcoholics (Sobell & Sobell, 1978). These criticisms have been refuted successfully (Dickens, Doob, Warwick, & Winegard, 1982; Sobell & Sobell, 1984), and the details of the arguments are beyond the scope of this chapter. What many alcoholism treatment personnel do not realize is that, even if the Sobell's study were totally disregarded (and we do not believe it should be), a large literature reviewed in detail by Heather and Robertson (1981) shows (1) that a small proportion of alcoholics treated in abstinence-oriented programs do successfully engage in nonproblem drinking for various lengths of time, and (2) that behavioral self-control training can be used successfully to teach controlled drinking skills to *some* alcoholics. On the basis of this evidence, behavior therapists and other empirically oriented clinicians have turned their attention to identifying the patients for whom abstinence is the most appropriate goal and those for whom controlled drinking might be considered. Although empirical data on which to base this decision are still being gathered, detailed rational guidelines are available (Heather & Robertson, 1981, pp 215–240; Miller & Caddy, 1977) and should be considered carefully prior to implementing a controlled drinking treatment. In our opinion, at this time pursuit of a controlled drinking treatment generally is not advisable during most inpatient treatment programs because (1) the majority of alcoholics treated on an inpatient basis have characteristics (e.g., physical addiction; social instability such as being unemployed, divorced, or homeless; medical problems related to alcohol abuse) thought to contraindicate such treatment; (2) a period of at least three to six weeks or more abstinence (the length of most inpatient programs) is considered advisable before beginning such treatment. This is done to allow at least partial recovery from neuropsychological deficits due to excessive alcohol intake that can interfere with the treatment, and to assess the patient's ability to maintain total control over drinking, a simpler task than partial control. Another factor influencing our opinion is a recent well-controlled study (Foy, Nunn, & Rychtarik, 1984) showing that for chronic alcoholics in a VA hospital treatment program, patients who received intensive training in controlled drinking in addition to a broad spectrum behavioral treatment program had significantly *fewer* abstinent days and *more* abusive drinking days in the six months after discharge than patients who did not get the additional controlled drinking treatment.

Related to the ideological controversy just discussed is the need for the behavior therapist to maintain a productive interface with Alcoholics Anonymous (AA). Difficulties can arise because AA and behavior therapy are based on different and sometimes contradictory values and beliefs (e.g., unitary disease model versus heterogeneous learning model, progress through scientific approach versus reliance on an established set of beliefs and practices, etc.). Our alcoholic patients can benefit from cooperation between AA and behavior therapists. Behavior therapists cannot afford to overlook the enormous advantages of so extensive a self-help system as AA: daily contact with thousands of alcoholics to whom traditional treatment is undesirable or unavailable, long-term maintenance by AA group support following treatment, and the low cost of this treatment approach. Further, some authors have suggested that in terms of actual treatment procedures, AA and behavior therapists have much in common (e.g., Burt, 1975; Miller, 1978). AA proponents inclined to dismiss behavior therapy for ideological reasons might do well to consider the evidence of favorable outcomes for behavioral treatments. They might also consider Miller and Hester's (1980) conclusion after reviewing available evidence on the effectiveness of AA that "certainly an exclusive or preferential reliance on AA as a treatment model for *all* problem drinkers is not justified by our present knowledge" (p. 53).

Another very important issue is the cognitive impairment in chronic alcoholics and the impact of these neuropsychological deficits on their ability to participate in and fully benefit from inpatient behavioral treatment programs of the type described in this chapter. An exhaustive review by Ryan and Butters (1983) indicates consistent evidence of neuropsychological deficits in chronic alcoholics affecting functions of learning and memory, abstract reasoning, and perceptual organization. What happens to these deficits once the alcoholic stops drinking? Another recent review (Goldman, 1983) summarizes available evidence on this topic:

> The patterns of psychological recovery may be summarized as follows across the range of studies completed to date: existing verbal abilities (vocabulary) are not impaired following drinking cessation. Most other abilities, especially when any new learning is involved, are impaired during the first week or two of abstinence. New verbal learning then recovers. Visual-spatial abilities, abstraction and problem solving, short-term memory, and perhaps some simple sensory reception show persistent impairment, particularly in older alcoholics. It is possible that with prolonged abstinence, some of these abilities also recover. In general, the more novel, complex, and rapid the information processing that a task requires, the longer it takes to recover (pp 1050–1051).

Only recently have studies begun to examine the treatment implications of alcoholics's cognitive deficits and the temporal pattern of recovery from these deficits. It is known that the more extensive the cognitive deficit during the first few weeks of abstinence, the poorer the long-term treatment outcome is (Abbott & Gregson, 1981). Little is known about specifically how cognitive impairment affects the treatment of hospitalized alcoholics, even though cognitive functioning tends to be at its worst during the beginning of abstinence when the alcoholic starts inpatient treatment. A recent study (Becker & Jaffe, 1984) addressed this question by assessing how much treatment-relevant information hospitalized chronic alcoholics remembered from a 55-minute film on the disease of alcoholism that was a routine component of an inpatient alcoholism treatment program. The authors conclude:

> The results of this study are clear. During the first week of treatment, the inpatient alcoholics were virtually unable to extract any important information from the film. By the third week of hospitalization, however, performance on the recall and recognition tests were comparable to that of other hospitalized veterans. . . . These results suggest that alcohol education programs need to be adjusted to compensate for the impaired cognitive functioning that may adversely affect aspects of treatment having a strong cognitive component. These results also raise questions about the present trend of shortening the period of inpatient or residential care for alcoholism (p. 324).

If the results of the above-mentioned study are replicated across a variety of tasks that alcoholics are required to perform as part of a behavioral inpatient program, they would have significant implications for the design and implementation of such treatment programs. These might include neuropsychological screening to assess readiness for treatment; insurance that patients have a period of abstinence prior to treatment; inclusion as part of the treatment program methods to accelerate cognitive recovery or to enhance cognitive performance in areas not likely to recover quickly (e.g., Binder & Schrieber, 1980; Hansen, 1980); redesigning treatment components so that information is presented in small, easily encoded chunks using short learning sessions with frequent opportunity for rehearsal (Becker & Jaffe, 1984), and carefully assessing whether the patient indeed is learning the desired material.

SUMMARY

Alcoholism is a disorder marked by a pathological pattern of alcohol use that has serious negative life consequences and, in some cases, by physical addiction to alcohol. Alcoholism is not a unitary disorder but rather a heterogeneous problem, so that alcoholics vary considerably in the nature, pattern, antecedents, and consequences of their drinking. After detoxification has been completed (if needed), a comprehensive assessment of the individual patient's drinking and other problems is the first step in inpatient behavioral treatment of alcoholism. On the basis of the assessment results, treatment is planned and delivered in an individualized manner to achieve three major goals. The first goal of treatment is to facilitate and consolidate the patient's commitment to change by carefully reviewing the evidence from the assessment of negative consequences of the patient's drinking. Alcohol education about the long-term negative consequences of drinking, and the use of a decision matrix to clarify the patient's reasons for not drinking, also are useful in pursuit of this first goal. The second goal is to stabilize the change in the drinking that occurred when the patient decided to enter the inpatient treatment program. Aversion therpy (i.e., nausea-producing drugs, aversive imagery) to decrease desire for alcohol, teaching alternative skills (e.g., relaxation, problem solving) to deal with likely precipitants of renewed alcohol use, and strengthening behaviors incompatible with alcohol abuse (e.g., satisfying job and marriage/family relationship) all can be used to help maintain abstinence. Antabuse, (including behavioral contracting procedures to increase compliance with this drug), along with psychotropic medication for additional psychopathology (e.g., depression) are pharmacologic interventions that often can be used in pursuit of this second goal. A final very important goal is the careful planning of aftercare and postdischarge life to help maintain the changes implemented during inpatient treatment.

REFERENCES

Abbott MW, & Gregson RAM. (1981). Cognitive dysfunction in the prediction of relapse in alcoholics. *Journal of Studies on Alcohol 42*, 230–243.

Azrin NH. (1976). Improvements in the community-reinforcement approach to alcoholism. *Behaviour Research and Therapy 14*, 339–348.

Azrin, NH, & Besalel VA. (1980). *Job club counselor's manual: A behavioral approach to vocational counseling.* Baltimore: University Park Press.

Azrin, NH, Flores T, & Kaplan SJ. (1975). Job-finding club: A group-assisted program for obtaining employment. *Behavior Research and Therapy 13*, 17–27.

Baker, TB, Cannon, DS, Stephenson GM, & Droubay E. (1978). Procedures for taste aversion therapy for alcoholism. *American Journal of Psychiatry 135*, 1439.

Becker JT, & Jaffe JH. (1984). Impaired memory for treatment-relevant information in inpatient men alcoholics. *Journal of Studies on Alcohol 45*, 339–343.

Billings AC, Kessler M, Gomberg CA, & Weiner S. (1979). Marital conflict resolution of alcoholic and nonalcoholic couples during drinking and nondrinking sessions. *Journal of Studies on Alcohol 40*, 183–195.

Binder LM, & Schrieber J. (1980). Visual imagery and verbal mediation as memory aids in recovering alcoholics. *Journal of Clinical Neuropsychology 2*, 71–74.

Burt DW. (1975). A behaviorist looks at AA. *Addictions 22*, 56–69.

Caddy GR. (1978). Toward a multivariate analysis of alcohol abuse. In Nathan PE, Marlatt GA, & Loberg T (Eds). *Alcoholism: New directions in behavioral research and treatment.* New York: Plenum Press, pp 71–117.

Cautela JR. (1984). General level of reinforcement. *Journal of Behavior Therapy and Experimental Psychiatry 15*, 109–114.

Cautela JR. (1966). Treatment of compulsive behavior by covert sensitization. *Psychological Record 16*, 33–41.

Chaney EF, O'Leary MR, & Marlatt GA. (1978). Skill training with alcoholics *Journal of Consulting and Clinical Psychology 46*, 1092–1104.

Cheek, FE, Franks CM, Burtle V, & Laucius J. (1971). Behavior modification training for wives of alcoholics. *Quarterly Journal of Studies on Alcohol 32*, 456–461.

Dickens BM, Doob AN, Warwick OH, & Winegard WC. (1982). *Report of the Committee of Enquiry into Allegations Concerning Drs. Linda & Mark Sobell*. Toronto: Addiction Research Foundation.

Eisler RM, Hersen M, Miller PM, & Blanchard EB. (1975). Situational determinants of assertive behaviors. *Journal of Consulting and Clinical Psychology 43*, 330–340.

Eisler RM, Miller PM, Hersen M, & Alford H. (1974). Effects of assertiveness training on marital interaction. *Archives of General Psychiatry 30*, 643–649.

Elkins RL, & Murdock RP. (1977). The contribution of successful conditioning to abstinence maintenance following covert sensitization (verbal aversion) treatment of alcoholism. *IRCS Medical Science: Psychology & Psychiatry: Social & Occupational Medicine 5*, 167.

Finney JW, Moos RH, & Mewborn CR. (1980). Posttreatment experiences and treatment outcome of alcoholic patients six months and two years after hospitalization. *Journal of Consulting and Clinical Psychology 48*, 17–29.

Fortang J, O'Farrell TJ, Cutter HSG, & Bayog RD. (1981). *Behavioral versus nonbehavioral group therapy for hospitalized alcoholics: Results at one year follow-up*. Paper presented at Grand Canyon International Conference on the Treatment of Addictive Behaviors (November), New Mexico.

Foy, DW, Massey FH, Duer JD, Ross JM, & Wooten LS. (1979). Social skills training to improve alcoholics' vocational interpersonal competency. *Journal of Counseling Psychology 26*, 128–129.

Foy DW, Miller P, Eisler R, & O'Toole DH. (1976). Social skills training to teach alcoholics to refuse drinks effectively. *Journal of Studies on Alcohol 37*, 1340–1345.

Foy DW, Nunn LB, & Rychtarik RG. (1984). Broad spectrum behavioral treatment for chronic alcoholics: Effects of training controlled drinking skills. *Journal of Consulting and Clinical Psychology 52*, 218–230.

Glasser W. (1976). *Positive addiction*. New York: Harper & Row.

Glatt MM. (1967). The question of moderate drinking despite "loss of control". *British Journal of Addiction 62*, 267–274.

Glatt MM. (1974). *A guide to addiction and its treatment*. New York: John Wiley.

Greeley A, & McReady WC. (1980). *Ethnic drinking subcultures*. New York: Praeger.

Goldfried MR, & Davison GC. (1976). *Clinical behavior therapy*. New York: Holt, Rinehart & Winston.

Goldman MS. (1983). Cognitive impairment in alcoholics: Some causes for optimism. *American Psychologist 38*, 1045–1054.

Goldstein S, & Marlatt GA. (1985). Behavioral techniques for dealing with alcohol problems. In Cox WM (Ed), *Treatment and prevention of alcohol problems: A resource manual*. New York: Academic Press.

Goodwin DW. (1979). *Is alcoholism hereditary?* New York: Oxford University Press.

Hansen L. (1980). Treatment of reduced intellectual functioning in alcoholics. *Journal of Studies on Alcohol 41*, 156–158.

Heath DB. (1975). A critical review of ethnographic studies of alcohol use. In Gibbons RJ et al. (Eds), *Research advances in alcohol and drug problems, vol. 2*. New York: John Wiley, pp. 1–92.

Heather N, & Robertson I. (1981). *Controlled drinking*. London: Methuen.

Hore, BD. (1971a). Life events and alcoholic relapse. *British Journal of Addiction 66*, 83–88.
Hore, BD. (1971b). Life events and alcoholic relapse. *British Journal of Addiction 66*, 89–96.
Horn JL, Wanberg KW, & Foster FM. (1974). The Alcohol Use Inventory—AUI. Denver: Center for Alcohol Abuse Research and Evaluation.
Horwitz M, Schaefer C, Hiroto D, Wilner N, & Levin B. (1977). Life event questionnaires for measuring presumptive stress. *Psychosomatic Medicine 39*, 413–431.
Hunt GM, & Azrin NH. (1973). A community-reinforcement approach to alcoholism. *Behaviour Research and Therapy 11*, 91–104.
Jackson JK. (1954). The adjustment of the family to the crisis of alcoholism. *Quarterly Journal of Studies on Alcohol 15*, 562–586.
Janis IL. (1982). *Counseling on personal decisions: Theory and research on short-term helping relationships*. New Haven: Yale University Press.
Jellinek EM. (1952). Current notes—phases of alcohol addiction. *Quarterly Journal of Studies on Alcohol 13*, 673–684.
Jellinek EM. (1960). *The disease concept of alcoholism*. New Haven: College and University Press.
Keller M. (1972). On the loss of control phenomenon in alcoholism. *British Journal of Addiction 67*, 153–166.
Knight RP. (1937). The dynamics and treatment of chronic alcohol addiction. *Bulletin of the Menninger Clinic 1*, 158–167.
Langenbucher JW, & Nathan PE. (1983). The "wet" alcoholic: One drink, then what? In Cox WM (Ed), *New directions in methodology for the social and behavioral sciences, #16*. San Francisco: Jossey-Bass, pp 21–36.
Lazarus AA. (1968). Behavior therapy and marriage counseling. *Journal of the American Society of Psychosomatic Dentistry and Medicine 15*, 49–56.
Locke HJ, & Wallace KM. (1959). Short marital-adjustment and prediction tests: Their reliabililty and validity. *Journal of Marriage and Family Living 212*, 251–255.
Lundwall L, & Baekeland F. (1971). Disulfiram treatment of alcoholism. *Journal of Nervous and Mental Disease 153*, 381–394.
Mann M. (1968). *New primer on alcoholism (2nd ed)*. New York: Holt, Rinehart and Winston.
Margolin G, Talovic S, & Weinstein CD. (1983). Areas of change questionnaire: A practical approach to marital assessment. *Journal of Consulting and Clinical Psychology 51*, 920–931.
Marlatt GA. (1982). Relapse prevention: A self-control program for the treatment of addictive behaviors. In Stuart RB (Ed), *Adherence, compliance and generalization in behavioral medicine*. New York: Brunner/Mazel, pp 329–378.
Marlatt GA, & Miller WR. (1983). *The drinking profile: A questionnaire for the behavioral assessment of alcoholism*. Albuquerque: University of New Mexico Press.
McLellan AT, Luborsky L, Woody GE, & O'Brien CP. (1980). An improved diagnostic evaluation instrument for substance abuse patients: The addiction severity index. *Journal of Nervous and Mental Disease 168*, 26–33.
Miller PM. (1978). Behavior modification and Alcoholics Anonymous: An unlikely combination. *Behavior Therapy 9*, 300–301.
Miller PM, & Mastria MA. (1977). *Alternatives to alcohol abuse: A social learning model*. Champaign, IL: Research Press.
Miller WR. (1976). Alcoholism scales and objective assessment measures: A review.

Psychological Bulletin 83, 649–674.

Miller WR. (1983). Motivational interviewing with problem drinkers. *Behavioural Psychotherapy 11*, 147–172.

Miller WR, & Caddy GR. (1977). Abstinence and controlled drinking in the treatment of problem drinkers. *Journal of Studies on Alcohol 38*, 986–1003.

Miller WR, & Hester RK. (1980). Treating the problem drinker: Modern approaches. In Miller WR (Ed), *The addictive behaviors: treatment of alcoholism, drug abuse, smoking and obesity*. New York: Pergamon Press pp 11–141.

National Council on Alcoholism, Criteria Committee. (1972). Criteria for the diagnosis of alcoholism. *American Journal of Psychiatry 129*, 127–135.

O'Farrell TJ. (1985). Marital and family therapy for alcohol problems. In Cox WM (Ed), *Treatment and prevention of alcohol problems: A resource manual*. New York: Academic Press.

O'Farrell TJ. (in press). Marital therapy in the treatment of alcoholism. In Jacobson NS, & Gurman AS (Eds), *Clinical handbook of marital therapy*. New York: Guilford Press.

O'Farrell TJ, & Bayog RD. (1984). *Antabuse contracts for married alcoholics and their spouses: A method to insure Antabuse taking and decrease conflict about alcohol*. (Manuscript submitted for publication.)

O'Farrell TJ, & Cutter HSG. (1984). Behavioral marital therapy couples groups for male alcoholics and their wives. *Journal of Substance Abuse Treatment 1*, 191–204.

O'Farrell TJ, Cutter HSG, Bayog RD, Dentch G, & Fortgang J. (1984). Correspondence between one-year retrospective reports of pretreatment drinking by alcoholics and their wives. *Behavioral Assessment 6*, 263–274.

O'Farrell TJ, Harrison RH, & Cutter HSG. (1981). Marital stability among wives of alcoholics: An evaluation of three explanations. *British Journal of Addiction 76*, 175–189.

O'Farrell TJ, Kleinke CL, & Cutter HSG. (1984). Sexual adjustment of male alcoholics: Changes from before to after receiving alcoholism counseling with and without marital therapy. (Manuscript submitted for publication).

Pattison EM. (1976). Non-abstinent drinking goals in the treatment of alcoholism. In Gibbons R et al. (Eds), *Research advances in alcohol and drug problems, vol. 2*. New York: John Wiley, pp 401–455.

Pendery ML, Maltzman IM, & West LJ. (1982). Controlled drinking by alcoholics? New findings and a reevaluation of a major affirmative study. *Science 217*, 169–175.

Plant MA. (1979). *Drinking careers: Occupations; drinking habits; and drinking problems*. London: Havistock.

Prochaska JO, & DiClemente CC. (1983). Stages and process of self-change of smoking Toward an integrative model of change. *Journal of Consulting and Clinical Psychology 51*, 390–395.

Rada RT, & Kellner R. (1979). Drug treatment in alcoholism. In Davis J, & Greenblatt DJ (Eds), *Psychopharmacology Update*. New York: Grune & Stratton, pp 105–144.

Ryan C, & Butters N. (1983). Cognitive deficits in alcoholics. In Kissin B, & Begleiter H (Eds), *The pathogenesis of alcoholism, vol 7*. New York: Plenum Press, pp 485–538.

Ryan C, & Butters N. (1980). Learning and memory impairments in young and old alcoholics: Evidence for the premature aging hypothesis. *Alcoholism 4*, 288–293.

Selzer ML. (1971). The Michigan Alcoholism Screening Test: The quest for a new diagnostic instrument. *American Journal of Psychiatry 127*, 1653–1658.

Skinner HA, & Sheu W. (1982). Reliability of alcohol use indices: The lifetime drinking history and the MAST. *Journal of Studies on Alcohol 43*, 1157–1170.

Sobell MB, Maisto SA, Sobell LC, Cooper AM, Cooper T, & Sanders B. (1980). Developing a prototype for evaluating alcohol treatment effectiveness. In Sobell LC, Sobell MB, & Ward E (Eds), *Evaluating alcohol and drug abuse treatment effectiveness: Recent advances*. New York: Pergamon Press, pp 129–150.

Sobell MB, & Sobell LC. (1984). The aftermath of heresy: A response to Pendery et al.'s (1982) critique of individualized behavior therapy for alcoholics. *Behavior Research and Therapy 22*, 413–440.

Sobell MB, & Sobell LC. (1978). *Behavioral treatment of alcohol problems: Individualized therapy and controlled drinking*. New York: Plenum Press.

Stalonas PM, Keane TM, & Foy DW. (1979). Alcohol education for inpatient alcoholics: A comparison of live, videotape and written presentation modalities. *Addictive Behaviors 4*, 223–229.

Steinglass P. (1976). Experimenting with family treatment approaches to alcoholism, 1950–1975. A review. *Family Process 15*, 97–123.

Straus MA. (1979). Measuring intrafamily conflict and violence: The Conflict Tactic (CT) Scales. *Journal of Marriage and the Family 41*, 75–88.

Vaillant GE. (1982). *The natural history of alcoholism*. Cambridge, MA: Harvard University Press.

Van Hasselt VB, Hersen M, & Milliones J. (1978). Social skills training for alcoholics and drug addicts: A reviw. *Addictive Behaviors 3*, 221–233.

Wanberg KW. (1983). *Differential assessment and treatment manual*. Denver: Colorado Department of Health, Alcohol and Drug Abuse Division.

Wechsler D. (1941). The effects of alcohol on mental activity. *Quarterly Journal of Studies on Alcohol 2*, 479–485.

Weiss RL, & Cerreto MC. (1980). The marital status inventory: Development of a measure of dissolution potential. *American Journal of Family Therapy 8*, 80–85.

Wheeler DD, & Janis IL. (1980). *A practical guide for making decisions*. New York: The Free Press.

Wiens AN, & Menustik CE. (1983). Treatment outcome and patient characteristics in an aversion therapy program for alcoholism. *American Psychologist 38*, 1089–1096.

8
Personality Disorders

Geary S. Alford and John A. Fairbank

Behavior is not random. Behavior is not a happenstance aggregate of physiokinetic events randomly occurring in space. Behavior, even of the most primitive organism has form and pattern. The more complex and differentiated the structure of an organism, the more complex and differentiated are the forms and patterns of events biobehavioral scientists call *behavior*. With increasing complexity comes increasing difficulty in clearly defining the characteristics or properties of events which, by one convention or another, are included or excluded from a particular abstracted category. *Right fore-paw maximum extension* is rather easy to define, though such an event is composed of millions of minute subcomponents. *Right fore-paw bar-press* is a bit more difficult in that we have added, as part of the defining characteristics an environmental effect, or consequence, or result of the *behavior* per se. More complex, hence more difficult still is a definition of bird nest-building behavior, or worse, human sexual seduction. But such behavioral events are infinitely easier to clearly describe or define than are private, experiential events: pain, hunger, dreaming, abstract reasoning. Such private events are universal among human beings, yet each individual instance is unique and observed or known only to the specific individual organism experiencing that specific occurance.

Difficulties in directly observing and directly measuring phenomena complicate but do not preclude definition or scientific investigation, as is perhaps most elegantly demonstrated by modern theoretical physics. Of all the diverse systems by which we conceptualize behavior, none is more complex, more

PRACTICE OF INPATIENT BEHAVIOR THERAPY
ISBN 0-8089-1715-3

difficult to define, to measure, to investigate, nor has a longer history in the study of human behavior than *personality*. Derived from the Latin word *persona*, the mask worn by ancient actors to signify their roles in the drama, *personality* has been variously used to refer to both broad as well as more narrowly circumscribed sets of events. For example, in common parlance the word personality is frequently used to refer simply to an individual's stylistic social behavior patterns. Philosophers and psychologists, on the other hand, have typically employed the term *personality* in reference to deeply ingrained, primary, fundamental patterns of perception, cognition, and emotive processes. In preparing their 1930, classic review article for *Psychology Bulletin*, Allport and Vernon claim to have identified several dozen different definitions of personality, which they subdivided into five categories ranging from those involving highly integrated, interactive, hierarchical, internal hypothetical components to less integrated, less interactive, clusters of behaviors more culturally and situationally determined (Allport & Vernon, 1930). Since that time, one could probably add a few dozen more definitions of personality (and associated personality theories) to Allport and Vernon's count. Needless to say, the diversity of definitions, models, and theories is accompanied by equally diverse and numerous theoretical debates. What has not changed is the fact that the term *personality* (conceptualized in one form or another) has endured these theoretical vagaries and even harsh criticisms aimed at expunging such notions from modern psychology. Indeed, every current major theoretical system includes some version of personality theory.

Although a review of the numerous historical and current theories of personality is beyond the intent and scope of the present chapter, several features are common to the diverse theoretical models. First, each definition and theory of personality either explicitly or at least implicitly acknowledges that it is addressing complex, multifacited, rather global patterns of behavior, including both inferred, mediational elements (e.g., ego, memory, behavioral repertoire, etc.) as well as more overt, publicly observable events. Second, each model acknowledges to a greater or lesser degree that many complex behavior patterns tend to be rather consistent, though not invariant, over time and across a variety of stimulus situations. Third, each model entails a dynamic (not necessarily psychodynamic) integration of its subcomponents such that behavior patterns or response classes or "internal events" are considered to influence other classes of behavioral events. Fourth, each model includes one or more dimensions of adjustment along which specific behavioral events, response classes, habits, and behavior patterns can be and are ordered (normal versus abnormal or deviant, adaptive versus maladaptive, healthy versus pathological, desirable versus undesirable, effective versus ineffective, skilled versus unskilled, and so forth). Each model implicates etiological factors thought to account for the development and occurrence of these behavior patterns. Finally, each model implicitly if not explicitly suggests methods by which personality–behavior patterns may be modified.

Of the more contempory models of personality, the one most closely aligned with cognitive behavioral therapies is a conceptualization of personality disorders based upon the principles of cognitive social learning theory (Mischel, 1968, 1973, 1984). This conceptualization of personality development emphasizes the importance of the interaction between idiosyncratic "person" variables and situational/contextual variables in determining the behavior of individuals. Mischel (1973) proposes that an individual's person variables can be analyzed in terms of five interdependent component variables: (1) construction competencies, (2) encodings, (3) expectations, (4) goals and values, and (5) self-regulatory systems. The first of these person variables, construction competencies, describes the individual's abilities to generate diverse cognitive and social responses when necessary. These competencies reflect the individual's potential ability to construct adaptive, skillful behavior that will produce beneficial consequences for himself or herself. Generally correlated with intellectual abilities (e.g., IQ and mental age), construction competencies range from the ability to cognitively generate lists of creative solutions for various problems to the ability to flexibly act upon these solutions and self-regulate one's behavior as a function of consequences. Mischel (1984) hypothesizes that cognitive and social competencies are relatively stable and enduring and serve as the basic foundations of coherence in the individual.

The second person variable describes the encoding strategies and personal constructs used by the individual to categorize particular situations. Hypothetically, encoding strategies describe the cognitive procedures by which individuals process, categorize, selectively attend to, and integrate information to fit with existing cognitive structures. Encoding variables thus encompass the covert cognitive behaviors engaged in by the individual as a result of any simple or complex stimulus input. Encoding variables are determined by inferences made from the individual's overt behavioral acts. For example, the clinician might observe that a patient on the inpatient ward continuously makes unrealistic demands of the ward staff and concurrently shows disregard for the legitimate needs of other patients on the ward. After repeated observations of this type of overt behavior, the clinician may begin to make testable inferences about the patient's encoding strategies as well as his existing cognitive structures. For instance, the clinician may speculate that this patient performs cognitive transformations on relevant stimuli such that they provide confirmation of a grandiose sense of self-importance and uniqueness.

The third person variable describes the individual's specific expectations about contingencies operating in different situations. Mischel (1968, 1973) proposes that an individual's previously learned expectations about various environmental contingencies guide his or her performance in specific situations. Importantly, however, an individual's expectancies about the contingencies operating in the environment may not be in accord with the actual objective contingencies in the situation. For example, a patient on the ward may engage in inappropriate, disruptive attention-seeking behavior because he or she expects that medical and psychological services are provided to him or her because of special entitlement (i.e., "the doctors owe it to me"). Actual contingencies for staff attention, such as severity of clinical symptoms relative to other patients on the ward, are not considered. Often, an individual's expectancies can be determined through the identification of specific "If . . . then . . ." statements that govern the individual's social interactions, or through observation of the individual's ability to recognize new contingencies when presented.

The fourth and fifth person variables in cognitive social learning theory describe the individual's method for ascribing subjective values to the outcomes that they expect, and their self-regulatory systems, respectively. Subjective values are critical since the degree of importance that an individual places upon his or her perceptions and expectancies may affect his or her level of effective functioning. Thus, although two individual's may have similarly fallacious expectations (e.g., the world owes me a living), the degree of actual social impairment experienced by each may differ greatly as a function of differences in the subjective importance attached to this expectation. Regarding the fifth person variable, the individual's self-regulatory systems include his or her covert rules that specify performance standards and consequences for achievement of, or failure to achieve, standards (Mischel. 1973).

The basic elements of Mischel's personality theory and Bandura's (1969, 1977a, 1977b) more general social learning theory serve as common ground for a number of contempory cognitive therapies (e.g., Bandura, 1977b; Beck, 1976; Beck, Rush, Shaw, & Emery, 1979; Ellis & Grieger, 1977; Mahoney, 1974; Mahoney & Arnkoff, 1978; Meichenbaum, 1977), though not all of these derive directly from social learning theory, per se. Indeed, it is interesting to note that while subtle differences in conceptualizations and in the specificity and systemization of clinical tactics vary among current cognitive-behavioral approaches (see Kendall & Bemis, 1983), their basic tenets are remarkably similar, though arrived at from separate, relatively independent avenues of approach. While Bandura's (1969) classic *Principles of Behavior Modification* served as a clinical spring board for the social learning based cognitive therapies, that book contains not a single reference to the works of Albert Ellis or Aaron Beck. Nor do Ellis' or Beck's publications at that time contain extensive crossreference to each other, to Bandura, Mischel or to other "neocognitivists." The point is not to suggest any lack of scholarship in these early works, but rather to emphasize that these investigators appear to have independently observed similar clinical phenomena from which they drew similar theoretical inferences that were to be brought together, merged, and refined in the subsequent decade. It is within this general "neocognitivist" framework (see Kendall & Bemis, 1983) that personality disorders are conceptualized and treatment procedures are formulated in the present chapter.

DESCRIPTION, DIAGNOSIS, AND EVALUATION

DSM-III lists 12 types of personality disorders, including one classification for "atypical" "mixed," or "other personality disorder." Each type is accompanied by a list of criterion behavior patterns for making diagnostic judgments. As with most concepts or sets of concepts, rules and examples for class exclusion as well as for class inclusion are provided. For example, "pervasive, unwarranted suspiciousness" along with sample manifestations occurs under *paranoid personality disorder*. However, differential diagnoses, such as schizophrenia in which similar behaviors may also occur, must be ruled out. Some of the criteria enumerated in *DSM-III* entail observable events such as truancy and angry tantrums. Other criteria, for example, "expectation of trickery or harm" and "magical thinking" require clinical inference. Publication of *DSM-III* was met with mixed reviews (Kaplan, 1983; McLemore & Benjamin, 1979; Millon, 1983; Williams & Spitzer, 1983; Wulach, 1983). As with many other clinicians and clinical researchers, the present authors are not entirely satisfied with *DSM-III*. However, *DSM-III* is the current system most broadly accepted and utilized. For this reason, as well as for conservation of space, we will assume that the reader is familiar with *DSM-III*. Therefore, we will not reproduce the defining characteristics and decision rules for each of the 12, *DSM-III* types of personality disorders. Instead, an adjunctive system for clustering problematic or symptomatic behaviors is suggested. In this system, classes of behaviors included as "symptomatic" components of personality disorders in *DSM-III* and/or otherwise evidenced by individuals diagnosed as personality disordered are assigned to one of three categories, each associated with a different set of intervention procedures.

I. Problems Associated with Behavioral Skill Repertoire

Included in this category are those behavioral problems that involve patients lacking specific sets of skills requisite to their natural environmental conditions (e.g., various classes or educational, occupational, and social skills deficits) and/or those behavioral problems that involve the patient having acquired or developed ineffectual, inappropriate, or otherwise maladaptive behavioral skills (e.g., objectionable social behaviors). Although *behavioral repertoire* can, and often is, defined in a fashion to include *all* acquired behaviors, the inverted term *behavioral skill repertoire* is used in this chapter in a more restrictive sense to refer to relatively circumscribed sets of skills such as "job-interview-skills," "study habits," "hetero-social dating skills," and so forth.

II. Problems Associated with Conditioned Emotional Reactions

Assignment in this category is limited to those autonomic-emotional reactions that function essentially as conditioned reflexes (e.g., phobic or relatively discrete aversion reactions; autonomic components in sexual inhibition, deficient arousal to appropriate sexual stimuli or inappropriate arousal to deviant sexual stimuli, etc.). Emotional reactions that are almost entirely *secondary* to Categories I and/or III are not included under Category II. For example, frustration at not getting a job due to vocational skills deficits or depression resulting from inaccurate negative self-perceptions and invalid beliefs are not included here. However, emotional behaviors associated with problems in Categories I and III are also listed under Category II to the extent that an autonomic reflexive component appears present (e.g., the job applicant interviewee may be apprehensive because he or she isn't sure what to do or how to act, but may *also* be disruptively symphathetically aroused in response to the interview-situational stimuli per se).

III. Problems Associated with Cognitive Content and Information Processing, including Secondary, Aversive, Affectual Behaviors

Included in this category are behavioral problems judged to result from inaccurate perception of stimulus events, fallacious or illogical information processing, erroneous information or beliefs, and emotional reactions associated with those distored cognitions. Included in this category, for example, would be angry, hostile behavior judged to result from a patient mistakenly interpreting a playful pat as a threatening, aggressive act intend to injure or harm. Similarly included would be a patient's tendency to engage in logically fallacious reasoning such as deriving A or E proposition-conclusions from I or O proposition premise-events (e.g., "Those people do not like me"; "therefore, nobody likes me").

Thus, observed overt and inferred covert behavioral events are classified both according to the criteria for personality disorders enumerated in *DSM-III* and also according to these three categories. We frequently employ a fourth category with other behavioral disorders, but only occasionally with personality disorders: that is "Problems Associated with Identified or Probable Organic Pathology." With respect to personality disorders, this would include such things as drug-induced psychotic behavior. This fourth category, of course, is most relevant to major thought and affective disorders or to brain injured patients. Each of these categories is addressed with different intervention packages appropriate to the nature of the targeted problems included.

Initial Inpatient Evaluation

All patients admitted to an inpatient psychiatric unit undergo a relatively standard initial clinical evaluation. This includes interviews and mental status examinations, medical history and physical examination, routine laboratory studies (e.g., SMA-12), personal and social history, and usually a toxicology drug screen. Where indicated, special laboratory tests such as EEG, thyroid function, dexamethasone suppression test, or sleep studies are conducted. General psychological testing is common, though not universal during the initial evaluation, often utilizing the MMPI. Preliminary interviews with significant others (e.g., spouse, parents, older or adult children) also take place during this time. Results of these data-gathering procedures form the basis for diagnostic determinations. If this evaluation produces findings that match the inclusive and exclusionary criteria for personality disorder, either as a primary or secondary diagnosis, then evaluation proceeds aimed at delineating and assessing the various subcomponents of the particular personality disorder in the particular patient.

Many personality disordered patients have histories or exhibit evidence of poor social skills, phobic and anxiety behaviors, alcohol and/or drug abuse, sexually injudicious or even deviant behavior, or other collateral behavioral disorders. Such behaviors may or may not be components of their personality disorder, though such behavior patterns may interact with the central features of personality disorder, per se. By *central features*, we mean those inferred perceptual and cognitive processes by which the human organism perceives, abstracts, and organizes its internal representation of the stimulus universe and the emotional behaviors elicited, occasioned, evoked, or which otherwise collaterally occur secondary or parallel to those processes. Differentiated, though not defined as mutually exclusive, from these processes are: (1) sets of integrated, effector-behavioral skills (e.g., playing the violin, "social skills effector repertoire," etc.); and (2) simple stimulus-stimulus-conditioned reflexive reactions of the autonomic nervous system. According to this convention, then, we define the *core* or *central* features of personality disorder as those observed or inferred behavioral phenomena that match the inclusive and exclusionary criteria in *DSM-III* for personality disorder and that fall into Category III. Patients' behavior patterns, then, are evaluated with respect to each of the three general categories, while those of Category III are considered the central features of *personality disorder*.

The process of individual patient evaluation typically includes interviews with the patient. Interviews by a senior therapist are conducted repeatedly and usually entail both relatively structured aspects (e.g., specific discrete and open-ended questions about a patient's family, friends, home-life, etc.) and relatively unstructured formats (e.g., "what would like to talk about today?") Patients are also interviewed by other staff personnel such as residents, social workers, nurses and students. Incidental observation of the patient's behavior on the ward are also noted and recorded. Patients are observed not only with respect to specific behavioral events (e.g., angry outbursts, refusal to attend group therapy sessions, etc.), but also with respect to stylistic features of their behavior (e.g., "appears to act insultingly and hostile toward other patients"). In fact, spontaneous comments by other patients in reference to particular patients are often recorded.

In addition to the MMPI, psychological testing usually includes a standard intelligence test (e.g., Wechsler Adult Intelligence Scale) and one or more self-report inventories (e.g., Beck Depression Scale).

Collateral Sources

Persons intimately involved with the patient (e.g., spouse, parents, older children) are interviewed with an eye to gathering both specific information about the patient and also to determining thematic features or patterns that appear to characterize significant and important fractions of his or her behavior across time. Information generated from these sources is clustered according to the categories described above, and is subjected to a somewhat finer level of analysis.

Problems Associated with Behavioral Skill Repertoire

As previously noted, patients diagnosed as having personality disorder often display evidence of deficiency or impairment in one of more classes of behavioral skills that are necessary or at least of major utility in their natural environment. If the second phase of evaluation suggest such a problem, then specific assessment procedures are conducted. Such skills-repertorial problems occasionally involve occupational-vocational skills and educational limitations, but by far the most common are various social skill deficiences.

Where occupational or vocational problems are indicated, a vocational rehabilitation counselor is consulted. This counselor usually meets with the patient on the unit and begins a vocational rehabilitation assessment. Based on this assessment, the patient may be placed in a vocational training program, placed in an employment program that includes an on-the-job training phase, or assisted in locating employment in which the job descriptions match the patient's training and abilities. Similarly, individuals with severe educational limitations are seen by adult education consultants who assist patients in enrolling in such programs as evening classes for improving reading and basic mathematic competencies.

Evaluations and treatments of various social skill problems have received considerable research attention over the past decade. These studies have provided clinically useful as well as efficacious methods for assessment (e.g., Curran & Mariotto, 1980; Kelly, 1982) and remediation (e.g., Kelly, 1982; Scott, Himadi, & Keane, 1983). In utilizing these procedures, we also attempt to distinguish between repertorial deficits and performance problems. That is, a *deficit* per se is not automatically assumed on the basis that an individual displays poor or inappropriate social behaviors within certain social-stimulus contexts. Rather, alternative bases are also considered, including conditioned autonomic reflexive contributors and, particularly with personality disorders, cognitive-mediational variables.

For example, a woman taking a night-college course arrives home much later than usual accompanied by a female classmate with whom she has been studying for an exam. The husband of the late-arriver acts in what appears to be a cold, sullen, yet anxious and agitated manner, and generally behaves toward the visitor in a socially unskilled fashion. It is possible that this man simply lacks appropriate, effective social skills, in other words has a behavioral repertoire deficit. Alternately, it is also possible that this husband has an excellent social skills repertoire, but that *performance* of these skills is impaired under certain types of circumstances. This hypothetical husband might, for example, have developed an extreme anxiety response to meeting new people or to strangers visiting his home. It is also possible that performance of his social skills was altered because he erroneously believed his wife unfaithful and suspected her of being sexually involved with this female classmate. Each of these three diverse conditions could contribute to similar overt behavior patterns, yet each would entail different diagnostic considerations and, similarly, would require different procedures for remediation.

When a patient with a personality disorder is also found to have significant Category I problems (e.g., "social skill deficits"), then these are concomitantly assessed and treated with appropriate, current methods (e.g., Kelly, 1982).

Although there are many variants of autonomic-reflective behaviors, those most commonly seen in conjunction with personality disorders involve disruptive reflective anxiety reactions and inadequate and deviant sexual arousal. As in the case of social skills deficits, an extensive body of evaluation and treatment research literature is available to guide clinical intervention with Category II, anxiety-based dysfunctions (e.g., Bandura, 1969; Barlow & Beck, in press; Bellack & Hersen, 1977; Leitenberg, 1976; Mavissakalian & Barlow, 1981) and sexual disorders (e.g., see: Barlow, 1977; Brownell & Barlow, 1980). Behavior problems that fall into this category are addressed with these current, empirically based evaluative and treatment methods.

Category III: Problems Associated with Cognitive Content and Information Processing, including Secondary, Aversive Affectual Behavior.

Evaluation and assessment of personality and personality disorders is a complex, and controversial enterprise (e.g., Mischel, 1968). By what objective criterion can one determine when or where *suspicion* becomes *paranoid ideation* or paranoid ideation can be considered to constitute a *delusional system?* Few experienced clinicians would argue, for example, that an individual's suspicions that his or her boss did not like him or her was equivalent to and indiscriminable from an individual's belief that his or her boss was trying to poison him or her, or that these were equivalent to and indiscriminable from an individual's belief that aliens from Alpha Centuria had taken control of their employer's brain by means of "Orgone teletransmission." The domains are discriminable, but the boundaries are unclear. Lacking empirically established norms and guidelines for these events, we are often left to rely, however reluctantly, on our own subjective models against which to gauge the nature, intensity, frequency, "normalcy," and functional relationships or consequences of such phenomena. Hopefully, our training, experience, and extrapolative application of what empirical data do exist provide some basis for our "educated" estimations. From a strictly scientific point of view, this state of the art is not very advanced. But it will not be further advanced by either ignoring these phenomena or by attempting to operate on the pretense that they are equivalent to rather simple, discrete verbal-motor acts. Scientist-practitioners seek empirical bases for our clinical actions, but ethical clinicians cannot ignore or put on indefinite hold patients whose disordered behavior patterns result in pain and suffering for themselves and others; nor can we ethically agree to attempt to treat only what is clear, clean, and easy. Defining a malignant melanoma as just another mole because we know more about common moles and how to treat them in pseudoscience at its worst. Perhaps we are unsure of the mechanisms and have no well documented efficacious treatment for many of these diseases, but until the mysteries are unraveled and the definitive treatments are derived, we must use what limited knowledge and skill we do have in attempting to help our patients. Clinicians who work with personality disorders *qua* personality disorders are faced with extraordinarily complex, subtle, even elusive phenomena: the elements and processes entailed in an individual's perception, organization, and understanding of his or her stimulus universe (i.e., epistemology and cosmology).

Cognitive knowledge is nothing more than a set of abstractions derived from sensory input. At the most basic level of analysis, this set can be viewed as relatively enduring molecular changes resulting primarily from chemical events occurring throughout the sensory system. Stimulus transduction in a sensory receptor cell is, itself, the first level of abstraction; and this *abstracting* continues throughout the sensory system up through those relatively few bundles of sensory signals that emerge as consciously perceived sensory images. The vast majority of events in the human sensory-nervous system, including the vast majority to which the biological system has learned to discriminantly respond, do not typically reach the level of verbalizable awareness (i.e., "consciousness awareness" with self-conscious, volitional response selection) in the ongoing, routine functions of the central nervous system. Those sensory events that are consciously experienced are already abstractions when they are experientially detected. Such sensory events are also further abstracted into imaginal and/or symbolic (e.g., linguistic) coding systems (e.g., Bandura, 1969; Luria, 1961). Indeed, there exists a substantial body of evidence that "lower animals," including insects, develop internal sensory "images" that subsequently guide overt response patterns, (see Hinde, 1970). From such internal sensory events, inferential images or models and their associated coding systems are constructed, which serve as abstract reflections of the stimulus universe. To the extent that these abstractions reliably and proportionately reflect the actual timing, sequence, frequency, intensity, duration, and elemental relationships of events occurring in the stimulus universe (though, of course, not necessarily in a monomorphic, isomorphic, or isotonic manner: see Hake & Rodwan, 1966; Mountcastle, 1967), they are considered accurate representations. Significant lack of correspondence between perceptual events (or recalled or recollected perceptual events) and actual reality (i.e., the external, independent stimulus universe) usually results in maladaptive or inappropriate effector behavior. By way of simple example, misestimation of the distance, speed, (hence vector-closing-time of an oncoming vehicle) may result in death for a driver attempting to pass another car. Likewise, misremembered directions may result in failure to arrive at the desired destination.

In addition to their fundamental properties, stimulus events may also function as signs or symbols or indications of other events. This is so when one set of stimulus events meets one of four criteria: (1) has a relatively reliable sequential relationship with other sets of stimulus events (e.g., clouds before the rain or glowing coals after a fire); (2) relatively reliably occurs parallel to, in concert with, or as an integral component of some other set of events (e.g., lightening and thunder, elevated body temperature with elevated white blood count and infection); (3) is itself an abstraction of salient features of another set of stimulus events (e.g., drawings or photographs of objects, a reflection in a mirror); or (4) is assigned by convention a symbolic or representational value (e.g., a red light hanging over an intersection means to stop, the word *dot* represents or stands for ●).

Significant lack of correspondence between perceptual events and their respective cognitive representations (or models or codes) and actual reality (i.e., the external, independent stimulus universe) results in maladaptive acquisition and/or dysfunctional performance of effector behaviors. Poor correspondence between events in reality (i.e., the stimulus universe) and their organismic representations may occur in a variety of ways:

1. Failure to detect the stimuli at receptor or sentient level.
2. Failure to become aware of and/or attend to specific sets of stimuli or their actual magnitude or frequency.
3. Inaccurate or insufficient imaginal or symbolic coding of stimuli.
4. Failure to accurately associate ("recognize") patterns or sequences in clusters of stimulus events. That is, for example, failure to identify stimulus-stimulus associations and cause-effect relationships; failure to appropriately generalize.
5. Inaccurate or invalid attributions of associations among patterns or sequences or stimulus events. For example, inaccurate and invalid attribution of stimulus events; stimulus-stimulus associations and cause-effect relationships where no, little or weak, or low probability relationships actually exist; failure to appropriately discriminate, cf: overgeneralization.
6. Misattribution of signal or symbolic value to stimulus events and egocentric personalization of external events.
7. Failure to appropriately discriminate beween intraorganismic stimulus events. At basic sensory-perceptual level, this would include hallucinations; at cognitive-symbolic level it would include existential import of symbolic-linguistic constructions: The statement, "Because of the antiunicorn light, there are no unicorns in this room," carries the latent implication that there exist unicorns somewhere, if not in this room; or that external reality is externally structured or altered by an act of internal thinking per se.
8. Faulty or erroneous hypothesis formulation and testing processes, e.g., simple errors in formal logic.

As discussed earlier, there are as yet no well defined, objective methodologies for calibrating such events. Clinical evaluation consists of careful scanning of the information generated within the second phase of assessment described earlier for evidence of: (1) systematic distortions in the patient's description of circumscribed external, potentially publicly verifiable events; (2) significant errors of logic in information processing with special notation of the content areas in which such errors are most prevalent or most extreme; (3) significantly inaccurate complex cognitive models or representations (e.g., "belief systems"); (4) recurrent patterns wherein behaviors entailed in, guided by, or associated with (1), (2), and (3) have resulted in significant aversive consequences (e.g., excessive, aversive autonomic reactions, impaired performance of various behavioral skills, negative social reactions and sanctions).

A clinically significant pattern of such events is considered to exist where the evidence indicates either a high frequency of such epistemological errors or the degree of inaccuracy is very high *and* the pattern is judged to be related to significantly adverse consequences. To illustrate, most human beings will occcasionally mistake a clerk's harried, brusk behavior for "rudeness," but most human beings do not believe that they are "insulted" several times almost every day. Likewise, the perhaps mistaken opinion that one's boss does not particularly like one is a different order of magnitude from the opinion that he or she is controlled by evil aliens who are plotting murder. Finally, whether one privately believes in a creationist versus evolutionary model of the universe is unlikely to result in significant adverse consequences in one's daily life. Frequent misperception of innocuous events as "insulting" or even "threatening," however, is quite likely to evoke disquieting and unpleasant antonomic arousal and may contribute to socially offensive, retaliatory overt behaviors. Thus, clinical significance is not determined solely by the frequency of "distortion," the degree of distortion, or by its degree of narrowness or comprehensiveness, but with consideration for the *consequences* of the invalid content and erroneous cognitive processes.

Specific, observable behavioral events upon which clinical inferences and judgments are based are systematically gathered and collated. The patient's primary therapist records many of the patient's remarks verbatim. With the patient's permission, this is sometimes accomplished via audio or video recordings. Ward personnel keep descriptive frequency counts of selected target events (e.g., requests for medication, dramatic or explosive outbursts, general complaints, etc.), as well as noting incidental observations about a patient's behavior (e.g., "talked more about her own behavior in group therapy today"). Family members are asked to describe specific historical examples of "problem behaviors" and to provide estimates of frequency, magnitude, and the kinds of consequences resulting from such behaviors. During treatment, patients are asked to self-monitor and rate selected behavioral events. Information generated through these methods is used not only in conceptualizing certain "personality" functions, but is also used in the treatment process.

TREATMENT

Inaccurate cognitive representations and processes occurring in personality disorders are considered, as discussed above, to result from developmental-environmental experience (i.e., are "learned") in contrast to similar behaviors that probably arise out of biological pathology (i.e., in schizophrenias). As such, they should be potentially modifiable by new learning experiences. The emergence of the cognitive-behavioral therapies provides a starting point from which tactics designed to modify personality disorders can be developed.

In their review of cognitive-behavioral approaches, Kendall and Bemis (1983) introduce their chapter by enumerating six points that generally characterize the underlying assumptions and basic operational models of cognitive therapies. Among these are a conceptualization of the human animal as an information processing organism that responds primarily to internal representations of its environments rather than to the environment per se; that these internal (e.g., "cognitive") representations mediate or subserve most human learning; that cognitions, feelings, and overt effector behaviors are functionally-casually interrelated; and that the task of the cognitive therapist is to modify these internal representations and processes via designing new learning experiences (Kendall & Bemis, 1983). It can be seen, then, that the model of personality disorder proposed in the present chapter is essentially consistent with the cognitive-behavioral framework. In particular, the kinds of subjective epistemological errors described earlier closely correspond to the characteristic errors in information processing postulated by Beck and his associates as underlying depression (e.g., Beck, 1976; Hollon & Beck, 1979). Beck and co-workers argue that depressed patients tend to draw arbitrary inferences or conclusions based on minimal or ever contrary evidence, engage in gross overgeneralization, magnify or minimize the significance or meaning of discrete events, and view impersonal events as having specific personal import.

Although the early developers of cognitive-behavioral approaches such as Albert Ellis (1962, 1970) focused on "attacking" irrational cognitions and fallacious information processing, the newer cognitive behavior therapists developed more explicit, systematic procedures designed to modify somewhat more operationally defined target behaviors. For example, Beck's form of cognitive therapy teaches patients how to identify and self-monitor negative cognitions and related mood states and to recognize the functional relationships among thoughts, feelings, and overt actions; trains patients how to formulate and test simple hypotheses and how to replace unfounded negativistic cognitions with more valid, reality-oriented ones; and educates patients in how to identify and modify their more global, "higher order" (cosmological in our terms) conceptualizations of themselves and their world (cf: basic irrational beliefs in Ellis).

In developing a cognitive-behavioral treatment model for personality disorders, we sought to frame the concepts in a form and language that would be relatively easily comprehended by the average patient and yet would capture the essential clements.

Treatment Steps

Step 1

The patient is instructed in a simple epistemology and cosmology. The main points can be summarized briefly as follows: There is an independent universe. You are a small entity in that universe. You learn and know some things about that universe through your senses. You can think and imagine; but your thoughts and images do not, in themselves, create or modify the universe outside yourself. Your images (representations) of and thoughts about the universe are only valid to the extent that they correspond to actual, independent reality, including natural law. One subset of natural law includes principles of behavior. i.e., psychology. One of the most crucial aspects of behavioral laws is that of functional behavior-effect relationships: e.g., similar behaviors occurring in similar environments tend to result in similar effects of consequences. In general, natural environments (e.g., society, culture, government, social laws, other people, etc.) are less amenable to modification by the individual than are his or her own behavior patterns. Further, natural environments and their associated behavioral contingencies are, with some significant but relatively infrequent exceptions, remarkably similar across cultures and individuals. Natural law, of course, is assumed to be universal. Thus, modification of one's behavior-contingent experiences (positive and negative reinforcers and punishers) is most pragmatically accomplishable via modification of one's own behavior (cognitive behavior, emotive behavior, overt behavior).

This step begins after the therapist has seen the patient for at least six to eight individual sessions, during which the information-gathering described earlier was conducted and in which the therapist developed a therapeutic relationship with the patient. The philosophical educative phase usually requires three or four sessions and is conducted in part as lecture, in part as Socratic dialogue. Of course, each of the points is discussed in simple language and numerous examples are used to illustrate the concepts. Explicit examples drawn from the patient's own behavior are initially avoided, however, since the patient may "miss the point" while defending his or her specific actions. The patient is asked to take notes during these sessions and to review these between sessions, to identify some new examples of each point (though not necessarily involving themselves), and to be prepared to "teach these points" to the therapist as if he or she knew nothing about them. Disagreement with or rejection of one or more of these tenets is dealt with by returning to extremely simple examples of the disputed notion, and slowly, systematically shaping and presenting the evidence. Since specific content areas thought to be involved in the patient's own particular disorder are avoided, less atypical, idiosyncratic interpretations or violations of basic logic occur.

Once the patient can discuss each of these points clearly, exhibits no evidence of significant disagreement with the basic ideas, and otherwise appears accepting of this fundamental "world view," the focus of individual therapy sessions narrows to the patient's particular behavior and his or her natural environment.

Step 2

The patient is given a between session "homework" assignment in which he or she is asked to write out a list of "goals, experiences and everyday things" that he or she considers important, valuable, and pleasurable in and for their lives. The patient is instructed to be as specific as possible in defining these items and is asked to give examples. In the following treatment session, the therapist and patient collaborate in clustering these items into four groups: Necessary or Extremely Important, Valuable or Pleasurable or Important (but not necessary), Somewhat Pleasurable or Valuable (but not unnecessary and of minor importance, and a fourth group, consisting of those items whose group assignment the patient and therapist could not agree upon. At this time, the patient's list may also be supplemented or particular items restated. After a brief discussion of an item, either the patient or therapist can "set aside" (i.e., place in Group 4) an item "for later discussion."

Step 3

The next homework task involves the patient evaluating each item on his or her list with respect to two dimensions: (1) to determine "how realistic" or "actually attainable in the real world" an item is (ranging on a 10-point scale from Probably Impossible to Probably Easily Attainable); (2) to determine to what extent the patient himself or herself (e.g., his or her own behavior) could influence or bring about or disrupt attainment of each item. Then, the patient is to describe and discuss in this written homework task what he or she perceives, as his or her own "strengths" and "weaknesses" or "faults" that would or could contribute "positively" or "negatively" to achieving each item. Accomplishment of this step usually requires two or three therapy sessions with repeated between-session homework assignments to "be more specific," "elaborate more or discuss this more," and so forth. As in Step 2, treatment sessions are used to collaborate with the patient in estimating "achievability" and suggesting patient-behavior contributions.

Step 4

Again employing a mixture of lecture presentation and Socratic dialogue, the therapist reviews Step 1 and then focuses on individual subjective perception and cognition. The patient is taught that "events in reality" and "events as we see and interpret them" are *not* the same thing; that all human knowledge is only a "reflected image" of "real events"; that all humans tend to misperceive and misunderstand some of what they experience, and "sometimes we develop patterns of such errors more in some aspects of our lives than in others"; that these misperceptions can lead us to overreact emotionally and to overtly react ineffectually or maladaptively to certain "real world events." The patient is instructed in the kinds of perceptual-cognitive errors discussed earlier; however a briefer, simpler system is used, for example:

Overgeneralization. Where some event is perceived as occurring much more often or much less often (or with much greater of lesser magnitude) than is, in fact, the actual case. All-or-none thinking is an extreme example of this type of error.

Oversymbolization. Where an event is interpreted as having symbolic meaning or sign-signal value far beyong what is, in fact, inherent in the event itself.

Overconsequation. Where an event is interpreted as having a high probability of leading to, producing, or otherwise resulting in severe, adverse even catastrophic aversive consequences, when, in fact, such probability is low or zero.

In each case, numerous examples are used to illustrate these distortions. Of particular value in exemplifying these processes are common, idiomatic linguistic constructions (e.g., "Everything's gone wrong today"; "If he really cared about me he would not have . . ."; "If I don't get this chapter finished by the deadline, the editor is going to kill me").

The patient is requested to make careful notes and to memorize these definitions. Homework assignments require that patients write out a list of examples from their everyday lives exemplifying each of the general categories of perceptual-cognitive distortions. Individual therapy sessions are used, at this point, to assist the patient in identifying personal examples specific to each category. The therapist, however, avoids most material derived from his or her own evaluation, considered to be highly emotionally evocative or likely to be rigidly resisted by the patient. In addition, the patient is asked to make two other descriptive lists of situations or events to which they respond with aversive emotion: anxious, angry, or depressive feelings. One list includes events that tend to occur with a high frequency but to which the patient internally reacts with "mild to moderate" level of emotion. This list includes the patient's "pet peeves" and such common events as "waiting in a long, slow moving line when you are in a hurry," "losing money in a coke machine that turns out to be broken," etc. The second list includes events that may (though not necessarily) occur relatively less frequently, but to which the patient reacts with strong ("moderate to strong") internal, aversive emotions.

Step 5

Utilizing the lecture-and-Socratic-dialogue style, the therapist reviews with the patient how our own private, personal perceptions and interpretations of events in reality can result in our generating feelings and overt reactions "disproportionate" to and "maladaptive" for the actual events and realities. Items from the patient's own list of examples and those from the mild to moderate (high frequency/low intensity) list are used to demonstrate this perceptual-cognitive reaction pattern.

At this point, the therapist instructs the patient in a method designed to increase the accuracy of his or her cognitive-perceptual representations. The patient is asked to practice being "hyperaccurate" in the use of language, including refraining from using idiomatic expressions. "Low intensity" but relatively high frequency events from their daily lives are designated for the initial targets (for inpatients these include as many items as can be constructed that occur in the hospital setting). When a designated event (or one very similar in nature) occurs, or the patient experiences mild to moderate aversive feelings in rection to "any event," he or she is instructed to covertly ask and answer the following questions exactly as stated, in the exact sequence, and with answers constrained by the guidelines for responding to each question.

Question 1. What was (is) the real event?

Answer 1. Brief, clear, accurate description of the event itself with no interpretive or emotionally loaded language, rather like an ideal reporter or legal witness should do.

Example. "The nurse said, It is very late; you need to be in bed." Not, "The nurse insulted me, treating me like a child" or even "The nurse said I was 'staying up too late and ordered' me to bed" (since that was not literally accurate).

Question 2. What does the event mean or symbolize in reality?

Answer 2. This answer must be restricted to the most conservative interpretation possible with no speculation as to subtle or hidden meanings and not "what it means to me."

Example. Based on the sample event under Question 1: "The nurse thinks I should be in bed" or "The nurse wants me to go to bed"; *not* "The nurse thinks I'm a child" or "The nurse is just trying to swing her weight around."

Question 3. What is going to happen in reality because of the event?

Answer 3. By *happen in reality* is meant what is going to happen independent of the patients feelings or emotional reaction, i.e., what effects or consequences are going to result from the *event itself* independent of the patient. Again, for purposes of practice, the patient is to respond covertly with the most conservative interpretation possible with no speculation as to "possible" effects.

Example. "Nothing is going to happen (result, change) in reality"; not "It's going to make me mad" or even "I'm going to feel perturbed," since the event cannot *cause* the patient's anger and, in any event, is something the patient is doing and is not something that is happening or would happen independent of the patient's own behavioral reaction to it. By these constraints, even a patient's answer to Question 3 such as "I guess I'll go to bed" would be incorrect, though of course the patient may well elect the course of action.

Training the patient in this task is very difficult. Exaggerated, overstated, idiomatic phrases are such basic components of our language that they occur with relatively high frequency in common parlance. Likewise, inaccurate conceptions of cause-effect relationships are an integral part of Indo-European languages. We ask "What's got you down?" and "What made you do it?" when we really mean "Why did you do it?" and "To what are you reacting with 'down' feelings?" We say "He pissed me off" and "She hurt my feelings" when we really mean "I got mad at or felt hurt over what he or she did." Thus, much modeling and corrective feedback is necessary in this step. The therapist now utilizes this same "hyperaccurate" language in talking with the patient. It is repeatedly pointed out that patients' feelings will be different as they more accurately perceive-encode and more validly interpret external events. Throughout treatment, the relationship between patients' own behaviors (thoughts, feelings, overt actions) and consequences of those behaviors are repeatedly described and stressed.

The following excerpts exemplify how this procedure is actually conducted. The reader is asked to bear in mind that this and other brief vignettes are very brief samples taken out of much longer interactions. This caveat is important because one might erroneously conclude that clinical inferences are drawn from very limited, even minor bits of information or that modification of Category III problem behaviors can be achieved via brief, persuasive argument.

These two excerpts are drawn from two separate sessions that occurred in the early phases of Step 5 in the treatment of a 37-year-old male diagnosed as paranoid personality. The patient's wife had been to visit him on several occassions during his first three weeks in the hospital. The patient repeatedly complained that his wife "doesn't visit any more than she has to".

T: How many times has she been to visit?
P: She's been up here a couple of times.
T: How many times is "a couple?"
P: I don't know; maybe three or four.
T: Joe, the notes in your chart say she has been here seven times.
P: That's not true! Besides, I didn't see her one time because they had me down in X-Ray.
T: Well, OK . . . but that leaves six visits with you that are noted on the chart.
P: I don't think that's right. Besides, that's not very often if you are *in* here!
T: That may not be as often as you would like or as often as she might like; but six is a lot more times than "a couple"—wouldn't you agree?
P: I don't see what's the big difference between four and six.
T: You know how we've been talking about the importance of seeing things as clearly and accurately as we can? Well, let's look at this together. First, you said you were upset because she "visits only when she has to"; then, you said she had been up here "a couple" of times. The fact is, she doesn't really *have to* visit at all. I mean no one is really forcing her to visit. So every time she does visit, she must want to or she wouldn't be here. Secondly, to most human beings, you and I included, "a couple" usually means *two* or *twice*, not four, much less six or seven. Still, when asked exactly how many times she had come to visit, you said "three or four", when, *in reality*, she had come to visit seven times and, *in fact*, did visit with you six times.
P: I just meant she wasn't coming to visit very often.
T: OK, but look at how you thought about it. You talked about "a couple" of visits and you interpreted this as meaning that she did not want to visit you. The kinds of feelings you expressed appeared more consistent with "a couple" and "doesn't want

to visit," than with the actual reality or facts of the situation. I mean, the type of feelings and the level of feelings you had would be relatively natural if what you said to yourself were true. I think if you had seen the actual number of visits more accurately and had not concluded that your wife didn't want to visit you, that you would not have felt so bad. You might still wish she could or would visit more often, but you would not feel like you did . . . Here is a good example of how our misperceptions of things and our distorted thoughts or conclusions about them can result in our reacting excessively or disproportionately to them . . .

The second excerpt is drawn from a session that occurred three days later. The evening before this session, the patient had come to the primary therapist's office and angrily announced, "That bitch head nurse cussed me out in front of all those nuts down there . . . " Asked what had happened, the patient replied, "She threw a screaming fit because I changed the God-damned television station." Asked if the head nurse had, in fact, "screamed" at him, he said, "Yeah, I'd call it screaming; everybody could hear her, that's for sure." Brief interviews with the head nurse, an orderly, and two medical students who had been close enough to observe this event, independently denied the patient's version of the episode. The head nurse had simply, but firmly instructed the patient not to change the television station without asking the other patients who were already watching the television. There had been no "cursing" or raised voices, except by the patient, who reportedly had shouted at the head nurse, calling her a "bitch." Several other patients had previously complained about this patient's habit of walking into the television room and changing stations even though others were already watching something. Picking up in mid-session, and having reiterated the Question-Answer "homework" assignment, the therapist, in the following excerpt, uses material from the patient's behavior in the hospital. The patient claimed he wasn't upset over not watching a particular television program. He said he didn't even know what was on. He stated that he was upset in reaction to the head nurse's rebuke.

T: I'd like for the two of us to reexamine that incident, to give us an opportunity to practice this exercise. What I'd like you to do is to start by describing exactly what occurred in the TV Room.
P: You mean when the head nurse crawled my ass?
T: I mean when the head nurse talked to you about changing the stations. Start, if you would, at the point the head nurse spoke to you. Start by asking Question 1 out loud, if you would, and then go on through the exercise.
P: "What was the real event?" The head nurse crawled all over me because I changed the television station.
T: Did she literally crawl on top of you?
P: OK Doc; she didn't crawl on top of me. She just cussed me out.
T: Did she, in fact, use any curse words?
P: You don't have to use cuss words to cuss somebody out!
T: You mean you don't have to use curse words to reprimand someone?
P: That's right.
T: Did she use curse words?
P: I don't remember.

T: I was a little troubled by what you told me that happened . . . do you remember what you said yesterday. Let me read you these notes I took yesterday. *(Reads verbatim the patient's report of the incident.)* So, I went to the ward. I talked to the orderly and two medical students about the incident, then I talked to the head nurse. She did not "scream" at you and she did not use any "curse" words. Let's start again and you describe exactly what happened using very simple, literal language. OK. What was the real event?

P: The head nurse told me not to change the television station without asking the other patients first. Is that what you wanted me to say?

T: Is that exactly what happened?

P: Yeah, that's it.

T: Then, that is what I wanted you to say. Now, let's go to Question 2.

P: "What does it mean or symbolize?" It means she's a bitch. No *(laughing)*, it means, I guess it means she doesn't want me to change the television station without asking the other patients. I guess it means she thinks I'm an inconsiderate son of a bitch.

T: *(Smiling)* Well, that was pretty good, except that last part. Can you or anyone conclude for a fact that she thinks you are a S.O.B. based *only* on the fact that she asked you not to change the television station—I mean from the event in and of itself?

P: Not just from that, maybe.

T: Well, we are talking, at this point, only about that single event.

P: Then, I guess not.

T: Does that event have any other meaning, in and of itself?

P: What it means to me?

T: No, what it means itself.

P: I don't know of any, if you put it that way.

T: OK, Question 3.

P: "What is going to happen because of that event?" I guess I won't change the damn station.

T: You might decide to act that way. That would certainly be the sociable and considerate way to act; and, of course, the other people would appreciate you for it; but the question is what is the event itself going to *cause* or *result* in itself—regardless of what you do. Let's stop a second and re-read the instructions for answering Questions 2 and 3 . . .

P: I guess her saying that isn't going to make anything happen by itself, except make me mad.

T: Of course, you may become angry; but the event itself isn't going, by itself, to make anything happen independent of your own behavior . . . your own reaction to it.

P: If you put it that way.

T: Isn't that the way it is? If we exclude your own behavior, including your feelings, then nothing is going to happen, by itself, right?

P: OK, I guess that's right.

T: Fine, now, together, we are getting a pretty accurate picture. Let's go on. Anyone might react with a little anxiety, or a little irritation at being reprimanded, but you really got quite upset. One of the reasons, I suspect, has to do with your own thoughts and feelings about yourself and what you think criticism implies about you. We will talk more about that later on. Another reason you got so upset has to do with the way you perceived and interpreted exactly what happened. I think the way you talked about it in here yesterday pretty much reflects how you saw it at that time. Let's compare what you said yesterday with what you said today . . . (*Quotes patient's descriptive phrases from the first report, then his wording arrived at in the session).* So, you see a big difference in what actually happened and how you said it and the strength of emotions that you had. Your original emotional level pretty closely matched how you originally described the events. I think if you had seen it as clearly and accurately yesterday as you do right now, you would not have had such a strong reaction. You would still have had some negative reaction, perhaps; but nothing like the intensity you experienced yesterday. This exercise is not designed to make you feel good or nothing about something. It's designed to help you develop a clearer more accurate way of viewing things so that your emotional and other behavioral reactions are more in response to the actual events and not so much in response to our misperception and misinterpretations of them. Let's now go back to those little, low intensity events and talk about how to practice on them.

Step 6

Once the patient has demonstrated that he or she can correctly perform the task of identifying and "reality testing" (i.e., applying the three-part question-answer sequence) to frequent, "minor" events to which he or she responds with aversive emotions, the therapist selects one or two of the more moderate-severe items for which there is externally validated, persuasive evidence that the patient's previously self-reported subjective interpretation is significantly distorted or erroneous. In individual therapy sessions, the therapist asks the patient to perform the "self-challenge-reality testing" questions to these, and coaches the patient in strictly adhering to the conservative and constraining descriptive and interpretive guidelines. This process is repeated across sessions until all items have been "tested." During the latter sessions in this step, the therapist begins to introduce more material from the clinical diagnostic evaluation, initially selecting items thought to be relatively less emotionally evocative and for which potentially persuasive *contrary* evidence (i.e., contrary to the patient's prior interpretations) exists. Every effort is made to reassure the patient that he or she is not being asked to "blindly accept other people's opinions," rather that he or she is learning a way to be "a more careful, conservative, accurate observer" and how not to confuse "what you think with the actual external events themselves." This therapeutic enterprise is similar to Beck's *collaborative empiricism* model (see: Beck, 1976; Hollon & Beck, 1979).

Step 7

"Higher order," "cosmological" dysfunctional beliefs are identified. During Step 6, the therapist begins to suggest to the patient that he or she "appears" to "tend" to hold some "inaccurate general, thematic beliefs" about himself or herself, about other people, and about the "world in general." (For example: T: "Joe, you seem to believe that most people are not only out to take advantage of each other, but also that they really dislike or would even hurt each other if they could." P: "Why do you say that? T: "Well, for example, on several occasions, you, yourself have told me that 'everybody is out to screw everybody else' and that 'you've got to get them before they get you'. You've said several times that you 'really don't think anybody is trustworthy', and the session before last you made the comment that if you let your guard down for a minute, somebody's liable to stab you in the back.")

The therapist discusses such issues at length with the patient, reviewing the evidence implicating such beliefs and encourages him or her to reexamine the evidence for or against such beliefs. Further, the therapist points out the relationship between global beliefs and how individuals interpret-misinterpret discrete events. Importantly, the therapist repeatedly discusses how "misinterpretations" and "false beliefs" result in aversive arousal ("bad feelings") for the patient and in maladaptive, ineffectual overt behaviors, much of which is associated with negative social sanctions.

General thematic beliefs are inferred from the patient's own verbal statements and from observations reported by other people (e.g., spouses, ward personnel, etc.) For example, a husband may say "I don't know what she is saying to you, but she constantly claims that since 'everybody believes what they want to believe', her opinions are 'just as good as anybody elses'." The therapist may ask "You mean whether she likes something or not?" *Spouse:* "No, I mean whether something is true or not. Her idea is that if you don't believe something then it's not true for you." *Therapist:* "I think I see, she tends to think everybody's reality is what they believe." *Spouse:* "Yea, that's right. If I tell her scientists have discovered that smoking causes cancer , she will say: 'Well, that's their opinion'." *Therapist:* "That if you don't believe it, then smoking won't cause cancer in you?" *Spouse:* Exactly, and she does this in lots of things." *Therapist:* Can you give me some actual examples of where you think she's done this . . . especially examples that involved some important issues or that resulted in significant problems."

Such information is then compared to other data about the patient, including the therapist's own observations. If the evidence does suggest a pattern of behavior from which a thematic belief can be reasonably inferred, then the therapist includes that on the list of "higher order" or more global beliefs to be explored with the patient.

As in the former steps, the therapist selects global belief items for the initial therapeutic examination for which substantial and seemingly persuasive evidence exists and which, in the therapist's judgment, are most likely to be those the patient would more readily recognize and acknowledge. The relationship between global beliefs and specific instances of "distorted perception-misinterpretation" of events is thoroughly discussed and stressed, as is the relationship between "misperception" and excessive or "disproportionate" emotional reactions and maladaptive overt reactions. As the patient appears to grasp these more multifacited cognitive-emotive relationships, demonstrates increased skill in identifying and "challenging" his or her own cognitive-interpretive processes, and very importantly, appears increasingly desensitized to finding errors in these behaviors and then practicing to modify them, the therapist introduces newer, potentially more conflictual material from further up the hierarchy.

Step 8

During the latter sessions in Step 7, the therapist more explicitly begins a systematic review of all the former steps, stressing a philosophical integration of them. The patient is instructed to apply the Step 5 question-answer exercises "every time" he or she feels "more than slightly upset" (e.g., irritated, frustrated, anxious, or depressed) in reaction to any event. Although discussed earlier during treatment, during Step 8 increased emphasis is placed on the patient noting how other people have begun to react differently, in more positive ways, to changes in the patient's behavior patterns. In addition, items from Steps 2 and 3 are reviewed in the light of the patient's "new philosophy," with specific emphasis placed on not defining goals as "necessary for happiness or well-being" if, in fact, they actually are only "desirable," and focusing on "reasonably and realistically achievable" changes in, or additions to, the patient's behaviors, which can "increase the chances of attaining reasonably, realistically achievable goals." Further in this step, the patient is instructed in a method to increase the frequency and intensity of pleasurable life experiences (see Alford, 1981). Finally, the patient is repeatedly reinforced for his or her progress to date, in part, by noting observations by other people commenting on desirable changes. However, the patient is repeatedly warned that such changes are "at this stage" very tenuous and that reversion to previous patterns of functioning can and will occur unless the patient maintains active, daily practice. The need for continued outpatient therapy is stressed.

ADJUNCTIVE TREATMENT ACTIVITIES

Group Therapy

Where possible, personality disordered inpatients are placed in a therapeutic group that includes other nonpsychotic patients, particularly other patients with a primary or secondary diagnosis of personality disorder. These groups are led by a trained group therapist who utilizes a constructive confrontational approach. That is, patients are encouraged to discuss their problems, what they are working on in individual psychotherapy, and to ask for help in identifying and modifying their problem behaviors. Thus, in addition to personal disclosure, group therapy explicitly guides patients in providing constructive feedback to each other. For example, patients are encouraged to recognize that if one's family, individual therapist, group therapist, other treatment staff, and other patient group members agree on an observation about a specific patient's behavior, then it is quite likely a valid observation in spite of that patient's personal perceptions or beliefs to the contrary. Patients are encouraged to reinforce each other for carrying out therapeutic assignments and for consensually agreed upon evidence of progress.

Bibliotherapy

Some patients are given reading assignments that they are asked to be prepared to discuss with their individual therapist and in group therapy. The emphasis is on relating the patient's problem behaviors with the ideas expressed in the reading assignments. Specific reading material is selected by the individual therapist for the patient. Sections or chapters from Ellis and Harper (1975) and Glasser (1965) are frequently used. Further, sections from a work in progress, tentatively titled "Reality, Experience, and Adaptation," by one of us (GA), are also used with selected patients. Patients are also encouraged to read from their own religious texts.

Discharge

Patients are discharged to outpatient status when (1) they have begun working on Step 8 material, (2) they have demonstrated behavior changes that suggest that the patient both intellectually understands the treatment concepts and is actively and successfully practicing them, and (3) when any related or collateral problem which itself would warrant inpatient treatment has progressed to the point at which discharge would be indicated. Determination of (2) is based upon an accumulation of evidence from individual therapists, group leaders, ward personnel, and family members from which inferences about the patient's "symptomatic" perceptual cognitive-emotive processes and content are made. This is done in the same fashion described previously under *Evaluation and Diagnosis.* In particular, treatment staff observes for evidence of significant changes in both the targeted Category III cognitive-behavioral events and incidental behaviors in part by comparing therapists' observations, on-ward frequency counts and notations, and family members' observations across the course of hospitalization.

Following discharge from the hospital, treatment continues on an outpatient basis. This consists of repeated reviews of the various steps with emphasis on the patient detecting and noting how their modified ("more realistic") perceptions-interpretations-reactions to various life experiences result in less "self-generated" or "self-exacerbated" aversive feelings, increased capacity for positive pleasurable sensations, and in more effective, adaptive overt responses in the natural environment.

SUMMARY

While there is a substantial and growing body of research supporting the efficacy of cognitive therapeutic procedures similar to those presented in the present chapter (Kendall & Bemis, 1983; Meichenbaum & Cameron, 1982), systematic research investigating cognitive behavioral therapies for personality disorder and the particular procedures described here has only recently begun. Thus, this approach is only in the experimental stage of development. Further, it is extremely important for clinicians and clinical researchers to bear in mind that modification of cognitive processes and information-belief systems is much more akin to, say, training someone in a new language, than it is like modifying a rather circumscribed behavioral skill. It therefore entails a relatively long acquisition period during which frequent review, corrective feedback, and systematic shaping are combined with extensive personal practice. While one may learn a few simple, handy phrases with little effort, to understand and communicate spontaneously with facility even at a rudimentary level in a new language requires extensive training and practice. Similarly, knowing the rules of grammar, having a basic vocabulary, and even being able to struggle through a translation does not constitute linguistic competence. Rather, it is when one reaches that point where comprehension occurs without translation, and verbal expressions are formed and uttered spontaneously and unself-consciously that true mastery begins. This is analogous to our view of personality functions and their modification. For this reason, clinical studies investigating personality changes will necessitate rather long acquisition (treatment) phases and will require creative methods of assessment. For example, if one is truly fluent in a language, one can assess someone else's functional fleuncy in that language better in a single 50-minute conversation, then by seeing a transcript documenting that person's "masters degree" in it. This is not to argue that unstructured, unsystematic "clinical studies" are sufficient. Rather, it is to suggest that no matter how well designed, tightly controlled, or rigorously conducted, research studies that fail to recognize the subtlety, complexity, and integrative nature of the phenomena ostensibly under investigation, will likely fail to capture the central features of personality and personality disorders. Put simply, the difference between the phenomena that we consider central to "personality functions" and, say, "social skills deficits" is analogous to the difference between classical mechanics and plasma physics. The former remains useful for many things, as does behavioristic behavior therapy; the latter requires an expanded theoretical point of view, as does cognitive learning therapy.

We have no doubt that many patients who meet the *DSM-III* criteria for personality disorder can be significantly helped by narrowly focusing on those behavioral problems we define as Categories I and II (e.g., traditional targets for traditional behavioral therapeutics). There are also more complex and more subtle behavioral phenomena that are complex, indirectly observable, and even elusive in nature, and thus subject to controversy and, indeed, to questions of scientific legitimacy. The approach and techniques described in this chapter are, therefore, in the experimental stage of development and are, likewise, open to the same controversy and questions that surround the phenomena ostensibly being "treated." Space limitations precluded more extensive discussion of important topics integrally involved in this treatment. These include *resistance* (e.g., see Wachtel, 1982), *conscious* and *unconscious* mechanism (e.g., see Hilgard, 1977; Kahneman, 1973), and at a more basic level, human neurophysiology and sensory systems (e.g., see Brown, 1973; Gazzaniga, 1979) and social learning and cognition (see e.g., Rosenthal & Zimmerman, 1978). The procedures presented in this chapter represent the central structure of our treatment approach. It is hoped clinicians will find these useful in their work with this class of behavioral disorders and that clinical researchers might find this fertile ground for programmatic investigation.

REFERENCES

Alford GS. (1981). Behavior therapy and the good life. In Michaelson L, Hersen M, & Turner SM (Eds), *Future perspectives in behavior therapy*. New York: Plenum.

Allport GW, & Vernon PE. (1930). The field of personality. *Psychological Bulletin 27*, 677–730.

Bandura A. (1977a). Self-efficacy: Toward a unifying theory of behavior change. *Psychological Review 89*, 191–215.

Bandura A. (1977b). *Social learning theory*. Englewood Cliffs, NJ: Prentice-Hall.

Bandura A. (1969). Principles of behavior modification. New York: Holt, Reinhart, & Winston.

Barlow DH. (1977). Assessment of sexual behavior. In Ciminero AR, Calhoun KS, & Adams HE (Eds), *Handbook of behavioral assessment*. New York: John Wiley.

Barlow DH, & Beck JG. (in press). The psychosocial treatment of anxiety disorders: Current status, future directions. In Williams JBW, & Spitzer RL (Eds), *Psychotherapy research: Where are we and where do we go?* New York: Guilford Press.

Beck AT. (1976). *Cognitive therapy and the emotional disorders*. New York: International Universities Press.

Beck A, Rush AJ, Shaw B, & Emery G. (1979). *Cognitive therapy of depression*. New York: Guilford Press.

Bellack AS, & Hersen M. (1977). *Behavior modification: An introductory textbook*. Baltimore: Williams & Wilkins, pp 37–99.

Brown JL. (1973). *Sensory systems*. Baltimore: Williams & Wilkins.

Brownell KD, & Barlow DH. (1980). The behavioral treatment of sexual deviation. In Goldstein A, & Foa EB (Eds), *Handbook of behavioral interventions*. New York: John Wiley.

Curran JP, & Mariotto MJ. (1980). A conceptual structure for the assessment of social skills. In Hersen M, Eisler RM, & Miller PM (Eds), *Progress in behavior modification, vol. 10*. New York: Academic Press.

Ellis A. (1970). *The essence of rational psychotherapy: A comprehensive approach to treatment*. New York: Institute for Rational Living.

Ellis A. (1962). *Reason and emotion in psychotherapy*. New York: Lyle Stuart.

Ellis A, & Greiger G (Eds). 1977). *Handbook of rational-emotive therapy*. New York: Springer Verlag.

Ellis A, & Harper RA. (1975). *A new guide to rational living*. Hollywood, CA: Wilshire.

Gazzaniga MS (Ed). (1979). *Behavioral neurobiology, vol. 2: Neuropsycology*. New York: Plenum Press.

Glasser W. (1965). *Reality therapy: A new approach to psychiatry*. New York: Harper & Row.

Hake HW, & Rodwan AS. (1966). Perception and recognition. In Sidowski JB (Ed), *Experimental methods and instrumentation in psychology*. New York: McGraw-Hill.

Hilgard ER. (1977). *Divided consciousness: Multiple controls in human thought and action*. New York: Wiley-Interscience.

Hinde RA. (1970). *Animal behavior: A snythesis of ethology and comparative psychology*. New York: McGraw-Hill.

Hollon SD, & Beck AT. (1979). Cognitive therapy of depression. In Kendall P, & Hollon S (Eds), *Cognitive behavioral interventions: Theory, research, and procedures*. New York: Academic Press.

Kahneman D. (1973). *Attention and effort*. Englewood Cliffs, NJ: Prentice-Hall.

Kaplan M. (1983). A woman's view of DSM-III. *American Psychologist 38*, 786–792.

Kelly JA. (1982). *Social skills training: A practical guide for intervention*. New York: Springer Verlag.

Kendall PC, & Bemis KM. (1983). Thought and action in psychotherapy: The cognitive-behavioral approaches. In Hersen M, Kazdin AE, & Bellack AS (Eds), *The clinical psychology handbook*. New York: Pergamon Press.

Leitenberg H. (1976). Behavioral approaches to the treatment of neuroses. In Leitenburg H (Ed), *Handbook of behavior modification and behavior therapy*. Englewood Cliffs, NJ: Prentice-Hall.

Luria AR. (1961). *The role of speech in the regulation of normal and abnormal behavior*. New York: Lippincott.

McLemore CW, & Benjamin LS. (1979). Whatever happened to interpersonal diagnosis? A psychosocial alternative to DSM-III. *American Psychologist 34*, 17–34.

Mahoney M. (1974). *Cognition and behavior modification*. Cambridge, MA: Ballinger.

Mahoney M, & Arnkoff D. (1978). Cognitive and self-control therapies. In Garfield S, & Bergin A (Eds), *Handbook of psychotherapy and behavior change*. New York: John Wiley.

Mavissakalian M, & Barlow DH. (Eds). (1981). *Phobia: Psychological and pharmacological treatment*. New York: Guilford Press.

Meichenbaum D. (1977). *Cognitive-behavior modification: An integrative approach*. New York: Plenum.

Meichenbaum D, & Cameron R. (1982). Cognitive behavior therapy. In Wilson GT, & Franks CM (Eds), *Contemporary behavior therapy*. New York: Guilford Press.

Millon T. (1983). The DSM-III: An insider's perspective. *American Psychologist 34*, 804–814.

Mischel W. (1984). Convergences and challenges in the search for consistency. *American Psychologist 39*, 351–364.

Mischel W. (1973). Toward a cognitive social learning reconceptualization of personality. *Psychological Review 80*, 252–283.

Mischel W. (1968). Personality and assessment. New York: John Wiley.

Mountcastle VB. (1967). The problem of sensing and the neural coding of sensory events. In Quarton, GC, Melnechuk T, & Schmitt FO (Eds), *The neurosciences*. New York: Rockefeller Press.

Rosenthal TL, & Zimmerman BJ. (1978). *Social learning and cognition*. New York: Academic Press.

Scott RR, Himadi W, & Keane TM. (1983). A review of generalization in social skills training: Suggestions for future research. In Hersen M, Eisler RM, & Miller PM (Eds), *Progress in behavior modification, vol. 15*. New York: Academic Press.

Wachtel PL (Ed). (1982). *Resistance: Psychodynamic and behavioral approaches*. New York: Plenum Press.

Williams JBW, & Spitzer RL. (1983). The issue of sex bias in DSM-III: A critique of "a woman's view of DSM-III" by Marcia Kaplan. *American Psychologist 38*, 793–798.

Wulach JS. (1983). Diagnosing the DSM-III antisocial personality disorder. *Professional Psychology 14*, 330–340.

PART 3

Treatment of Children and Adolescents

9
Acting-Out Disorders

William I. Gardner and Christine L. Cole

There are some children and adolescents whose patterns of aggressive, defiant, oppositional, and similar problems of social conduct occur with such frequency, magnitude, and/or duration that removal from the home and placement in a psychiatric treatment facility is necessitated.[1] This placement may be of a short- or long-term nature and may involve such facilities as public or private community psychiatric hospitals, state or regional public psychiatric hospitals, highly structured boarding schools, children's psychiatric day hospitals, psychiatric units affiliated with medical schools, or community and state facilities serving the mentally retarded.

Psychological treatment procedures based on various behavior therapy models represent one of the therapeutic approaches used in these inpatient settings. The increasing popularity of behavioral procedures among clinical staff is related to (1) their potential effectiveness and efficiency in attaining various therapy goals and (2) the fact that the procedures can be implemented in the day-by-day milieu by a range of residential treatment staff members. Further, use of behavior therapy procedures with acting-out disorders has appeal in an inpatient

[1] As the focus of this chapter is on inpatient treatment of acting-out disorders in psychiatric facilities, only peripheral attention is provided those behavioral intervention programs offered for conduct disordered delinquents in various nonpsychiatric programs associated with educational, correctional, or criminal justice agencies. The reader interested in this literature is invited to consult such works as Kirigin, Braukmann, Atwater, and Wolf (1982) and Stumphauzer (1979).

PRACTICE OF INPATIENT BEHAVIOR THERAPY
ISBN 0-8089-1715-3

psychiatric treatment facility because these procedures can be used in combination with various other psychiatric and psychological treatment approaches such as psychopharmacology and psychotherapy.

TERMINOLOGY

The term "*acting-out*" is used in a descriptive sense to emphasize the disruptive nature of the child's problem behaviors. Terms such as "destructive," "verbally and physically assaultive," "violent," and "extreme negativism" portray the disruptive interpersonal dimension of the acting-out behaviors. Other terms such as "antisocial," "socially aggressive," and "sociopathic personality," used by various mental health professionals, emphasize the disruptive social nature of the child's problems.

More formal clinically- or empirically-based diagnostic and classification systems include a variety of disorders or categories that involve acting-out symptoms. These difficulties may represent the central feature of the disorder (e.g., conduct disorder) or be only one of a complex of other symptomatic features requiring treatment (e.g., schizophrenia). Diagnostic categories included in *DSM-III*, Quay (1979), and Weiner (1982) in which serious acting-out difficulties are, or may be, present include conduct disorder, oppositional disorder, attention deficit disorder, adjustment disorder with disturbance of conduct, socialized aggressive disorder, pervasive developmental disorders, specific developmental disorders, intermittent explosive disorder, mental retardation, psychomotor epilepsy, depression, and schizophrenic disorders. Thus, acting-out difficulties take many different forms, may represent features of various syndromes of pathology, and may require either primary or secondary intervention.

DIAGNOSTIC AND CLASSIFICATION SYSTEMS

Current diagnostic and classification systems in psychology and psychiatry that include categories of acting-out behavior have been developed either through clinically- or empirically-derived procedures. *DSM-III* is the most current and popular example of a clinically-derived system. Within *DSM-III*, various symptom clusters have been developed from extensive clinical experiences and are conceptualized as diagnostic categories of mental disorders. For each disorder, a set of diagnostic criteria or rules are provided to guide the clinician in arriving at a diagnosis. Thus, the clinician initially decides what symptoms of pathology are present and then applies the diagnostic rules for selecting a specific mental disorder category.

Within the *DSM-III* system, most children and adolescents with persistent and serious acting-out difficulties are provided a diagnosis of *conduct disorder*. The major behavioral characteristic of this disorder is a repetitive and persisting pattern of conduct that violates the basic rights of others or disregards societal norms or rules. Subtypes of aggressive and nonaggressive violations are included. To meet the diagnostic criteria for the aggressive category, the child or adolescent demonstrates repetitive and persistent (at least six months duration) acting-out behaviors involving physical violence toward other persons (e.g., assault, mugging, rape) or property (e.g., vandalism, fire-setting, breaking-and-entering), or thefts outside the home involving confrontation with a victim (e.g., purse-snatching, extortion, hold-up of a store). The nonaggressive subtype, in contrast, is characterized by such behaviors as persistent truancy, stealing, substance abuse, or running away, none of which involves confrontation with a victim.

Conduct disorder is further divided into undersocialized and socialized subtypes. The undersocialized conduct disordered child does not establish adequate social bonds involving affection or empathy and has no, or only minimal or superficial, relationships with peers. As a result, feelings of guilt or remorse following acting-out behaviors are generally absent. The socialized subtype, in contrast, shows evidence of social attachment to others and does show concern for the welfare of friends or companions.

A second popular classification system, and one that appeals to the behaviorally-oriented clinician, is that based on a multivariate statistical analysis approach. Quay (1979) describes various acting-out difficulties as depicting either a *conduct disorder* or a *socialized aggressive disorder*. These empirically-derived categories are based on Quay's analysis of a large number of factor analytic studies of child psychopathology. The *conduct disorder* factor includes such specific acting-out behaviors as fighting, disobedience, destructiveness, disruptiveness, negativism, rowdiness, irritability, and hyperactivity. The *socialized aggressive disorder* includes such personal features as has bad companions, steals in the company of others, belongs to a gang, is loyal to delinquent friends, and is truant from school. These disorders may be identified by means of the Behavior Problem Checklist (BPC), a three-point rating scale containing 55 problem behaviors (Quay, 1977). Typically filled out by parents or teachers, the BPC represents a valuable source of information for the behavior therapist in identifying the specific acting-out behaviors presented by a child or adolescent.

As noted, acting-out disorders may accompany a variety of other psychiatric disorders described in *DSM-III*. For example, Puig-Antich (1982) report that 33 percent of a sample of prepuberty boys with major depression also met *DSM-III* criteria of conduct disorder. Satterfield, Hoppe, and Schell (1982) report a high correlation between attention deficit disorder and conduct disorder among institutionalized adolescents. Acting-out difficulties described in children with specific developmental disorders (Pfeffer, Plutchik, & Mizruchi, 1983), psychoses (Lewis, Shanok, Grant, & Ritvo, 1983), psychomotor epilepsy (Lewis, Pincus, Shanok, & Glaser, 1982), mental retardation (Gardner & Cole, 1984), and pervasive developmental disorders (Johnson & Baumeister, 1981) provide other illustrations of this interrelationship.

Although the behavioral clinician is prone to eschew psychiatric diagnosis and focus on direct behavioral assessment and treatment of the acting-out behaviors as these occur under specific conditions, this approach may be problematic in individual cases. As emphasized by Kazdin (1983), children with similar presenting problems (e.g., aggression) may differ widely in responsiveness to behavioral interventions and in prognosis depending on factors other than the current presenting problems. For example, a number of writers indicate that acting-out problems of children and adolescents with long-standing conduct disorder are more difficult to manage in residential settings and more difficult to treat successfully then acting-out problems presented by children with other mental disorders as defined by *DSM-III* (e.g., McAuley, 1982; Plapp, 1983; Weiner, 1982). As another illustration, the inefficiency of extinction and differential attention procedures in influencing negativistic behaviors of oppositional children is well documented (Herbert, Pinkston, Hayden, Sajwaj, Pinkston, Cordua, & Jackson, 1973; Hersen & Barlow, 1976). Being sensitive to the diagnosis provided the child in the psychiatric setting thus may have utility both in the development of realistic behavioral program objectives and in selection of effective treatment procedures.

In fact, the relationship between acting-out disorders and a range of other psychiatric conditions that involve major problems of affect, cognition, and perception would suggest that behavioral treatments be closely interfaced with psychiatric treatment approaches. In some instances, successful medical treatment of a syndrome pattern such as depression may have a significant impact on the child's acting-out difficulties. This was illustrated by Puig-Antich (1982), who reported, following successful drug treatment (imipramine) of major depressive disorders in prepuberty boys who also presented conduct disorders, that the conduct problems in most cases also abated. In other instances, improvement may be optimized by a combination of drug and behavior therapies. This was illustrated by successful inpatient treatment of an adolescent with problems of seizure activity and concomitant aggressive outbursts. A combination of antiseizure medication (carbamazepine) and behavior therapy procedures resulted in successful control of both the seizures and related acting-out difficulties (Rapport, Sonis, Fialkov, Matson, & Kazdin, 1983).

BEHAVIORAL ASSESSMENT

In conducting an assessment of acting-out disorders, two themes should guide the behavioral clinician's activities. First, the behavioral assessment should be client-specific: that is, designed to identify and understand critical factors relating to the problematic behaviors in individual children. For example, one child may act aggressively in an impulsive manner when angry or overly anxious, while another child's aggression may be more deliberate and goal-directed. Second, when attempting to understand the child's acting-out difficulties, the clinician simultaneously should be pinpointing those specific coping skills and related cognitive, emotional, and motivational supports that the child will need for successful social and interpersonal functioning following return to the community. The general view, and a laudable one, in inpatient facilities is to return the person to his or her home environment as quickly as possible. With this set, however, the clinical staff with a behavioral orientation has a tendency to ask: "What behavioral procedures are available to most rapidly suppress the acting-out behaviors?" Such program experiences, if initiated prior to an understanding of client-specific contributing factors, seldom have durable effects.

In our experiences with various inpatient programs using behavioral procedures, the clinical staff is prone to rely excessively on deceleration procedures and to minimize skill-building ones. From an ethical as well as practical position, however, the critical assessment question is "How can the acting-out problem behaviors be replaced with more socially appropriate ones that are criticial to the child's present or future adjustment in naturalistic settings?" It is evident that, in most instances of chronic acting-out disorders, socially and personally significant and durable behavior change will not occur in a short period of time. Various symptoms may be reduced in severity by drug therapy or by suppressive behavioral techniques. However, if used as the major treatment approaches, the controlling effects of these procedures most typically are shortlived following termination of treatment. Consistent therapeutic program experiences provided over an extended period of time typically are required for development of both the social skills competency and the motivational and affective supports needed to insure that these will replace the acting-out behaviors. With this competency development orientation to guide assessment and intervention activities, the inpatient experience will more likely assist the child and his or her family in arriving at that psychological growth needed for adequate adjustment following discharge from this setting.

In most instances, acting-out problems requiring inpatient treatment result from a complex of factors. Both assessment and intervention activities should reflect this complexity. In our clinical assessment and treatment activities, we have approached acting-out disorders from a multicomponent view using constructs and procedures drawn from a variety of behavioral and related models. This Multicomponent Behavioral Model of Acting-Out Disorders is represented in Figure 9-1. The model results from our personal experiences indicating that acting-out difficulties cannot be understood, managed appropriately, or modified successfully unless consideration is given to a complex of factors that may contribute to the acquisition, instigation, and persistent recurrence of such problems.

Behavioral assessment based on this model is focused on the acting-out behaviors that precipitated the inpatient placement. The major concern is with understanding the multitude of factors currently influencing these excessively occurring actions. The objectives of the behavioral assessment are threefold: (1) to identify the various internal and external stimulus conditions under which the acting-out behaviors are likely to occur, (2) to identify the functions served by the acting-out behaviors, and (3) to identify various client-specific personal characteristics that contribute to the problem behaviors. In our view, an understanding of these child-specific personal characteristics is essential if *effective* and *durable* behavior change is to occur.

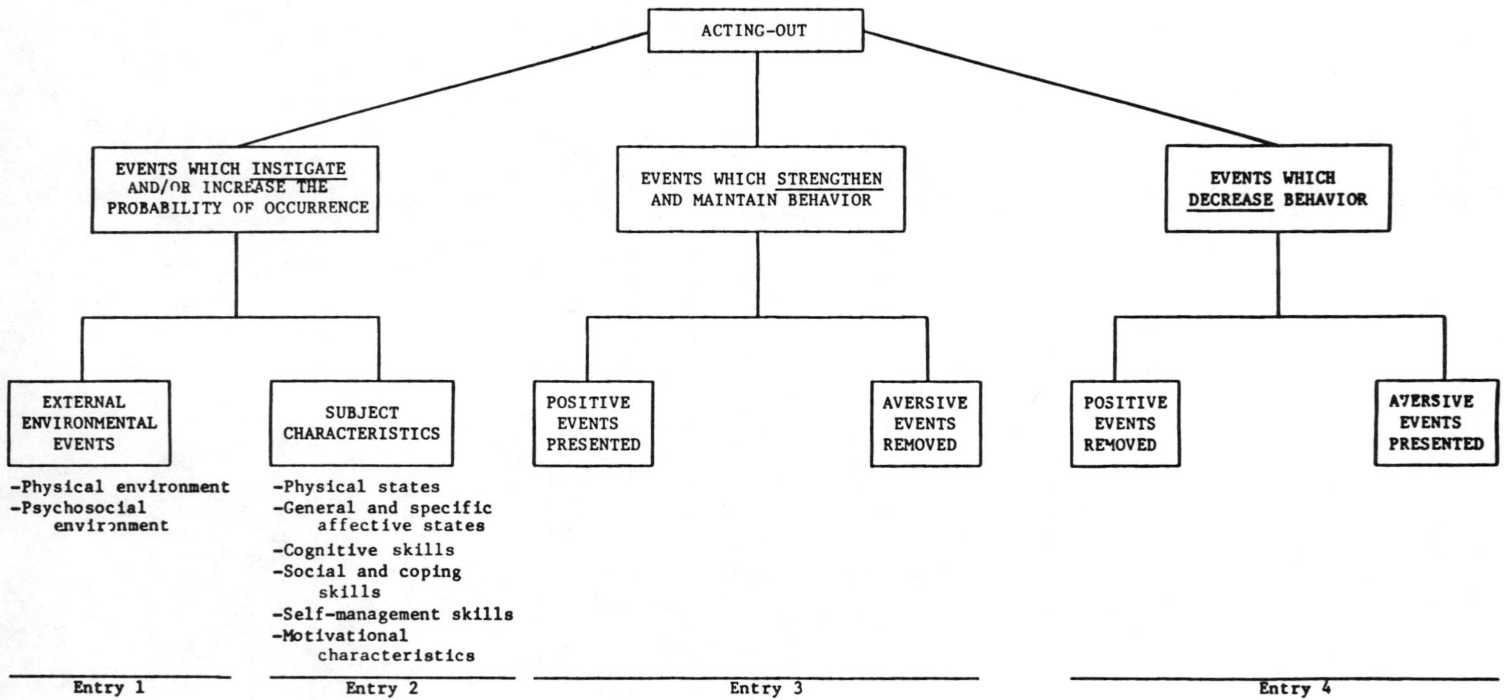

Fig. 9-1. Multicomponent behavioral model of acting-out disorders.

This multicomponent view represents the traditional operant explanations of acting-out behaviors as well as more recently developed social skills, anxiety management and cognitive behavioral and coping skills models. Entries 3 and 4 of the model focus on the effects on acting-out problems of various procedures that manipulate contingent consequences. These include both positive and negative reinforcement and punishment procedures. Entry 1 includes description of factors that, when present, instigate or increase the likelihood that acting-out behaviors will occur.

Entry 2 variables include those internal stimulus conditions that, when combined with external stimulus events, instigate or increase the likelihood of acting-out behaviors. Examples of these events include physical states (e.g., pain, fatigue), affective states (e.g., anger, anxiety), and cognitive variables (e.g., covert verbal ruminations of a provoking nature, paranoid ideas). Entry 2 also includes consideration of skill areas and characteristics that, due to their low strength or absence, increase the likelihood of problems in those inclined to behave disruptively. In illustration of these behavior deficits, an adolescent, when taunted by peers or criticized by adults, may react aggressively because he either does not have alternative interpersonal skills in his repertoire or, if present, the skills to self-manage these are absent or inefficient. A final subject characteristic of significance in understanding acting-out difficulties and in selecting effective interventions is the child's motivational features. Knowledge of positive reinforcers (e.g., adult approval, peer acceptance, having control over others) as well as the variety and relative influence of aversive events that influence behavior (e.g., rejection by peers, adult reprimand, anxiety) are of central importance in behavioral programming.

In summary, some Entry 2 subject characteristics such as excessive negative emotional arousal may, *by their presence*, increase the likelihood of acting-out behaviors. Other subject variables, such as conflict-resolution skills and motivation to please adults or to abide by rules of social behavior, *by their absence or low strength*, render the child more vulnerable to conduct problems under conditions of provocation.

Assessment data relative to Entries 1, 2, and 3 are obtained through direct observation of the child in the settings in which the acting-out problems occur. These observations may be made by the behavior therapist, the child him or herself, or by living area and program staff. Additionally, interviews with family members and with the child provide valuable information relative to the generality and chronicity of the problem behaviors.

It has been our practice to provide residential living and program staff with a Behavior Recording Form (BRF) designed to obtain narrative information about each occurrence of target behaviors defined specifically for each child. The BRF includes columns for recording the immediately preceding conditions, the specific acting-out behavior, and the immediate consequences produced by the behavior. Additionally, staff are requested to describe any other circumstances or conditions that appeared to influence the acting-out episode. This latter inquiry is designed to uncover any recurring setting events (e.g., being depressed) that may increase the likelihood of the problem behaviors under specific discriminative stimulus events (Gardner, Karan, & Cole, 1984).

This direct observational approach is emphasized because the acting-out problems occur in relation to specific persons or requirements and must be understood in this context. Acting-out behaviors are not solely a function of the child's pathology, but rather of the child in interaction with various social and physical environments. The problem behaviors can be understood only within this context.

The assessment data gathered from these variety of sources are used by the therapist to develop a series of hunches about current factors that contribute to problem behaviors. Even though the therapist may attempt to reconstruct previous history in an effort to understand how the current problem areas developed over time, this "understanding" typically is not critical to the development of program hypotheses or to the realization of therapy goals. This assessment strategy is based on the assumption that there is no necessary relationship between these historical factors involved in the initial development of problem behaviors (etiology) and those curent factors that are functional in instigating and maintaining them.

Again, hypotheses are developed about current environmental conditions and child characteristics that increase the likelihood that acting-out behaviors will occur (e.g., anger, adult reprimand), as well as about the functions served by the behaviors (e.g., aggression produces peer approval and staff distress, staff demands are removed). Hypotheses are developed about factors in each of the three entry points of Figure 9-1, as each repesents potential targets of behavioral intervention.

Following development of a complex of hypotheses concerning factors contributing to the acting-out behaviors, the therapist translates these into program implications and then into specific intervention procedures relevant to each of these hypothesized influential variables. For example, if it is assumed that a child acts out to obtain adult attention when with a group of peers, this hypothesis translates into the following program implications: (1) remove or minimize adult social attention following acting-out behavior; (2) provide adult social attention at frequent other occasions following appropriate behavior; and, if needed, (3) provide specific skills training to insure that the child has appropriate attention-gaining skills for use in group settings. These program implications next are translated into specific approaches involving (1) an extinction procedure, (2) differential reinforcement procedures, and (3) a social skills training program. As a second example, the hypothesis may be developed that at least one function served by the highly disruptive behaviors of an adolescent toward a specific teacher is that it produces negative reactions from the teacher and other staff. This hypothesis could then be translated into program implications and related intervention procedures aimed at removing or reducing the negative reactions of staff, increasing the positive reinforcement value of the teacher, and teaching the adolescent other social skills that could be used to more appropriately exert personal influence over his or her teacher or other adults in authority roles.

To summarize, steps involved in the assessment and program development process are as follows:

Step 1. Gather data in Entries 1, 2, and 3 of Figure 9-1.
Step 2. Develop hypotheses relative to influential variables in each entry point.
Step 3. Translate hypotheses into program implications.
Step 4. Select specific behavioral intervention procedures and combine these into a comprehensive behavior therapy program.
Step 5. Following initiation of the program, monitor client progress and modify program as needed. Add generalization and maintenance approaches as therapy goals are being realized.

TREATMENT

Most of the behavior therapy literature addressed to treatment of acting-out disorders in children and adolescents has been devoted to evaluating the effects of various contingent consequences on rate of acting-out behavior. As previously described, these procedures are represented in Entries 3 and 4 of Figure 9-1 and include consideration of consequences that strengthen appropriate behavior (positive reinforcement procedures), as well as those that reduce the strength of inappropriate behavior (extinction and punishment procedures). More recently, a number of subject characteristics, depicted in Entry 2, have been considered in development of behavioral treatment approaches to acting-out disorders in children and adolescents.

Positive Reinforcement Procedures

Procedures involving the contingent presentation of valued consequences (e.g., social praise, preferred activities, tokens) to increase desired behavior frequently have been used with acting-out children and adolescents. The most commonly used positive reinforcement approaches include differential reinforcement procedures, token economies, and contingency contracting.

Differential Reinforcement

Several types of differential reinforcement procedures, in which adult praise and attention or other reinforcers are provided for appropriate behavior while inappropriate behavior is ignored, have been used to decrease acting-out disorders in children. With differential reinforcement of other behavior (DRO), the undesired behavior is carefully specified, and reinforcement is provided following periods of nonoccurrence of the behavior. An obvious consideration in use of this procedure is whether or not the child has the prosocial replacement behaviors in his or her repertoire that will appear spontaneously and be reinforced during periods of nonoccurrence of the undesired behavior. More specific positive reinforcement procedures are those of differential reinforcement of alternative responses (DRA) and differential reinforcement of incompatible behavior (DRI). DRA provides reinforcement for specific appropriate behaviors, while DRI involves reinforcing specific behaviors that are physically incompatible with the target response. Finally, the child may be reinforced for engaging less frequently in the undesired behavior. This procedure, called differential reinforcement of low rates of behavior (DRL), involves administering reinforcement on an interval basis (Kazdin & Frame, 1983).

When using any of these differential reinforcement procedures, the possibility of recurrence of the acting-out behavior remains. Although the inappropriate behavior may occur less frequently and may even eventually disappear as other replacement behaviors become relatively stronger, the maladaptive behavior remains in the child's repertoire. Acting-out behaviors may reappear if alternative behaviors are not maintained through positive reinforcement. The positive effects of therapy programs using differential reinforcement procedures may be short-lived because the child's environments do not consistently reinforce the desired behaviors for a sufficient period of time to insure their continued strength.

Token Economies

Token economies are positive reinforcement programs that involve the presentation of objects that initially have no particular value of their own (e.g., marks, stamps, poker chips) contingent on specific appropriate behavior. These token reinforcers may be saved and later exchanged for backup reinforcers (e.g., privileges, special food items, records). An example of a token economy implemented in psychiatric hospital school classes for unsocialized aggressive and schizophrenic children is provided by Drabman (1973). Each child received tokens at regular intervals for compliance with the classroom rules. Tokens could be exchanged for prizes (e.g., edibles, toy trinkets) available from the class store. Both teacher- and student-administered token economies reduced the children's acting-out behaviors. In a second example of successful use of a token economy (Moss & Rick, 1981), adolescent patients in a psychiatric hospital earned points for engaging in a variety of specific desirable behaviors and forfeited points for undesirable behaviors (e.g., incorrigibility, drug abuse, criminal acts). Points could be spent for various privileges and activities.

Token economies can be a valuable asset to the behavior therapist if used as a supportive component of a comprehensive behavior program. One central problem in treatment of chronic acting-out disorders is that of motivating the child or adolescent to participate in program activities and to engage in prosocial behaviors. It is evident that many inpatients place only minimal value on becoming involved simply to obtain adult social approval or praise. The token economy, with its potential for providing immediate, frequent, and meaningful consequences, can be invaluable in the early stages of program initiation to insure participation in potentially therapeutic experiences. Also, through repeated association with the delivery of tokens and backup reinforcers, the therapist is likely to gain some secondary reinforcing qualities.

Contingency Contracting

Contingency contracting typically is used with older children and adolescents as it involves mutual negotiation between the child or adolescent and adults. Generally, a contingency contract is a precise statement of the behaviors and responsibilities expected and the reinforcement and/or penalties associated with each (Stuart, 1971). It may be quite valuable in working with negativistic and argumentative children and adolescents, as there is reduced opportunity for confrontation relative to expected behaviors and associated contingencies. Behavioral contracting potentially reduces the "controlling" aspects of behavior therapy by dividing responsibility and consequences equally between the client and the therapist (Ayllon & Skuban, 1973). When contracts are used with children, the required behavior should be clearly specified, the total task should be broken down into components, and small approximations should be reinforced initially.

Extinction Procedures

When behavior is maintained by either positive or negative reinforcement, it will decrease in strength if no longer followed by these reinforcing consequences. Thus, one method of reducing a child's acting-out behavior is to identify and eliminate the reinforcers that maintain its occurrence, an extinction procedure. This is sometimes difficult, especially with acting-out behaviors of high strength that have occurred over a long period of time. A specific behavior pattern frequently is maintained by multiple sources of possible positive and negative reinforcement: peer attention, adult attention, and removal of aversive consequences. Thus, any particular acting-out behavior may serve a variety of functions. In fact, the behavior may even be self-maintaining due to its previous frequent association with contingent reinforcing consequences. Such acting-out behavior thus would be maintained for a period of time independent of other sources of contingent reinforcement. It also is apparent that the previous schedules of reinforcement associated with the acting-out behavior will influence the effectiveness of an extinction procedure. Most acting-out behaviors have developed and are maintained under an intermittent reinforcement schedule. As a result, the behavior is likely to persist through numerous experiences of nonreinforcement. In fact, it is not unusual to observe that the frequency and intensity of the behavior increases during the early stages of extinction. Also, as noted earlier, there is evidence that extinction and differential attention may even intensify the problem behaviors to an intolerable level. In our experience with acting-out behaviors, extinction seldom works in isolation and must be combined with other tactics that provide reinforcement for alternative behaviors.

Punishment Procedures

Punishment procedures, involving the presentation of unpleasant consequences or the removal of pleasant events following an undesired response, frequently have been used to reduce acting-out behaviors in children and adolescents. These procedures include time-out, response cost, overcorrection, and presentation of aversive consequences.

Time-Out

Time-out from positive reinforcement (TO) refers to the removal of the opportunity to experience or earn positive reinforcement. TO typically involves procedures that temporarily remove the child for a specific period of time from access to reinforcing situations. In illustration, Lisa, who is making taunting comments to a peer, is required to move away from the group activity, sit in a nearby chair, and observe the group as they continue to watch a favorite film. Staff deliberately provide positive social feedback to those children who are behaving appropriately. This TO procedure is referred to as contingent observation. Other variations of TO involve seclusion or social isolation of the child following misbehavior. These procedures of removing the person from the current social/physical environment contingent upon acting-out and placing him or her alone in a room with the door closed and usually locked serve as a major treatment component in a large number of inpatient treatment programs (Matson, Ollendick, & DiLorenzo, 1980; Thomas & Maus, 1983). An assumption underlying the use of this procedure is that the child's environment is highly reinforcing and that removal from it for a period of time will be aversive. Drabman and Spitalnik (1973) provide an example of the use of social isolation TO with a class of 9- and 11-year-old aggressive boys in a residential psychiatric setting. Following each target aggressive behavior, the child was immediately escorted to a small, dimly lit room for 10 minutes. Aggressive acts decreased dramatically using this procedure.

In other variations of TO, an ongoing source of positive reinforcement is removed for a period of time following acting-out behavior. For example, whenever Mark screams and strikes out in a fit of anger, staff may turn away from him and ignore him until he regains control. Another child who throws her food during meals will lose access to the food tray for a short period of time. TO procedures may be effective in reducing acting-out behaviors even in children with severe developmental difficulties who may appear to be relatively unresponsive to social reinforcement (e.g., Foxx & Shapiro, 1978; White, Nielson, & Johnson, 1972).

Response Cost

Acting-out behavior patterns may be reduced by using a response-cost procedure in which a previously acquired reinforcer is removed contingent upon an undesired response. Inappropriate behaviors cost the person. He or she is fined for engaging in these through loss of specific reinforcing events that he or she possesses. As an example, following tantrum behavior, Karen may lose her off-grounds privileges, may not have access to the special leisure room for three days, or may lose the privilege of being staff assistant for a day. A response-cost procedure is easy to manage whenever a token economy program is in operation. This is illustrated by Phillips (1968), who used response cost in combination with token reinforcement to reduce a variety of acting-out behaviors in adolescents.

Overcorrection

Overcorrection is a combination of procedures designed to suppress undesired behaviors while providing opportunities to practice more appropriate behavior. This is done by requiring the child or adolescent, following acting-out behavior, to (1) overcorrect the environmental effects of the disruptive behavior by restoring it to an improved state (restitution), and (2) repeatedly practice relevant appropriate behavior in situations where the problem behaviors typically occur (positive practice) (Foxx & Bechtel, 1982). For example, if a child physically injures a peer, he or she might be required to assist in cleaning, medicating, and bandaging the wound, to assist in filling out the necessary reports, and to apologize to each person on the unit. If the child refuses to comply, he is physically guided in the corrective response. Variations of the overcorrection response have been used to suppress a wide range of acting-out behaviors (Foxx & Bechtel, 1982; Ollendick & Matson, 1978).

Implementation of overcorrection procedures may become highly problemmatic with the acting-out adolescent who might find it extremely provocative if physically guided through an overcorrection procedure. In our view, a major theme of the acting-out child's past experiences probably has been that of physical confrontation with adults. It would appear, in order to reduce the resistive nature of the child's interactions with adults, that confrontation should be minimized and positive adult–child experiences maximized. This, perhaps, can best be accomplished by positive reinforcement procedures.

Presentation of Aversive Consequences

The presentation of aversive consequences (PAC) involves the contingent application of some unpleasant event (e.g., verbal reprimand, loud noise, unpleasant taste, tickling, noxious odor, aversive electrical stimulation) following acting-out behavior. Greene and Hoats (1971) describe an aversive tickling procedure used to reduce physical aggression in a mentally retarded adolescent. Staff approached her from the rear and tickled her under the arms "forcefully and somewhat aggressively" for three to five seconds following each target behavior. Brief electric shock has also been shown to be effective in suppressing various acting-out behaviors in mentally retarded residents (Ball, Sibbach, Jones, Steele, & Frazier, 1975; Birnbrauer, 1968; Burcher & King, 1971).

Although such PAC procedures may successfully eliminate acting-out behaviors in children, treatment effects may not generalize to new situations (e.g., Burcher & King, 1971) and intervention may produce negative effects in some clients. In the Birnbrauer (1968) study, for example, the client began wetting himself and "when shock was 'due,' Mike ran to a corner of the room, jumped in place, hit himself and yelled" (p 206). Thus, it cannot be assumed that a particular procedure will automatically produce the same effects in different individuals. The unique characteristics of each child or adolescents must be carefully assessed prior to selection and implementation of any therapy procedure. especially a punishment procedure such as PAC.

Skill Training Approaches

While behavior therapists typically have focused on direct suppression of acting-out disorders, it is evident that skill deficits frequently underlie many of these children's problems (Clarizio & McCoy, 1983; Patterson, Reid, Jones, & Conger, 1975). Thus, a number of recent investigations reflect this assumption that acting-out disorders in children and adolescents are related to the absence or low strength of alternative social and cognitive behavioral/coping skills.

Social Skills Training

Social skills training programs typically have combined procedures of instruction, modeling, role-playing, and performance feedback (Goldstein, 1981). The child or adolescent is informed of the specific desired skill behaviors for a particular situation (instruction), provided examples of a person performing these behaviors (modeling), encouraged to rehearse or practice these behaviors (role-playing), and provided positive feedback or approval for his or her behavior (performance feedback). A number of recent studies illustrate the efficacy of these procedures in treatment of various clinical groups including children in inpatient psychiatric settings (Bornstein, Bellack, & Hersen, 1980), mentally retarded boys in an inpatient unit for emotionally disturbed children (Matson, Kazdin, & Esveldt-Dawson, 1980), adolescent psychiatric patients (Elder, Edelstein, & Narick, 1979), and incarcerated juvenile delinquents (Ollendick & Hersen, 1979).

A common problem, however, with social skills training, as with other behavior therapy procedures, is limited generalization to the natural environment of skill behaviors trained. Children may be taught to respond appropriately in role-play situations, but their behavior in the natural setting frequently does not change (e.g., Berler, Gross, & Drabman, 1982; Cooke & Apolloni, 1976; Singleton & Asher, 1977). One approach used to increase the likelihood for generalization across situations concerns the selection of target behaviors. Berler et al. (1982) and Kazdin (1983) suggest that target behaviors be selected on the basis of a child's performance in the natural environment rather than, as is typically done, on the basis of deficits observed in role-play situations. The child or adolescent would be taught those specific problem-solving skills required in interpersonal situations in which acting-out problems are likely to occur. Thus, specific target behaviors would be selected on the basis of their relevance and potential usefulness for the child in his or her daily interactions with others in the natural setting. An additional method of facilitating generalization of newly acquired behavior skills is to practice these with the client *in vivo*. The clinician can assume, following social skills training experiences, that the new skills are in the child's behavioral repertoire, but cannot assume that these will automatically appear in untrained environments. Our clinical experiences suggest that performance of these behavior skills in the presence of the actual stimulus conditions in the naturalistic environment must be prompted and repeatedly reinforced to insure their continued occurrence in these settings.

Cognitive Behavioral/Coping Skills Training

Other skill training approaches have focused on teaching acting-out children and adolescents self-regulation strategies and skills for effectively coping with stress. A variety of cognitive behavioral/coping skills training procedures have been developed and are currently available to the behavioral clinician. Adolescents, for example, may be taught specific skills of interpersonal transaction (problem-solving), assuming another person's point of view (role-taking), and inhibiting their own impulses (self-control) (Little & Kendall, 1979).

Novaco (1979) describes the use of a "stress inoculation" program of controlling one's own anger. In this program, an adolescent initially would be encouraged to identify circumstances that arouse anger and to discriminate between justified and unjustified anger. Following this, alternative coping skills are taught by modeling and rehearsal. Finally, the adolescent would practice the skills in imaginal and role-played interactions. Although research demonstration of the effectiveness of this program with acting-out problems is limited, this cognitive approach offers an exciting alternative to the therapist. In our own clinical experience, we have made use of a graduated exposure procedure in which the client, via audio and video presentations, is exposed to a variety of specific anger-provoking scenes. *In vivo* practice also is provided.

Other cognitive behavioral strategies focus on teaching various specific skills of self-management. Clients may be taught to self-monitor ("What did you do?"), self-evaluate ("Was that appropriate or inappropriate?"), and self-consequate ("What do you earn?") their own appropriate and inappropriate behaviors (Gardner, Cole, Berry, & Nowinski, 1983; Shapiro & Klein, 1980).

An integral component in several cognitive anger control programs in school settings is that of *self-instructional training*. Meichenbaum's original self-instructional training program involved teaching aggressive children self-verbalizations to direct their own task performance (Meichenbaum & Goodman, 1971). Specific self-instructions taught include identifying the problem, labeling alternative solutions, evaluating solutions, choosing one solution, correcting errors, and providing self-reinforcement. Training began with the adult modeling these self-statements while performing a task, and gradually shifted responsibility for self-instruction and task performance to the child. The ultimate goal was for the child to perform the task while making the statements covertly. The "think-aloud" program, developed for use with aggressive, impulsive children, also involves modeling and role-playing to teach self-instructions for problem-solving (Camp, Blom, Herbert, & vanDoorninck, 1977). Similarly, Schneider and colleagues (Schneider, 1974; Robin, Schneider & Dolnick, 1976) taught children to use covert problem-solving and to pretend to withdraw into an imaginary "turtle shell" when in provocative situations. Finally, a cognitive restructuring procedure has been used to reduce aggression in children. After identifying the thought patterns of children in aggression-provoking situations, the children were taught to engage in alternative thinking involving more adaptive behaviors (Foreman, 1980).

Although cognitive behavioral/coping skills training procedures have been shown to be effective in reducing the acting-out behaviors of some children and adolescents, results have been mixed (Hobbs, Moguin, Tryoler, & Lahey, 1980) and most studies have been conducted with impulsive and hyperactive children (Kazdin & Frame, 1983). However, these approaches currently are undergoing extensive research investigation and should be considered by the behavior therapist in devising treatment programs for the acting-out child.

GUIDELINES FOR BEHAVIOR THERAPY PROGRAMS

Even the most minimal standards for behavior therapy programs aimed at resolution of acting-out disorders in children require that treatment procedures reflect a close relationship to client assessment data. This is especially true considering the limited availability of empirically-based treatment packages or procedures that represent best approaches to influencing specific acting-out behaviors. Denoting the potential value of such "automatic application" procedures for remediating social skill deficits in adults, Hersen and Bellack (1977) state, "As research in this area accumulates, the most effective behavioral technique for a given deficit will have been identified, thus permitting its 'automatic' application, given the particular restrictions or contraindications of the case" (p 548).

Unfortunately, there is a noticeable absence of such "automatic application" approaches for treatment of acting-out disorders in the child and adolescent behavior therapy literature (Evans & Nelson, 1977; Fehrenbach & Thelen, 1982). The inpatient clinician, thus, when faced with these clients and problems is required to develop an individualized treatment program based on client assessment information.

From our perspective, the behavior therapy program should meet the following minimal criteria:

1. *The intervention program should be based on behavioral assessment data that suggest hypotheses concerning the functionality of the acting-out behaviors.* For example, use of an extinction procedure would be based on the hypothesis, generated from specific client assessment data, that at least one function of the child's acting-out behavior was that of producing social attention that was reinforcing to him or her. As a second example, use of a desensitization procedure to reduce or eliminate the aversive qualities of a required program activity may

be based on the hypothesis, derived from client assessment information, that an adolescent's aggressive outbursts are maintained by negative reinforcement, as these actions terminate or delay staff attempts to get him or her to attend and/or participate in the program activity.

2. *The treatment program should reflect assessment data concerning possible relationships between the problem behaviors and both (a) external stimulus control features and (b) various client features.* In illustration, studies indicate that various improvements in the physical and social environments of institutionalized mentally retarded children may result in reduction in problems of aggression (Boe, 1977; Levy & McLeod, 1978; Murphy & Zahm, 1978). The behavior therapy program would focus on changing such physical and social environmental conditions if assessment data indicated that these were present and were hypothesized to contribute to the problem acting-out behaviors. Assessment data also may suggest that a client who engages in frequent temper outbursts has minimal self-control skills when confronted with provocative stimulation by peers. The intervention focus in this case may be on teaching the person specific mediational skills that could be used to cue alternative conflict-resolution actions (Gardner & Cole, 1984).

3. *The program should include procedures for developing, strengthening, and/or maintaining prosocial behaviors that will replace the acting-out behaviors.* Procedures, such as social skills training, cognitive behavioral approaches, token economies, and contingency contracting, designed specifically to strengthen alternative adaptive behaviors, should be included in the child's program. If such procedures are not included, conceptual and empirical justification for the exclusion should be presented. That is, the program should include a rationale for assuming that alternative prosocial behaviors are in the child's repertoire and are likely to occur once the acting-out behavior is eliminated. As an example, use of only a behavior suppression procedure such as TO would be based on the speculation, gained from client assessment data, that alternative prosocial behaviors (a) were in the child's repertoire, (b) would occur when the punished behavior was sufficiently suppressed, and (c) would maintain predominance over the acting-out behavior once the suppressive functions of the TO procedure had dissipated. In addition, baseline and intervention data should be included to demonstrate that these prosocial behaviors have in fact increased in strength at a level significantly exceeding baseline strengths. The clinician thus should not be satisfied with the mere absence or reduction in strength of acting-out behaviors.

Barrett (1977) and Touchette (1978) further highlight the unacceptability of behavior therapy programs that emphasize only deceleration or elimination of inappropriate behaviors (e.g., acting-out behaviors), especially with inpatient populations such as young children or the mentally retarded who are characterized by numerous behavioral deficits and deficiencies. Barrett (1977) notes that if deceleration programs are: "not complemented by contingencies that strengthen adaptive and constructive alternative behaviors, decelerative behavior control risks eliminating the behavers' only effective means of manipulating their environments. The results may be not only counterproductive but also antithetical to the goals of behavioral normalization" (p 179). Touchette (1978) also suggested, "Drugs, punishment, and restraint may solve the immediate problems of those who must care for the child, but they do not alleviate the problem of the child. The problem is, and will continue to be, behavioral insufficiency. There is a real danger that procedures which suppress undesirable behavior and accomplish nothing else, will delay or prevent any constructive solution to the child's problems" (p 199).

4. *The behavior therapy program should initially use and evaluate the least intrusive or restrictive procedures prior to use of more intrusive ones.* Differential reinforcement, contingency contracting, skill training approaches, and other positive procedures designed to strengthen alternative adaptive behaviors should be used prior to implementing more intrusive punishment procedures such as TO, response cost, PAC, and overcorrection. If these less intrusive approaches are not used, the program should present a rationale, based on assessment data, that indicates that specific client characteristics dictate the more intrusive intervention procedures. For example, if in an attempt to suppress an adolescent's aggression toward peers, TO is used instead of a specific social skills training procedure, assessment data should be presented that would justify the use of the intrusive TO procedures with this person. In this case, it should be demonstrated that the adolescent does have the socially appropriate skills in his or her repertoire but, due to insufficient inhibitions, engages impulsively in aggressive actions.

It has been our experience that initiation of punishment contingencies early in a treatment program creates the risk of exacerbating rather than reducing the problem behaviors. Our approach has been one of initially increasing the reinforcement value of a variety of prosocial behaviors through differential reinforcement procedures, as well as of increasing the type and value of events that are reinforcing to the client. If the acting-out behaviors continue to occur and punishment is added to the program, the person now has viable alternatives. When confronted with a choice between socially appropriate behavior and reinforcement, and disruptive behavior and punishment, the client will be in a position to select the most preferred alternative.

As noted earlier, the intrusiveness of a procedure may be subject-specific and cannot be judged on its face characteristics. As a result, any punishment procedure, however innocent it may appear to be (a) should not be used in isolation, (b) should be monitored carefully for negative side effects, and (c) should be accompanied by equally, or more, powerful procedures to develop and strengthen prosocial replacement behaviors (May, Risley, Twardosz, Friedman, Bijou, Wexler, et al., 1975).

5. *The intervention program should use those procedures that offer the most promise of long-term benefits.* A suppressive procedure such as TO or overcorrection may well result in even rapid deceleration of various excessive behaviors. But unless alternative replacement behaviors are specifically trained and pro-

vided systematic reinforcement, the suppressive effects may dissipate over time, resulting in the reappearance of the inappropriate behavior. Procedures of teaching replacement behaviors also offer greater possibilities for generalization and maintenance of the desired behaviors, as such behaviors would be likely to result in naturally occurring social feedback (Marholin, Siegel, & Phillips, 1976).

Case Study

Shirley, a 13-year-old adolescent, and her family had been seen on an outpatient basis for a few weeks prior to placement for inpatient treatment. As a result, we were able to obtain some initial behavioral assessment data in the home and school settings. Both mother and special education teacher completed the BRF during a three-week period. Interviews with mother and teacher and a problem-focused interview with the young adolescent also were conducted. Prior to initiation of a behavior therapy program, the adolescent assaulted her mother while in a fit of rage and was hospitalized because "mother could no longer manage her." These assessment data, combined with those obtained following hospitalization, were most valuable in our understanding of the case and in development of short- and long-term goals for Shirley.

Shirley was an only child who lived with her mother. She was physically incapacitated due to a childhood injury and required some assistance with mobility, dressing, and toileting. Her father died of a heart attack when she was 10 years old. Mother reported a history of acting-out behaviors that began shortly after the death of the father. Shirley was described as demanding and impatient, and depended excessively on her mother to entertain her when at home. Mother admitted that she had spoiled Shirley, but frequently was unable to manage her unless she gave in to her demands. Rage reactions consisting of screaming, swearing, physical assault, property destruction, and self-abuse were likely to occur if her demands were not met. These tantrums had continued for extended periods of time when mother had attempted to "wait Shirley out." Following these episodes, Shirley frequently expressed remorse and resolved to control her temper in the future. Mother and daughter participated in an insight-based counseling experience for over a year prior to Shirley's hospitalization. Although some initial improvement was noted, the problems intensified in the few months prior to hospitalization. Mood, while variable, generally was negative or neutral. Although mother and teacher described Shirley as sociable, she had few friends due to her disruptive and demanding actions. She was described by the teacher as an overanxious child who excessively sought approval and reassurance and who was overly sensitive to criticism.

Following placement in the psychiatric treatment facility, Shirley's defiant, oppositional, and conduct problems continued. Her problem behaviors, defined by the facility staff, included verbal and physical aggression toward peers and staff, uncooperativeness in following living area routine and in complying with reasonable staff requests, refusal to attend and participate in the educational and therapy programs provided, excessive demanding of staff time and services, prolonged periods of excessive negative emotionality, prolonged temper outbursts, and frequent negative self-statements. She also displayed both nocturnal and diurnal enuresis, a problem that had been present on an irregular basis for about three years. The BRF, completed by living area and program staff, direct observation of and interaction with Shirley by the behavior therapists in living and program areas, and interviews with Shirley relative to her problems were used to obtain the assessment data.

On the basis of these data, supported by the preadmission information, a number of program hypotheses were developed relative to Entry 1, 2, and 3 factors influencing her acting-out and oppositional behaviors:

1. The aggressive behaviors were functional in that these resulted in (a) compliance with her demands, (b) valuable staff and peer attention, (c) distress in staff who ignored her demands, and (d) the removal/postponement of requests or directives that she did not find to her liking.
2. Shirley required a frequent schedule of social interaction with staff and frequent feedback relative to her acceptability. If this was not provided, she insured attention through her acting-out behavior.
3. Her remorse and apologies following disruptive actions, while reflecting guilt or shame, also were functional in that they resulted in affectionate reactions from others.
4. The prolonged tantrum behavior had been shaped by mother and currently was being maintained by intermittent positive and negative reinforcement.
5. The acting-out behaviors were more likely to occur under conditions of negative emotional arousal (e.g., anxiety, anger, jealousy).
6. Shirley had a limited repertoire of socially appropriate means of obtaining and maintaining positive social interaction and feedback from adults or peers.
7. Shirley had a limited repertoire of skills for coping with frustration, peer conflict, or anxiety.
8. As a result of her physical limitations and social skills, Shirley was limited in means of controlling or exerting influence over her physical and social environments. Her experiences had taught her that various of her disruptive behaviors did result in her exercising control over others.
9. Various frustrations produced by her physical limitations and dependency on others produced frequent negative emotional arousal. When negatively aroused, she had an increased likelihood of responding disruptively to minor sources of aggravation.
10. Physical limitations resulted in poor self-esteem and generalized anxiety over her competency. She was likely to react in an impulsive and disruptive manner to any criticism or failure.

These hypotheses next were translated into program implications and then into detailed program approaches. These approaches were followed by living area and program staff as they interacted with Shirley throughout the day. They focused on teaching and strengthening a variety of social, coping, and self-management skills designed to replace the acting-out behaviors:

1. Provide Shirley with a schedule card of her daily activities. Review the schedule with Shirley each morning and at times throughout the day prior to each activity. Prompt Shirley to describe the program activity and remind her of some positive features of program attendance and participation. Use the card to emphasize that she is managing aspects of her own life, e.g., "Shirley, what program are *you* attending this afternoon?"
2. Provide a lead time when reminding Shirley of her scheduled activities, especially prior to activities that she does not prefer. Avoid confrontation or arguments. Your interactions should reflect interest and positive concern.
3. Following each period/activity, Shirley will be prompted to label her social behaviors relative to those expected in the setting, decide if she "did meet" or "did not meet" the expected behaviors, and then self-record her evaluation on her schedule card. Staff will initial the card to verify its correctness and to record any differences in opinion relative to the appropriateness of her behavior. Staff will prompt Shirley to describe her behaviors that resulted in her evaluation. Praise her for prosocial behaviors. Do not reprimand or otherwise react to inappropriate behaviors. Shirley will keep her schedule card with her throughout the day.
4. Staff are encouraged to prompt Shirley to show her schedule card and describe what she is doing. Comment on the positive behavior marks and ignore the negative ones. Our strategy is to focus her attention on prosocial behaviors and to minimize attention for inappropriate actions.
5. Prior to bed each evening, Shirley will count the number of marks attained for prosocial behaviors throughout the day. She will transfer these to a Reinforcer Preference Card (RPC). These cards, depicting back-up reinforcers previously selected by Shirley and cost (number of positive evaluations) of each, will be placed in a three-ring binder located in Shirley's room. Shirley will deposit the earned marks on the RPC of her choice.
6. After the transfer has been completed, staff will describe the number of marks on each card needed for exchange for the depicted reinforcer. Provide a casual, noncritical comment about the number of "did not meet" marks obtained that day. Follow this with a comment of encouragement relative to earning a larger number of marks for expected behaviors during the next day.
7. After a RPC has been completed, Shirley may exchange the card for the depicted item or activity. A range of back-up reinforcers reflecting her preferences will be available for exchange. This is especially essential during the early weeks of the program to ensure adequate incentives for her to inhibit her inappropriate behaviors and to select desired ones.
8. It is essential that staff interactions with Shirley be as positive as possible. Model desired behavior and a positive demeanor, and demonstrate a helpful attitude. Label appropriate behaviors (e.g., positive affect, initiating positive peer and staff interactions, following staff requests, being independent) and express your satisfaction. To enhance her self-esteem, use positive self-labels, e.g., "Wow, Shirley, *you* did it," "That's really using *your* head,"

"*You* really worked hard on that one. I'll bet *you're* proud of yourself." Also, provide Shirley with frequent opportunities to make choices, and to be in a position of being in charge and having specific personal responsibility. Make such statements as "Shirley, *you* decide," or "What would *you* choose to do?" Label and praise appropriate choices and independent actions.

9. Provide Shirley with specific routine responsibilities in living and program areas. These responsibilities will provide her with experiences of being in charge of and influencing aspects of her environment. A positive sense of personal value and accomplishment should develop.
10. Relate to Shirley in a *calm* manner, even when she is being inappropriate. A reprimand, sharp tone of voice, criticism, an aggravated grimmace, or a sign of despair all serve to provoke, and potentially reinforce, inappropriate behavior. When she is disruptive, be as calm and deliberate as possible. Demonstrate that her inappropriate demands, yelling, or swearing will not have a negative effect on you.
11. As there is a correlation between her negative, depressive-like moods and her disruptive behaviors, it is essential that we provide Shirley with numerous mood-elevating positive experiences. A predominantly positive mood state serves as an emotional background for a range of prosocial behaviors that currently are in her repertoire. Approach Shirley positively, prompt positive affect, interact with her in a personable manner, and spend individual time with her. Vary conversational topics to ensure that she will focus on activities and events other than her own limitations. Label positive affect and express your delight, e.g., "Shirley, what a pretty smile! Did you know that your brown eyes dance when you smile?" . . .
15. Identify specific situations that result in negativistic and other acting-out behaviors. Use these in developing training scenes in desensitization, cognitive restructuring, and social skills training. An emphasis will be placed on such interpersonal behaviors as initiating and maintaining appropriate peer and adult interactions, coping with frustration, expressing emotions, making friends, expressing disagreements, handling criticism, and leisure skills involving peers. Basic self-management skills of self-labeling, evaluating behaviors as appropriate or inappropriate, self-reinforcement, self-punishment, standard setting, and self-instruction will be taught and used in training the interpersonal social skills. Psychological Services staff will consult with living and program area staff in developing specific training experiences.
16. Following training, staff will be in a position to anticipate problem situations and prompt Shirley to use appropriate social skills. Also, when observing Shirley behaving negatively, staff can prompt Shirley to *label* her behavior ("Shirley, what are *you* doing?"), *evaluate* it ("Shirley, is that appropriate or not appropriate?"), *describe its consequences* ("Shirley, what happens when you threaten your peers?"), and *self-instruct* and *demonstrate* more

> appropriate behaviors ("Shirley, what is a better way to show your anger. Show me please."). If successful, staff will be in a position to provide positive feedback and prompt Shirley to self-reinforce with positive self-statements . . .

The program also included specific procedures for managing episodes of physical aggression and prolonged tantrums. These involved prompting Shirley to remove herself to a quiet area until she had calmed herself. She then was prompted to describe and demonstrate alternative means of expressing her aggravations and concerns.

Shirley responded quite positively to the program and was returned to the community within three months following hospitalization. Mother was provided training in the rationale and procedures of the program. Additionally, the behavior therapist consulted with the public school system and provided a set of guidelines for managing any recurrence of her acting-out problems and for support of her newly developed social skills.

Problem Areas

Although Shirley did respond positively to the behavior therapy program, these gains were not attained without difficulty. Brief description of these difficulties is provided, as they are representative of recurring problems encountered or observed in our association with various public, private, and university inpatient psychiatric facililties. Similar problems have been described by others and should be consulted by those interested in a more detailed presentation (Hersen, 1979; Hersen & Bellack, 1978).

The initial problem encountered was that of suitably interfacing the behavior therapy program with the psychoactive drug therapy provided by the medical staff. Changes in the type and dosage levels of drugs were made frequently without adequate communication between the psychiatrist and the psychology staff responsible for preparation and monitoring of the behavior therapy program. Initially, it was difficult to determine what treatment procedures or combinations of procedures might be responsible for, or contributing to, the behavior changes obtained. This problem was reduced by a mutual commitment that no treatment changes would be made without prior consultation. The monitoring system offered by the behavior therapists was then used to meaningfully evaluate the specific effects of treatment changes as these were made.

The second set of problems related to the differences of opinion among the staff concerning the factors that "caused" Shirley's acting-out difficulties. Few of the medical and nursing staff were behavioral in their views, and most preferred to use dynamic explanations. When pressed to translate these explanations into treatment procedures that could be used by a range of living area and program staff, however, the shortcomings of many of the explanations were accepted. However, the behavior therapists incorporated as many of the notions as possible into the approaches developed. As noted in the exerpts from the behavioral program, technical jargon was minimized. Also, the rationale for each program component was carefully described to staff, and each approach was modeled. In this presentation, effort was made again to use the explanatory terms offered by staff and to demonstrate how these were addressed in the program.

A third problem, and a perennial one in all behavioral programming implemented in naturalistic settings, related to the competency of the staff in implementing the approaches. A closely related problem was the lack of motivation to consistently follow the program approaches. These problems were present in the professional staff (e.g., nursing, educational, recreational) as well as in the living area assistants. When working with children and adolescents with acting-out difficulties, it has been our experience that staff too frequently react with anger and aggravation when personally insulted by the foul language of patients or when physically assaulted. It is quite difficult to train staff to remain calm and neutral with the victim of negativism or assault. Variations of anger control procedures described by Novaco (1980) have been used with varying degrees of success. In most cases, although time-consuming, it is relatively easy to prepare therapeutically sound behavior therapy programs. Their success or failure, however, is quite related to the therapists' effectiveness in influencing authentic and consistent implementation of these program components by *in vivo* staff.

SUMMARY

Acting-out difficulties presented by children and adolescents in inpatient settings may take different forms representing features of a variety of formal diagnostic categories of pathology. Since acting-out behavior involves a variety of characteristics rather than a unitary disorder with a single etiology, no single assessment method is adequate and there is no single best treatment for it. Instead, multicomponent client-specific behavioral assessment that provides direction to development of individualized behavior therapy programs is recommended.

In viewing acting-out disorders in children and adolescents from this multicomponent behavioral perspective, it becomes evident that many of these difficulties are related to deficits in adaptive behavior skills. Many of these clients do not have the social, coping, self-management, affective, or motivational features necessary for successful functioning in their natural environments. Thus, it is essential that behavioral procedures designed to teach alternative adaptive skills to replace the acting-out responses be included in any behavior therapy program. Guidelines for behavioral programming consistent with this skill-building orientation were presented in this chapter. In addition, the behavior therapist must be aware of problems encountered in implementing behavioral programs in inpatient psychiatric settings and must address these directly to maximize the likelihood for client progress.

REFERENCES

Ayllon T, & Skuban W. (1973). Accountability in psychotherapy: A test case. *Journal of Behavior Therapy and Experimental Psychiatry 4*, 19–30.

Ball TS, Sibbach L, Jones R, Steele B, & Frazier L. (1975). An accelerometer-activated device to control assaultive and self-destructive behaviors in retardates. *Journal of Behavior Therapy and Experimental Psychiatry 6*, 223–228.

Barrett BH. (1977). Behavior analysis. In Wortis J (Ed), *Mental retardation and developmental disabilities: An annual review, Vol. IX*. New York: Brunner/Mazel.

Berler ES, Gross AM, & Drabman RS. (1982). Social skills training with children. *Journal of Applied Behavior Analysis 15*, 41–53.

Birnbrauer JS. (1968). Generalization of punishment effects—a case study. *Journal of Applied Behavior Analysis 1*, 201–211.

Boe RB. (1977). Economical procedures for the reduction of aggression in a residental setting. *Mental Retardation 15*, 25–28.

Bornstein M, Bellack AS, & Hersen M. (1980). Social skills training for highly aggressive children. *Behavior Modification 4*, 173–186.

Burcher B, & King L. (1971). Generalization of punishment effects in the deviant behavior of a psychotic child. *Behavior Therapy 2*, 68–77.

Camp BW, Blom GE, Herbert F, & vanDoorninck WJ. (1977). "Think aloud": A program for developing self-control in young aggressive boys. *Journal of Abnormal Child Psychology 5*, 167–169.

Clarizio HF, & McCoy GF. (1983). *Behavioral disorders in children* (3rd ed). New York: Thomas Y. Crowell Company.

Cooke TP, & Apolloni T. (1976). Developing positive social-emotional behaviors: A study of training and generalization effects. *Journal of Applied Behavior Analysis 9*, 65–78.

Drabman RS. (1973). Child versus teacher administered token programs in a psychiatric hospital school. *Journal of Abnormal Child Psychology 1*, 66–87.

Drabman RS, & Spitalnik R. (1973). Social isolation as a punishment procedure: A controlled study. *Journal of Experimental Child Psychology 12*, 178–188.

Elder JP, Edelstein BA, & Narick MM. (1979). Adolescent psychiatric patients: Modifying aggressive behavior with social-skills training. *Behavior Modification 3*, 161–178.

Evans IM, & Nelson RO. (1977). Assessment of child behavior problems. In Ciminero AR, Calhoun KS, & Adams HE (Eds), *Handbook of behavioral assessment*. New York: John Wiley, pp 603–681.

Fehrenbach PA, & Thelen MH. (1982). Behavioral approaches to the treatment of aggressive disorders. *Behavior Modification 6*, 465–497.

Foreman SG. (1980). A comparison of cognitive training and response cost procedures in modifying aggressive behavior of elementary school children. *Behavior Therapy 11*, 594–600.

Foxx RM, & Bechtel DR. (1982). Overcorrection. In Hersen M, Eisler RM, & Miller PM (Eds), *Progress in behavior modification: Vol. 13*. New York: Academic Press, pp 227–288.

Foxx RM, & Shapiro ST. (1978). The timeout ribbon: A nonexclusionary timeout procedure. *Journal of Applied Behavior Analysis 11*, 125–136.

Gardner WI, & Cole CL. (1984). Aggression and related conduct problems in the mentally retarded: A multicomponent behavioral model. In Breuning SE, Matson JL, & Barrett

RP (Eds), *Advances in mental retardation and developmental disabilities, Vol. 2*. Greenwich, CT: JAI Press, pp 41–84.

Gardner WI, Cole CL, Berry DL, & Nowinski JM. (1983). Reduction of disruptive behaviors in mentally retarded adults: A self-management approach. *Behavior Modification* 7, 76–96.

Gardner WI, Karan OC, & Cole CL. (1984). Assessment of setting events influenicng functional capacities of mentally retarded adults with behavioral difficulties. In Halpern AS, & Fuhrer MJ (Eds), *Functional assessment in rehabilitation*. Baltimore: Paul H. Brookes Publishing, pp 171–186.

Goldstein AP. (1981). Social skill training. In Goldstein AP, Carr EG, Davidson WS, & Wehr P (Eds), *In response to aggression: Methods of control and prosocial alternatives*. New York: Pergamon Press, pp 159–218.

Greene RJ, & Hoats DC. (1971). Aversive tickling: A simple conditioning technique. *Behavior Therapy 2*, 389–393.

Herbert EW, Pinkston EM, Hayden ML, Sajwaj TE, Pinkston S, Cordua G, & Jackson C. (1973). Adverse effects of differential parental attention. *Journal of Applied Behavior Analysis 6*, 33–47.

Hersen M. (1979). Limitations and problems in the clinical application of behavioral techniques in psychiatric settings. *Behavior Therapy 10*, 65–80.

Hersen M, & Barlow DH. (1976). *Single case experimental designs: Strategies for studying behavior change*. New York: Pergamon Press.

Hersen M, & Bellack AS. (1977). Assessment of social skills. In Ciminero AR, Calhoun KS, & Adams HE (Eds), *Handbook of behavioral assessment*. New York: John Wiley, pp 509–554.

Hersen M, & Bellack AS. (1978). *Behavior therapy in the psychiatric setting*. Baltimore: Williams & Wilkins.

Hobbs SA, Moguin LE, Tryoler M, & Lahey BB. (1980). Cognitive behavior therapy with children: Has clinical utility been demonstrated? *Psychological Bulletin 87*, 147–165.

Johnson WL, & Baumeister AA. (1981). Behavioral techniques for decreasing aberrant behaviors of retarded and autistic persons. In Hersen M, Eisler RM, & Miller PM (Eds), *Progress in behavior modification: Vol. 12*. New York: Academic Press, pp 119–170.

Kazdin AE. (1983). Psychiatric diagnosis, dimensions of dysfunction, and child behavior therapy. *Behavior Therapy 14*, 73–99.

Kazdin AE, & Frame C. (1983). Aggressive behavior and conduct disorder. In Morris RJ, & Kratochwill TR (Eds), *The practice of child therapy*. New York: Pergamon Press, pp 167–192.

Kirigin KA, Braukmann CJ, Atwater JD, & Wolf MM. (1982). An evaluation of Teaching-Family (Achievement Place) group homes for juvenile offenders. *Journal of Applied Behavior Analysis 15*, 1–16.

Levy E, & McLeod W. (1977). The effects of environmental design on adolescents in an institution. *Mental Retardation 15*, 28–32.

Lewis DO, Pincus JH, Shanok SS, & Glaser GH. (1982). Psychomotor epilepsy and violence in a group of incarcerated adolescent boys. *American Journal of Psychiatry 139*, 882–887.

Lewis DO, Shanok SS, Grant M, & Ritvo E. (1983). Homicidally aggressive young children: Neuropsychiatric and experiential correlates. *American Journal of Psychiatry 140*, 148–153.

Little VL, & Kendall PC. (1979). Cognitive-behavioral interventions with delinquents: Problem solving, role-taking, and self-control. In Kendall PC, & Hollon SD (Eds), *Cognitive-behavioral interventions*. New York: Academic Press.

Marholin D, Siegel LJ, & Phillips D. (1976). Transfer and treatment: A search for empirical procedures. In Hersen M, Eisler RM, & Miller PM (Eds), *Progress in behavior modification: Vol. 3*. New York: Academic Press.

Matson JL, Kazdin AE, & Esveldt-Dawson K. (1980). Training interpersonal skills among mentally retarded and socially dysfunctional children. *Behaviour Research and Therapy 18*, 419–427.

Matson JL, Ollendick TH, & DiLorenzo TM. (1980). Time-out and the characteristics of mentally retarded institutionalized adults who do or do not receive it. *Mental Retardation 18*, 181–184.

Moss GR, & Rick GR. (1981). Application of a token economy for adolescents in a private psychiatric hospital. *Behavior Therapy 12*, 585–590.

May JG, Risley RR, Twardosz S, Friedman P, Bijou SW, Wexler D, et al. (1975). Guidelines for the use of behavioral procedures in state programs for retarded persons. *Mental Retardation Research 1*, 1–73.

McAuley R. (1982). Training parents to modify conduct problems in their children. *Journal of Child Psychology and Psychiatry and Allied Disciplines 23*, 335–342.

Meichenbaum DH, & Goodman J. (1971). Training impulsive children to talk to themselves: A means of developing self-control. *Journal of Abnormal Psychology 77*, 115–116.

Murphy MJ, & Zahm, D. (1978). Effect of improved physical and social environment on self-help and problem behaviors of institutionalized retarded males. *Behavior Modification 2*, 193–210.

Novaco RW. (1979). The cognitive regulation of anger and stress. In Kendall PC, & Hollon SD (Eds), *Cognitive-behavioral interventions: Theory, research, and procedures*. New York: Academic Press.

Novaco RW. (1980). Training of probation counselors for anger problems. *Journal of Counseling Psychology 27*, 385–390.

Ollendick TH, & Hersen M. (1979). Social skills training for juvenile deliquents. *Behaviour Research and Therapy 17*, 547–554.

Ollendick TH, & Matson JL. (1978). Overcorrection: An overview. *Behavior Therapy 9*, 830–842.

Patterson GR, Reid JG, Jones RR, & Conger RE. (1975). *A social learning approach to family intervention, Vol. 1*. Eugene, OR: Castalia.

Pfeffer CR, Plutchik R, & Mizruchi MS. (1983). Predictors of assaultiveness in latency age children. *American Journal of Psychiatry 40*, 31–35.

Phillips EL. (1968). Achievement place: Token reinforcement procedures in a home style rehabilitation setting for "predelinquent" boys. *Journal of Applied Behavior Analysis 1*, 213–223.

Plapp JM. (1983). Some characteristics of adolescents who present significant management problems in residential psychiatric treatment. *Australian Psychologist 18*, 107–115.

Puig-Antich J. (1982). Major depression and conduct disorder in prepuberty. *Journal of the American Academy of Child Psychiatry 21*, 118–128.

Quay HC. (1979). Classification. In Quay HC, & Werry JS (Eds), *Psychopathological disorders of childhood* (2nd ed.). New York: John Wiley, pp 1–42.

Quay HC. (1977). Measuring dimensions of deviant behavior: The Behavior Problem Checklist. *Journal of Abnormal Child Psychology 5*, 227–289.
Rapport MD, Sonis WA, Fialkov MJ, Matson JL, & Kazdin AE. (1983). Carbamazepine and behavior therapy for aggressive behavior. *Behavior Modification 7*, 255–265.
Robin A, Schneider M, & Dolnick M. (1976). The turtle technique: An extended case study of self-control in the classroom: *Psychology in the Schools 12*, 120–128.
Satterfield JH, Hoppe CM, & Schell AM. (1982). A prospective study of delinquency in 110 adolescent boys with attention deficit disorder and 88 normal adolescent boys. *American Journal of Psychiatry 139*, 795–798.
Schneider M. (1974). Turtle technique in the classroom. *Teaching Exceptional Children 8*, 22–24.
Shapiro ES, & Klein RD. (1980). Self-management of classroom behavior with retarded/disruptive children. *Behavior Modification 4*, 83–97.
Singleton LC, & Asher SR. (1977). Peer preferences and social integration among third-grade children in an integrated school district. *Journal of Educational Psychology 69*, 330–336.
Stuart RB. (1971). Behavioral contracting within the families of delinquents. *Journal of Behavior Therapy and Experimental Psychiatry 2*, 1–11.
Stumphauzer JS (Ed). (1979). *Progress in behavior therapy with delinquents*. Springfield, IL: Charles C. Thomas.
Thomas DR, & Maus ME. (1983). Duration characteristics of locked-room time-out with behavior contingent release: A seven-year analysis. *Behavioral Engineering 8*, 116–121.
Touchette PE. (1978). Mental retardation: An introduction to the analysis and remediation of behavioral deficiency. In Marholin D II (Ed), *Child behavior therapy*. New York: Gardner Press.
Weiner IB. (1982). *Child and adolescent psychopathology*. New York: John Wiley.
White GD, Nielson G, & Johnson SM. (1972). Timeout duration and the suppression of deviant behavior in children. *Journal of Applied Behavior Analysis 5*, 111–120.

10
Pervasive Developmental Disorders

Sandra L. Harris and Carolyn A. Thorwarth

Providing care for any patient carries with it a major sense of responsibility for the clinician. We need to make choices and decisions on behalf of another person who, no matter how carefully informed about the nature of treatment, still is unlikely to be as fully informed as we can be as professionals. This responsibility is especially sobering when the individual is an inpatient, and even more so when he or she is a child. The child with a pervasive developmental disorder is often totally unable to communicate, to protect himself or herself from abuse, or to express pain or pleasure in any but the most elemental ways. Aware of the limitations of our current technology and fully cognizant of the depth of the therapeutic needs of these youngsters, we must nonetheless design and execute treatment plans to the best of our ability.

DESCRIPTION AND DIAGNOSIS

An endless stream of diagnostic categories has been generated to describe psychotic behavior in childhood. Some of these terms have found an enduring place in the professional literature, while others remain idiosyncratic to a small audience. The American Psychiatric Association recently provided an important new organizational schema for the psychopathology of childhood, the *Diagnostic and Statistical Manual of Mental Disorders (DSM-III)*. This is a major departure from the previous editions of the diagnostic manual in that it provides a more

PRACTICE OF INPATIENT BEHAVIOR THERAPY
ISBN 0-8089-1715-3

extensive and detailed description of the various psychological disorders of childhood.

Many of the children previously described with a hodge-podge of labels are now incorporated into *DSM-III*'s "Pervasive Developmental Disorders." The authors of *DSM-III* avoided the term "psychotic disorders in childhood" because these childhood behaviors bear little clear connection to adult psychotic behavior.

Pervasive developmental disorders, because they begin in childhood, have a more pervasive impact upon behavior than do psychotic disorders of adulthood. The adult who becomes schizophrenic has had 20 or more years in which to process and store information in a more or less "normal" fashion, while the child who has a pervasive developmental disorder may have suffered from gross distortions of external reality from earliest infancy. Even if we could modify this child's dysfunction to allow him or her to understand the world in more conventional ways, we would still be faced with the major challenge of remediating years of distorted information processing. *DSM-III* recognizes two subcategories of pervasive developmental disorder: infantile autism and childhood onset developmental disorder.

Infantile Autism

Leo Kanner first described infantile autism in 1943. Since that time the diagnosis has been used, with more or less rigor, by a growing number of child clinicians. In defining infantile autism, *DSM-III* points to several key features of the disorder. These include the early onset (before 30 months of age), pervasive lack of response to other people, gross deficits in speech (muteness, echolalia, pronominal reversal), bizarre responses to the environment (resistance to change, preoccupation with objects), and an absence of thought disorder (no delusions, hallucinations, etc.)

Many autistic children look physically normal; they bear none of the stigmata that mark mentally retarded children. The autistic child often appears alert and thoughtful and may have good motor coordination. This apparently normal facade makes all the more puzzling the gross distortions of language, cognition, affect, and social behavior that characterize these youngsters.

The behavioral excesses and deficits of autistic children pose major problems for intervention. Among the excesses, such behaviors as self-stimulation (stereotyped behavior), self-injury, and resistance to change with accompanying tantrums, all demand special treatment. The deficits, such as lack of speech, play behavior, self-care skills, and other adaptive behaviors, will only respond to a comprehensive treatment program.

Childhood Onset Pervasive Developmental Disorder

The youngster with childhood onset pervasive developmental disorder, while in many ways resembling the autistic child, has a different set of symptoms. According to *DSM-III*, childhood onset pervasive developmental disorder begins after 30 months of age and before 12 years, while infantile autism begins before 30 months. The youngster with childhood onset pervasive developmental disorder exhibits gross deficits in interpersonal relationships, which may include clinging behavior, relative indifference to other people, lack of appropriate affect, and limited capacity for empathic response. Like the autistic child, they show none of the hallucinations, delusions, and other signs of thought disorder that are part of the schizophrenic picture. In addition, the authors of *DSM-III* indicate that these children exhibit at least three of the following seven features: (1) sudden, excessive anxiety; (2) constricted or inappropriate affect; (3) resistance to change; (4) peculiarities of motor movement (e.g., odd hand movements, toe-walking); (5) abnormalities of speech; (6) over- or under-sensitivity to sensory stimulation; (7) self-injury.

It is important to note that many of the behaviors of infantile autism or childhood onset pervasive developmental disorder can be found in other categories of child psychopathology as well. The presence of self-stimulation, self-injury, lack of speech development, and so forth do not by themselves provide a diagnostic decision. One must take care to discriminate these children from others who are mentally retarded, hearing impaired, developmentally language delayed, or schizophrenic.

Schizophrenia in Childhood

DSM-III notes that if a child or adolescent meets the criteria for a diagnosis of schizophrenia, one should apply that diagnosis regardless of the age of the individual. Thus, a child with hallucinations, delusions, and other key features of schizophrenia would not be diagnosed as having either infantile autism or childhood onset pervasive developmental disorder.

Cantor, Evans, Pearce, and Pezzot-Pearce (1982), in examining *DSM-III's* treatment of schizophrenia in childhood, note that these adult-oriented standards have serious limitations when applied to children. They studied 19 children and 11 adolescents who had been psychotic since childhood and found that the subjects met the criteria for schizophrenia except for the requirement that there be a deterioration in functioning from a previously higher level. Seven of their subjects were psychotic before 30 months of age, but the presence of thought disorder precluded a diagnosis of infantile autism. Cantor and his colleagues (1982) argue that symptoms and signs rather than age of onset should be the basis for diagnosis.

BEHAVIORAL ASSESSMENT

Although traditional diagnosis is helpful in placing children in categories that may be useful in organizing treatment units or conducting research, it offers less guidance when one addresses day-to-day problems of individualized treatment. For such purposes the therapist turns to behavioral assessment.

A comprehensive chapter on the behavioral assessment of autism by Newsom and Rincover (1981) discusses in detail issues we skim only briefly in the present chapter. These authors note that behavioral assessment plays a major part in decisions concerning placement, intervention, and research. The placement decision must include not only the child's level of functioning and the specific management problems posed by the youngster, but also an evaluation of resources available in the home and community. The child's degree of disruptive behavior, ability to communicate, physical handicaps, age, and size will all be factors in determining which classroom, group home, ward, or other unit is selected for placement. The availability of specialized services such as workshops, prevocational training, staff members who use manual signs, special programs to manage aggressive or self-injurious behavior, and so forth will also enter into this decision.

An assessment aimed at intervention defines precisely the nature of the child's behavioral excesses and deficits in terms of a behavioral description, circumstances under which the behavior occurs, ranking of priorities for intervention, assessment of environmental resources for implementing a specific treatment program, and so forth. A substantial professional literature exists describing how one assesses and treats many of the most frequent problems of the pervasively developmentally disordered individual including self-injury (Carr, 1977), language deficits (Harris, 1975; Lovaas, 1977, 1981), aggression (Favell, 1983), self-help deficiencies (Lovaas, 1981), and educational deficits (Koegel, Rincover, & Egel, 1982). The reader can consult these sources for detailed guides to intervention with specific problems in terms of measurement and treatment.

Self-Injurious Behavior

While we lack the space to discuss treatment for many of the problems of children with pervasive developmental disorders, we do wish to address self-injurious behavior. Because of its life-threatening severity, it is not unusual for children with self-injury to be placed in residential facilities where they have continual care and prompt medical attention. Schroeder, Schroeder, Smith, and Dalldorf (1978) found the prevalance of self-injury in one large state institution was consistently 10 percent over three years. The self-injurious residents were younger, had a longer history of hospitalization, had more seizure disorders, language handicaps, visual impairments, and severe or profound mental retardation than did other residents. Over 90 percent of the self-injurious residents improved during the three-year period. Among the children treated by behavior modification, 94 percent improved, while 32 percent responded to medication alone, and 21 percent improved with neither behavior modification nor drugs.

In 1982, a task force for the Association for the Advancement of Behavior Therapy published a report on the treatment of self-injurious behavior (Favell, Azrin, Baumeister, Carr, Dorsey, Forehand, Foxx, Lovaas, Rincover, Risley, Romanczyk, Russo, Schroeder, & Solnick, 1982). Its members included some of the most distinguished people in this field, and the report summarized much of what is currently known about self-injury. This task force identified the need for a careful assessment of the problem behavior, provision for reinforcement of adaptive behaviors, removal of reinforcement for self-injury, creating an environment that is not associated with self-injury, the careful use of punishment when essential, and ensuring that one provides for generalization of effects during treatment. The report urges that treatment of self-injury be planned and supervised by a trained professional. They call for a professional peer review of the treatment plan in terms of technical expertise, as well as a human-subject committee to ensure that the rights of the child are protected. The task force also asked for a rigorous and open evaluation of the treatment program.

Although initial behavioral treatment of self-injury relied to a large extent upon aversive techniques (Harris & Ersner-Hershfield, 1978), more recently there has been considerable interest in less punitive methods. For example, Horner (1980) and Favell, McGimsey, and Schell (1982) have provided data suggesting that offering self-injurious people a more stimulating and interesting environment and reinforcing their use of toys will decrease self-injury. Interrupting self-injury and reinforcing incompatible behaviors (Azrin, Basalel, & Wisotzek, 1982) and a water mist accompanied by the word "no" (Dorsey, Iwata, Ong, & McSween, 1980) each serve to diminish self-injury. Overcorrection has also been found helpful in reducing the behavior (Johnson, Baumeister, Penland, & Inwald, 1982; Wesolowski & Zawlocki, 1982).

Although protective devices have long been a part of institutional care for self-injury, Dorsey, Iwata, Reid, and Davis (1982) took a creative approach to the use of restraints when they demonstrated that brief application of these devices would reduce the frequency of self-injury. It is important to note that the equipment was used during a brief time-out, contingent upon self-injury, and not as a restraint for endless hours. While continuous application may protect the child, it also precludes a variety of desirable behaviors and thus hampers the child's learning of adaptive behavior.

PHARMACOTHERAPY AND BEHAVIOR THERAPY

It is not uncommon for a significant number of children in inpatient settings to receive medication as part of their treatment program. Although recognizing the potential contribution of such medication, both Fish (1976) and Campbell (1977) expressed concern about many of the drugs that have been used with pervasively developmentally disordered or schizophrenic children. As Campbell (1977) observed, "No currently available drug or other treatment for that matter, will result in dramatic improvement or changes in a severely impaired young autistic child or adolescent who has continuously shown severely deviant development and behavior since earliest life" (p 103).

It is important to know that a drug which works well with children at one age may not be effective at another (Campbell, 1973; Fish, 1976). One must also be sensitive to the problems of adjusting the child's dose to maximize benefits while reducing disruptive side effects.

McAndrew, Case, and Treffert (1972) examined the effects of prolonged phenothiazine medication on 125 hospitalized children ages 4 to 16 years. They found weight gain in 29 children related to taking thioridazine. Tardive dyskinesia was diagnosed in 10 children on high doses of phenothiazines over a prolonged period. Lens stippling occurred in five children. In response to these findings, McAndrew et al. (1972) indicated that in their clinical practice they use placebos periodically to determine the continuing need for medication.

The medication that has emerged as most frequently studied and apparently effective for some pervasively developmentally disordered children is haloperidol (Haldol). Serrano (1981) suggests that haloperidol is useful in treating hyperactivity, aggression, self-injury, rage, explosive outbursts, withdrawal, and stereotyped behavior in autistic children.

Interaction of Drugs and Behavior Therapy

Although medication may make a child more manageable, this will be of minimal value if the drug intrudes upon the child's ability to learn. Medication, while it may suppress behavior, will not teach a person how to be less aggressive, self-injurious, and so forth. Without other treatment there remains the risk that removal of the drug will reinstate the behavior problem (Favell, 1983). Thus, medication is most valuable when it is only one component of a comprehensive treatment package.

Unfortunately, only a few studies to date have examined the interaction of medication and behavior therapy for the pervasively developmentally disordered child. Campbell, Anderson, Small, Perry, Green, and Caplan (1982) found that haloperidol improved performance on a laboratory learning task by young autistic children. Other research from this same group (Campbell, Anderson, Meier, Cohen, Small, Samit, & Sachar, 1978; Campbell, Cohen, & Anderson, 1981) indicates that haloperidol combined with behavior therapy is superior to either one alone in facilitating the acquisition of imitative speech in young autistic children.

Durand (1982) treated self-injury in a 17-year-old profoundly retarded male and found that neither mild punishment nor haloperidol alone decreased the self-injury, but these two combined had a significant effect on the behavior.

It is premature to draw conclusions about the contribution of medication coupled with the use of behavior therapy in the treatment of pervasively developmentally disordered children. Nonetheless, the sophisticated work of Magda Campbell and her colleagues and a few other studies do point to the possibility that haloperidol makes a useful contribution to treatment. Enthusiasm for medication must be tempered by a recognition of the risks inherent in the long-term negative effects of drugs upon a child's development. It is also wise to be realistic about the fact that when a clinical researcher like Campbell undertakes treatment, she administers drugs with great care for the welfare of her young patients.

Doses are carefully monitored, and highly experienced staff observe closely for side effects. One cannot count on this quality of care in many contemporary child treatment centers.

STAFFING ISSUES

Many an elegant, well designed treatment plan has met a premature death because of lack of well trained people to carry out the intervention. Such problems are especially compelling in inpatient settings where there is continual responsibility for some of society's most handicapped children. On the outside, intelligent care by parents might compensate for a less dedicated teacher (or vice versa), but for the child in residential care, his or her total welfare rests in the hands of that institutional staff.

Reppucci (1977) spoke directly to these issues in his well considered article on how behavior therapists establish themselves in institutional settings. Among the issues he identified were finding a way to gain entry into the working system of the institution, establishing relationships with the existing staff, and adapting to political realities. As Reppucci (1977) notes most behavior therapy programs described in the literature are done in university settings, in newly created facilities, or in well-funded demonstration projects of existing programs. These are ideal settings for intervention where one is not forced to confront issues of union contracts, civil service rules, or a staff exhausted by years of frustration. Graduate students are often trained in these settings, and while they learn to hold high standards in terms of the quality of their interventions, these settings fail to teach them how to go about making changes in existing service delivery systems. We may not like the realities we see about us, but unless we deal with them our tenure as effective change agents is likely to be short indeed.

A small but significant body of research has developed addressing itself to the problem of training direct service staff and making structural modifications in residential staffing patterns to improve service delivery. While many of these studies were done in programs for the mentally retarded, some included youngsters with pervasive developmental disorders.

For example, one organizational change explored by Streifel, Smith, and Savino (1976) tested the benefits of a specialized intensive treatment team at the Behavior Development Center for the Autistic. They used a small team of highly trained behavioral specialists to intervene on two wards for autistic adolescents when management problems arose which disrupted the ongoing activities of the regular staff. This special team allowed the Center to offer a greater number and more versatile set of treatment plans for residents without increasing the demands on the nursing staff. It required no major administrative changes and led to increased job satisfaction on the part of the participants. The specialized team, because they could focus on a resident for a sustained period, achieved major changes that might otherwise have been impossible.

Staff Training

A number of attempts have been made to modify supervisory and training techniques to improve the performance of direct care staff. Iwata, Bailey, Brown, Foshee, and Alpern (1976) found that allowing staff who met performance criteria to enter a lottery to arrange their days off for the next week increased the percentage of time they spent on target behaviors and the frequency of their task completion.

Increasing the expression of approval for staff behavior by supervisors can increase the percentage of appropriate behavior (Montegar, Reid, Madsen, & Ewell, 1977). Page, Iwata, and Reid (1982) found that training supervisory staff to improve their teaching behaviors produced improved teaching by direct care staff. One need not confine changes in staff behavior to the level of supervisory staff. Teaching a direct care staff member self-monitoring, standard setting, self-evaluation, and self-reinforcement techniques can lead to increased staff-resident interaction (Burgio, Whitman, & Reid, 1983). Marshall and Marks (1981) note that it is important to define the staff member's job, provide appropriate supervision, and give the person feedback on his or her performance.

Ivancic, Reid, Iwata, Faw, and Page (1981) taught staff members to talk more to their young charges while bathing them. The staff increased their vocalizations, used no more time, and did not diminish the quality of routine care. There was also some increase in child vocalizations. Two other studies used direct care staff to teach manual signing to retarded and autistic residents (Faw, Reid, Schepis, Fitzgerald, & Welty, 1981; Schepis, Reid, Fitzgerald, Faw, van den Pol, & Welty, 1982). Such an approach is valuable in ensuring generalized use of communication beyond the classroom.

Issues of staff motivation and training are nowhere more compelling than when providing care for pervasively developmentally disordered children. These youngsters are often mute, may be content to be left alone in relative neglect, and may sometimes engage in highly frustrating behaviors that can push even well trained, caring staff members to anger. It is therefore urgent to ensure that a competent and highly motivated team carries out the treatment program.

FOLLOW-UP ON CHILDREN IN INPATIENT CARE

The term "inpatient" covers a multitude of settings. It incorporates large wards in state hospitals, small group homes, short-term intensive treatment facilities in general or psychiatric hospitals, intensive long-term residential facilities, and so forth. Some of these function as custodial facilities for youngsters who have exhausted community alternatives; others serve as brief, intensive programs to remediate acute problems and return the child to the community; still others provide long-term care while trying to incorporate the child into the community as fully as possible.

An important early report by Lovaas, Koegel, Simmons, and Long (1973) described their experience with 20 autistic children treated in an intensive behavioral program at UCLA. All of the children made significant gains as a result of treatment, but some of them lost these gains when they were discharged to other institutions, while others continued to make progress because they went home to families who were trained to work with them. This follow-up study documented persuasively the critical importance of ensuring that the people who work with a child after discharge be well trained to sustain the gains made during an inpatient program.

Browning (1971) wrote about his concern that some autistic youngsters are so impaired that it may be more realistic to aim toward preparing them for an effective life within an institution rather than expecting that they will be able to function in a less structured setting. His experience was consistent with the observations of Treffert, McAndrew, and Dreifuerst (1973), who followed up 57 children who had been treated in an inpatient program at Winnebago State Hospital. Two-thirds of the children were still in the hospital, and the remainder had made a poor-to-fair adaptation to life in the community. Treffert and his colleagues note that the degree of mental retardation in most of these children precluded their independent functioning.

Amy Lettick (1983), in her description of the Benhaven program for autistic children, adolescents, and adults, likewise notes that even with the best of educational and behavioral treatment, one must be realistic about what some autistic children can achieve.

Recognizing that there are limits on the potential growth of the severely impaired child does not mean that our treatment programs are ineffective. Far from it! Many of the most intrusive and disruptive behaviors of the pervasively developmentally disordered youngster can be controlled, and these children can lead a more comfortable and productive life than was thought possible in the past. Nonetheless, just as we cannot "cure" most causes of mental retardation, neither can we cure these disorders when they occur in conjunction with a severe cognitive deficit. We have found, like many others, that while high functioning children can frequently be mainstreamed into regular schools, or at least into classrooms for much less impaired children with special needs, this does not appear to be true for the child with a severe cognitive deficit. Many of these more impaired youngsters can move from a highly individualized treatment program to one where they work in small groups, or from a total care institution to a group home, but the likelihood of their living alone, holding a job, and so forth remains remote.

ETHICAL ISSUES

Child Rights

There is no definite listing of what constitute's an individual's "basic rights." Although there are certain standard items likely to appear on anyone's list—the right to food, sleep, clothing, protection from physical harm—a universal list of agreed-upon essential rights has yet to be developed. This is unfortunate, since there are few treatment settings more in need of such guidelines than residential care facilities for children with pervasive developmental disorders. The severity of their disorders, coupled with a tendency to display difficult-to-treat behaviors makes these children especially vulnerable to violation of basic rights.

Several strategies can be effective in assuring the rights of the developmentally disordered in residential settings. Since no standardized, nationally accepted list of rights exists, it is essential that service programs develop their own list (Ennis & Emory, 1978). These individually developed guidelines should be disseminated to all residential staff members to ensure that they are acutely aware of the standards as well as familiar with the administrative actions that would follow if a child's rights were violated. The direct care staff member should learn to regard himself or herself as a "child advocate."

The severity of disability seen in many developmentally disordered people may make it difficult to provide them with their basic rights. For example, some people might argue that it is impossible to provide the right to privacy for these youngsters. To some extent such a contention is valid; some developmentally disordered youth may require supervision during such private activities as showering, dressing, and toileting. Nevertheless, rather than define the right to privacy as inapplicable, service providers should make an increased effort to teach the skills that would ensure privacy in these domains.

The Individualized Treatment Plan is an important mechanism for protecting child rights (McClannahan & Krantz, 1981). These plans should include (1) a thorough assessment of the client's skills and deficits, (2) operational definitions of desired responses, (3) treatment procedures that are clearly written, and (4) information regarding data collection and analysis. Such Individualized Treatment Plans give the evaluator a global understanding of how well a client's right to treatment is being maintained.

Almost any list of client rights includes protection from physical harm. In the case of the developmentally disordered youth, this right has been under close scrutiny because of the use of aversive procedures. In the absence of a single set of standards for the use of aversive procedures, individual providers typically generate their own guidelines. Developing a set of such standards is imperative in residential settings, where direct service personnel are likely to be confronted by client behaviors such as aggression or self-injury that endanger client and staff. Without such guidelines aversive procedures may be used in a fashion that violates the child's right to protection from harm.

Standards regarding the use of aversive strategies need to include a general policy that they are not to be used without the written consent of both the residential supervisor and the child's parents. Additionally, any aversive program should include (1) a detailed, behaviorally-specific description of the target behavior; (2) a clear outline of the aversive treatment procedure; (3) provisions for data collection and analysis; and (4) plans for frequent follow-up.

Within the last decade there has been a growing cry for ethics committees to monitor the treatment of the developmentally disordered (Griffith & Henning,

1981; McClannahan & Krantz, 1981). One issue confronted in forming these committees is the question of membership. While most people propose a multidisciplinary group of professionals and laypeople (Treadway & Rossi, 1977), there are certain practical disadvantages to a heterogenous group. It may be difficult to obtain a general consensus, and lay members may lack a technical understanding of treatment techniques. These issues aside, such a committee seems an essential component of any residential treatment program.

Parents' Rights

The decision to place a child in residential care generates an array of emotions in parents. Guilt and regret are mixed with freedom and satisfaction that their child is obtaining appropriate services. Parents respond to this experience in various ways. Some parents terminate all contact with the child, others become over involved in residential programming, while the majority run a course somewhere between these extremes.

Regardless of the extent to which a parent remains involved in his or her child's treatment, certain parental rights must be respected: (1) the right to visit their child; (2) involvement in the Residential Treatment Plan; (3) informed consent for treatment procedures (Martin, 1975); (4) medical consent for medical procedures, including changes in medication; and (5) involvement in the Individualized Educational Plan if the residential program provides educational services.

CONSISTENT TREATMENT ACROSS SETTINGS

In comparison to other populations, the pervasively developmentally disabled are especially prone to overselect on specific characteristics of a teaching situation, therefore showing little generalization from one setting to the next (e.g., Handleman, 1979; Harris, 1975; Lovaas, Koegel, Simmons, & Long, 1973). As a consequence, one of the crucial mandates in working with this population is to provide consistent treatment across settings.

If a residential placement includes educational services, it is quite possible to provide such consistency by having residential and school staff meet on a frequent basis to ensure that they are implementing the same program for a child. Strategies to facilitate communication when treatment involves separate sets of caretakers include (1) daily checklists, which are sent back and forth between school and residential staff; (2) frequent phone calls and face-to-face meetings; and (3) sharing of written programs that have proved effective in either setting.

Residentially placed children also have difficulty generalizing newly acquired skills to their parents' homes. Again, consistent treatment across all settings is key; a home visit should not signal to the child that this is a time for inappropriate behaviors to resurface. The following tactics may be useful in promoting consistency between residential placement and home: (1) parent training is essential—do not expect parents to implement effective programs without training, (2) model procedures for parents during their visits to the residential setting, (3) have a staff member accompany the child on a home visit to provide support and training in the home, and (4) incorporate the parents' needs into the Individualized Residential Plan (e.g. teach a child how to use the phone to call home).

Whether working with school staff or parents, it is important for residential staff to maintain an atmosphere of open-mindedness and collaboration. Too often an adversarial relationship develops between individuals in different settings. Such relationships can only decrease the efficiency of treatment.

CASE REPORTS

The Case of Susan

Susan, an adolescent who had lived in a state institution for the past seven years, was being considered for a group-home setting. During the initial interviews her mother provided a detailed developmental history. Susan was the product of an uneventful pregnancy. The only occurrence of note was that Susan's mother received injections to induce the onset of menstruation prior to discovering she was pregnant. During delivery the umbilical cord was wrapped around Susan's neck, but there were no signs of respiratory distress and her APGAR score was 10. She weighed a healthy 8 pounds, 7 ounces.

Susan was frequently ill during the first three years of her life. She had many bouts with influenza, and had a grand mal seizure after her temperature reached 105 degrees. As a consequence she was given phenobarbital for several years. Susan's developmental milestones were typically in the normal range. The only exception was her speech development; she tended to parrot what others said without any apparent comprehension.

As a toddler Susan demanded little attention; in fact, one of her mother's earliest concerns was that she did not appear to react to pain. She rarely enjoyed cuddling and would actively push away from her parents if they initiated physical contact. The only activities she seemed to enjoy were twirling flat objects on her fingertips, rocking, and repeatedly opening and shutting doors. When presented with the usual array of toddler toys, Susan would either flap them quickly in front of her eyes or toss them across the room.

When Susan was five, her parents divorced and her mother had difficulty managing the child on her own. As a consequence, Susan was placed in a state residential facility, where she remained for five years. Her mother visited her sporadically.

As the deinstitutionalization movement grew across the state, her mother explored the possibility of placing Susan in a community-based group home. After two years on a waiting list, Susan was slotted for placement in a home relatively close to her mother's residence. A special advantage of the home was that it was affiliated with an educational program serving pervasively developmentally disordered youth.

During the preplacement interviews the examiner observed many of the behaviors described by Susan's mother: She spent much of the time rocking on the floor while flapping a rattle in front of her eyes. She did not respond to her name, and moved to the other side of the room when the examiner touched her shoulder. Her language consisted almost exclusively of exact mimicry of the examiner's questions.

During the early weeks in the group home, daily behavioral assessments were conducted. This assessment process facilitated the development of Susan's Residental Treatment Plan (RTP) outlining the behavioral objectives for the coming year. A major goal in the RTP was to decrease self-stimulatory behavior, since both the group home and school staff identified her rocking and flapping of objects as behaviors that inhibited learning. After baseline data were collected, a formal, data-based program was developed that incorporated the following treatment strategies: First, a Differential Reinforcement of Other Behavior (DRO) program was initiated whereby Susan was given primary and secondary reinforcement every five minutes for the absence of rocking and flapping. The second component of the treatment plan was to teach Susan activities that were incompatible with self-stimulatory behavior. The staff developed two skill-acquisition programs; one focused on teaching Susan to sit still, while the other taught her how to play with simple toys.

Subsequent group-home data reflected significant changes in Susan's self-stimulatory behavior. During baseline, time-sampling data indicated that she exhibited self-stimulatory behaviors 80 percent of the time. Two months after the initiation of the program, self-stimulation had decreased to 15 percent. The data collected during her "appropriate play" and "sitting still" programs also reflected notable success; for Susan was responding correctly 83 percent of the time when instructed to "sit still" or "play with the toys."

Unfortunately, Susan did not demonstrate similar gains in school. Although she showed increases in good sitting and play behavior, the time-sampling of her self-stimulatory behaviors had declined only to 67 percent. Furthur assessment of the school environment suggested that the higher student-to-teacher ratio made it difficult to implement the DRO component of the program. In order to help school staff remember to reinforce Susan, an egg timer was set to ring every five minutes. This proved effective, and within six weeks Susan's self-stimulation in school had dropped to the low levels observed in the group home.

The Case of Joey

Although Joey was almost 12 years old, he had spent only two years of his life in school. Again and again he had been deemed "inappropriate" by the few special education programs that had allowed him to attend their schools. As a consequence, he stayed at home, tutored each year by Home Bound instructors.

Frustrated, his parents sought alternative means of treatment. They eventually found themselves pursuing the possibility of a group-home placement.

Joey's developmental history indicated that he had been admitted to the hospital several times as an infant with a variety of acute conditions including pneumonia, anemia, and respiratory infections. Some of his developmental milestones were within normal limits, while others were delayed. For example, although Joey did not walk until he was 16 months old, he was toilet trained at 30 months. His most significant delay was in speech development, for he did not speak his first word until he was seven. In fact, at age 11, Joey had never learned to express himself verbally, although he could label over 30 objects using American Sign Language.

Of special concern were Joey's aggressive and self-abusive behaviors. From an early age he demonstrated tantrums that included hitting, kicking, and biting. Self-abusive behaviors were observed as well; for Joey frequently hit his head, pulled his hair, and pinched his arms until he was quite bruised. Joey's family was understandably distressed by these behaviors and tended to "give him anything he wanted just to make him stop."

After several interviews and visits to the group home, Joey became a resident at a community-based home not far from his family. Following standard procedures, the staff spent the first few weeks collecting baseline data. A wide range of skills were assessed including self-help, social/interpersonal, language, and prevocational and home-maintenance abilities. All of these data were essential for a comprehensive Residential Treatment Plan (RTP).

One of the primary goals of the group-home staff was to decrease Joey's aggressive and self-abusive behaviors. These behaviors posed a danger to Joey and other people, and made teaching new skills virtually impossible.

Baseline data indicated that Joey was having an average of 12 aggressive and/or self-abusive tantrums per day, each lasting approximately 26 minutes. A behavioral analysis suggested that aggressive tantrums almost invariably followed a sequence: Joey would come running into the room, attempt to grab an object or food, and become aggressive when this was taken away from him. If the staff did not give in to his demand, he would become self-abusive. Interestingly, baseline data indicated that self-abuse only occurred subsequent to aggressive behaviors; therefore, it was predicted that a behavior reduction program focused on aggressions would in turn decrease self-abuse.

The group-home staff met with Joey's parents to develop the treatment program. In order to facilitate behavioral change, the group decided to implement a treatment package with several components. The major component was an overcorrection procedure to be initiated each time Joey became aggressive. Since his aggressions involved a lack of instructional control and inappropriate use of hands, the staff and parents designed a procedure to address both of these factors. The overcorrection procedure selected required Joey to follow a randomly presented set of instructions (e.g., "touch your head," "look at me," "take a deep breath"). Joey had to respond correctly to at least 20 commands before the procedure was terminated.

A second component of the treatment package was to examine the behaviors that preceded Joey's tantrums. As noted, tantrums almost invariably occurred after Joey had run into a room. Consequently, the staff began to react to the behavior of running in order to break the chain of behavior. As soon as Joey ran, staff members stopped him and required him to practice walking into the room. As a second means of alleviating running, the staff implemented a formal skill-acquisition program that focused on teaching Joey to walk from room to room of the group home.

The final component of the treatment package emphasized development of Joey's skills. For example, the behavioral analysis indicated that Joey's tantrums usually took place after he attempted to grab food or objects. Therefore, a data-based skill-acquisition program was implemented to teach Joey to sign: "I want *(food or object)*, please."

Three months after the implementation of the comprehensive treatment package, Joey's behavior in the group home was significantly improved. Frequency of aggressive tantrums had dropped to two per week, and the average duration was down to one minute. As his aggressions decreased, self-abusive behavior became essentially nonexistent.

One problem that developed during treatment involved implementing the programs during Joey's visits to his parents' home. His parents viewed themselves as unable to control their son, and Joey quickly learned to discriminate his parents' home as a setting where aggression still led to desired consequences. Home visits were often chaotic, and his parents brought him back to the group home earlier than expected. The group home staff realized that Joey's parents needed additional support and, consequently, assigned staff members to go with Joey on his home visits. During these visits, staff members modeled the behavioral techniques used in the group home and observed Joey's parents as they implemented the programs. Eventually the staff members were faded from the home visits, for Joey's parents had gained sufficient skills and confidence to assure successful interactions with their son.

Summary

Clients with pervasive developmental disorders pose extraordinary demands for the staff who work with them. As a consequence it is essential that staff be well trained, well supervised, and have a clear sense of their mission and responsibilities in working with their clients. It is also urgent that clients be appropriately assessed during the placement process to ensure that they are placed in a setting appropriate to their individual needs. The profound withdrawal, lack of speech, self-injury, and other troublesome behaviors exhibited by many of these youngsters create a need for sophisticated, ongoing assessment and intervention. Given the appropriate context for treatment, it has been our experience that many of these individuals can benefit in substantial ways from our interventions. Nonetheless, given the limits of our present technology and understanding of these disorders, our hopeful expectations for each client must be tempered by our realistic understanding of likely limits.

REFERENCES

Azrin NH, Besalel VA, & Wisotzek IE. (1982). Treatment of self-injury by a reinforcement plus interruption procedure. *Analysis and Intervention in Developmental Disabilities 2*, 105–113.

Browning RM. (1971). Treatment effects of a total behavior modification program with five autistic children. *Behaviour Research and Therapy 9*, 319–327.

Burgio LD, Whitman TL, & Reid D. (1983). A participative management approach for improving direct care staff performance in an institutional setting. *Journal of Applied Behavior Analysis 16*, 37–53.

Campbell M. (1977). Treatment of childhood and adolescent schizophrenia. In Wiener JM (Ed), *Psychopharmacology in childhood and adolescence*. New York: Basic Books, pp 101–115.

Campbell M. (1973). Biological interventions in psychoses of childhood. *Journal of Autism and Childhood Schizophrenia 3*, 347–373.

Campbell AM, Samit C, & Sachar EJ. (1978). A comparison of haloperidol and behavior therapy and their interaction in autistic children. *Journal of the American Academy of Child Psychiatry 17*, 640–655.

Campbell M, Anderson LT, Small AM, Perry R, Green WH, & Caplan R. (1982). The effects of haloperidol on learning and behavior in autistic children. *Journal of Autism and Developmental Disorders 12*, 167–175.

Campbell M, Cohen IL, & Anderson LT. (1981). Pharmacotherapy for autistic children: A summary of research. *Canadian Journal of Psychiatry 26*, 265–273.

Cantor S, Evans J, Pearce J, & Pezzot-Pearce T. (1982). Childhood schizophrenia: Present but not accounted for. *American Journal of Psychiatry 139*, 758–762.

Carr EG. (1977). The motivation of self-injurious behavior: A review of some hypotheses. *Psychological Bulletin 84*, 800–816.

Dorsey MF, Iwata BA, Ong P, & McSween TE. (1980). Treatment of self-injurious behavior using a water mist: Initial response suppression and generalization. *Journal of Applied Behavior Analysis 13*, 343–353.

Dorsey M, Iwata BA, Reid DH, & Davis PA. (1982). Protective equipment: Continuous and contingent application in the treatment of self-injurious behavior. *Journal of Applied Behavior Analysis 15*, 217–230.

Durand VM. (1982). A behavioral/pharmacological intervention for the treatment of severe self-injurious behavior. *Journal of Autism and Developmental Disorders 12*, 243–251.

Ennis BJ, & Emory RD. (1978). *The rights of mental patients*. New York: Avon Books.

Favell JE. (1983). The management of aggressive behavior. In Schopler E, & Mesibov GB (Eds), *Autism in adolescents and adults*. New York, Plenum, pp 187–222.

Favell JE, Azrin NH, Baumeister AA, Carr EG, Dorsey MF, Forehand R, Foxx RM, Lovaas OI, Rincover A, Risley TR, Romanczyk RG, Russo DC, Schroeder SR, & Solnick JV. (1982). The treatment of self-injurious behavior. *Behavior Therapy 13*, 529–554.

Favell JE, McGimsey JF, & Schell RM. (1982). Treatment of self-injury by providing alternate sensory activities. *Analysis and Intervention in Developmental Disabilities 2*, 83–104.

Faw GD, Reid DH, Schepis MJ, Fitzgerald JR, & Welty PA. (1981). Involving institutional staff in the development and maintenance of sign language skills with profoundly retarded persons. *Journal of Applied Behavior Analysis 14*, 411–423.

Fish B. (1976). Pharmacotherapy for autistic and schizophrenic children. In Ritvo ER, Freeman BJ, Ornitz EM, & Tanguay PE (Eds), *Autism. Diagnosis, current research and management*. New York: Spectrum, pp 107–119.

Griffith RG, & Henning DB. (1981). What is a human rights committee? *Mental Retardation 19*, 61–63.

Handleman JS. (1979). Generalization by autistic-type children of verbal responses across settings. *Journal of Applied Behavior Analysis 12*, 273–284.

Harris SL. (1975). Teaching language to nonverbal children—with emphasis on problems of generalization. *Psychological Bulletin 82*, 564–580.

Harris SL, & Ersner-Hershfield R. (1978). The behavioral suppression of seriously disruptive behavior in psychotic and retarded patients: A review of punishment and its alternatives. *Psychological Bulletin 85*, 1352–1375.

Horner RD. (1980). The effects of an environmental "enrichment" program on the behavior of institutionalized profoundly retarded children. *Journal of Applied Behavior Analysis 13*, 473–491.

Ivancic MT, Reid DH, Iwata BA, Faw GD, & Page TJ. (1981). Evaluating a supervision program for developing and maintaining therapeutic staff-resident interactions during institutional care routines. *Journal of Applied Behavior Analysis 14*, 95–107.

Iwata B, Bailey, JS, Brown KM, Foshee TJ, & Alpern M. (1976). A performance-based lottery to improve residential care and training by institutional staff. *Journal of Applied Behavior Analysis 9*, 417–431.

Johnson WL, Baumeister AA, Penland MJ, & Inwald C. (1982). Experimental analysis of self-injurious, stereotypic, and collateral behavior of retarded persons: Effects of overcorrection and reinforcement of alternative responding. *Analysis and Intervention in Developmental Disabilities 2*, 41–66.

Kanner L. (1943). Autistic disturbances of affective content. *Nervous Child 2*, 217–240.

Koegel RL, Rincover A, & Egel AL. (1982). *Educating and understanding autistic children*. San Diego, CA: College-Hill.

Lettick AL. (1983). Benhaven. In Schopler E, & Mesibov GB (Eds), *Autism in adolescents and adults*. New York: Plenum, pp 355–379.

Lovaas OI. (1981). *Teaching developmentally disabled children. The me book*. Baltimore: University Park Press.

Lovaas OI. (1977). *The autistic child*. New York: Irvington.

Lovaas OI, Koegel RL, Simmons JQ, & Long JS. (1973). Some generalizations and follow-up measures on autistic children in behavior therapy. *Journal of Applied Behavior Analysis 6*, 131–166.

Marshall AM, & Marks HE. (1981). Implementation of "zero reject" training in an institutional setting. *Analysis and Intervention in Developmental Disabilities 1*, 23–35.

Martin R. (1975). *Legal challenges to behavior modification*. Champaign IL: Research Press.

McAndrew JB, Case Q, & Treffert DA. (1972). Effects of prolonged phenothiazine intake on psychotic and other hospitalized children. *Journal of Autism and Childhood Schizophrenia 2*, 75–91.

McClannahan LE, & Krantz PJ. (1981). Accountability systems for protection of the rights of autistic children and youth. In Hannah G, Christian W, & Clark H (Eds), *Preservation of client rights*. New York: The Free Press, pp 83–106.

Montegar CA, Reid DH, Madsen CH, & Ewell MD. (1977). Increasing institutional staff to resident interactions through in-service training and supervisor approval. *Behavior Therapy 8*, 533–540.

Newsom C, & Rincover A. (1981). Autism. In Mash EJ, & Terdal LG (Eds), *Behavioral assessment of childhood disorders*. New York: Guilford Press, pp 397–439.

Page TJ, Iwata BA, & Reid DH. (1982). Pyramidal training: A large-scale application with institutional staff. *Journal of Applied Behavioral Analysis 15*, 335–351.

Reppucci ND. (1977). Implementation issues for the behavior modifier as an institutional change agent. *Behavior Therapy 8*, 594–605.

Schepis MM, Reid DH, Fitzgerald R, Faw GD, van den Pol RA, & Welty PA. (1982). A program for increasing manual signing by autistic and profoundly retarded youth within the daily environment. *Journal of Applied Behavior Analysis 15*, 363–379.

Schroeder SR, Schroeder CS, Smith B, & Dalldorf J. (1978). Prevalence of self-injurious behaviors in a large state facility for the retarded: A three-year follow-up study. *Journal of Autism and Childhood Schizophrenia 8*, 261–269.

Serrano AC. (1981). Haloperidol—its use in children. *Journal of Clinical Psychiatry, 42*, 154–156.

Streifel JA, Smith PA, & Savino LJ. (1976). The intensive treatment team in a residential setting. *Hospital and Community Psychiatry 27*, 697–698.

Treadway JT, & Rossi RB. (1977). An ethical review board: Its structure, function and province. *Mental Retardation 15*, 28–29.

Treffert DA, McAndrew JB, & Dreifuerst P. (1973). An inpatient treatment program and outcome for 57 autistic and schizophrenic children. *Journal of Autism and Childhood Schizophrenia 3*, 138–153.

Wesolowski MD, & Zawlocki RJ. (1982). The differential effects of procedures to eliminate an injurious self-stimulatory behavior (digito-ocular sign) in blind retarded twins. *Behavior Therapy 13*, 334–345.

11
Eating Disorders

L.K. George Hsu and Francis C. Harris

This chapter is concerned primarily with the inpatient behavior therapy of two eating disorders: anorexia nervosa and bulimia nervosa. The diagnostic criteria of the two disorders are summarized in Tables 11-1 and 11-2. Detailed descriptions of the clinical features may be found elsewhere (e.g., Bruch, 1973; Russell, 1979). Anorexia nervosa is characterized by a morbid mental attitude termed variously "the relentless pursuit of thinness" (Bruch, 1973), "weight phobia" (Crisp, 1980), or "fear of fatness" (Russell, 1970). In addition, there is the presence of emaciation, amenorrhea, and a set of behaviors calculated toward weight loss, such as starvation, vomiting, purging, and excessive exercising. Bulimia nervosa is also characterized by fatness phobia (although most patients do not aim at reaching an unreasonably low weight), but in addition there are discreet episodes of binge-eating, during which the patient experiences loss of control over eating, followed by guilt and depression after the binge-eating episode. Most bulimia patients also induce vomiting after a binge, and may take laxatives or diuretics in an attempt to dispose of the calories. The bulimic patient is, by definition, at normal or above normal weight. Menstration is usually normal but may be irregular. If an emaciated patient presents with weight phobia, amenorrhea, binge-eating, vomiting, and purging, she should be given a diagnosis of anorexia nervosa with bulimic features.

The two disorders share common factors: (1) they affect mainly women between the ages of 15 to 40, and (2) the patients are always intensely preoccupied with food, dieting, shape, and weight. Many are depressed, although the depres-

PRACTICE OF INPATIENT BEHAVIOR THERAPY
ISBN 0-8089-1715-3

Table 11-1
Diagnostic Criteria for Anorexia Nervosa

A. Intense fear of becoming obese, which does not diminish as weight loss progresses.

B. Emaciation as a result of weight loss of at least 15 percent of original body weight:
   1. Grade 1: Body weight less than 85 percent of average weight for height.
   2. Grade 2: Body weight less than 75 percent of average weight for height.

C. Behavior directed toward weight loss.

D. Amenorrhea in the female.

E. Subgroup:
   1. Bulimic: Presence of bulimic episodes.
   2. Restrictor: Absence of bulimic episodes.

F. No known physical illness that could account for the weight loss and emaciation.

sion is almost always related to the eating problem. The patients are usually perfectionistic and tend to come from a higher social economic background. Onset of the two disorders is identical in that the earliest feature is conscious dieting to lose weight. In anorexia nervosa the dieting proceeds to severe emaciation, whereas in bulimia nervosa episodic binge-eating follows and the patient remains at a reasonable weight. Binge-eating and vomiting also develops in about 50 percent of anorexia patients after they have been ill for several years, and many then gain weight and develop bulimia nervosa instead.

The nosology of the two disorders is still unclear, and emaciation may not be the best feature to distinguish between the two disorders (Table 11-3). Many researchers (e.g., Garfinkel, Garner & O'Shaghnessy, 1983; Strober, Salkin, Burroughs, & Morrell, 1982) have found that bulimia, whether or not accompanied by anorexia nervosa, is associated with emotional lability and impulsivity,

Table 11-2
Diagnostic Criteria for Bulimia Nervosa

A. Recurrent episodes of binge-eating (rapid consumption of a large amount of food in a discrete period of time, usually less than two hours), frequency of at least once a week over the previous four weeks.

B. Awareness that the eating pattern is abnormal and fear of not being able to stop eating voluntarily once the binge-eating begins.

C. Intense fear of fatness; depressed mood, and self-deprecatory thoughts following eating binges.

D. Termination of binge-eating episodes by abdominal pain, sleep, social interruption, self-induced vomiting, or use of cathartics or diuretics.

E. Repeated attempts to lose weight by severe dieting, self-induced vomiting, or use of carthartics or diuretics.

F. The bulimic episodes are not related to a concurrent anorexia nervosa or any known physical disorder.

Table 11-3
Comparison of Anorexia Nervosa and Bulimia Nervosa

	Restrictor Subgroup (60%)	Anorexia Nervosa	Bulimic Subgroup (40%)	Bulimia Nervosa
Cardinal features		Emaciation drive for thinness behavior directed to weight loss		Normal or overweight Fear of fatness Bulimic episodes
Weight		Low		Normal or overweight
Amenorrhea (female)		Present		Variable
Binge-eating	Absent		Present	Present
Vomiting/Purging	Usually absent		Usually present	Usually present

premorbid obesity, and a family history of obesity, alcoholism, and depression. From an operational and treatment point of view, however, it is probably still best to regard the two disorders as separate and distinct.

EVALUATION

The purposes of an evaluation are (1) to make a diagnosis of whether the patient has anorexia nervosa (with or without concurrent bulimia) or bulimia nervosa; (2) to assess the severity of the condition and decide whether immediate inpatient treatment is necessary; (3) to determine the presence of other concomitant psychiatric disorders, such as depression, or alcohol or substance abuse; (4) to engage the patient in treatment and to outline the treatment options. An outpatient session coupled with several laboratory tests may generally be sufficient to accomplish these purposes. Only in cases of diagnostic uncertainty is an inpatient evaluation necessary. The content of this evaluation is outlined in Table 11-4.

Inpatient treatment is necessary for anorexia nervosa when the following occurs: (1) body weight is below 80 percent of average weight for height; (2) there is electrolyte disturbance such as a low potassium level (less than 3.5 mEq/L); (3) there are abnormal cardiac findings either on physical examination or on electrocardiogram; (4) there is daily vomiting or laxative abuse; (5) there is severe depression. Other indications of inpatient treatment are relative, and include failure to respond to outpatient treatment and inability of the family to cope with the situation.

Inpatient treatment for bulimia nervosa is usually not necessary. However, if the binge/vomiting is frequent (more than once a day), or if the patient is

Table 11-4
Assessment of Eating Disorders

1. Body Weight
   What is her current weight and height?
   How long has she been at this weight?
   What would she like to weigh?
   How does she feel about her present weight?
   Does she see herself as being overweight?
   Has there been a weight loss? How much? Over what period of time?
   Is she extremely frightened at the prospect of gaining weight?
   What has been her highest weight? When? For how long was she at this weight?
   What has been her lowest weight? When? For how long was she at this weight?
2. Binge Eating
   Does she experience uncontrollable urge to eat?
   How often does she experience these urges? And how long do they last?
   At what times of the day do these urges occur?
   What does she think of prior to an urge to binge?
   What activity was she engaging in prior to an urge to binge?
   When she binges in response to these urges:
      What types and quantities of food does she consume?
      At what rate does she consume such foods?
      What other activities does she engage in while eating?
      How long does a binge last?
      Where does she binge?
      Does she binge alone or with others?
      What does she think of when she binges?
      How does she feel during a binge?
      How frequently does she binge?
      What were the circumstances of the first binge episode?
   After a binge:
      How does she terminate a binge?
      What is her mood after a binge?
      What are her "self-statements" after a binge?
      What activity does she engage in after a binge?
3. Vomiting
   How frequently does she vomit?
   What procedures does she employ to induce vomiting?
   How long after eating does she vomit?
   Is vomiting difficult and/or painful?
   What were the circumstances of the first episode?
   How does she feel after vomiting?
4. Laxatives
   What type of laxative does she use?
   How frequently does she use them?
   How much does she ingest at one time?
   What were the circumstances of the first episode?
   How does she feel afterwards?

5. Diuretics
   What type of diuretic does she use?
   How frequently does she use them?
   How much does she ingest at one time?
   What were the circumstances of the first episode?
   How does she feel afterwards?

6. Diet Pills
   What type of diet pill does she use?
   How frequently does she use them?
   How much does she ingest at one time?
   What were the circumstances of the first episode?
   How does she feel afterwards?

7. Eating Habits and Activities
   At what times of the day does she eat?
   Does she plan what she eats?
   Does she eat regular meals?
   Does she cook her own meals or cook for others?
   What types and quantities does she consume?
   What is the nutritional composition (in terms of calories and food types) of her diet? Does she selectively avoid carbohydrates and fat?
   Does she eat alone or eat with others?
   How does she feel when she eats a regular meal?
   How much fluid does she consume in one day?
   What types of fluids does she consume?
   What exercise activities does she engage in? How much and how frequently does she exercise?

8. Medical Considerations
   The following must be assessed by a competent physician:
   - Physical and neurological status
   - Electroytes, BUN, creatinine
   - Thyroid function
   - Electrocardiogram
   - Electroencephalogram

9. Other Psychiatric Features
   A standardized interview should be used to assess the following:
   - What is her predominent mood?
   - Does she have low self-esteem and worth?
   - Does she feel guilty about her eating behavior as well as her behavior in general?
   - Is there any change in her energy level?
   - Is there any change in her interest level?
   - Is there any social withdrawal?
   - Does she feel hopeless and suicidal? Has she engaged in any self-injurious behavior?
   - How is her sleep?
   - Does she use alcohol? How much?
   - Does she use any drugs? What type are they and how much does she use?

Table 11-4 *(continued)*

Are there any obsessive compulsive features?
Are there any anxiety features?
Are there any psychotic features?
10. Treatment
Outpatient or inpatient?
Where?
By whom?
What type of treatment (e.g., medication, psychotherapy, etc.)?
What was the outcome?

severely depressed, or if electrolyte disturbances occur, then inpatient treatment is necessary. The eating disorders usually require long-term treatment and care. Inpatient treatment is always to be followed by outpatient treatment.

ENGAGING THE PATIENT AS A COLLABORATOR

Eating disorder patients, particularly those with anorexia nervosa, are notoriously resistant to the suggestion of treatment. An explanation of the effects of starvation (Keys, Brozek, Henschel, Mickelson, & Taylor, 1950), the nature of the disorder and the course and outcome, may serve to educate the anorectic patient regarding the illness, and she will generally be receptive to such factual information. The clinician should then attempt to make a therapeutic alliance with the patient by stating that he or she can appreciate the importance of being slim. Information on the current sociocultural emphasis on slimness may be useful at this juncture (Garner, Garfinkel, Schwartz, & Thompson, 1980). However, the clinician should then point out the negative aspects of the illness (i.e., "the price she has to pay" to stay slim), such as the depression, the insomnia, the restlessness, the intense preoccupation with food and dieting, and the social withdrawal. A treatment plan may then be outlined. An initially resistant patient may respond to the offer of inpatient treatment after a few more outpatient sessions. Several easy to read books may also be recommended to the patient (e.g., Bruch, 1978; Crisp, 1980).

The bulimic patient, at least those who present for an evaluation, appears to be more motivated for help. It is also essential that the nature of the illness should be explained, the complications and danger outlined, and a treatment plan offered.

Anorexic patients are usually brought to treatment by family members. In such cases the clinician should ask for the patient's permission to meet with the family, whether separately or together with the patient. Educating a family regarding the illness and engaging their support are the primary tasks. If the patient came to the session unaccompanied, it is important to explore the family's attitude toward the illness and also to ask for permission to speak with the family members. Sometimes the patient refuses permission for the clinician to contact the family, who, however, contact the clinician to find out about the patient's condition. Under such circumstances the patient's confidentiality should be respected, but the family's concern may become a topic that can be explored with the patient.

INPATIENT BEHAVIOR TREATMENT OF ANOREXIA NERVOSA

The inpatient treatment of anorexia nervosa is twofold: (1) weight restoration and establishment of healthy eating habits, and (2) psychotherapy aimed at the "fatness phobia." Behavior therapy is effective in weight restoration, and numerous reports have appeared within the last 15 years (for review, see Garfinkel & Garner, 1982). It is however important to state at the outset that weight restoration successfully achieved in hospital is not necessarily followed by permanent cure. In one series (Hsu, Crisp, & Harding, 1979), 40 percent of patients relapsed within one year after successful weight restoration in hospital. While no hard data exist, behavior therapy is probably most effective if (1) the patient is aware that treatment does not merely consist of eating and weight gain; (2) the patient knows that the treatment will not let her become overweight (a great fear); (3) the patient knows that the treatment does not encourage her eating to get out of control (another great fear); and (4) the patient's self-defeating behavior, such as vomiting or purging, is controlled.

The Treatment Contract

A treatment contract is signed by both the patient and members of the treatment team at the beginning. The contract should stipulate the following:

1. *The target weight.* An age-appropriate, low average weight is selected as the target weight by the clinician at the outset. This is important, as the patient will then know how much weight she has to gain. It is generally futile to negotiate an agreed weight with the patient, as she will always argue for an unreasonably low weight. Most clinicians will require the patient to reach target weight before discharge, although some discharge the patient after she has achieved some weight gain (e.g., Collins, Hodas, & Liebman, 1983).
2. *Meal size.* It is important not to overfeed the patient, particularly at the beginning, as this may lead to medical complications such as dilatation of the stomach and peripheral edema. While large meals may encourage intake and increase the rate of weight gain, it also heightens the fear of loss of control. Thus, the patient should be given frequent (6 meals a day), smaller (300 calories per meal initially increasing to 500 calories later), balanced (50% carbohydrate, 25% protein, 25% fat) meals. Some clinicians advocate the use of liquid diet supplements. While this may be necessary for some

resistant patients during the beginning, the aim is for the patient to eat normal balanced meals. The help of a dietician in meal planning and nutritional education is advisable.

3. *Weight gain.* An average gain of 0.2 kg/day (0.5 lb/day) is medically safe. Larger gains create fear in the patient and may precipitate complications. Most patients will gain weight rapidly in the first few days as their dehydration is corrected. In those abusing laxatives, diuretics, and vomiting, the gain may be very rapid. In such cases it is very important to monitor intake and output, and serum electrolytes carefully. The patient should be weighed daily in the morning before breakfast and after she uses the bathroom. This allows monitoring of the patient's physical state. Less frequent weighing (such as once a week) has been recommended, but there is no evidence to suggest that this decreases preoccupation with weight. Wide fluctuations in weight from day to day should lead one to suspect surreptitious vomiting/purging or binging/water-loading.
4. *Information feedback.* The patient should keep a weight chart that records her daily weight. Information feedback improves weight gain (Elkin, Hersen, Eisler, & Williams, 1973).
5. *Reinforcement.* Weight gain should be the contingent variable for reinforcement, and as already mentioned, a gain of 0.1 to 0.2 kg/day is normally safe, and less likely to induce fear. Number of bites per meal or amount of food consumed may also be used as the contingent variable, but doing so may inadvertently reinforce undesirable behavior such as binging. The nature of the reinforcers should be established and stipulated in the treatment contract after a careful behavioral analysis, so that after each morning's weighing the patient and the staff know exactly what the privilege status for the day is. Reinforcers generally include privileges (positive reinforcers), such as access to the television and visitors, and restrictions (negative reinforcers) such as bed rest or confinement to the bedroom. Tube-feeding or intravenous feeding may also be used as punishment, but are generally unnecessary. Inexperienced clinicians are sometimes surprised how most patients will eat voluntarily and gain weight provided that the conditions set forth above are fulfilled.
6. *Control of vomiting/purging/binging.* The patient should eat only food that is provided in the contract by the hospital, and family or friends should not bring in extra food. This policy not only gives the patient a sense of control but also prevents battles surrounding food between the patient and her family. Following each meal the patient should not be allowed to use the bathroom for one hour. Bed rest after meals for one hour may control vomiting. If vomiting/binging is suspected, the patient should be confronted directly and gently.

Supportive treatment. The contract is easier to implement if an experienced nurse can sit with the patient during and after her meals. She can discuss any anxieties that she may have and the nurse may gently encourage her to finish her meals (Russell, 1977). Presence of the nurse may also deter the patient from secretly disposing of the food.

Overcoming resistance. When presented with the contract the patient usually objects to the restrictions and sometimes frankly refuses to cooperate. The clinician should attempt to find out what she objects to and address the same directly. One commonly expressed fear is that she will inevitably become obese. This may be countered by explaining to her that once she reaches her target weight, her intake will be reduced and she will be given a period of time to adjust her intake and her activity level to maintain her target weight. Another commonly expressed fear is the loss of control, the fear that she is no longer her own master. This may be countered by informing her that the teatment contract merely stipualtes the *consequences* of her behavior and that she retains complete control over whether to gain weight or not. A third fear is that the target weight is too high. This may be countered by informing the patient that she has to attain a physiologically normal, healthy weight in order to overcome the effects of starvation and allow her to work on whatever other issues that may be important to her. Such resistance usually lessens after a few days, when rapport begins to develop between the patient and the treatment team. It is thus important to assign a small, experienced team of staff to work with these patients. The importance of engaging the family, particularly with the younger patients, already has been mentioned, and the family's support of treatment may be crucial in overcoming resistance.

After the initial difficulties, progress is usually smoother until the patient approaches her target weight. Some patients become anxious as their weight approaches 100 lbs (a three-figure weight). Usually by this time some progress will have been made in the psychotherapy and the fatness phobia may be addressed directly.

LEARNING TO KEEP A HEALTHY WEIGHT

After the patient has reached her target weight, she should stay in the hospital for another two weeks, during which she learns to maintain her target weight with appropriate amounts of food and activity. This period will allow her to consolidate the gains and help her to overcome the fear that once she gains weight she will inevitably become overweight. Control is gradually relaxed during this period, and the patient is allowed to choose her own food or eat out in a restaurant accompanied by a nurse. If wide fluctuations in weight (more than 1 kg/day) occur, the patient may be indicating that she is not yet ready for the increased responsibility of keeping her weight at a healthy level, and a longer period of inpatient stay may be necessary.

Cognitive Therapy

The value of psychotherapy is endorsed by many clinicians (e.g., Bruch, 1970; Crisp, 1980; Garfinkel & Garner, 1982; Palazzoli, 1974). Although there is no clear evidence that psychotherapy changes the long-term outcome of the illness, common sense suggests that the patient's attitudes toward herself and others are so distorted that to leave them unchanged and unchallenged is simply unwise. More recently, Garner and Bemis (1982), have developed many cognitive therapy techniques aimed specifically at the distorted cognitions of the patient. In this approach the patient is asked to examine the validity of her beliefs on a moment-to-moment basis. Cognitions such as selective abstraction, overgeneralization, magnification, dichotomous thinking, personalization, and superstitious thinking are first examined by helping the patient to define and operationalize them, and they are then challenged by a variety of techniques (such as decentering, and the "what if" technique). Such evaluation may then lead the patient to modify her thoughts and underlying assumptions.

In practice the fear of fatness and preoccupation with weight and shape may be altered by several approaches, all attempted within the context of a trusting therapeutic relationship (Garner & Bemis, 1982): (1) *reattribution*–the clinician informs the patient that all eating disorder patients perceive themselves as too fat and that she should tell herself that she can expect to feel fat, as this is a part of her illness (i.e., the misperception is not real); (2) *trusting her body*–her body knows how to keep at a healthy weight if she feeds it properly; (3) *avoid frequent weighing*–in the hospital she should only be weighed as often as the contract allows, and should not weigh herself at other times, and after discharge she should only be weighed when she returns for her outpatient appointments; (4) *recognize fear of fatness as a cover-up*–the clinician may inform the patient that the fatness fear and preoccupation with shape may sometimes act as a cover-up for unpleasant feelings or thoughts that she may be trying to avoid. Attempts should be made to identify what bothers her apart from her weight.

Behavior therapists have not contributed much to the literature on family therapy in anorexia nervosa. Family therapy is particularly useful when the patient is young or resistant to individual therapy.

Pharmacotherapy

Several medications have been used in the treatment of anorexia nervosa, but the specific purposes of their use are often unclear. Chlorpromazine, a neuroleptic, was first used in the late 1950s (Dally & Sargant, 1960) to promote sedation and decrease resistance and restlessness, and to promote weight gain through its possible direct effect on the hypothalamus. Unfortunately, it has several potentially serious side effects (such as hypotension and the tendency to induce epileptic seizures), and it has never been subjected to a proper trial. Amitriptyline, an antidepressant, and cyproheptadine, an antihistaminic with many possible central nervous system actions, have been found to promote weight gain and improve depression in a three-month, double-blind, inpatient trial (Halmi, Eckert, & Falk, 1982). Lithium has also been found to increase the rate of weight gain in another double-blind inpatient trial (Gross, Ebert, Faden, Goldberg, Lee, & Kaye, 1981). It remains unclear whether medication alters the long-term outcome of the illness.

Medication should be used if there are clear indications (e.g., antidepressants for major depression, neuroleptics for severe anxiety and restlessness), and the purpose of their use should be explained to the patient. The fears that the patient may have toward the medication (e.g., addiction) should be addressed. Under such circumstances there is no conflict between the use of behavior therapy and the concurrent use of medication.

Other Aspects of Inpatient Treatment

The treatment of medical complications, the use of expressive arts therapy, and psychoeducational treatment for school-age patients are beyond the scope of this chapter. Many clinicians have written about the inability of anorectic patients to handle social situations (e.g., Bruch, 1973; Crisp, 1980; Palazzoli, 1974). It is, however, surprising that very little has been written on the use of social skills training for anorexia nervosa patients. The one study that has been published (Pillay & Crisp, 1981) did not find it useful. Clearly, many more studies are needed.

INPATIENT TREATMENT FOR BULIMIA

The treatment for bulimia is threefold: (1) to replace the binge/vomit cycle with normal eating habits; (2) development of alternative strategies to cope with antecedents for a binge; (3) psychotherapy aimed at the weight phobia. Generally, the treatment can be carried out on an outpatient basis. As already mentioned, inpatient treatment is necessary only when the binge/vomit behavior is out of control, when there are severe electrolyte disturbances, or when depression is severe.

Educating the Patient Regarding the Illness

Initially, the patient will usually claim that she does not know why she binges. The clinician should inform her that the urge to binge increases with starvation, and is a sign that her starving body is crying out for nutrition (Russell, 1979). The patient is usually able to identify with this and may then describe how the binges alternate with periods of fasting. When the first bite is taken, a sense of relief, even abandon, and the taste of the forbidden food combine to overwhelm the patient. She usually then says to herself, "Now that I have given in, I have failed, why not make the most of the failure by eating all I want. I'll start all over tomorrow again." The vomiting or purging simply serves to deplete the body of the food, and the starvation sets in again, only to be followed by another binge. The patient usually identifies willful fasting with self-control and power, and binging with a sense of liberation from all constraints. In time, she binges for other reasons. The most commonly identified antecedents are boredom, loneliness, depression, anxiety, tension, and anger or frustration. Sometimes she binges to celebrate or to punish herself or others. Vomiting or the purge are always to dispose of the calories and sometimes to relieve the physical discomfort.

Occasionally a patient may describe it as a way to release tension. Treatment is unlikely to succeed unless the patient grasps the significance of the starvation-binge-vomit-starvation cycle and begins to identify the antecedents.

The dangers of the illness should also be explained. Vomiting, purging, and diuretic abuse deplete the body of electrolytes, particularly potassium. Acute loss of potassium may lead to heart failure and sudden death; chronic hypokalemia may lead to renal tubular changes and kidney failure. Occasionally a bout of bulimia may cause acute gastric dilation, while severe vomiting may tear the esophagus, and both may lead to death. Less life-threatening medical complications include loss of hair, salivary gland swelling (from inflammation due to vomiting and excessive gum chewing), sore throat, rectal bleeding (from use of suppositories), and dry skin. The patient should learn that vomiting and purging are relatively ineffective means of weight control, while abuse of diuretics is completely useless, as it gets rid of fluids, not calories, and the weight loss from abuse of diuretics is an illusion. Furthermore, once the patient stops vomiting or purging, there is almost an inevitable rebound in weight due to retention of fluids, and the stage is set for a vicious cycle. While long-term outcome of bulimia is unknown, patients should be told that without treatment they are unlikely to improve.

Psychiatric complications are common and they may be outlined to the patient: depression, anxiety, insomnia (occasionally hypersomnia), tiredness, social phobia and withdrawal, alcoholism, and substance abuse. The price the patient has to pay to keep her bulimia is enormous.

Developing Normal Eating Habits

The bulimic usually starves during the day and feels proud, good, and superior that she can refuse the temptation to eat. By evening the hunger and craving is intense and she feels deprived. Thus, binges usually occur in the evening, but they may occur at other times (e.g., in the middle of the night). It is therefore essential that the patient should eat regular, balanced meals to prevent hunger and starvation. The help of a dietician is advisable in nutritional education and meal planning. The amount of calories each day should be enough for the patient to maintain her present weight and in any case should not be under 1200 calories/day. Meals should consist of roughly 50 percent carbohydrates, 25 percent protein, and 25 percent fat, and should be taken three times a day. Some may do better with an additional evening snack before they retire to bed. Resistance to such dietary advice is almost inevitable and mainly for the following reasons:

1. The patient feels that she will gain weight and become fat. The clinician and the dietician should patiently explain that eating the right amount of food regularly and not binging will not lead to obesity. The failure of her attempts to control weight and the price she is paying should again be emphasized. The patient may respond to suggestions such as "trusting her body." The

body usually has a weight that it will hold on to and will resist attempts to change it; normal eating will allow the body to find this weight. While this "set point" theory is still controversial, it makes common sense and many patients find it acceptable.

2. She does not feel hungry for most of the day, and thus she does not need to eat when she does not feel hungry. The vicious cycle of starvation-binge-vomit-starvation should again be outlined. The clinician should also inform her that her perception of hunger may be inaccurate (she will usually agree and say she never knows when she is full or hungry), and that normal perception will return after a period of normal eating.
3. She will compensate by overexercising. The patient is generally already very preoccupied with exercise to the point of compulsion and more exercising is counterproductive. She should not generally exercise for more than 30 minutes each day. Emphasis should be placed on the discomfort of overexercising.
4. She refuses to eat carbohydrates. Bulimics often identify carbohydrates as bad food, as junk. In fact, carbohydrates avoidance creates a sense of deprivation, and there is some evidence to suggest that carbohydrates may prevent craving (Wurtman, 1983). They are certainly essential for normal metabolism. Carbohydrates taken in proper amounts will not lead to more weight increase.

In the hospital the controlling environment usually ensures that the patient complies with eating three proper meals. Problems may arise upon discharge, and thus plenty of practice should be given for a patient to spend time outside the hospital as well as eating out prior to discharge.

Prevention of Binging, Vomiting, and Purging

In the hospital this treatment goal may be accomplished by not allowing food to be brought in from outside the hospital, not allowing the patient to use the bathroom for a period of an hour after meals, charting of intake and output, and daily weighing. If binging, vomiting, or purging is suspected, the treatment team should confront the patient. A nurse sitting with the patient during and after meals may help to alleviate the anxiety of eating. Bed rest after meals may prevent vomiting.

Self-monitoring of Eating

In hospital the patient should begin to monitor her intake and feelings associated with eating and binging. Each day she should fill out the time and amount of food eaten, the feelings afterwards, whether there are any urges to binge, and if so, what events or feelings or thoughts preceded and accompanied these urges. If she binges, she should record the foods eaten, the amount, and the feelings before, during, and after the binge. Vomiting or purging should also be recorded. Self-monitoring improves control and should be continued after her discharge until eating returns to normal.

Self-instruction

When an urge to binge occurs, the patient should literally try to talk herself out of it. She may try to do the following: (1) identify feelings associated with this urge and the situations, problems, and thoughts that preceded the urge. (2) identify the benefits (i.e., positive results such as a sense of satisfaction and oblivion) and the negative effects (such as guilt and fear of fatness) that she will experience through binging, and convince herself that binging is not the best solution to the problem; (3) explore alternative strategies to continue those feelings, thoughts, problems, or situations; (4) reassure herself that since she is eating regularly, she is not depriving herself of proper nutrition. Sometimes the patient may find it helpful to write down her thoughts and self-instructions. This also serves as a delay to the impulse to binge, which generally will decrease in intensity after a period of time, say 10 minutes.

Cognitive Therapy

Bulimics, like anorectics, are exceedingly fearful of weight gain and preoccupied with shape and fatness. This may be treated by the approach outlined for anorectics. In addition to this fear, bulimics often identify the following areas as being problematic:

1. *Control.* The patient often feels that the only area she can completely control is her weight and dieting. The sense of ineffectiveness is pervasive. As already mentioned, dieting is associated with a feeling of competence effectiveness, and achievement, while binging is associated with failure and guilt. Paradoxically, binging may be accompanied, at least initially, with a sense of triumph and liberation, an escape from the rigid controls of dieting and deprivation.
2. *Lack of asssertiveness and helplessness.* Lack of assertiveness is common, although occasionally such patients explode and become aggressive. The nonassertiveness is often associated with a sense of helplessness, and some may be aware that this is intended to be an entrapment for men (White & Boskind-White, 1981) and is associated with fantasies of being rescued. Anger and frustration because of the helplessness build up and are sometimes "taken out" on food. Sometimes the binge is a way of "getting back" at the person they are angry with ("see what I am doing to myself, you ought to feel guilty").
3. *Fear of failure and rejection.* Bulimics strive to suceed, often not so much to achieve perfection, but often out of a fear of failure that is equated with rejection. Living up to others' expectations and the need to please are related to this fear of failure. Paradoxically, there is also a fear of success, again related to a fear of rejection, or sometimes to a fear that they may not be able to maintain being successful. Such fears are often coupled with resentment, and feelings of yielding to others' expectations, or of losing control.

Binging is sometimes related to such resentment: "I don't care what you think, this (binging) is for myself."

4. *Acceptance and self-deprivation.* Bulimics tend to depend on others, usually males, to define their sense of worth. They seek, even crave acceptance, but paradoxically, they also resent the control that others have over them. Some perceive those who accept them as "weak," not believing how anyone who is "normal" can accept them. Since acceptance brings obligations of having to live up to expectations, rejection is sometimes welcomed with relief that they are freed from such obligations.

The clinician should review the daily intake chart each day with the patient. In an inpatient unit the urges to binge are likely to be rather infrequent, and this may help the patient to identify clearly the antecedent feelings and thoughts. Alternative strategies should be explored, and these generally included self-instruction (see above), discussing feelings and thoughts with a staff member, some form of distraction (which is most useful if there is a regular predictable pattern to the binges), and developing a set of behaviors to confront the situations. Role-play with a clinician in anticipation of such stressful situations, thoughts, or feelings, combined with appropriate social skills training, is helpful. Family therapy is indicated if the stressful situation occurs frequently in the family. Also, individual outpatient therapy should be implemented after the inpatient stay.

Pharmacotherapy

There are four medications that have been found to be useful for bulimia: phenytoin (Wermuth, Davis, Hollister, & Stunkard, 1977), imipramine (Pope, Hudson, Jonas, & Yurgelun-Todd, 1983), phenelzine (Walsh, Stewart, Wright, Harrison, Roose, & Glassman, 1982), and lithium carbornate (Hsu, 1984). The evidence for their efficacy is suggestive, particulary for imipramine and phenelzine, but not conclusive, and further trials are necessary. While some believe that bulimia is a variant of an affective illness (e.g., Pope et al., 1983), others have remained skeptical (e.g., Sabine, Yonace, Farrington, Barratt, & Wakeling, 1983). It is conceivable, however, that medications may serve to decrease the dysphoria that is a common antecedent to a binge, and patients usually accept this explanation. Medication should be tried if the depression is severe.

OUTCOME

The outcome of anorexia nervosa has been reviewed elsewhere (Hsu, 1980). Briefly, about 70 percent of patients followed four years after treatment have regained a healthy weight, 20 percent remained chronically ill, and 5 to 10 percent have died from the illness or suicide. Eating behavior remained abnormal in a large proportion of the patients who regained normal weight, and depression and social phobia are common. The long-term outcome of bulimia nervosa remains unknown. Preliminary data (e.g., Fairburn, 1981) suggest that it is more encouraging than that of anorexia nervosa.

CASE STUDY

Ann, a 17-year-old girl from a working class family, decided to lose a few pounds over the summer so that she could be slim when she began her senior year in high school. She soon became totally preoccupied with dieting and exercise, and within two months had lost 45 pounds to reach 75 pounds in weight. She then began to crave sweets and on one occasion ate a whole chocolate cake, which filled her with remorse and she vomited. She then developed a pattern of fasting during the day, and binging and vomiting at night. Her weight increased somewhat, to 85 pounds, but the amenorrhea, which began at the onset of the dieting, persisted. She took diet pills to curb her hunger but they were of no benefit in decreasing binges. With the onset of the bulimia, she became increasingly depressed.

The family sought help through a private psychiatrist, and Ann attended weekly sessions for a year without significant improvement. She was referred for inpatient treatment.

Evaluations established a diagnosis of anorexia nervosa with bulimia. There was also a concurrent major depression. Treatment was aimed at establishing a target weight of 115 pounds, development of normal eating habits without binging and vomiting, and psychotherapy focused on her distorted congnitions regarding weight and shape. She signed a treatment contract and agreed to take a tricyclic antidepressant for her depression. Ann began eating six meals a day, each containing 300 calories initially and gradually increasing to 500 calories. She ate with other eating disordered patients in the unit and discussed her food choices with a dietician on several occassions. On the days that she gained weight, she earned privileges, such as taking part in unit social activities and having phone calls and visitors. On the days that she did not gain weight or had lost weight, she was confined to her room, although she could attend group and family therapy sessions as well as vocational guidance sessions. Vomiting was prevented by not allowing access to the bathroom for up to one hour after each meal, and talking with a nurse who sat with the patient during and after each meal. Her progress was uneventful and she reached her target weight two months after admission. She then began eating three meals and one evening snack, with appropriate adjustments in the calories to allow weight maintenance. After about a week she began eating her meals in the patient cafeteria, and chose her foods initially with the help of a dietician. She also ate in outside restaurants on several occasions, either with the family or a member of the staff.

Her preoccupation with weight and shape responded to cognitive restructuring, and she began to accept that such preoccupations often served to hide her low self-esteem and her fear of men. She learned to avoid the urges to binge by eating regular meals, and learned to manage such urges by examining the thoughts and feelings associated with them. Developing alternative strategies for coping with stressful situations was difficult for her, but she made plans to go to college. Family therapy focused on issues such as a critical mother who handed over much responsibility to the patient, a distant father, favoritism, and lack of communication. She was discharged three months after admission.

Follow-up nine months later found Ann to be at normal weight with regular menses, eating normal meals, and not binging or vomiting. She was working in a boutique and had plans to leave home to attend an out of state college. She continued to see the private therapist who referred her but had stopped taking her antidepressant.

SUMMARY

The clinical features of anorexia nervosa and bulimia are discussed, and the assessment and inpatient behavioral treatment for both disorders is described. Commonly encountered difficulties and techniques for overcoming them are presented. The treatment of a case of anorexia nervosa with bulimia features is presented to highlight the principles described.

REFERENCES

Bruch H. (1978). *The golden cage*. Cambridge, MA: Harvard University Press.

Bruch H. (1973). *Eating disorders*. New York: Basic Books.

Bruch H. (1970). *Psychotherapy in primary anorexia nervosa. Journal of Nervous and Mental Disease 150*, 51–67.

Crisp AH. (1980). *Anorexia nervosa—Let me be*. London: Plenum Press.

Collins M, Hodas, GR, & Liebman R. (1983). Interdisciplinary model for the inpatient treatment of adolescents with anorexia nervosa. *Journal of Adolescent Health Care 4*, 3–8.

Dally PJ, & Sargant W. (1960). A new treatment of anorexia nervosa. *British Medical Journal 1*, 1770–1774.

Elkin T, Hersen M, Eisler RM, & Williams JG. (1973). Modification of caloric intake in anorexia nervosa. *Psychological Reports 32*, 75–78.

Fairburn CG. (1981). A cognitive behavioral approach to the management of bulimia. *Psychological Medicine 11*, 707–711.

Garfinkel PE, & Garner DM. (1982). *Anorexia nervosa: A multidimensional perspective*. New York: Brunner/Mazel.

Garner DM, & Bemis K. (1982). A cognitive behavioral approach to anorexia nervosa. *Cognitive Therapy and Research 6*, 1–27.

Garner DM, Garfinkel PE, & O'Shaghnessy M. (1983). Clinical and psychometric comparison between bulimia in anorexia nervosa and bulimia in normal weight women. In *Understanding anorexia nervosa and bulimia: Report of the Fourth Ross Conference on Medical Research*. Columbus, Ohio: Ross Laboratories.

Garner DM, Garfinkel PE, Schwartz D, & Thompson M. (1980). Cultural expectations of thinness in women. *Psychological Reports 47*, 483–491.

Gross HA, Ebert MH, Faden VB, Goldberg SC, Lee LE, & Kaye WH. (1981). A double-blind controlled trial of lithium carbonate in primary anorexia nervosa. *Journal of Clinical Psychopharmacology 1*, 376–381.

Halmi KA, Eckert E, & Falk JR. (1982). Cyproheptadine for anorexia nervosa. *Lancet 1*, 1357–1358.

Hsu LKG. (1984). Treatment of bulimia with lithium. *American Journal of Psychiatry 141*, 1260–1262.

Hsu LKG. (1980). Outcome of anorexia nervosa: A review of the literature (1954–1978). *Archives of General Psychiatry 37*, 1041–1046.

Hsu LKG, Crisp AH, & Harding B. (1979). Outcome of anorexia nervosa. *Lancet 1*, 61–65.

Keys A, Brozek J, Henschel A, Mickelson O, & Taylor HL. (1950). *The biology of human starvation: Vols. I & II.* Minneapolis: University of Minnesota Press.

Palazzoli MS. (1974). *Self-starvation.* New York: Jason Aronson.

Pillay M, & Crisp AH. (1981). The impact of social skills training for anorexia nervosa. *British Journal of Psychiatry 139*, 533–539.

Pope HG, Hudson JI, Jonas JM, & Yurgelun-Todd D. (1983). Bulimia treated with imipramine: A placebo-controlled, double-blind study. *American Journal of Psychiatry 140*, 554–558.

Russell G. (1979). Bulimia nervosa: An ominous variant of anorexia nervosa. *Psychological Medicine 9*, 429–448.

Russell GFM. (1977). General management of anorexia nervosa and difficulties in assessing the efficacy of treatment. In Vigersky RA (Ed), *Anorexia nervosa.* New York: Raven Press, pp 277–289.

Russell GFM. (1970). Anorexia nervosa: Its identity as an illness and its treatment. In Price JH (Ed), *Modern trends in psychological medicine: Vol II.* London: Butterworths, pp 131–164.

Sabine EJ, Yonace A, Farrington AJ, Barratt KH, & Wakeling A. (1983). Bulimia nervosa: A placebo-controlled double-blind therapeutic trial of mianserin. *British Journal of Clinical Pharmacology 5*, 195–202.

Strober M, Salkin B, Burroughs J, & Morrell W. (1982). Validity of the bulimia-restricter distinction in anorexia nervosa. *Journal of Nervous and Mental Disease 170*, 345–351.

Walsh BT, Stewart JW, Wright L, Harrison W, Roose SP, & Glassman AH. (1982). Treatment of bulimia with nomoamine oxidase inhibitors. *American Journal of Psychiatry 139*, 1629–1630.

Wermuth BM, Davis KL, Hollister LE, & Stunkard AJ. (1977). Phenytoin treatment of the binge-eating syndrome. *American Journal of Psychiatry 134*, 1249–1253.

White WC, & Boskind-White M. (1981). An experiential-behavior approach to the treatment of bulimarexia. *Psychotherapy: Theory, Research and Practice 18*, 501–507.

Wurtman RJ. (1983). Behavioral effects of nutrients. *Lancet 1*, 1145–1147.

12
Pediatric Medical Problems

Carol S. Hickman, Karen L. Thompson, Wendy S. Feldman, and James W. Varni

The child hospitalized for surgery, other medical procedures, or intensive rehabilitation experiences a number of stressful situations, which are often manifested as biobehavioral problems (Varni, 1983). This chapter presents recent work in behavioral pediatrics on topics relevant to the biobehavioral assessment and management of pediatric inpatients, including (1) a description of the problems associated with pediatric intensive care units; (2) presentation of recent work in the area of preparation for hospitalization and surgery; and (3) a discussion of recent work in two areas of pediatric pain management—postoperative pain and pain secondary to aversive medical procedures.

PEDIATRIC INTENSIVE CARE UNITS

As reported by Melamed, Robbins, and Graves (1982), behavioral difficulties occur in approximately 92 percent of hospitalized children and include behaviors such as extreme fears, sleep and eating disturbances, regression in toilet training, and increased dependency needs. The most dramatic of these effects occur to patients in a pediatric intensive care unit (PICU). PICUs are environments that have been attributed with high risk for the development of psychiatric and psychological trauma (Cataldo, Jacobs, & Rogers, 1982). Children hospitalized in PICUs experience dramatic changes in their environments, including unfamiliar and/or painful but necessary biomedical interventions, isolation from their

PRACTICE OF INPATIENT BEHAVIOR THERAPY
ISBN 0-8089-1715-3

families, witness of other children undergoing critical medical procedures, and exposure to vital-sign monitoring devices and intravenous procedures (Cataldo et al., 1982). Cataldo and associates report that as a result of these changes, non-medical, behavioral, and psychological problems arise, and have been termed the *ICU syndrome*. In their review of past interventions for ICUs, Cataldo et al. (1982) note that psychiatric referrals were the most common, with psychiatric treatments, including changes in the ICU environment, counseling, and medication. Also mentioned in their review were preventive strategies, including environmental redesigning and normalization through socialization and provision of play materials, and preparation of children for hospitalization and surgery, the latter of which is discussed in detail in a later section of the present chapter.

Cataldo et al. (1982) note that several reviews of the literature on hospitalization and PICUs find research in these areas not sufficiently theoretically minded nor experimentally sound. These criticisms prompted Cataldo and his colleagues to formulate a theoretically based approach to the problems of hospitalization. Their approach is founded on the principles of learning theory, with specific reference to the aversive-conditioning literature. Within this framework events that occur in a PICU (painful and frightening procedures, separation from families, etc.) are conceptualized as being quite similar to experimentally produced aversive stimuli. As such, these events are capable of providing the same conditioned response suppression and learned helplessness that result from exposure to experimentally aversive stimuli.

In their review of the basic animal literature, Cataldo et al. (1982) report that strong, inescapable, and unavoidable aversive stimulation leads to adverse biological reactions (e.g., catecholamine release and gastric secretions) and general behavioral suppression. Their review also suggests that certain events can mitigate the effects of aversive stimulation (i.e., strong, positive stimuli that counteract the aversive stimuli, and warning signals that make the aversive stimulus more predictable).

Several studies support the model put forth by Cataldo and associates. A behavioral observation study (Cataldo, Bessman, Parker, Pearson, & Rogers, 1979) was made of the PICU. Ninety-nine patients with a mean age of 6 years and a mean length of hospital stay of 4.9 days were observed. Results showed that children did not verbalize 82 percent of the time, did not attend to anything 37 percent of the time, and were not engaged in any activity 54 percent of the time. The authors noted that such neutral affect and noninteraction is characteristic of the aversive stimulation research findings, especially the conditioned suppression and learned helplessness literatures. They also noted, however, that the results of the study are open to alternative explanations. For instance, behavioral and affective suppression could be the result of poor medical status. Since in general patients are discharged as their medical status improves, if behavioral and affective suppression were the result of poor medical status, such suppression should be negatively correlated with length of stay; however, they were positively correlated with length of stay. A second part of the study by Cataldo et al. (1982) further supports the finding that patient behavior is a function of the aversive PICU environment and not merely a function of poor medical status. In this investigation positive stimulation (toys and positively attending adults) was programmed in an attempt to mitigate the adverse effects of the PICU environment. A within-subjects reversal design was used to show that affect (smiling), interaction, and other behaviors were increased in the experimental condition. Obviously, if such behaviors were determined by medical status alone they should not have changed as a function of environmental manipulation. This last study is of particular interest because it shows that even with such minor changes as the presence of toys and positively attending adults, aversive events of the PICU were, albeit for a short time, mitigated.

In summary, Cataldo et al. (1982) contend that "while still quite speculative, this approach to studying the iatrogenic effects of hospitalization suggests that solutions can be found in the basic literature on classical and operant conditioning and from studies on learned helplessness" (p 293). It seems apparent that PICU patients could benefit from an application of the early animal work that showed how to lessen the effects of aversive stimuli. According to Cataldo, this research implies two changes that should take place in the PICU environment: (1) a PICU environment should include some positive events and stimuli to elicit and maintain new behavioral repertoires, and (2) periods of time should be identified during which the patient is "safe" from aversive procedures.

PREPARATION FOR HOSPITALIZATION AND SURGERY

An increasing number of health care professionals have recommended psychological preparation for hospitalization and surgery to alleviate the potential distress and to enhance the effectiveness of medical care. A recent survey reported that over 70 percent of the hospitals providing chronic pediatric care provide some preparation for hospital procedures (Peterson & Ridley-Johnson, 1980). However, it was estimated that only 42 percent of hospitalized children were actually receiving the available preparation procedures.

Assessment

In order to evaluate children's reactions to hospitalization and to evaluate the effectiveness of various procedures, a multidimensional assessment must be performed. A number of physiological measures are easily observable and can be included, such as sweaty palms, flushing, pulse rate, sleeping difficulties, and irregular breathing patterns (Melamed et al., 1982). Melamed et al. (1982) also suggest that physical recovery measures may be informative, including vomiting, swelling, reports of pain, use of pain medication, time until first voiding, eating of solids, and wound healing. These variables may be affected by psychological factors and may be helpful in providing a physiological assessment of various preparation procedures.

Behavioral measures, such as observer rating scales of cooperation during medical procedures (Johnson & Melamed, 1979) and anxiety during medical procedures (Melamed & Siegel, 1975), are utilized, as are self-report measures of anxiety. However, younger children may have difficulty with the conceptualization of fear and anxiety, thereby making self-report difficult. This is supported by Johnson and Melamed's (1979) conclusions from the literature reviews, that self-report measures tend to be less reliable than observational measures.

Preparation Techniques

As reviewed by several authors (Elkins & Roberts, 1983; Melamed et al., 1982; Peterson & Brownlee-Duffeck, 1984; Varni, 1983), preparation techniques have involved several types of play, puppet and group therapy, desensitization, hypnosis, imagery, and behavioral rehearsal. Two techniques that have received much attention are filmed modeling and self-regulation techniques.

Melamed and Siegel (1975) evaluated the effectiveness of filmed modeling as a preparatory technique for hospitalization and surgery. The film portrays a child, who also narrates the film, progressing through a hospitalization experience. During the film the child displays some anxiety. In this manner he serves as a peer model, one who expresses fear and anxiety but who is able to acquire mastery of the situation. Subjects were 60 children between the ages of 4 and 12 who were hospitalized for elective surgery for the first time. A variety of self-report, behavioral, and physiological measures showed evidence of a reduction in fear, behavior problems, and postsurgical complications in the film-prepared as compared to routine-prepared children.

Peterson and Shigetomi (1981) compared the effectiveness of four preparation protocols that consisted of self-control techniques, modeling, and information. The self-control techniques included relaxation, mental imagery, and self-talk. Subjects were 66 children between the ages of two and ten who were being hospitalized for elective tonsillectomies. The results indicated that children who received self-control training plus filmed modeling were more cooperative and calm during invasive procedures than children receiving self-control training alone, or filmed modeling alone. Also, self-control training alone was more effective than modeling alone for both parents and children. An advantage of self-control strategies is that they are not as situationally specific as filmed modeling may be, and therefore are more likely to generalize the different hospital settings and a variety of stressful situations during hospitalization.

In the utilization of hospital preparation techniques, the issue of timing and length of preparation needs to be considered. Visintainer and Wolfer (1975) compared two identical preparation procedures: one was a 45-minute single preparation session, conducted shortly after admission; the other was conducted as a series of six stress-point preparation contacts, involving the same components of information and preparation as the other preparation, but extended over a period of critical times during hospitalization. They found that stress-point preparation was more effective than single-session preparation, results that are substantiated by numerous other studies (Peterson & Brownlee-Duffeck, 1984).

A variety of patient-related factors such as age, hospital experience, and parenting style have been shown to influence children's responses to hospitalization. The age range of subjects involved in preparation research has varied greatly, making it difficult to determine age-related responses. However, several studies have found that regardless of treatment interventions, younger children generally exhibited greater upset and less cooperation during hospitalization (Melamed & Siegel, 1975, 1980; Visintainer & Wolfer, 1975; Woilfer & Visintainer, 1975, 1979). Melamed, Meyer, Gee, and Soule (1976) found that younger children responded best to immediate as opposed to delayed preparation. Later, Melamed, Dearborn, and Hermecz (1983) found that younger children who viewed a peer-modeling film tended to report increased medical concerns, and this was particularly evident in younger children who had already had surgery. Also, they tended to exhibit decreases in these medical concerns if they were shown an unrelated film rather than one that dealt with the upcoming surgery. This suggests the need to evaluate not only the presence or absence of previous hospitalizations but also the nature of the hospitalization and whether it produced negative responses in the child.

Another possible factor to consider is parenting style. Zabin and Melamed (1980) found that children of parents who used positive reinforcement, modeling, and persuasion as ways of encouraging their child to deal with fearful situations were low in anxiety during hospitalization, whereas children whose parents used punishment, force, or reinforcement of dependency had higher anxiety during hospitalization.

Although the literature indicates that psychological factors influence cooperation with medical procedures and postoperative recovery, Melamed et al. (1982) note that there often is difficulty in making treatment recommendations because of the inability to demonstrate a functional relationship between specific factors and behavior. There is, however, considerable evidence to suggest that hospital preparation needs to be sensitive to children's individual characteristics.

Melamed and her colleagues identify problems with research in this area: the tendency for multiple treatment packages to be offered to children, making it difficult to assess the effectiveness of individual treatment components, and the use of unique assessment batteries with few measures in common across studies. They further suggest that rather than comparing one treatment package to another, treatment components must be identified. Since various treatment techniques overlap, many may be equally effective in reducing anxiety.

The literature indicates that pediatric preparation has become an established routine in many hospital settings and although extensive research has been developed, many areas need further investigation.

PEDIATRIC PAIN MANAGEMENT

Pain in children represents a complex process involving cognitive developmental level, emotions, motivations, neurochemical states, sensations, and socioenvironmental influences (Varni, 1983). These multidimensional factors combine to produce varying degrees of pain perception in children (Varni, Katz, & Dash, 1982). For example, children in different cognitive developmental stages will conceive of pain differently, an older adolescent may be able to effectively communicate her concept of pain to others, while a young child in the pre-abstract stage of development may find the term "pain" incomprehensible (Varni, 1983). The young child may nevertheless have a neurophysiological sensation of pain but be unable to communicate this adequately.

Definition and Categories of Pain

Varni et al. (1982) defined four categories of pediatric pain: (1) pain associated with a disease state, such as hemophilia or arthritis; (2) pain associated with an observable injury or trauma, such as burns or fractures; (3) pain not associated with an identifiable cause, such as recurrent abdominal pain syndrome or migraine headaches; and (4) pain associated with aversive medical and dental procedures, such as bone marrow aspirations, lumbar punctures, or tooth extractions. This section presents research most relevant to inpatients, that is, postoperative pain and pain associated with aversive medical procedures.

Pediatric pain can also be differentiated along the acute and chronic continuum. Acute pain operates as an adaptive biological warning system, directing attention to an injury or disease. At times, however, the pain sensation may be much greater than necessary for a mere signaling device, the original sensation being modified by the reaction to the neurophysiological sensation. Varni (1983) states that it is precisely the severe intensity of pain and its associated anxiety that may most parsimoniously distinguish acute and chronic pain.

Chronic pain consists of an adaptive response to the initial experience of acute pain. The fearful and anxious response, present in acute pain, is absent or greatly reduced in chronic pain. Chronic pain behaviors may consist of mood changes, decreased physical activity, or regression to developmentally inappropriate behaviors (Varni, 1983; Varni et al., 1982). In addition, chronic pain reactions are often reinforced by socioenvironmental influences (Varni, Bessman, Russo, & Cataldo, 1980) and may be maintained independent of the original pathology.

A further distinction between acute and chronic pain lies in the biobehavioral treatment techniques utilized with the two pain responses. Pain perception regulation is the primary biobehavioral treatment mode in the management of acute pain processes and includes self-regulatory techniques such as guided imagery, meditation, biofeedback, and progressive muscle relaxation. Pain behavior regulation, primarily used in the treatment of chronic pain, focuses on socioenvironmental factors that may influence pain expression and rehabilitation (Varni et al., 1982).

Assessment

Biobehavioral pain assessment ideally involves physiological assessments (pulse and respiratory rate, blood pressure), self-reports, behavioral observation, and consideration of socioenvironmental factors that may affect pain reports.

However, special problems arise in the assessment of pediatric pain that require some adjustment of the ideal assessment battery.

With special reference to self-reports of pain by children, it is interesting to note that Mather and Mackie (1983) report that children do suffer pain but seem reluctant to show it. A child may become withdrawn when suffering pain, thinking that he or she must put up with the pain, not knowing medical relief is available.

Verbalization is the principal means to determine the subjective aspect of pain; however, effective verbal communication is limited in some pediatric patients. As an alternative, multiple biobehavioral assessment techniques allow children to effectively communicate their perception of pain. Abu-Saad and Holzemer (1981) examined children's self-assessment of pain and were able to categorize parameters of verbal and nonverbal expression of pain in the following ways: (1) placement of an X on a body outline to localize a pain source; (2) vocalizations (e.g., sighing, moaning, screaming, crying) to communicate distress; (3) facial expressions (e.g., clenched teeth, tightly shut lips, wrinkled forehead, biting of the lower lip) to indicate the presence of pain; (4) motor behaviors (e.g., unusual immobility, purposeless rhythmic rubbing or protective body movements) to alleviate discomfort.

Another subjective measure called the Visual Analogue Scale (VAS), involves cross-modality matching, in which line length is the response continuum. VAS have been used by several investigators to derive sensitive measures of pain intensity (Abu-Saad & Holzemer, 1981; Price, McGrath, Rafii, & Buckingham, 1983). The VAS consists of a 10-cm line with endpoints typically designated as *free of pain* and *most intense pain possible*. Although the VAS was found to be a valid and reliable assessment of effective magnitude as well as sensation intensity of pain (Price et al., 1983), its effectiveness with children is still under investigation.

Objective assessment of pain, usually consisting of behavioral observation, was first proposed by Fordyce (1976) for use with adults. This work has since found an application with pediatric populations (Miller & Kratochwil, 1979; Sank & Biglan, 1974; Varni et al., 1982). With this model the frequency of such statements as "It hurts," "Ouch," etc., are measured, as are items like attention, anxiety, skeletal muscle responses, perspiration, sounds, and nausea. As Teske, Daut, and Cleeland (1983) point out, in the observation of pain behaviors, both reliability and validity must be considered. Although observer rating scales for patient's pain behavior may be reliable, the problem of validity is more complex. The observer must be concerned about the extent with which his or her behavioral observations of the patient measure what they are supposed to measure (i.e., pain.)

Another problem in the assessment of pain, mentioned earlier, is the difficulty in separating pain from anxiety. Given that both self-report and observational measures of anxiety and emotional responses in children seem to overlap with acute pain measures, (e.g., Dearborn & Melamed, 1982; Glennon & Weisz, 1978; Melamed & Siegel, 1975; Spielberger, 1973) the suggestion by Katz, Kellerman, and Siegel (1981) that the general term "behavioral distress" be used to refer to the behaviors of negative affect including anxiety, fear, and pain, seems warranted. Katz and associates developed an observer rating scale of acute behavioral distress. This instrument is comprised of 11 distress behaviors, such as crying, resistance, muscular rigidity, and so on, whose occurrence is scored as present or absent during an aversive procedure.

Postoperative Pain

Within the four categories of pain outlined by Varni et al. (1982) there exist several good examples of pain management research (e.g., in the management of chronic arthritic pain associated with hemophilia). However, these problems are typically treated on an outpatient basis. This present discussion is limited to programs implemented primarily on an inpatient basis.

The incidence of pain in children recovering from surgery is unknown (Mather & Mackie, 1983). Part of this neglect is due to difficulties in assessing an abstract concept such as pain, and part is due to the difficulties inherent in assessing a pediatric population.

Treatment. Administration of analgesics has been the standard approach to postoperative pain management; however, recent investigations have questioned the adequacy of the analgesic approach (Beyer, DeGood, Ashley, & Russell, 1983; Mather & Mackie, 1983). Mather and Mackie (1983) surveyed the incidence of pain in 170 children recovering from surgery. Estimates of pain scores were made using a questionnaire with modifications for recording responses from very young patients. Medications ordered and administered (analgesic and nonanalgesic) were tabulated. Results showed that in aproximately 40 percent of the cases, the primary drugs ordered were not given; non-narcotic analgesics were substituted for narcotic analgesics or no analgesic was given. Of the patients receiving no analgesic medication, 34 percent were without pain, 40 percent reported mild pain, 21 percent reported moderate pain, and 6 percent reported severe pain. The investigators concluded that (1) the incidence of moderate or severe pain reported in the postoperative period is high, (2) the prescribing patterns of the medical staff managing the patients is far from uniform, and (3) the interpretation of the analgesic medication orders by nursing staff often contributed to poor analgesia.

To date there is no specific biobehavioral strategy to alleviate postoperative pain in children. However, biobehavioral treatment methods used with other pediatric pain disorders may be applicable to postoperative pain management. The techniques of progressive muscle relaxation, meditative breathing exercises, guided imagery, biofeedback, socioenvironmental contingency planning, and parent-child preoperative education are all suitable for use in a recovery setting (see Varni, 1983, for a review of these biobehavioral treatment approaches).

Pain Secondary to Aversive Medical Procedures

In the course of their hospitalization, a proportion of all pediatric patients will undergo repeated medical procedures, several of which are painful and anxiety-provoking. Often, the pain and anxiety associated with aversive procedures is anticipatory, occurring prior to the procedure (Katz, Kellerman, & Siegel, 1980). At times, anticipatory anxiety can be so severe that patients (and sometimes parents) report symptoms of nausea, vomiting, skin rashes, and insomnia days before the procedures are scheduled (Jay, Ozolins, Elliott, & Caldwell, 1983). Anxiety may even develop into a generalized response, occurring in the presence of the original provoking stimuli as well as other, related stimuli (Katz et al., 1980). In this manner, personnel who administer the procedure (Zide & Pardoe, 1976), as well as sights, smells, and sounds of the medical procedures (Katz et al., 1980) become anxiety-provoking. The pediatric patient's response to aversive medical procedures (procedural distress) is thus a difficult problem, involving the conditioning of pain and anxiety and conditioning that extends beyond the times, places, people, and things associated with the original procedure.

Certain psychosocial variables correlate with procedural distress. Age is inversely related to distress (Katz et al., 1980), with distress levels dropping dramatically at around age six to seven (Jay et al., 1983). Sex has also been correlated with procedural distress, with females exhibiting higher anxiety than males (Katz et al., 1980). Consistently, parental anxiety has been linked with child anxiety during a painful procedure (Jay et al., 1983). Finally, cognitive development is related to the anxiety a child experiences during painful and aversive procedures. A child's perception of the causes of illness vary markedly with the stage of cognitive development (see Varni, 1983, for review). The resulting lack of understanding exacerbates the pain and anxiety associated with the required treatment regimen. To make matters worse, children may not only misunderstand, they may actually perceive illness causality, treatment, and hospitalization as punishments for transgressions from societal and parental rules and regulations (Nagera, 1978; Weis, 1975).

Treatment. Distress associated with aversive procedures is unique in that it contains problems associated with both acute and chronic pain. In acute pain high levels of anxiety exist along with a severe and intense painful stimulus that is disproportional to its function as a signaling stimulus (Varni, 1983). With chronic pain the child learns to adapt to the initial acute experience and learns a whole set of pain behaviors, such as regression and inactivity (Varni, 1983). With respect to procedural distress, there is an intense, painful stimulus the child reacts to, and the repetitive nature of the procedure is such that the child learns a whole repertoire of pain behaviors, the expression of which may be so severe that administering personnel are often unable to complete the procedure. Furthermore, if such pain behaviors are reinforced, they may persist and occur even in the absence of the aversive procedure (Varni et al., 1982).

Self-regulatory techniques for the management of acute pain, and pain behavior regulation for the management of chronic pain behaviors are discussed here as they apply to burn patients. Similar work with cancer patients is presented below.

Burn patients typically maintain their inpatient status for weeks or months.

During this time they are exposed to extremely aversive procedures, such as wound debridement and grafting. Wound debridement, or "tanking," is performed in the majority of U.S. burn facilities (Perry & Heidrich, 1982). This is a daily procedure during which the wound is washed and necrotic epithelium is cut away with forceps and scissors. Afterward, medications are applied to the wounds (some cause pain and burning), and there is possibly further debridement and application of dressings. Children often respond to the tanking procedure with hysterical screaming, physical resistance, requests for postponement, and so on; they may even become less tolerant of the pain as time progresses.

Perry and Heidrich (1982) surveyed U.S. burn facilities to determine how analgesics were utilized in the management of pain during wound debridement. They found that fewer facilities used narcotic analgesics with children, even though such analgesics were used with adults and even though pediatric pain was rated by the facilities as equal to that of adults.

Even when properly administered, pain medication is neither totally safe nor effective; hence, other methods for reducing pain and anxiety during debridement have been tried. Muscle relaxation, deep breathing, and attention diversion have been successful in facilitating pain management in adult burn patients (Wernicke, Jaremko, & Taylor, 1981). Wakeman and Kaplan (1978) were successful with hypnosis in treating children, adolescent, and adult burn patients enduring painful debridement procedures. They found that children aged seven to eighteen who were trained in self-hypnosis techniques required significantly less pain medication when compared to both a medication-only control group and to adult burn patients receiving the same self-hypnosis training.

In addition to pain perception regulation such as hypnosis, burn patients may require treatment for chronic pain behaviors. A burn patient is at risk for developing a whole repertoire of maladaptive and interfering pain behaviors. Such patients are exposed to intense pain, daily aversive procedures, and are hospitalized for extended periods. Staff reports indicate that burn patients are especially difficult to care for. One case study of a 13-year-old boy with extensive second- and third-degree burns includes a detailed description of how pain behaviors can be manifested: "The nurses described him as depressed, demanding, and whining. He asked for analgesics incessantly, used abusive language with nurses, refused meals and fought and moaned when tubbed." After six weeks he was transferred to another hospital for continued care, where he remained for six months, after which he was readmitted to the original hospital. "When we warned our staff of his imminent readmission, many went into a state of sheer panic" (Zide & Pardoe, 1976, p 380).

Case Study

Varni et al. (1980) worked with a three-year-old child who had been hospitalized for 10 months for the treatment of second- and three-degree burns to her buttocks, legs, and peroneum. At the time of referral for pain regulation, the patient was exhibiting an array of chronic pain behaviors that interfered significantly with her rehabilitation and constructive patient-caregiver interactions.

During baseline assessment, it was apparent that the child's behavior was a function of adult attention and demand situations (see Figures 12-1 and 12-2).

In the absence of adults, chronic pain behaviors were noticeably infrequent. Also, when the child was engaged in interesting activities with accompanying staff attention for this appropriate behavior, pain complaints were reciprocally low. Since baseline assessment suggested that pain behavior was influenced by socioenvironmental factors, treatment consisted of rearranging the existing contingencies. Social praise and a treat were contingent upon such well behavior as helping to put on the splints, positive verbalizations, and smiling. All pain responses were ignored. Reliable behavioral data on pain and appropriate, well, or rehabilitative behaviors obtained throughout the baseline and treatment conditions indicated a successful program (Fig. 12-1 and 12-2). In addition, other clinically significant changes were observed. At the beginning of the study, the child's behaviors had severely disrupted her physical as well as emotional rehabilitation, and physical therapy was essentially terminated because of the patient's interfering pain behaviors. Following the behavioral intervention, a number of concomitant responses were noted. Whereas the child initially resisted splinting attempts, she subsequently began requesting to assist, saying, for example, "I'll do it. I want to help you." Rather than seeking attention from caregivers for pain behaviors, there was a shift to the utilization of "well" behaviors to attract social attention and praise.

Comment

The techniques utilized for burn patients have also been used with cancer patients who must undergo lumbar punctures, chemotherapy, and bone marrow aspirations, each of which are extremely aversive procedures. These procedures are reported by both parents and children to be the most painful and traumatic events in the entire treatment regimin (Jay et al., 1983). Such procedures may even be perceived as worse than the disease (Zeltzer & LeBaron, 1982). Typical reactions to bone marrow aspirations (kicking, screaming, and resistance to the point of having to be carried into the treatment room) make the procedures difficult to perform (Jay et al., 1983).

Typically, local anesthetics injected intramusculary have been used to reduce the pain associated with such procedures as bone marrow aspirations, even though the degree of perceived anesthesia varies widely from child to child and even when some children report the anesthesia injection to be worse than the procedure itself (Katz et al., 1980). Tranquilizers, narcotic analgesics, physical restraint, and general anesthesia are also commonly used to deal with procedural distress (Zeltzer & LeBaron, 1982). Each of these techniques contain obvious drawbacks, especially for use with children.

Hypnosis has proven effective in reducing procedural distress in child and adolescent cancer patients (Ellenberg, Kellerman, Dash, Higgens, & Zeltzer, 1980). Zeltzer and LeBaron (1982) found hypnosis to be more effective than nonhypnotic techniques (such as deep breathing and distraction) in reducing pain and anxiety experienced by pediatric patients. The authors reasoned that, par-

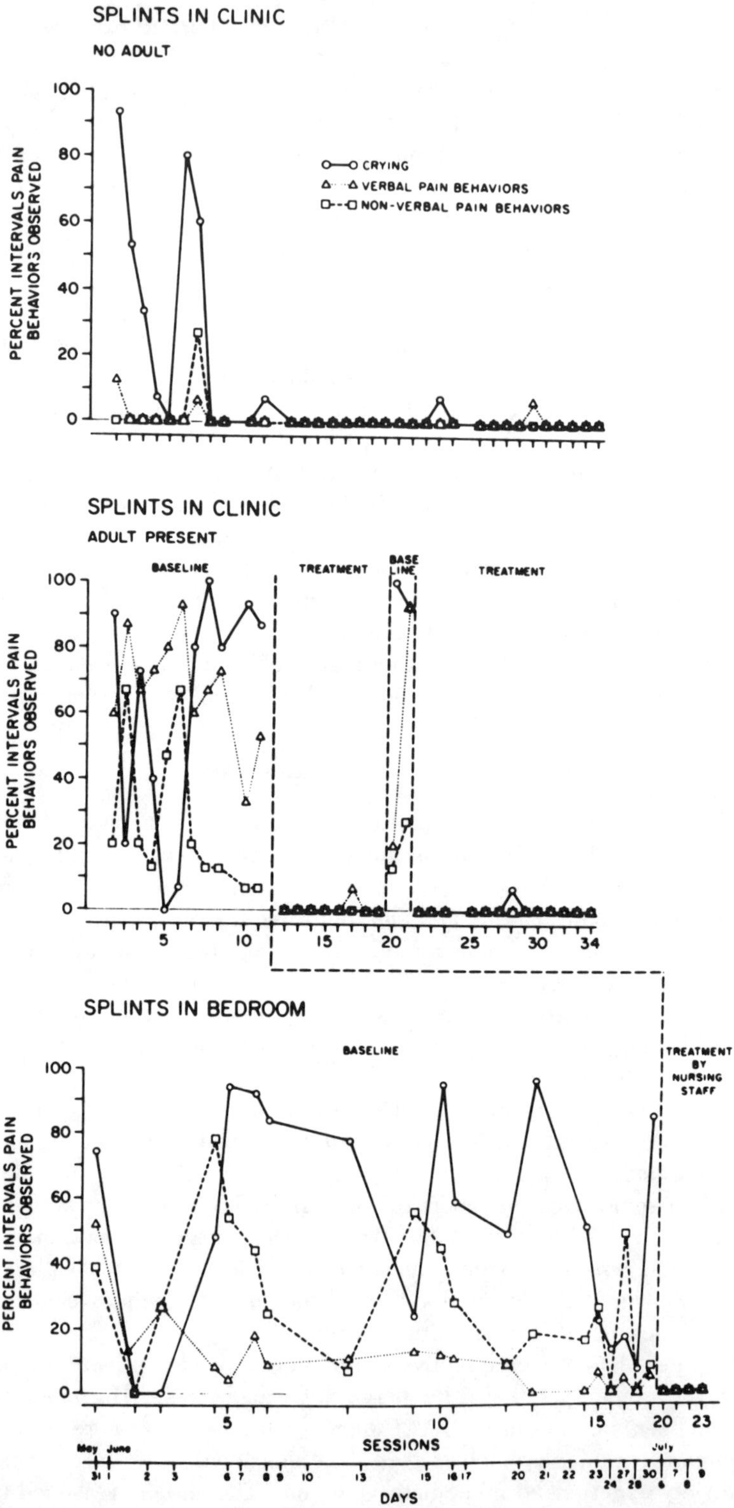
SPLINTS IN CLINIC
NO ADULT
CRYING
VERBAL PAIN BEHAVIORS
NON-VERBAL PAIN BEHAVIORS
PERCENT INTERVALS PAIN BEHAVIORS OBSERVED
SPLINTS IN CLINIC
ADULT PRESENT
BASELINE
TREATMENT
BASE LINE
TREATMENT
SPLINTS IN BEDROOM
BASELINE
TREATMENT BY NURSING STAFF
SESSIONS
May June
July
DAYS

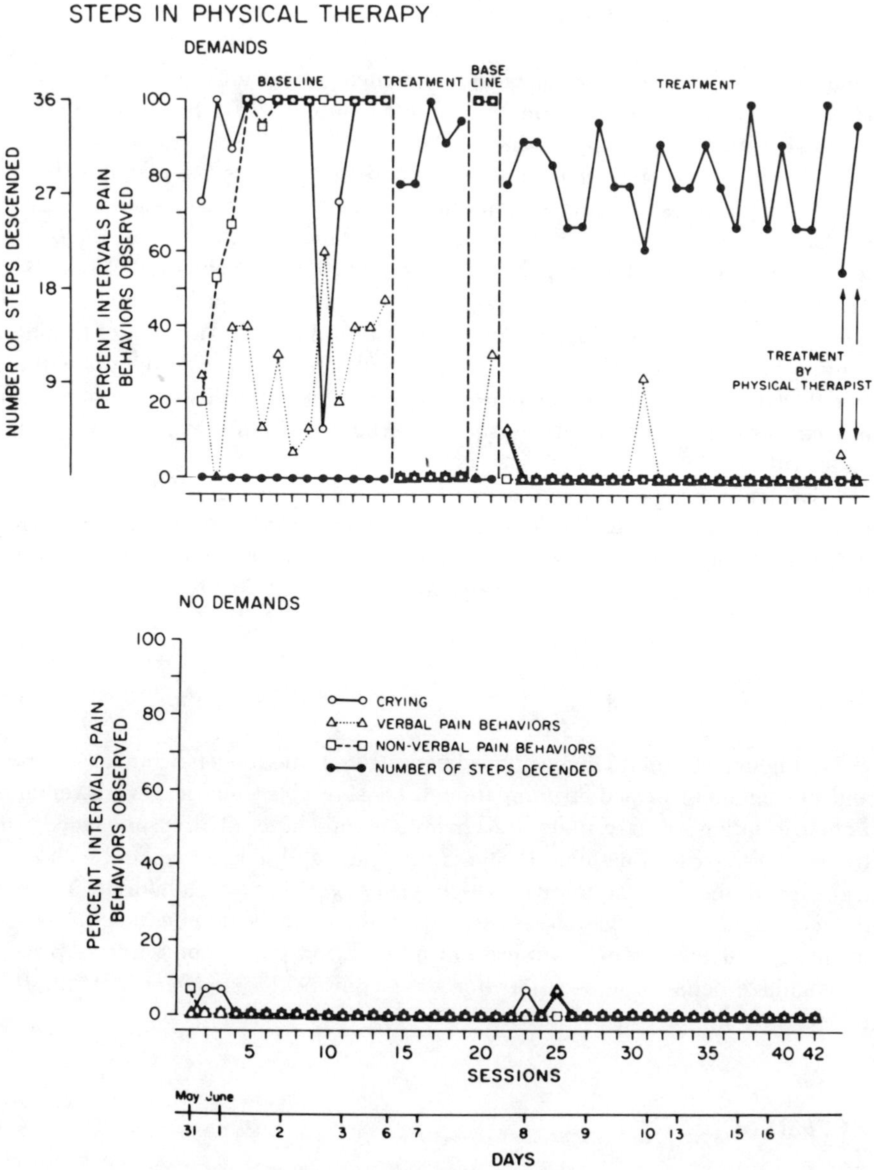

Fig. 12-2. Number of steps descended and percent of observation intervals in which chronic pain behaviors were noted. (From "Behavioral Management of Chronic Pain in Children: Case Study," by J. W. Varni, C. A. Bessman, D. C. Russo, & M. F. Cataldo, 1980, *Archives of Physical Medicine and Rehabilitation*, *22*, p 171. Copyright 1980 by the American Congress of Rehabilitation Medicine. Adapted by permission.)

←

Fig. 12-1. Percent of observation intervals in which chronic pain behaviors were noted in each of three situations. (From "Behavioral Management of Chronic Pain in Children: Case Study," by J. W. Varni, C. A. Bessman, D. C. Russo, & M. F. Cataldo, 1980, *Archives of Physical Medicine and Rehabilitation*, *22*, p 171. Copyright 1980 by the American Congress of Rehabilitation Medicine. Adapted by permission.)

ticularly with children, the imagery component of hypnosis was crucial to its success over nonhypnotic techniques. (For a comprehensive review of the use of hypnosis with children see Gardner, 1980).

One intervention package for cancer patient's distress associated with bone marrow aspirations and lumbar punctures utilizes a very comprehensive, multimodal approach, combining self-regulatory techniques with operant techniques for the regulation of chronic pain behavior (Jay, Elliott, Ozolins, & Olson, 1982). The package consists of five components: film modeling, reinforcement, breathing exercises, emotive imagery, and behavioral rehearsal. The goal of the intervention is to enable the child to cope with the repeated aversive procedures. Initial analyses show that the intervention package reduces distress during painful procedures, and a comprehensive controlled-outcome evaluation is now underway.

Evidence for the effective use of behavioral technology in the treatment of procedural distress in pediatric patients is accumulating and, as Redd and Hendley (1983) point out, behavioral techniques are clear improvements over traditional methods of treatment, such as narcotics and physical restraint.

SUMMARY

Although recent advances have been made in the biobehavioral assessment and management of pediatric inpatients, considerable empirical work remains. Pediatric intensive care units are environments where children are faced with tremendous stress situations. Postoperative pain and pain associated with medical procedures are frequently occurring aversive events for children. Yet very limited cognitive-behavioral research has thus far been conducted. Consequently, pediatric inpatients represent a childhood population where a priority for cognitive-behavioral research efforts must now be directed in order to improve the clinical care of these children.

REFERENCES

Abu-Saad H, & Holzemer WL. (1981). Measuring children's self-assessment of pain. *Issues in Comprehensive Pediatric Nursing 5*, 337–349.

Beyer J, DeGood D, Ashley L, & Russell G. (1983). Patterns of postoperative analgesic use with adults and children following cardiac surgery. *Pain 17*, 71–81.

Cataldo MF, Bessman CA, Parker LH, Pearson JE, & Rogers MC. (1979). Behavioral assessment for pediatric intensive care units. *Journal of Applied Behavior Analysis 12*, 83–97.

Cataldo MF, Jacobs HE, & Rogers MC. (1982). Behavioral/environmental considerations in pediatric inpatient care. In Russo DC, & Varni JW (Eds), *Behavioral pediatrics: Research and practice*. New York: Plenum Press, pp 271–298.

Dearborn MJ, & Melamed BG. (1982). *The self-assessment mannequin as a measure of emotional reactions in children.* Unpublished Manuscript. University of Florida, Miami.

Elkis PD, & Roberts MC. (1983). Psychological preparation for pediatric hospitalization. *Clinical Psychology Review 3*, 275–295.

Ellenberg L, Kellerman J, Dash J, Higgens G, & Zeltzer L. (1980). Use of hypnosis for multiple symptoms in an adolescent girl with leukemia. *Journal of Adolescent Health Care 1*, 132–136.

Fordyce WE. (1976). *Behavior methods for chronic pain and illness.* St. Louis: C.V. Mosby.

Gardner GG. (1980). Hypnosis with children: Selected readings. *The International Journal of Clinical and Experimental Hypnosis 28*, 289–293.

Glennon B, & Weisz JR. (1978). An observational approach to the assessment of anxiety in young children. *Journal of Consulting and Clinical Psychology 46*, 1246–1257.

Jay SM, Elliott CH, Ozolins M, & Olson RA. (1982). *Assessment of children's distress during painful medical procedures.* Paper presented at the annual meeting of the American Psychological Association, Washington, D.C., August.

Jay SM, Ozolins M, Elliott CH, & Caldwell S. (1983). Assessment of children's distress during painful medical procedures. *Health Psychology 2*, 133–147.

Johnson SB, & Melamed BG. (1979). The assessment and treatment of children's fears. In Lahey B, & Kazdin A (Eds), *Advances in clinical child psychology, vol 2.* New York: Plenum Press, pp 107–139.

Katz ER, Kellerman J, & Siegel SE. (1981). Anxiety as an affective focus in the clinical study of acute behavioral distress: A reply to Shacham and Daut. *Journal of Consulting and Clinical Psychology 49*, 470–471.

Katz ER, Kellerman J, & Siegel SE. (1980). Distress behavior in children with cancer undergoing medical procedures: Developmental considerations. *Journal of Consulting and Clinical Psychology 48*, 356–365.

Mather L, & Macie J. (1983). The incidence of postoperative pain in children. *Pain 15*, 271–282.

Melamed BG, Dearborn M, & Hermecz DA. (1983). Necessary considerations for surgery preparation: Age and previous experience. *Psychosomatic Medicine 45*, 517–525.

Melamed BG, Meyer R, Gee C, & Soule L. (1976). The influence of time and type of preparation on children's adjustment to hospitalization. *Journal of Pediatric Psychology 1*, 31–37.

Melamed BG, Robbins RL, & Graves S. (1982). Preparation for surgery and medical procedures. In Russo DC, & Varni JW (Eds), *Behavioral pediatrics: Research and practice.* New York: Plenum Press, pp 225–267.

Melamed BG, & Siegel LJ. (1980). *Behavioral medicine: Practical applications in health care.* New York: Springer Verlag.

Melamed BG, & Siegel LJ. (1975). Reduction of anxiety in children facing hospitalization by use of filmed modeling. *Journal of Consulting and Clinical Psychology 43*, 511–521.

Miller AJ, & Kratochwil TR. (1979). Reduction of frequent stomach ache complaints by time-out. *Behavior Therapy 10*, 211–218.

Nagera H. (1978). Children's reactions to hospitalization and illness. *Child Psychiatry and Human Development 9*, 3–19.

Perry S, & Heidrich G. (1982). Management of pain during debridement: A survey of U.S. burn units. *Pain 13*, 267–280.

Peterson L, & Brownlee-Duffeck M. (1984). Prevention of anxiety and pain due to medical and dental procedures. In Roberts MC, & Peterson L (Eds), *Prevention of problems in childhood: Psychological research and applications.*

Peterson L, & Ridley-Johnson R. (1980). Pediatric hospital responses to survey on post-hospital prepartion for children. *Journal of Pediatric Psychology 5*, 1–7.

Peterson L, & Shigetomi C. (1981). The use of self-control techniques to minimize anxiety in hospitalized children. *Behavior Therapy 12*, 1–14.

Price D, McGrath P, Rafii A, & Buckingham B. (1983). The validation of visual analogue scales as ratio scale measures for chronic and experimental pain. *Pain 17*, 45–56.

Redd WH, & Hendley CS. (1983). Behavioral medicine in comprehensive cancer treatment. *Journal of Psychosocial Oncology 1*, 3–17.

Sank LI, & Biglan A. (1974). Operant treatment of a case of recurrent abdominal pain in a 10-year-old boy. *Behavior Therapy 5*, 677–681.

Spielberger CD. (1973). *State-trait anxiety inventory for children.* Palo Alto, CA: Consulting Psychologists Press.

Teske K, Daut RL, & Cleeland CS. (1983). Relationship between nurses' observations and patients' self-reports of pain. *Pain 16*, 289–296.

Varni JW. (1983). *Clinical behavioral pediatrics: An interdisciplinary biobehavioral approach.* New York: Pergamon Press.

Varni JW, Bessman CA, Russo DC, & Cataldo MF. (1980). Behavioral management of chronic pain in children: Case study. *Archives of Physical Medicne and Rehabilitation 22*, 171–174.

Varni JW, Katz ER, & Dash J. (1982). Behavioral and neurochemical aspects of pediatric pain. In Russo DC, & Varni JW (Eds), *Behavioral pediatrics: Research and practice.* New York: Plenum Press.

Visintainer MA, & Wolfer JA. (1975). Psychological preparation for surgical pediatric patients: The effect on children's and parents' stress responses and adjustment. *Pediatrics 56*, 187–202.

Wakeman RJ, & Kaplan JZ. (1978). An experimental study of hypnosis in painful burns. *American Journal of Clinical Hypnosis 21*, 3–12.

Weis DP. (1975). Children's cognitive development—or how children draw "maps." *Child Welfare 54*, 565–580.

Wernicke RL, Jaremko ME, & Taylor PW. (1981). Pain management in severely burned adults: A test of stress innoculation. *Journal of Behavioral Medicine 4*, 103–109.

Wolfer Ja, & Visintainer MA. (1979). Prehospital psychological preparation for tonsillectomy patients: Effect on children's and parents' adjustment. *Pediatrics 64*, 646–655.

Wolfer JA, & Visintainer MA. (1975). Pediatric surgical patients' and parents' stress responses and adjustment as a function of psychological preparation and stress-point nursing care. *Nursing Research 24*, 244–255.

Zabin M, & Melamed BG. (1980). The relationship between parental discipline and children's ability to cope with stress. *Journal of Behavioral Assessment 2*, 17–27.

Zeltzer L, & LeBaron S. (1982). Hypnosis and nonhypnotic techniques for the reduction of pain and anxiety during painful procedures in children and adolescents with cancer. *The Journal of Pediatrics 101*, 1032–1035.

Zide B, & Pardoe, R. (1976). The use of behavior modification therapy in a recalcitrant burned child. *Plastic and Reconstructive Surgery 57*, 378–382.

Index